THE JAPANESE ECONOMY

THE JAPANESE ECONOMY

Takatoshi Ito

The MIT Press
Cambridge, Massachusetts
London, England

Fifth printing, 1994

© 1992 Massachusetts Institute of Technology

Set in Trump Medieval by Asco Trade Typesetting Ltd., Hong Kong.
Printed and bound in the United States of America.

Library of Congress Cataloging-in-Publication Data

Ito, Takatoshi, 1950–
  The Japanese economy / Takatoshi Ito.
    p.   cm.
  Includes bibliographical references and index.
  ISBN 0-262-09029-5
    1. Japan—Economic conditions—1945– 2. Japan—Economic
policy—1945– 3. Japan—Commerce. I. Title.
HC462.9.I79   1992
330.952'04—dc20   91-13596
                                                              CIP

dedicated to my wife, Keiko

CONTENTS

Preface   xiii
Preliminary Notes   xv
Acknowledgements   xvii

Part I

BACKGROUND

Chapter 1
AN INTRODUCTION TO THE JAPANESE ECONOMY   3

Chapter 2
**HISTORICAL BACKGROUND OF THE JAPANESE
ECONOMY**   7

The Tokugawa (Edo) Era: 1603–1868   8

Foreign Pressure and the Fall of Tokugawa   11

From the Meiji Restoration to World War II   12

Summary   28

Appendix A: Case Studies   29

Appendix B: Japan as an Example for Developing Countries   34

Appendix C: Sources of Data   35

Notes   37

Bibliography   38

Part II

ECONOMIC ANALYSIS

Chapter 3
ECONOMIC GROWTH   43

Analyzing Sources of Economic Growth   46

Growth in Aggregate Demand   50

Reform and the Beginning of Strong Growth: 1945–1950   52

Rapid Growth: 1950–1973   61

The Slowdown   69

Summary   72

Appendix: Guide to GNP Data   73

Notes   74

Bibliography   76

Chapter 4
BUSINESS CYCLES AND ECONOMIC POLICIES   77

Dating of Business Cycles   77

Regularities among Business Cycles   78

Postwar Business Cycles in Japan   78

Theory and Estimation   79

Political Business Cycles   89

Summary   95

Appendix: Theories of Business Cycles   96

Notes   100

Bibliography   101

Chapter 5
FINANCIAL MARKETS AND MONETARY POLICY   103

Institutional Characteristics   107

Japan's Financial Markets in the 1950s and the 1960s   114

Disequilibrium in Financial Markets   119

Contents

Changes in the 1970s   119

The Short-Term Financial Market   121

Deregulation   124

The "Mistake" of Japanese Monetary Policy, 1971–1975   125

A Comparison of Japanese and American Monetary Policies, 1975–1989   128

Summary   134

Appendix A: Guide to Financial Data   134

Appendix B: Theories of Monetary Policy   138

Notes   140

Bibliography   142

Chapter 6
PUBLIC FINANCE AND FISCAL POLICIES   145

The Tax Structure   150

Government Spending   159

The Rise and Fall of the Government Deficit, 1975–1989   165

Ricardian Neutrality   167

Summary   173

Appendix: Guide to Data   174

Notes   174

Bibliography   176

Chapter 7
INDUSTRIAL STRUCTURE AND POLICY   177

Industrial Structure   177

Industrial Policy   196

Anti-Monopoly Law and Depression Cartels   204

Appendix: Sources of Data   205

Notes   206

Bibliography   207

Chapter 8
THE LABOR MARKET   209

Basic Statistics   209

Conventional Wisdom   210

Lifetime Employment and Seniority Wages   214

Enterprise Unions   226

Do the Japanese Work Too Much?   228

The Female Labor Force   231

Bonuses and the Share Economy   231

The Spring Offensive [Shunto]   239

Why Is the Japanese Unemployment Rate So Low and
Inflexible?   241

Summary   246

Appendix A: Concepts and Theories of Unemployment   248

Appendix B: Guide to Japanese Labor Statistics   253

Notes   255

Bibliography   257

Chapter 9
SAVING AND THE COST OF CAPITAL   259

Definitions and Japanese Data   260

US-Japan Comparison   262

Data from a Cross-Sectional Survey   264

Stylized Facts   267

Why Is the Japanese Saving Rate So High?   268

The Cost of Capital and Investment   277

Appendix A: Guide to Data on Consumption and Saving   280

Appendix B: The Saving-Investment Identity   282

Appendix C: The Life-Cycle Hypothesis of Saving   284

Notes   285

Bibliography   286

Chapter 10
INTERNATIONAL TRADE   289

Trade Structure   291

Exchange-Rate Adjustment and the J-Curve Effect   299

New Trade Theory and Trade Policy   300

Intra-Industry Trade   305

Summary   308

Notes   309

Bibliography   310

Chapter 11
INTERNATIONAL FINANCE   313

From the Bretton Woods System to the Floating-Rate Regime   313

Japanese Capital Controls   316

Covered Interest Parity   321

A Yen for Yen?   327

Exchange-Rate Dynamics and News   333

News Analysis: One Year after the Plaza Agreement   341

The Target Zone   349

Concluding Remarks   356

Appendix: The Forward Market and the Futures Market   357

Notes   358

Bibliography   361

Part III

CONTEMPORARY TOPICS

Chapter 12
US-JAPAN ECONOMIC CONFLICTS   365

The "Japan as Number One" Syndrome   367

American Frustrations   369

The Super-301 Clause and Structural Impediments Initiatives   375

The Use of "Gaiatsu"   378

Concluding Remarks   380

Notes   381

Bibliography   383

Chapter 13
THE DISTRIBUTION SYSTEM   385

The Conventional Wisdom   386

Measures of Efficiency in the Distribution Sector   398

Concluding Remarks   403

Notes   404

Bibliography   405

Chapter 14
ASSET PRICES: LAND AND EQUITIES   407

An International Comparison   408

Evidence from Land-Price Time Series   414

Policy Implications   421

Why Are Japanese Stock Prices So High?   426

Concluding Remarks   435

Appendix: Guide to Data   437

Notes   438

Bibliography   439

Index   441

PREFACE

This book, intended as a broad introduction, presents basic facts about the Japanese economy and then subjects those facts to modern economic analyses, both theoretical and empirical. Japanese institutions and policies are compared with their American counterparts, and the two countries' economies are compared in terms of performance. Relevant aspects of Japan's history, culture, and politics are explored briefly, and current issues—including US-Japan trade conflicts—are surveyed.

Part I presents background information. The first chapter is devoted to the basics of the current Japanese economy. Chapter 2 is a short review, from an economic perspective, of the long history of Japan up to the Second World War.

Part II is the core of the book. Each chapter in this part explains an important aspect—corresponding roughly to a "field" of economics—of the Japanese economy. The approach is that of mainstream economics. Cultural factors are not emphasized here, and these chapters are selective rather than comprehensive. The essential findings are summarized at the level of an introductory course in the principles of economics. Macroeconomic growth and business cycles are dealt with in chapters 3 and 4. Monetary and fiscal policies are discussed in chapters 5 and 6. These chapters cover standard macroeconomic topics with reference to Japanese data. Institutional aspects of financial markets are also discussed in chapter 5. Chapters 7–11 take up sectoral topics: industrial structures and policy, the labor market, saving and investment, and international trade and finance.

Japan's large trade surpluses and its foreign investments have become political issues. The traditional way of dealing with these issues is to analyze export and import structure; this is done in chapter 10. A newer approach is to investigate international movements of capital, which are based on decisions made by the managers of financial portfolios. This latter approach is taken in chapter 11, where an original analysis is put forth.

Part III takes up contemporary topics: US-Japan economic conflicts, the distribution system, and asset prices.

PRELIMINARY NOTES

NAMES OF JAPANESE PERSONS

In Japan, the family name comes first and the given name comes next, with no middle name. Many Japanese, in their English writing, reverse the order of names to conform with the Western tradition. In many books, however, the native ordering is adopted for persons in the old times or novelists, and sometimes mixed with the Western ordering for contemporaries. In this book the Western ordering is used throughout.

JAPANESE PRONUNCIATION

Vowels

There are only five vowels in Japanese. The vowel "a" is pronounced approximately as in "father"; "i" is similar to the vowel in "sit"; "u" is pronounced as in "book", "e" as in "pet", and "o" as in "omit". Japanese vowels are much closer to Spanish or Italian vowels than to English ones.

Double vowels are pronounced as a string of single vowels; for example, "Seiko" is pronounced "say-ko", not "see-ko". Long-tone vowels are sometimes indicated by adding an "h" after the vowel or a macron (¯) above the vowel, but sometimes not.

Consonants

The letter "f" (as in "Mt. Fuji") is commonly used in transliteration, although the actual Japanese pronunciation is more like "h".

Another well-known feature of Japanese consonants involves the difference (or lack of difference) between "r" and "l". The sound that is commonly transliterated as "r", as in "Sayonara", is actually a sound between "r" and "l".

ACKNOWLEDGEMENTS

My students at the University of Minnesota and at Harvard University suffered through the rough lecture notes that ultimately became this book, raising numerous questions that led to revisions. I thank them here.

Many friends commented on the various drafts of the manuscript. My greatest intellectual debt is owed to Thomas A. Barthold and Connel Fullenkamp, who read the entire manuscript more than once and who improved every aspect. Peter Boone, Takeo Hoshi, Anil Kashyap, Konosuke Odaka, Shinji Takagi, Georgia Villaflor, and Martin Weitzman gave me detailed comments on the chapters covering topics of their respective fields of expertise.

Some of chapters contain research results of my own studies and my joint research with my colleagues. I am indebted and grateful to my past co-authors: Kazumi Asako, Thomas Barthold, Fumio Hayashi, Masayoshi Maruyama, Vance Roley, Joel Slemrod, and Kazuo Ueda.

Part I

BACKGROUND

Chapter 1

AN INTRODUCTION TO THE JAPANESE ECONOMY

A standard measure of the size of a nation's economy is gross national product. In 1990 the GNP of the United States was about 5.5 trillion dollars, while that of Japan was 3.0 trillion dollars. The sheer size of an economy, however, is sometimes misleading. Since the United States has about twice Japan's population, the *per-capita* GNP is now higher in Japan ($23,382 in 1988) than in the United States ($19,813 in 1988).

Japan first surpassed the United States in per-capita GNP in 1986, after a long period of rapid growth. The real GNP growth rate (GNP growth adjusted for inflation) of Japan averaged more than 10 percent per year between 1955 and 1973; it slowed down to an average of 5 percent per year from 1973 to 1988. As a result, the Japanese economy in 1988 was 9 times its 1955 size (in real GNP). During the same 33 years, the United States' economy grew to 2.67 times its 1955 size.

Japan's higher per-capita GNP means that the average Japanese is producing (in flow) more than the average American, but it probably does not mean that Japan has as much social wealth as the United States. Accumulating social capital, infrastructure, and residential housing stock takes time, and it is generally accepted that housing, parks, and highways are more advanced in the United States.

Japan's rapid economic growth has been a popular topic of investigation. Some scholars point out that Japan's high rates of saving and investment led to a rapid accumulation of capital. Some labor economists point to the long-term relationship between worker and employer in Japan, which makes it possible to accumulate firm-specific human capital and which is supported by a flexible compensation scheme. The unique industrial structure, with its competing enterprise groups, is often cited as another factor in the high performance of Japan. An enterprise group acts as a coordination unit for diversification. Moreover, the cross-holding of stocks allows the management of a firm to focus on long-term projects rather than short-term performance. All these factors combined to propel Japanese firms to produce great amounts of products, which were then sold to foreign markets as well as to the domestic market. Exports were regarded as crucial to Japan's economic development and growth during the era of fixed exchange rates, since the resource-poor country had to import most of its raw materials. If exports lagged, economic growth had to be halted so that payments for imported raw materials could be saved. The balance of payments therefore acted as a constraint on economic growth. After 1973, when the exchange rate became flexible, the balance of payments became less of a problem.

The role of monetary and fiscal policies in Japan's success has been emphasized by some scholars. Monetary policy has succeeded in keeping inflation under control, except in the years 1973–1975. Fiscal policy has been used successfully in creating infrastructure for large-scale manufacturing projects. Economic policies are also credited with moderating economic fluctuations after the mid 1970s. Whether Japan's economic achievements are due more to autonomous saving and investment in the private sector or to economic policies guiding the private sector remains unresolved.

Controls on foreign investment (inflow and outflow) were gradually lifted in the second half of the 1970s. The 1980s were marked by a rapid increase in the outflow of Japanese capital. In the mid 1970s most of Japan's foreign investments had gone into US treasury bonds and American stocks, but recently Japanese direct investment in the United States has become more conspicuous. By the end of the 1980s Japan had become the world's "wealthiest" nation in the sense that its net holdings of foreign assets were the largest. The United States had accumulated the world's largest debt.

The Japanese economy, however, is not without its shortcomings as the twenty-first century nears. For many citizens, the standard of living or economic welfare has not improved as much as might be inferred from the nation's strong macroeconomic performance. The expression "rich Japan, poor Japanese" is sometimes heard. There are several dimensions to this problem. First, Japanese workers on average work much longer than their American counterparts. Many

Japanese work Saturday mornings, and on weekdays they stay at work longer. The typical summer vacation is less than ten days. Second, many Japanese feel that their long working hours are not sufficiently rewarded with a high standard of living. Prices are high, and the real purchasing power of the average worker did not rise as much as the yen's value did against the dollar in the latter half of the 1980s. (The relative value of the yen more than doubled from 1985 to 1986.) The value of the yen made foreign assets a bargain for Japanese investors, and contributed to a surge in foreign investment. The price of imported goods, on the other hand, did not go down as much as the yen appreciated—in one well-known case, the price of a made-in-Japan camera was found to be lower in New York than in Japan. Some scholars believe that the distribution system in Japan has kept the prices of imports—and prices in general—from going down when costs decrease. Third, housing prices, and particularly the price of land used for housing, became extraordinarily high toward the end of 1980s. As a result, a typical employee living in the greater Tokyo area is unable to own a single-family house without the benefit of a sizable inheritance. The problem of land prices has become the first priority of Japanese economic policy. What has driven up the price of real estate is the shortage of usable land. The total value of the land in Japan is now roughly 3 times the value of the land in the United States, despite the $1:25$ ratio of area—that is, the unit price of Japanese land is 75 times that of US land.

Trade conflicts have resulted in difficult diplomatic relations between the United States and Japan in recent years. The United States is Japan's largest trading partner, measured either by exports or by imports. For the United States, Japan is second only to Canada as a destination for its exports, and is the number one supplier of its imports. In 1989, the trade deficit with Japan accounted for about 40 percent of the total US trade deficit. This irritates many American policy makers.

Trade conflicts have taken various forms. "Voluntary exports restraints" on several commodities (most notably automobiles) have been negotiated. The United States has successfully demanded that Japan lift import restraints on beef, citrus fruit, lumber products, and other goods. The United States has asked Japan to deregulate its financial markets. In the second half of the 1980s, the United States demanded certain changes in the market shares of American products in Japan, under a threat of retaliatory measures.

Chapter 2

HISTORICAL BACKGROUND OF THE JAPANESE ECONOMY

After many years of rule under an imperial court and an aristocracy, Japan entered an age of feudalism around the thirteenth century. During this age, which lasted three centuries, local warlords fought one another continually.[1] Eventually, in 1603, the Tokugawa *Shōgun* (military general) succeeded in establishing a strong central government. This was the beginning of the rule of the Tokugawa family, which endured for 250 years. The Tokugawa era was marked by a policy that isolated Japan from the rest of the world. Foreign contact and trade were prohibited except at a single island.

The year 1868 is the benchmark of the modern history of Japan. In that year, it was formally declared that the Meiji emperor replaced the Tokugawa Shōgun as ruler of Japan. In the following twenty years, Japan was hastily transformed from a feudal state to a modern, Western-style state. Railroads were built, a postal system was set up, and a central bank was established. The civilian government was formed in 1885, the constitution was adopted in 1889, and the first election of a parliament took place in 1890.

Although relatively sophisticated irrigation and road systems had been constructed toward the end of the Tokugawa era, more than 250 years of isolationist policy had left Japan lacking in Western technology. Japan's transformation from a predominantly agricultural economy to a modern industrial power around the turn of the twentieth century was based on the good infrastructure inherited from the Tokugawa era as well as on the successful introduction of foreign technology after the restoration of the emperor.

The economic state of Japan between 1920 and 1939 was above the standard for that period, since Japan had been catching up with the United Kingdom and the United States in terms of industrialization. Through foreign trade and international financial transactions, Japan was integrated into the world economic order. The yen was traded on the major markets of the world, and some Japanese firms had opportunities to raise capital abroad. In some respects Japan's economy was more laissez-faire during this period than after World War II.[2]

This chapter will emphasize how the Tokugawa period's social structure contributed to the Meiji period's economic development and how some of Japan's prewar economic institutions and practices were carried over to the postwar Japanese economy.

THE TOKUGAWA (EDO) ERA: 1603–1868

After a crucial battle in 1600, Ieyasu Tokugawa emerged as the national leader. In 1603, Tokugawa formed his government in the city of Edo (which in 1868 became Tokyo). Although all political and military power now rested with the Tokugawa family, the appearance was maintained that the emperor had appointed Ieyasu Tokugawa to be a Shōgun. In fact, the imperial family (residing in Kyoto) had only formal political power; the Tokugawas had the real political power. The imperial family was respected for its cultural heritage, the Tokugawa family for its economic power. The Tokugawa family governed Japan without a major political crisis for more than 250 years.

The social structure of the Tokugawa era was marked by *Sakoku* (isolation from foreign countries), *Shinō-Kōshō* (a kind of caste system), and *Sankin-Kōtai* (the alternating attendance of local lords). The policy of Sakoku, introduced in 1639 and abolished in 1854, prohibited all trade and contacts with foreigners except at Dejima, an island off Nagasaki where Dutch and Chinese merchants were allowed to trade. If a Japanese citizen was found to have gone abroad and then returned, he was executed. This policy, though good for political stability, caused Japanese technology to lag behind that of the Western nations. There are two hypotheses as to why the Sakoku system was introduced. Both assume that the Tokugawa government was aware of the superior military technology of the Western countries. One hypothesis suggests that the Tokugawa government was concerned that a local lord might get help from a foreign country in order to topple the Tokugawa Shōgun; the other maintains that the Tokugawa government was afraid of a direct threat from foreign countries, which had already invaded China and the Philippines.

The Shinō-Kōshō system divided the citizenry into warriors (*samurai*), peasants, artisans, and tradesmen, and an underclass of untouchables. The peasant class, which accounted for 70–80 percent of the population, produced enough rice to sustain the entire population. This class was officially divided into freeholders and landless peasants. Between 10 and 30 percent of the land, depending on the region, was cultivated by tenant peasants. Landless peasants had to pay (in rice) a tax to the provincial lord (*Daimyō*); there was also a land-use (tenancy) fee to be paid to their landlord. There is an estimate that in the late Edo years "about 37 percent of the harvest went to taxes, with 20–28 percent going to the landlord, with 35–43 percent for the cultivator" (Nakamura 1971, p. 49). Some of the rice paid as taxes was resold on the rice market to help finance local governments. Osaka became a center of commercial trading, especially in rice. Local lords supplied three-fourths of the rice bought to market, the farmers one-fourth. The rice market was well organized—there was even a rice futures market with a clearing house.[3]

The various territories of Japan were governed by Daimyōs. *Shinpan* (relatives of the Shōgun) were placed in charge of territories near Edo, *Fudai daimyō* (old allies) were given strategically important areas, and *Tozama daimyō* (recent allies, gained only after the battle of 1600) were given frontier territories. A Daimyō was required to alternate his residence between Edo and his home territory every year, while his family was required to live in Edo all the time. This system, Sankin-kōtai, was introduced in 1635 to prevent major revolts, and it worked. The Shōgun could keep an eye on the behavior of the Daimyōs when they were in Edo. Furthermore, the Daimyōs had to spend money for transportation, so they could not accumulate enough wealth to finance a revolt. (As a by-product, the Sankin-kōtai system fostered the development of a nationwide road system.) Requiring the Daimyōs to keep their wives and children in Edo discouraged them from plotting rebellions.

The members of the samurai class, literate and educated but materially poor, were supposed to have the Confucian virtues of loyalty, righteousness, and propriety. They had the honor of the ruling class, but no economic wealth. On the other hand, artisans and tradesmen accumulated capital over the Tokugawa years, and they used part of their wealth to educate their children. Tradesmen's capital would become crucial for modern economic growth and industrialization in the Meiji era.

Monetary Conditions

The Tokugawa government introduced gold, silver, and copper currency. Whereas the value of a silver coin depended on its particular weight, gold and copper coins were standarized. Exchange rates for the three metals were determined daily.

Paper money emerged earlier in Japan than in Britain, but later than in China (where it first appeared at the end of the tenth century). The first paper money in Japan was issued around 1600 by a merchant in the Ise region in lieu of change for silver coins. Later many Daimyōs printed local paper money that was backed by national currencies. The long coexistence of national coins and local paper money is unique to Japan.

Japan's economic policy of the Tokugawa era resembles its modern counterpart to a surprising degree. For example, in the late seventeenth century Japanese silver, gold, and then copper were being traded to foreigners on the island of Dejima. In 1715, the government reduced the number of Dutch and Chinese ships allowed to come to Dejima. This parallels an import quota triggered by a reduction in foreign reserves. Also—partly because of the shortage of silver and gold that resulted from the trading of these metals to foreigners and partly because of the government's deficit (which was financed by borrowings from the tradesman class)—the Tokugawa government reduced the content of gold and silver in coins on two occasions: once in 1695 and once again during the period from 1706 to 1711. These are classic examples of seigniorage (profiting from recoinage), and of course the increases in the monetary stock created inflation.

In 1713, Hakuseki Arai, a Confucian scholar, recommended to the government that the gold and silver content in coins be raised to combat inflation. The government's adoption of this recommendation in 1714 and 1715 led to severe deflation. The subsequent drop in the price of rice had adverse effects not only on the peasants but also on the warriors, who taxed the peasants in rice. In 1736 the government reversed its course in order to increase the money supply, and prices were more or less stabilized for the next 80 years.

In the nineteenth century the government tightened its budget because of natural disasters, the Tokugawa family's extravagance, and military expenditures. Large amounts of seigniorage were collected in 1818–1829 and in 1832–1837. The money stock increased by 60 percent and 20 percent, respectively, on these occasions. As a result, prices more than doubled between 1820 and 1837.[4]

FOREIGN PRESSURE AND THE FALL OF TOKUGAWA

In 1853 the United States dispatched Commodore Matthew Perry to force Japan to open a port for free trading. The United States wanted ports to supply food and fuel for commercial ships sailing to and from China and for whaling fleets sent around Japan. In 1854 the Tokugawa government signed a treaty with the United States to open diplomatic ties. From 1854 to 1858, a series of treaties were signed between the Shōgun and other countries, including the British Empire, Russia, France, and the Netherlands. In 1859 the Tokugawa Shōgun opened three ports: Kanagawa (near Edo), Nagasaki (in Kyushu), and Hakodate (in Hokkaido). This was the end of the policy of isolation.

The treaties between the Tokugawa government and the foreign countries specified one-to-one exchange (in weight) of domestic gold and foreign gold, and of domestic silver and foreign silver. However, at the time of the signing a gram of gold was exchanged for approximately 5 grams of silver in Japan and for approximately 15 grams on the world market. This is a perfect example of a rare apportunity for profitable arbitrage. Right after the three ports were opened in 1859, many gold coins flowed out of Japan in exchange for silver coins, and this continued until the Tokugawa government changed the value of gold and silver coins in 1860.[5] Despite the outflow of gold coins from Japan between 1859 and 1868, the minting of gold and silver coins increased the number in circulation by 250 percent. Prices increased by 500 percent during this period.

Several Daimyōs criticized the Shōgun for his handling of these foreign demands. They wanted to restore imperial power. From 1859 to 1866 the conflicts between the Sonno-joi ("revere the emperor and expel the barbarians") and the adherents of Kaikoku ("open the country") intensified. Chōshū and Satsuma clansmen tried to attack the American, French, and British fleets, but it was clear that the country could not be kept closed. Seeing that the opening of Japan was inevitable, the Choshu and the Satsuma joined the anti-Tokugawa camp. The pro-Tokugawa camp orchestrated a more to unify the imperial court and the Tokugawas by arranging a marriage between Iemochi, the fourteenth Tokugawa Shōgun, and Princess Kazu. In 1867 Emperor Meiji, then 16 years old, succeeded Emperor Komei, who had died suddenly. In 1868 the imperial court, now with the backing of the Chōshū and Satsuma warriors, moved from Kyoto to Tokyo, and the Tokugawa Shōgun surrendered.

FROM THE MEIJI RESTORATION TO WORLD WAR II

The Meiji Restoration

The *Meiji Ishin* (Meiji Restoration) was the closest Japan came to a revolution. It is difficult, however, to make an analogy to any Western revolution. The Meiji Restoration was carried out mainly by those who wanted to protect Japan from foreign threats; it was triggered by the appearance of Perry's ship. The reform was not led by a religious sect or a particular economic class.

Morishima (1982, pp. 74–80) argues that the Meiji Restoration was neither an aristocratic revolution nor a primarily economic one. It is certainly difficult to see the Meiji Restoration as a proletarian revolution like the Russian revolution of October 1917. Nor was it quite a bourgeois revolution, such as the English revolution, the American revolution, the French revolution, the German revolution of March 1848, or the Russian revolution of February 1917. Morishima argues that a combination of intellectual elites and low-ranking warriors carried out the Meiji Restoration without a clearly defined plan.

Morishima (1982, pp. 80–87) elaborates his point by comparing the development of Japanese capitalism after the Meiji Restoration with the British experience. In Britain (as Max Weber pointed out) the accumulation of capital was encouraged by the Protestant ethic of thrift and frugality; in Japan it was advanced by Confucianism. The entrepreneurs in Britain were independent of the state and came to consider their own profession òr occupation as a mission given to them by God. The Japanese version of Confucianism, which stresses loyalty to parents, elders, and the state, promoted cooperation between entrepreneurs and the state.

Major Political Events[6]

The constitution adopted in 1889 created a bicameral national assembly modeled after the British parliament, with a House of Peers and a House of Representatives. Peerage had been created in 1884 for former court nobles, feudal lords (high-ranking samurai), and members of the new leadership. The right to vote for representatives was limited to males who paid more than 15 yen in taxes, who made up not much more than 1 percent of the population. The base of voters was broadened in 1900, in 1919, and again in 1925, when all adult males received the right to vote.

The task of the Meiji government was to catch up with the Western world in the aftermath of the Tokugawa isolation. Economic conditions at the end of the Tokugawa era were not as unfavorable as one might think. Still, there was a lot to learn from Europe and the United States in terms of technology and political institutions. The Meiji government's two favorite slogans were "Shokusan-Kōgyō" ("industrialization") and "Fukoku-Kyōhei" ("a wealthy nation and strong army").

Japan successfully demonstrated its emerging military power in a war with China (1894–1895), gaining reparations of 311 million yen (equal to 225 million 1895 dollars), control over Taiwan, and the southern peninsula of Manchuria. (The latter had to be given up when Russia complained.) This was the start of the building of the Japanese empire. Ten years later, Japan fought Russia. The Russo-Japanese War of 1904–05 gave Japan complete control over Korea, the southern half of Sakhalin Island, the southern tip of Manchuria, and the Manchurian railway. Japan entered the First World War and came out as a big victor in the Treaty of Versailles, becoming the major colonial power in Asia. In 1910, Japan annexed Korea.

The Taisho period (1912–1926) was a time of relative political stability and democracy in Japan. The economy did not grow quickly during the 1920s, when the United States was in the midst of a boom. Japan tried to maintain an overvalued exchange rate in the hope of returning to the gold standard at the parity that had existed before World War I; however, the gold standard was not reinstated

---

Dynastic Years

A calendar year is also known in Japan as a "dynastic year." In fact, government documents must bear a dynastic year instead of a "Western year." The year 1991 is also known as Heisei year 3, the third year of the Heisei period (i.e., the period since Prince Akihito assumed the position of emperor upon the demise of the Showa Emperor, Hirohito). Since the Meiji Restoration, one emperor, while he is in the reign, is assigned one dynastic year. (Before Meiji, it was not uncommon for a new dynastic year to be declared every few calendar years under the same emperor.)

The "Meiji years" are the years during which the Meiji emperor was in reign (1868–1912); the "Taisho years" are 1912–1926; the "Showa years" are 1926–1989. The year in which an emperor dies and is replaced belongs to two dynastic years, with the division at the day of the demise.

The emperor is addressed simply as "the emperor," or as "his majesty Emperor" [Tenno Heika]; his first name is rarely used in public. The form exemplified by "Showa emperor" comes into use only after an emperor has died.

---

by Japan until 1930 (partly in response to the great earthquake of 1923 and partly in response to the financial crisis of 1927).

Although the Great Depression had a significant impact on the Japanese economy, the drop in output was not as severe in Japan as in the United States. There are several reasons for this. First, the year 1929 was not the peak of the cycle in Japan. Second, a strong expansionary fiscal policy was pursued in 1931, thanks to Finance Minister Korekiyo Takahashi. Third, the devaluation of the yen after the abandonment of the just-reinstituted gold standard in 1931 helped the rate of Japanese exports recover quickly to its peak level of the 1920s. Fourth, military expenditures grew very rapidly after 1933.

As the worldwide depression worsened in the 1930s, the major powers tried to secure their respective economic empires for their markets. As the Western powers raised tariffs to secure markets, Japan increased its dependence on Asian countries and territories as export destinations and import origins. This policy only accelerated Japan's military expansionism. The military, especially the army, had increased its political power in the cabinet during the 1930s. Japan set up a puppet government in Manchuria in 1932. In 1933, when criticized in the League of Nations for aggression in China, Japan withdrew from the assembly, isolating itself from the world political community. In 1937 Japan began a full-scale war against China, and in 1940—after the outbreak of war in Europe—Japan signed the Tripartite Pact with Germany and Italy.

The United States did not approve of Japan's invasion of China or its other forays in Asia. When Japan captured Vietnam from France in 1940–41, the United States, fearing that Japan was becoming a dominant power in Asia, imposed economic sanctions and an oil embargo against Japan. Realizing that its oil supplies would dwindle rapidly, Japan chose to launch a full-scale war to obtain the oil of Indonesia and to maintain its interests in Southeast Asia.

Economic Growth since the Meiji Reform

There is a subtle difference between economic growth and economic development. The idea of economic *growth* emphasizes a quantitative expansion of economic size, most often measured by real GNP. The concept of economic *development* emphasizes qualitative changes in an economy: a change in industrial structure, a movement of resources from agriculture to manufacturing, and a shift of workers from rural areas to cities. This section will describe the start of Japan's modern economic growth—that is, its economic development from a stagnant condition to a state in which its economy could expand continuously.[7]

In many cases there has been a tendency for growth to accelerate, and for structural change to become rapid, when an economy has reached some critical point in its development. The critical point is called the "takeoff" by Rostow (1960) and the "start of modern economic growth" by Kuznets (1959).

Rostow (p. 39) defines the takeoff by three conditions: (1) The ratio of productive investment to GNP rises from 5 percent or below to 10 percent or above. (2) At least one strong manufacturing industry grows at a high rate. (3) The political, social, and institutional framework exists to take advantage of economic externalities for expansion in modern sectors. Rostow dates the takeoff of Japan's economy to the period 1878–1900.[8]

Kuznets (1959, lecture 1) lists the characteristics of modern economic growth as the following: (1) the application of modern scientific thought and technology to industry, (2) a sustained and rapid

Table 2.1
International comparison of long-term economic growth up to 1963–67 from the start
of modern economic growth (MEG).

	Start of MEG	Duration (years)	Growth rate of		
			Income (A)	Population (B)	Per-capita income (C)
Britain	1765–85	180.5	2.2	1.0	1.2
France	1831–40	128.5	2.0	0.3	1.7
United States	1834–43	125.5	3.6	2.0	1.6
Germany	1850–59	110.5	2.7	1.0	1.7
Netherlands	1860–70	100.5	2.5	1.3	1.2
Australia	1861–69	100.5	3.2	2.2	1.0
Sweden	1861–69	100	3.2	0.6	2.6
Denmark	1865–69	98	2.9	1.0	1.9
Norway	1865–69	98	2.8	0.8	2.0
Canada	1870–74	93	3.5	1.8	1.7
Japan (Kuznets)	1874–79	88.5	4.0	1.1	2.9
Japan (Ohkawa)	1885–89	78	3.6	1.1	2.5
Italy	1895–99	68	2.8	0.7	2.1
Belgium	1900–04	63	1.9	0.5	1.4

Sources: Kuznets 1971; Ohkawa et al. 1974, p. 249; Minami 1986, p. 37.

increase in real product per capita, usually (but not always) accompanied by a high rate of population growth, (3) a rapid transformation of the industrial structure (changing sectoral output, labor
force, and capital stock distribution), and (4) an expansion of international contacts. Kuznets dates the start of modern economic
growth in Japan to the period 1874–1879.

Ohkawa and Rosovsky (1973) date the start of modern economic
growth to the mid 1880s, when there was a sudden increase in the
speed of economic growth. The (annual) rate of economic growth
between 1879 and 1885 was 1.2 percent; the growth rate from 1885
to 1898 was 4.3 percent. Therefore, from the Meiji Restoration of
1868, Japan needed only 20–30 years to complete its "transition"
from a feudal state to the starting point of a modern state. The transition was a period of trial and error on the part of the Meiji government, as we shall see.

Table 2.2
Annual rates of Japanese economic growth.

	Population	Capital	Real GNP	GNP deflator
1880–1940	1.07	3.37	3.41	2.78
1955–1970	1.01	9.95	10.35	4.28

Source: Emi and Shionoya 1973, p. 55.

Table 2.3
Average growth rates of real GNP in Japan (annual percentages).

1885 (T)–1898 (P)	4.33
1898 (P)–1905 (T)	2.27
1905 (T)–1919 (P)	4.21
1919 (P)–1931 (T)	3.56
1931 (T)–1938 (P)	6.00

Source: Ohkawa and Rosovsky 1973.
Note: Growth rate is for 7-year moving averages of GNP around peak or trough of business cycle.

From a review of the studies cited above it is fair to conclude that Japan entered a phase of modern economic growth around 1880. Table 2.1 gives the average rate of economic growth in thirteen countries from the start of modern economic growth to the period 1963–1967. In terms of per-capita income, Japan experienced the highest rate of growth; with a different definition of a growth period, Japan comes out second to Sweden. An important point to be learned from this is that Japan's rate of economic growth was very high from the beginning (that is, from the mid 1880s). Its high rate of economic growth after the Second World War was a continuation, with some acceleration, of the expansion that had started before the war. Table 2.2 compares Japan's economic growth in the prewar and postwar years.[9]

Economic growth is accompanied by business cycles. Table 2.3 summarizes the booms and depressions that occurred before the war, with the average growth rate calculated for a period from a peak (P) to a trough (T) or from a trough to a peak. Note that growth was accelerating in the 1920s and the 1930s, even for a contractionary period.

The Initial Conditions and the Meiji Government's Policies

Ohkawa and Rosovsky (1973) describe the favorable economic conditions for modern economic growth during the mid 1880s as a combination of the heritages from the Tokugawa period and the policies taken by the Meiji government during the "transition period." Factors that contributed to the successful takeoff of the Meiji economy are listed below.

Heritages from the Tokugawa Era

High Educational Level. The educational level of the labor force at the very beginning of the Meiji Restoration was relatively high. Dore (1965) estimated that 43 percent of males and 10 percent of females had received some schooling outside of their homes in 1868, and concluded that the educational level of Japan at that time was higher than those of many developing countries in the 1960s. This was due largely to *Terakoya* (temple schooling), which was available in towns and villages during the Tokugawa era.

Capital Accumulation. Capital accumulated by tradesmen was available for economic investment at the beginning of the Meiji Restoration. Some of the capital was lent to the Meiji government, and some was invested privately to create railroads, power companies, and textile companies.

High Technological Level of Agriculture. The southwestern regions had higher agricultural technology than the northeastern regions. Technology transfers between feudal lords (Daimyōs) were rare during the Tokugawa era. The Meiji Restoration would make it possible to disseminate modern technology nationwide. Even at the beginning of the Meiji years, Japan's rice productivity was about 1.6 koku (1 koku = 4.69 bushels) per tan (1 tan = 0.245 acres); this exceeded the crop yields of most Asian countries in the 1960s (Nakamura 1971, p. 49). The silk and textile industries also had high levels of technology.

Infrastructure. A network of major roads had been developed because of the Sankin-Kōtai system during the Tokugawa era. The irrigation system was improved during this period, as well. This social capital would be put to greater use with the introduction of modern technology from the West during the Meiji period.

Policies of the Meiji Government during the Transition

Strong Central Government. Political power was transferred from the last Tokugawa Shōgun to the young Emperor Meiji in 1867. The Meiji government, set up in January 1868, moved toward establishing strong central authority, although it took about 10 years to suppress uprisings of small rebellious groups. (The last major rebellion, the Seinan War, occurred in 1877.)

Mobility of Labor. The abolition of the Shinō-Kōshō class system in 1869 increased labor's vertical mobility. Improved domestic transportation enhanced labor's geographic mobility. (During the Tokugawa period, *Sekisho*—checkpoints between Daimyōs' territories—had been set up to prohibit unauthorized trips by lower-ranking citizens.) The Meiji government also permitted some foreign travel. Labor mobility was crucial in supplying factories with workers from the rural areas to carry out the industrial revolution. Members of the samurai class were compensated for loss of their special privileges. The very high-ranking samurai became members of the newly created noble class; the others were given pensions.

Education. Compulsory education was introduced in 1879. As table 2.4 shows, compliance with the law was rapid. Of course, a disciplined and literate work force is essential for economic growth.

Fiscal Reform. Fiscal reforms instituted between 1873 and 1881 established a new source of revenues for the government. A major

Table 2.4
Percentage of children in school in Japan, 1873–1915.

	Primary (grades 1–6)	Secondary (grades 7–11)	Advanced
1873	28.1	no data	no data
1880	41.1	no data	no data
1895	61.2	4.3	0.3
1905	95.6	8.8	0.9
1915	98.5	8.1	1.0

Source: Yasuba and Dhiravegin, in Ohkawa and Ranis 1985, p. 27.

revenue source was a land tax now paid in currency, rather than in produce as had been the case during the Tokugawa era. The tax rate was a uniform 3 percent of the land's assessed value, and all landowners (now identified by land certificates) were obliged to pay every year.

Infrastructure. The Meiji government built Japan's modern infrastructure. Telegraph service between Tokyo and Yokohama began in 1870. In 1871, the postal system was initiated. The first Japanese railroad, connecting Yokohama and Shinbashi, was built in 1872, and by 1900 Japan had 6200 kilometers of railroad.

Introduction and Diffusion of Foreign Technology. The Japanese government actively introduced foreign technology in a variety of industrial sectors and in agriculture. Scarce foreign currencies and specie were often used to purchase modern machines and hire foreign technological advisers. New machines and technologies were displayed in various exhibitions and expositions [hakurankai].

Industrial Policy. The government identified and subsidized key industries and built model factories, such as the Tomioka silk factory and the Sakai spinning mill (both built in 1872).[10] The government also trained technicians and sent them to private factories to help run modern equipment introduced from European countries. Furthermore, the government sold or leased public land for modern factories at a discount. It also protected certain industries (including shipbuilding) from foreign competition, via licensing and implicit and explicit regulations.

Establishing a Central Bank and Curbing Inflation. The Meiji government proclaimed a new currency law in 1871, setting 1 yen equal to 1.5 grams of gold. (In practice, however, the convertibility was not honored.) Silver coins were issued to finance foreign trade. (In the Pacific region, silver coins—particularly Mexican ones—were the standard currency for trade.) On the other hand, paper monies issued by the Tokugawa government, by local lords, and by the Meiji government before 1871 were still circulating. To absorb these monies, the Meiji government issued new paper money (printed in Germany) in 1872. The government copied the National Banking Law of the United States and allowed private banks to issue paper money backed by reserves of gold. ("National banks" were nationally chartered banks and are not to be confused with the central bank.) In 1878, as silver became the standard currency, Japan shifted to a monetary regime with two standards in principle. In practice, the yen was tied to the value of silver, and the exchange rate floated against the British sterling, which was tied to gold.

To finance the Seinan War of 1877, the government and the national banks issued money without restraint. A period of severe inflation followed, and fiscal contraction was necessary to combat it. This experience convinced the government of the necessity for a central bank that would monopolize the issuance of money. Hence, the Bank of Japan was established on October 10, 1882.

Money, Prices, and the Exchange Rate

In 1885 the Bank of Japan issued its first note, a one-yen note that was convertible to the standard one-yen silver coin. The European countries and the United States went off the silver standard, and there was a significant increase in world silver production. The value of silver relative to gold decreased substantially. The value of the yen, which was tied to silver, dropped. Therefore, the price of foreign goods in terms of yen increased—that is, the prices of imported goods increased. These increases spread to other goods and caused inflation.

In 1897 the gold standard was adopted, setting one yen equal to 0.75 gram of gold. In 1899 the Bank of Japan became the sole bank authorized to issue paper money in Japan; other monies were suspended from circulation. The gold acquired from China as a result of the war of 1894–95 was used as a part of the gold reserve. The gold standard functioned well. The value of the yen against the British pound was stable around 10.1 yen per pound until 1920, even though Britain (along with the United States) suspended the gold standard in 1917. At the end of World War I the Western countries resumed gold convertibility. Japan, however, was hit by depression in 1920, the great Tokyo earthquake in 1923, and a financial crisis in 1927, all of which delayed the resumption of the convertibility of yen. The gold standard for the yen, resumed in January 1930, lasted only until December 1931.

As table 2.5 shows, prices and the exchange rate were relatively stable between the establishment of the Bank of Japan and World War I. During the 1920s the exchange rate was kept near the prewar level, which caused the domestic price level to drop about 35 percent from 1920 to 1929. The fact that domestic prices were not par-

Table 2.5
Prices and exchange rate.

	WPI	Pounds/100 yen	US$/100 yen
1874		20.9	101.5
1884		18.2	88.6
1894		8.1	55.4
	(1897: Gold standard established)		
1904	53.0	10.1	48.9
1914	61.8	10.1	49.2
	(1917: Gold standard suspended)		
1920	167.8	12.8	49.2
1924	133.6	8.1	43.1
1929	107.5	9.5	46.3
	(1930: Gold standard reestablished)		
	(1931: Gold standard suspended)		
1934	97.0	5.9	29.4
1939	146.6	6.0	25.3

WPI (wholesale price index): Toyo Keizai, Keizai Tokei Nenkan, 1980 (100 = 1934–36).
Exchange rates: Nakamura 1971, pp. 33–34.

ticularly stationary was due to the gold standard. The change in prices seems to have been gradual.

The Changing Industrial Structure

It has always been the case that an economy experiences a significant change in industrial structure during a period of rapid economic growth. Production and employment shift from agriculture to the manufacturing sector, and then from manufacturing to the service sector. Japan was no exception.

Table 2.6 shows the shares of income and employment accounted for by agriculture, forestry, and fishing (columns I), manufacturing (columns II), and service industries (columns III) for selected years. A shift of population from agriculture to manufacturing occurred without causing any severe shortage in the food supply; this was made possible by increases in land productivity, mainly through technological advances.

Table 2.6

	Employment ratio			National income ratio		
	I	II	III	I	II	III
1878–1882	82.3	5.6	12.1	63.9	10.4	25.7
1898–1902	69.9	11.8	18.3	47.1	21.3	31.6
1913–1917	59.2	16.4	24.4	35.6	26.5	37.9
1933–1937	47.7	19.5	32.8	21.8	35.9	42.3
1955	41.0	23.5	35.5	20.4	34.5	45.2
1960	32.6	29.2	38.2	12.9	41.2	45.8
1965	24.7	31.9	43.4	9.8	40.7	49.4
1970	17.4	35.2	47.4	6.5	44.4	49.0

Sources: Ohkawa 1957 for data through 1937; Emi and Shionoya 1973 (p. 124) for later data.

From 1880 to 1930, agricultural production (in value after inflation) increased by 120 percent while the number of workers declined slightly, arable land increased by 25 percent, and inputs of machinery and livestock doubled (Umemura et al. 1966, table 37). This shows that the productivity of land and labor improved greatly thanks to more capital and to technological advancement.

Agriculture played four main roles in the development of the Japanese economy.[11] First, agricultural production grew to fill the domestic need for food, so that foreign exchange was not spent on agricultural imports. Agricultural imports remained low, and the domestic price of agricultural goods relative to industrial goods stayed constant. The agricultural policy was very important politically, since rice shortages often caused riots. Second, traditional agricultural products, such as tea and silkworm cocoons, supported export growth in the early stages of economic development. Silk cocoons and tea accounted for 71 percent of the exports in 1867, for example. The share of agricultural products in exports, however, declined rapidly, amounting to 38 percent in the 1870s and 11 percent in the 1890s. Third, some researchers believe that savings from agriculture were invested in the development of the industrial sector, and that agricultural products were taxed more heavily to support the government, while other researchers believe that the financial flow was from the industrial sector to the agricultural sector.[12] Fourth, labor flowed from agriculture to the industrial sector as

Table 2.7
Japanese trade, 1859–1867, in units of Mexican silver dollars.

	Exports	Silk %	Tea %	Imports	Cotton %	Wool %
1859	891,000	—	—	603,000	—	—
1860	4,713,000	66	8	1,659,000	53	40
1862	7,279,000	81	14	3,882,000	50	30
1865	18,490,000	84	10	15,144,000	36	44
1867	12,124,000	54	17	21,673,000	25	22

Source: Emi and Shionoya 1973, p. 37.

technological progress in agriculture freed the rural population from agriculture without disrupting the food supply.

International Trade

Japan changed its export-import structure very rapidly. During the Tokugawa era, tea and silk were the two major exportable products. Table 2.7 shows the pattern of international trade immediately after the Tokugawa Shōgun reopened Japanese ports to foreign trade.

It was not long before textiles and other light industrial goods became Japan's primary exports. Just before the Second World War, textiles and other light industrial goods accounted for two-thirds to three-fourths of all Japanese exports. Clearly, the textile industry passed its peak as a dominant exporter sometime before the Second World War. Imports show a parallel pattern for textile goods. As more light manufactured goods were exported, more raw materials were imported. Table 2.8 shows how the import-export pattern changed from 1890 to 1965.

Figure 2.1 clearly shows how cotton cloth went from an import to an export between 1870 and 1930. (The vertical axis is on the logarithmic scale, so that the slope of a line shows a rate of growth. See the accompanying box "Interpreting the Semi-Logarithmic Scale.") A surge in imports was followed by an increase in domestic production. Eventually the domestic production surpassed domestic consumption, which meant that Japan went from being a net importer to a net exporter; this is well illustrated by the figure. This pattern was repeated in various industrial sectors.

Table 2.8
Trade structure, 1890–1965.

	Export percentage				Import percentage		
	Agr. forest. & fishery	Manufactured goods			Food	Raw mat. coal & oil	Manuf.
		Textile	Light	Heavy			
1890	32.5	36.2	11.5	19.8	24.6	12.7	62.7
1913	15.3	55.0	16.1	13.6	15.2	36.9	47.9
1925	12.6	66.1	11.2	10.1	19.8	42.2	38.0
1935	8.6	49.2	17.3	24.9	17.2	44.5	38.3
1955	15.7	32.3	14.3	37.7	28.8	59.7	11.5
1965	6.0	16.9	13.8	63.3	18.7	59.3	22.0

Source: Emi and Shionoya 1973, pp. 202, 206.

Interpreting the Semi-Logarithmic Scale

When a logarithmic scale of an economic variable is used on the vertical axis and time is measured on the horizontal axis, a straight upward-sloping line implies a constant *rate* of growth. For example, 10 percent growth of $Y(t)$ is a straight line on a plot of $(\ln Y(t), t)$, where ln means "natural logarithm." In order to see this, recall that, by definition,

$$\ln(XZ) = \ln X + \ln Z$$

and

$$\ln X^a = a \ln X.$$

Suppose that X is a growth factor, $X = (1 + x)^t$, that Z is a constant, and that $Y(t) = X(t)Z$. By definition,

$$\ln X = t \ln(1 + x).$$

Hence, a plot of $(\ln\{(1 + x)^t Z\}, t)$ is a plot of $(t \ln(1 + x) + \ln Z, t)$. As t increases by one unit, the vertical difference increases by $\ln(1 + x)$. This is a straight line on $(\ln Y(t), t)$.

On a semi-logarithmic scale, a value of 2 on the vertical scale is the power of 2 in the level of the variable. In particular, if a logarithm with base 10 rather than base e is chosen, then the vertical scale of 1, 2, 3 corresponds to 10, 100, 10,000 of the underlying variables, because $\log(10) = 1$, $\log(100) = 2$, and $\log(10,000) = 3$.

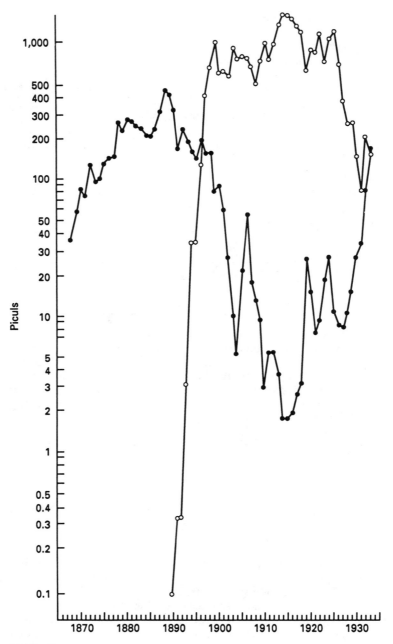

Figure 2.1
Japan's exports (○) and imports (●) of cotton cloth, in thousands of piculs (1 picul = 133.3 pounds avoirdupois). Source: *Long-Term Economic Statistics of Japan*, volume 11 (Toyo Keizai).

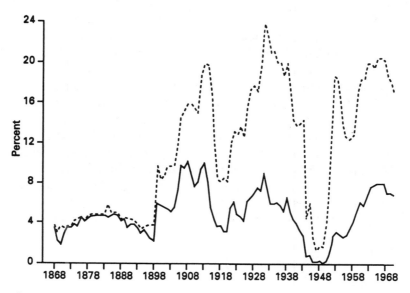

Figure 2.2
Average tariff rates, 1860–1970. Solid line: total imports. Broken line: dutiable imports. Source: *Long-Term Economic Statistics of Japan*, volume 14.

In sum, Japan developed from a primarily agricultural state to a light-manufacturing (including textiles) industrial state before the Second World War, first by import substitution and then by export substitution. Japan repeated the same process for heavy manufacturing industries after the war. The path of Japan's economic development is a classic example of a development economist's view of the world.

Figure 2.2 illustrates how the tariff rate has been changing in Japan. The solid line shows the average tariff rate for all imports; the broken line shows the average tariff rate for dutiable imports. The average tariff rate was below 5 percent until 1906. The low tariff rate was actually forced upon Japan by other countries in the treaties, signed at the end of the Tokugawa period, in which Japan promised to open her ports for trade. In 1906 Japan regained the right to set tariffs. Since then the tariff rates have fluctuated wildly. The discrepancy between the solid and broken lines implies that tariffs were imposed selectively.

A tariff rate of about 5 percent is very low by any standard. If one takes the tariff rate alone as evidence, one might think of Japan as a country that promoted free trade. This prompted Milton Friedman (1979, p. 39) to make the following observation: "Such controls have often been defended, particularly for underdeveloped countries, as essential to provide development and progress. A comparison of the experience of Japan after the Meiji Restoration in 1867 and of India after independence in 1947 tests this view. It suggests, as do other examples, that free trade at home and abroad is the best way that a poor country can promote the well-being of its citizens." It is ironic that the low tariff rates Friedman praises were not freely chosen by Japan. Western nations forced them upon Japan. Although competition from abroad usually provides a good incentive to be more efficient (and this was a factor during the Meiji era), it is an overstatement to attribute Japan's success to free trade alone.[13]

SUMMARY

The Pre-Meiji Era

• The Japanese demonstrated an ability to adopt elements of other cultures, such as languages and religions, with some modifications. They managed to have dual values, such as supporting both an imperial court and a military regime during the Kamakura and Tokugawa eras and maintaining an economically poor ruling class to govern wealthy lower-status citizens in the Tokugawa era.[14] These historical and cultural developments seem to have fostered technology transfers from and through China.

• The Japanese had a relatively secure territory and fought foreign powers on only a few occasions. The absence of foreign intervention before the Tokugawa era and the Sakoku (isolation) policy of the Tokugawa era ensured political stability. However, Sakoku cut Japan off from the technological advancements taking place in the West.

• Sankin-kōtai created a nationwide network of roads as one of its by-products.

• The education level among members of the samurai caste and the economic power of the artisans and tradesmen were both relatively high toward the end of the Tokugawa era.

• The Meiji Reform was triggered, if not caused, by foreign (especially American) pressure. This seems to have set a precedent that

major changes in Japan are forced or suggested by foreign pressure
rather than by internal pressure.

The Post-Meiji Era

• The Meiji Revolution was needed mainly so that Japan could
accommodate changes in the external conditions, such as the foreign demands to open ports for trade.

• Japan's economic growth since the Meiji Restoration has been
very rapid and respectable by any international standard. This high
rate of economic growth did not begin after the Second World War.
Growth had been rapid ever since about 1900. There was an acceleration in the growth rate during the 1950s and the 1960s.

• A key to Japan's fast economic growth seems to be the combination of favorable conditions inherited from the Tokugawa era and
economic policies of the Meiji government. The former category includes the high educational level, the amount of accumulated capital, the high technological level of agriculture, and the network of
roads and irrigation; the latter includes a strong central government,
labor mobility across regions and economic classes, compulsory
education, fiscal reform, the government's enhancement of the infrastructure, and the establishment of the Bank of Japan.

APPENDIX A: CASE STUDIES

This appendix presents three special topics which are digressions
from the main flow of the book and which may be interesting to
some but not all readers. The first topic is the Dōjima rice futures
market, which was the first futures market in the world. The second
topic is the establishment of a central bank—an example of the
movement toward strong, centralized political power by the Meiji
government. The third case study examines whether the sucessful
introduction of cotton-spinning factories to Japan was due to the
government's industrial policy or to the efforts of the private sector.

The Rice Futures Market[15]

The economy during the Tokugawa period was not as backward as
one might imagine for a feudalistic, isolated nation. In fact, as the

economy grew, markets for various commodities developed. Osaka became a center for commodity trading, and rice was the major crop not only for the Japanese diet but also for government revenues and expenditures. The Daimyōs imposed taxes in rice on peasants. After retaining the amount necessary to support their subordinate samurai class, the Daimyōs sold rice on the spot market. Since Osaka was the center of commercial activities, Daimyōs from rice-rich regions, sometimes far away, transported the crop to Osaka in order to sell it. There was a large demand for rice in Osaka from the city people in the artisan and merchant classes. Although there were local markets for rice, the price of rice set in Osaka became the national standard.

In order to enhance trading activity, a warehouse issued a rice coupon [*kome kitte*] that entitled the bearer to rice stored in the warehouse with a deposit of one-third of the value. The balance was to be paid at the time of delivery, which was supposed to take place within 30 days. Local merchants-turned-brokers bought coupons and acted as intermediaries in the market. Since they were not interested in taking delivery, they soon developed a market for arbitrage activity, buying and selling coupons for profit.

As arbitrage became widespread, delivery was often not taken after 30 days, and warehouses started to issue coupons even if rice was not stored. Thus, rice coupons acted as securities. Moreover, the warehousers were interested in hedging the risk of price fluctuations. Although the issuing of rice coupons without storage and the speculation of the brokers were often criticized by the government of the Tokugawa Shōgun, it became clear that the rice market would not function properly without such organized markets or such widespread participation by brokers.

In 1730 the government approved a plan by Osaka merchants to establish a futures market in the Dōjima area. The world's first futures market, it had all the modern features: a clearing house, a membership system, expiration dates (three times a year), margin requirements, and the practice of squaring members' positions before the expiration date (to avoid delivery).

The futures market functioned properly until the 1930s, when rice production and distribution came under government control. Today the rice market is one of the most backward markets in Japan. The producer price, the consumer price, and the production schedule are all under government control.

The Bank of Japan

The major Western countries established their central banks in the following years: Sweden, 1668; Britain, 1694; the (First) Bank of the United States, 1791–1811; France, 1800; the Netherlands, 1814; the Second Bank of the United States, 1816–1832; Belgium, 1850; Germany, 1875; Japan, 1882; Italy, 1893; the current Federal Reserve System of the United States, 1913. Most Western countries created their central banks because the governments needed either seigniorage or control of inflation.

In 1791 the United States established the Bank of the United States, which functioned as a central bank until 1811, when Congress refused to renew its charter. In 1816, however, Congress chartered the Second Bank of the United States to service the debt incurred during the War of 1812. In 1832, President Andrew Jackson vetoed the bill that would have renewed the charter of the bank and consequently killed the second central bank. A period of state-chartered banking, called the *free-banking era*, followed. Under this banking system, those businessmen who had enough reserves could create a bank and issue currency. During the free-banking era, paper money issued by many banks was often traded at different exchange rates. It is the traditional view that "free banking" did not work well and that President Jackson's decision to veto the Second Bank's renewal arose from confusion and a misunderstanding of economic theory.[16] The current Federal Reserve system was established in 1913.

The Japanese government, which emulated the United States' national banking system in the 1870s, established a central bank much earlier than the United States. Japan's National Banking Act was promulgated in November 1872, and the Bank of Japan was created in 1882. Did Japan have better foresight? Was it a coincidence that Japan experienced an internal war during the decade after 1872, and the government, in order to raise revenue, had to rely on seigniorage by a central bank?

Cotton Spinning

The Satsuma Daimyō in Kyushu introduced the first two cotton-spinning mills in Japan during the last year of the Tokugawa period, 1867. The first private-sector mill was introduced in 1872, in Kashima. The new Meiji government promoted the cotton industry as strategically important. Its assistance to the industry took several forms: It set up and ran "model" factories, made loans to cover payments for machines and factories (sometimes in connection with sales of government factories), dispatched technicians to install and break in new machines, and sponsored public exhibitions of cotton products to facilitate technological exchange. Cotton products accounted for 25–40 percent of Japan's exports during the first ten years of the Meiji era.

From 1878 to 1886, the Meiji government imported cotton-spinning machines and built several factories. In some cases a factories was run by the government for several years and then sold to the private sector. Some factories were sold even before their completion.

In 1886 the government more or less abandoned the policy of promoting the cotton industry. There were four main reasons for this. First, after 1881, fiscal deficits made it impossible to pour much money into subsidization. Second, the "model" factories were technologically obsolete, because they were too small (2000 spindles) and because they were water-powered. Third, government loans were limited to machines and factories, and there were other significant costs of operating a factory (such as labor costs). Fourth, the technical competence of the government technicians was not very high.

The first truly successful cotton-spinning factory in Japan was the result of private enterprise. The Osaka Boseki Company started operating in 1883 and grew very rapidly. The company received no direct protection and no subsidies from the government. It initially chose a scale of operation five times that of the government-run factories (10,000 spindles). It chose steam power rather than water power, and it located the factory where a labor force was easily obtained. The company successfully imported contemporaneous technology, obtained proper training for its workers, and started with sound financial backing.

Once the factory started rolling, two interesting practices emerged. First, the company introduced night shifts right away. (Production was divided into two twelve-hour shifts, one day and one night.) Second, the company used bank loans to cover operating costs. Both are evidence of the relative scarcity of "venture capital" at the time. The adoption of night shifts by this company preceded that of Western cotton-spinning factories. There was surplus labor that could put in long hours, even at night. Women increasingly filled the ever-growing demand for labor; in 1892, about 75 percent of mill workers were women. The private First National Bank supported the company, mainly because one of the important founders of Osaka Boseki was also the chairman of the bank. Merchants provided most of the equity capital. The initial shareholders of the company can be classified as follows: the peerage (noble) class held 38 percent, individuals (mostly merchants) in the Osaka area held 31 percent, individuals from the Tokyo area held 29 percent, and others held 2 percent. The percentage of shares held by the noble class fell to 11.3 percent in the next six years.

This case study illustrates several common factors between the experience of the Meiji period and the subsequent expansion of Japanese industry. First, the Meiji government gave various kinds of help to industries. This is what we now refer to as *industrial policy*. (In the case of Osaka Boseki, however, the private sector succeeded without government help.) Second, this example illustrates the development-induced pattern of movement from import substitution to export substitution. Third, companies were usually associated with a major bank, which provided an inexpensive source of operating funds. These developments would be repeated many times for different industries and are common to the postwar experience. Fourth, contrary to what one might expect, tariffs were very low (about 5 percent). Fifth, when demand fell or when too much was produced, a cartel was formed to shut down the factories for several days.

Although the "model" factories were not necessarily successful, and although the real success came from a factory initiated in the private sector, the government did not stop "helping" the private sector in the target industry. In this sense, the Meiji government's role in industrialization was indirect.

The development pattern of industry in Japan was very much established in the cotton industry. First, there occurred a strong demand for a product, which led to an increase in imports. Then the government encouraged domestic production, aiming at "import substitution." Domestic production surges lagged behind the import surges. The increase in domestic production eventually went beyond the self-supporting level until the country actually became a net exporter of the good, achieving "export substitution."

APPENDIX B: JAPAN AS AN EXAMPLE FOR DEVELOPING COUNTRIES

Economic-Development Typology: A Common Pattern

Can the Japanese experience serve as a lesson for the less-developed countries (LDCs)? Several research methods can be used to answer this question. First, a quantitative model of the Meiji economy could be estimated and used to answer hypothetical questions related to the secrets of success. (This technique is called *cliometrics*, or *quantitative economic history*.) Second, government policies and institutional environments could be compared between Meiji Japan and its (unsuccessful) contemporaries. Third, common features of Japan and other successful "latecomers" could be studied.

Kelley and Williamson (1974) constructed a quantitative model of the Meiji economy and tested several interesting hypotheses, such as whether there was "surplus labor" and whether exports were an engine for growth. For those who are interested in a quantitative approach to economic history, their book is excellent.

For an example of the second method, the period 1850–1914 in Siam (Thailand) and Japan could be compared, since at that time those two countries had similar political environments, were both free of Western colonialism, and had comparable initial economic conditions. They were both self-sufficient countries which were forced into trading with foreign nations.[17]

Examining common features (typology) of successful experiences is our third method of investigating the keys to successful industrialization. One hypothesis is that there is a unique path that every nation should follow to achieve modern economic growth, and that latecomers can travel this path at a faster pace.[18] Japan may be considered to have retraced the path running from light industries to heavy industries which Britain, the United States, and other Western countries had traveled. Hong Kong, Taiwan, Korea, and Singapore have more or less emulated the stages of the Japanese experience 50 to 60 years later: Traditional export expansion (tea and raw silk in the case of Japan) is closely followed by primary import substitution (cotton textiles). Then primary import substitution and export substitution develop. At this stage exports are concentrated in light industrial goods. The secondary import and export substitutions take place in heavy industrial goods. (See the

paper by Fei, Ohkawa, and Ranis in Ranis and Ohkawa 1985.)
According to this line of thought, India's unsuccessful attempt at
industrialization can be blamed on trying to develop heavy industries without have sufficient experience in light industry.

The rise in the 1980s of the "four tigers"—Hong Kong, Taiwan,
Korea, and Singapore—should give another clue to the ingredients
of Japan's success. Before these newly industrialized economies
(NIEs) emerged, Japan had been considered "unique" as the only
country in Asia to have achieved modern industrialization. But a
study of the NIEs may yield some common factors for success, including an emphasis on education, a disciplined workforce, a high
saving rate, and prudent monetary and fiscal policies. Still, there are
some caveats to this kind of typology. A close investigation would
reveal differences among the NIEs—for example, Korea actively introduced foreign capital, whereas Japan borrowed little from abroad
in the postwar period. Although a study of similarities and differences may give some clues, we cannot leave it at that. Each country
has a distinctive political and economic background, and prescrip-
tions for successful development may differ among countries. In any
case, the experiences of the NIEs should be investigated in addition
to the experience of Japan.

Summary

• The agricultural sector has to grow with the industrial sectors.
Higher productivity in this sector makes it possible to provide a
labor force to the industrial sectors without importing food. At the
initial stage, agricultural exports make it possible to earn foreign
exchange, too.

• There is a pattern of development: from import substitution to
export substitution, and from light industries to heavy industries.

• It is important for the government to build up the infrastructure,
including the systems of education, transportation, and irrigation.

APPENDIX C: SOURCES OF DATA

For prewar national-income series, a handy source is *Patterns of
Japanese Economic Development: A Quantitative Appraisal*, ed. K.
Ohkawa and M. Shinohara (Yale University Press, 1979); some of

the national-income series in that volume are revised over volume 1 of the LTES, mentioned below.

The fourteen volumes of *Estimates of Long-term Economic Statistics* (LTES) *of Japan since 1868* [*Choki Keizai Tokei*] provide wide-ranging economic statistics from the 1880s to 1940 and are standard references for that period. Almost all variables are in annual series, and sometimes their seven-year moving averages are given. The general editors of these volumes are Kazushi Ohkawa, Miyohei Shinohara, and Mataji Umemura; each volume has different editors in charge.

volume 1: *National Income* [*Kokumin Shotoku*], ed. K. Ohkawa, N. Takamatsu, and Y. Yamamoto

volume 2: *Manpower* [*Rōdōryoku*], ed. M. Umemura, K. Akasaka, R. Minami, N. Takamatsu, K. Arai, and S. Itoh

volume 3: *Capital Stock* [*Shihon stokku*], ed. K. Ohkawa, S. Ishikawa, S. Yamada, and H. Ishi

volume 4: *Capital Formation* [*Shihon Keisei*], ed. K. Emi

volume 5: *Savings and Currency* [*Chochiku to Tsūka*], ed. K. Emi, M. Ito, and H. Eguchi

volume 6: *Personal Consumption Expenditures* [*Kojin Shōhi Shishutsu*], ed. M. Shinohara

volume 7: *Government Expenditure* [*Zaisei Shishutsu*], ed. K. Emi and Y. Shionoya

volume 8: *Prices* [*Bukka*], ed. K. Ohkawa, M. Shinohara, and M. Umemura

volume 9: *Agriculture and Forestry* [*Nōringyō*], ed. M. Umemura, S. Yamada, Y. Hayami, N. Takamatsu, and M. Kumazaki

volume 10: *Mining and Manufacturing* [*Kōkōgyo*], ed. M. Shinohara

volume 11: *Textiles* [*Sen-i Kōgyō*], ed. S. Fujino, S. Fujino, and A. Ono

volume 12: *Railroads and Electric Utilities* [*Tetsudō to Denryoku*], ed. R. Minami

volume 13: *Regional Economic Statistics* [*Chiiki Keizai Tokei*], ed. M. Umemura, N. Takamatsu, and S. Itoh

volume 14: *Foreign Trade and Balance of Payments* [*Bōeki to Kokusai Shūshi*], ed. I. Yamazawa and Y. Yamamoto

NOTES

1. On political and social developments up to 1600, see chapters 4–6 of Reischauer 1988. Morishima (1982, chapters 1–4) offers a rather unorthodox interpretation of Japanese economic history.

2. For example, "lifetime employment," the long-term attachment of a worker to a firm, is mainly a postwar phenomenon, and bank failures—which were not uncommon before the war—never occurred in the postwar period. In other respects, however, prewar characteristics of the economy were carried over with some modifications. For instance, in some respects the postwar enterprise groups resemble the prewar Zaibatsu groups (see chapter 7).

3. See Grabbe 1986, p. 146. Some suggest that when the Chicago futures markets were established, a mission was sent to Japan to study the history of the Dojima rice market; I have not been able to document this.

4. See, for example, the wholesale price index for Osaka (Nakamura 1971, p. 50).

5. Economic historians in Japan argue that the misalignment in the parity was not caused by the government's ignorance of the basics of international finance but was forced by foreign trade negotiators. See Ohkura and Shimbo 1978 and page 4 of Eichengreen 1986. It is interesting to note that Sir Issac Newton, then England's Master of the Mint, made a similar mistake in 1717, setting too high a silver price for gold and driving new silver coins out of circulation.

6. A good summary of political events from the beginning of the Meiji era to the Second World War may be found in chapters 8 and 9 of Reischauer 1988.

7. Of course, the distinction between growth and development cannot be strict—many structural changes (such as a change from import substitution to export substitution) occur in the early stages of both economic development and economic growth. However, when we talk about the Japanese and US economies after the Second World War, we will be dealing exclusively in terms of economic growth. The problems faced by today's less-developed countries are still related to economic development.

8. In spite of Rostow's popular style of writing and his use of eye-catching terms such as "takeoff," his "theory" of stages of economic development is not generally accepted in development economics. Unlike Kuznets, Rostow appears not to have studied many countries carefully enough to deduce a general characteristic of economic development. It is not true that economic takeoff occurs with a "big push" and simultaneous growth in many sectors. The process of modern economic growth is known to be much more gradual, and to spread slowly from one industry to others. Thus, it may be inappropriate to juxtapose Rostow with Kuznets.

9. Prewar and postwar economic growth will be reviewed again in the next chapter.

10. The results of these efforts were mixed. The government's management was usually a failure. The Tomioka silk factory was sold to private interests in 1893. See appendix A to this chapter.

11. For a concise summary of competing hypotheses and further quantitative evidence, see section 4.3 of Minami 1986.

12. See pp. 94–97 of Minami 1986 for a summary of this controversy.

13. India's lack of success, noted by Friedman in the passage quoted, was due to its attempt to promote heavy industry at the wrong time rather than to its high tariff rate.

14. Morishima (1982) emphasizes this.

15. This subsection is based on Shohei Suzuki's *Dojima Kome Shijoshi* [*The Rice Market in Dojima*] (Nihon Hyoron Sha, 1940). See also U. Schaede, "Forwards and Futures in Tokugawa-Period Japan," *Journal of Banking and Finance* 13 (1989): 487–513.

16. See, for example, P. Temin, *The Jacksonian Economy* (Norton, 1969), pp. 28–37; J. K. Galbraith, *Money: Whence It Came, Whence It Went* (Houghton Mifflin, 1975), pp. 81–82.

17. Yasuba and Dhiravegin, in Ohkawa and Ranis 1985, describe the above-mentioned aspects of the Meiji government's policy, especially the government's role in building up the infrastructure.

18. An analogy could be drawn to the biological idea that ontogeny recapitulates phylogeny. (That idea is not to be regarded as a definite biological law. For an explanation and a critique, see p. 217 of Stephen Jay Gould's *Ever Since Darwin* [Norton, 1979].)

BIBLIOGRAPHY

Dore, R. 1965. *Education in Tokugawa Japan*. University of California Press.

Eichengreen, B., ed. 1986. *The Gold Standard in Theory and History*. Methuen.

Emi, K., and Y. Shionoya. 1973. *Nihon Keizai Ron* [*The Japanese Economy*]. Yuhikaku.

Friedman, M. 1979. *Free to Choose*. Harcourt Brace Jovanovich.

Grabbe, J. O. 1986. *International Financial Markets*. Elsevier.

Kelley, A. C., and J. G. Williamson. 1974. *Lessons from Japanese Development: An Analytical Economic History*. University of Chicago Press.

Kuznets, S. 1959. *Six Lectures on Economic Growth*. Free Press.

Kuznets, S. 1971. *The Economic Growth of Nations*. Harvard University Press.

Minami, R. 1986. *The Economic Development of Japan: A Quantitative Study*. St. Martin's.

Morishima, M. 1982. *Why Has Japan Succeeded?* Cambridge University Press.

Nakamura, T. 1971. *Economic Growth in Prewar Japan*. Yale University Press.

Ohkawa, K. 1957. *The Growth Rate of the Japanese Economy since 1878*. Kinokuniya.

Ohkawa, K., and H. Rosovsky. 1973. *The Economic Growth of Japan*. Stanford University Press.

Ohkawa, K., and G. Ranis, eds. 1985. *Japan and the Developing Countries*. Blackwell.

Ohkawa, K., N. Takamatsu, and Y. Yamamoto, eds. 1974. *Kokumin Shoto-ku [National Income]*. Toyo Keizai.

Ohkura, T., and H. Shimbo. 1978. "The Tokugawa monetary policy in the eighteenth and nineteenth centuries." *Explorations in Economic History* 15: 101–124.

Ranis, G., and K. Ohkawa. 1985. *Japan and the Developing Countries: A Comparative Analysis*. Blackwell.

Reischauer, E. 1988. *The Japanese Today: Change and Continuity*. Harvard University Press.

Rostow, W. W. 1960. *The Stages of Economic Growth: A Non-Communist Manifesto*. Cambridge University Press.

Umemura, M., S. Yamada, Y. Hayami, N. Takamatsu, and M. Kumazaki, eds. 1966. *Agriculture and Forestry [Nōringyō]* (Long-Term Economic Statistics, volume 9). Toyo Keizai.

Yasuba, Y., and L. Dhiravegin. 1985. "Initial conditions, institutional changes, policy, and their consequences: Siam and Japan, 1850–1914." In *Japan and the Developing Countries*, ed. K. Ohkawa and G. Ranis. Blackwell.

Part II

ECONOMIC ANALYSIS

Chapter 3

ECONOMIC GROWTH

The most remarkable aspect of the postwar Japanese economy is its rapid growth. Between 1950 and 1973 the economy grew at an average rate of 10 percent a year, doubling its size every seven years. The secret of rapid economic growth, or "high-speed growth" [Kōdo seichō], has attracted many researchers.

Figure 3.1 concisely illustrates the history of economic growth in Japan. With the logarithm of real GNP measured on the vertical axis, the slope of the solid line shows the rate of growth. (Recall the explanation of the semi-logarithmic scale in chapter 2.) The line shows slow but steady growth from the Meiji period to World War II, a sharp drop in productive capacity as a result of the war, rapid and accelerating postwar growth until the oil-price crisis of 1973–74, and a slowdown in growth (a kink in the slope) around 1973. The two broken lines in figure 3.1 show the level of the prewar peak and the prewar trend line (the line connecting 1917 and 1938) extrapolated through the postwar period.

Figure 3.2 compares US and Japanese economic growth since World War II. Notice that US growth has proceeded at a roughly constant rate (i.e., no trend), whereas Japanese growth dropped suddenly in 1974.

The postwar data in figure 3.2 are restated as five-year average growth rates in table 3.1. The table reinforces the impression of accelerating growth from the 1950s to the early 1970s, followed by slow and steady growth after the 1973–74 oil crisis.

From these data we can derive three observations. First, the rapid economic expansion in Japan was not unique to the postwar era. In fact, the average rate of economic growth from the Meiji Restoration to the 1930s exceeded 3 percent per year, which was respectable for

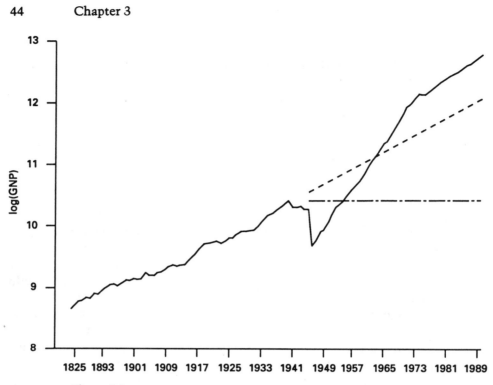

Figure 3.1
Japan's GNP. ——— log of GNP (billion yen, 1980 prices); ———— trend of prewar GNP extrapolated to postwar years; ———·— peak level of prewar GNP.

a country in the preliminary stages of economic development. Second, Japan's growth accelerated between the end of the war and the oil-price crisis of 1973–74. Since that oil crisis, however, growth has slowed noticeably, averaging only half the earlier rate. Third, Japan's economic growth has consistently outpaced that of the United States, although the gap has narrowed considerably since the oil-price shock of 1979. It is clear that Japan's growth before the oil crises was phenomenal. Even after the first oil crisis, Japan's economic growth rate exceeded that of the United States. Between 1977 and 1986 the average growth rate was 4.2 percent in Japan, while it was 2.7 percent in the United States; between 1986 and 1990, the average rate was 5.0 percent in Japan and 4.0 percent in the United States. These observations suggest that any satisfactory analysis of the Japanese experience should explain how prewar and

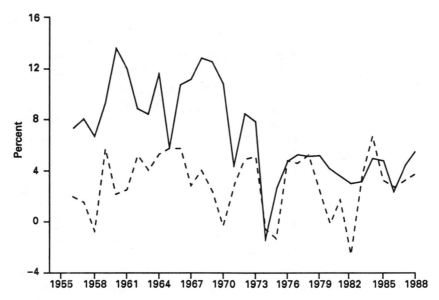

Figure 3.2
Growth rates of Japan (solid line) and United States (broken line).

Table 3.1
Real GNP growth rates of postwar Japan.

1953–55	1955–60	1960–65	1965–70	1970–75	1975–80	1980–85
7.0	8.6	10.6	11.2	4.6	5.1	3.9

Sources: Economic Planning Agency, National Income Accounts and Annual Report on National Accounts.

postwar growth are connected and why the first oil crisis affected Japan's growth so dramatically.

This chapter attempts to explain the secret behind Japan's rapid economic growth from the end of World War II to 1973, and the reasons for the slowdown after the first oil crisis.

It is important to emphasize the major constraints on growth, rather than only the major driving forces. It is often said that in the 1950s and the 1960s Japan's foreign-exchange reserves set a ceiling on growth. Since economic growth in Japan increased Japan's imports of raw materials and intermediate goods, while Japan's exports were determined by the growth of foreign countries' demands, too high a growth rate in Japan meant a deterioration of Japan's foreign-exchange reserves under the fixed-exchange-rate regime. When foreign reserves declined, policy measures were taken to slow down the growth of aggregate demand. In contrast, after the 1970s the constraint became effective on the aggregate supply side. The growth in technological progress as well as in capital and labor inputs defined the ceiling of growth for the 1970s and the 1980s. This gives a clue as to why Japan's average growth rate after the first oil crisis dropped to half of what it had been before.

A first thought on the rapid economic growth of postwar Japan might be that it was a result of recovery from the devastation of the war or of catching up to the prewar level. This hypothesis has two versions. According to the first version, Japan had abundant technology, capital, and labor at the end of war, idle from the halt of military production but easily convertible to nonmilitary production, and with these resources it was easy to grow rapidly back to the level of the prewar peak (i.e., the peak that was reached before productive factors were confiscated for military purposes). As figure 3.1 shows, the prewar peak of output was surpassed around 1954–55. But the rapid growth continued after 1955. The second version of the "catching up" hypothesis asserts that the prewar "trend line," not the level, was what the postwar Japanese economy was catching up to. If so, the Japanese economy would have grown up to the prewar trend line extrapolated through the postwar years, depicted by a broken line in figure 3.1. The trend line of the prewar period extrapolated through the postwar period was surpassed by actual output around 1963.[1] But the actual rapid growth continued for ten more years. Therefore, it is difficult to find support for either version of the simple recovery hypothesis in figure 3.1.

But if not mere recovery, what is the key to Japan's rapid postwar economic growth? This is the question we will explore in the present chapter.

ANALYZING SOURCES OF ECONOMIC GROWTH

Economic growth can be viewed from either the demand side or the supply side. Balanced growth can be achieved only if both demand and supply grow without disruptions, since output (aggregate supply) in the long run should be equal to aggregate demand. On the demand side, a small country must rely on exports in order to grow substantially. Therefore, developing international competitiveness is crucial to ensuring demand growth. Aggregate demand can be understood as the definition of GNP:

$$Y^d = C + I + G + (EX - IM),\qquad (3.1)$$

where aggregate demand (Y^d) is the sum of consumption (C), investment (I), government expenditures (G), and net exports (EM − IM). On the supply side, the accumulation of capital in the form of modern factories and machines is important for increasing productive capacity. The source approach to analyzing growth looks at output from the supply side. It attempts to decompose growth of output into growth of the factors of production, and to determine the relative contribution of each productive factor. The output when viewed from the supply side can be expressed as a (production) function dependent on inputs of capital (K), labor (L), and the technological level (A):

$$Y^s = F(K, L, A).\qquad (3.2)$$

Thus, growth can occur through capital accumulation, through increases in working hours and employment, or through technological progress that enhances the productivity of existing capital and labor. The question now is how to decompose growth into contributions from those growth factors. The exact formula for the econometric estimation required for any decomposition depends on the specification of the production function. (See the example of the Cobb-Douglas production function discussed in the accompanying box.)

In table 3.2, conventional estimates of the supply function are used to decompose growth into the amounts due to labor, capital, and technological progress in a comparison between Japan and the United States.[2] Table 3.3 compares the Japan of the 1960s with the Japan of the 1970s. These tables suggest five observations:

• Japan had a higher (absolute) contribution to its growth rate from every factor (labor, capital, and technological progress), and from almost all components of these factors. Therefore, the high growth rate of Japan depends on all three of the major factors.

• There are three subcategories that contributed more to US growth (in absolute terms) than to growth in Japan: number of persons employed, education, and international assets.

Table 3.2

Country	Japan		United States	
Period	1953–1971		1948–1969	
Average growth rate	8.81%		4.00%	
Contribution by factor	Absolute	Relative (to 8.81%)	Absolute	Relative (to 4.00%)
Labor	1.85	(21.0)	1.30	(32.5)
Employment	1.14	(12.9)	1.17	(29.3)
Hours	0.21	(2.4)	−0.21	(−5.3)
Sex, age composition	0.14	(1.6)	−0.10	(−2.5)
Education	0.34	(3.9)	0.41	(10.3)
Unallocated	0.02	(0.2)	0.03	(0.8)
Capital	2.10	(23.8)	0.79	(19.8)
Inventories	0.73	(8.3)	0.12	(3.0)
Nonres. struc. & equip.	1.07	(12.1)	0.36	(9.0)
Dwelling	0.30	(3.4)	0.28	(7.0)
International asset	0.00	(0.0)	0.03	(0.8)
Technological progress and residuals	4.86	(55.2)	1.91	(47.8)
Knowledge	1.97	(22.4)	1.19	(29.8)
Improved res. alloc.	0.95	(10.8)	0.30	(7.5)
Scale economies	1.94	(22.0)	0.42	(10.5)
Total, allowing for rounding errors		(100.0)		(100.0)

Source: Denison and Chung 1976a, pp. 98–99.

• From the 1950s to the 1960s, the "hours" component of labor input was a positive contributor to growth in Japan but not in the United States.[3] This trend reversed itself during the 1960s. According to the above observations, it would certainly be misleading to say that the major factor contributing to Japan's economic growth in the 1950s and the 1960s was an abundance of cheap labor. On the other hand, the effect of reallocating workers from the low-productivity agricultural sector to the high-productivity manufacturing sector is placed in the "improved resource allocation" subcategory, and Japan also enjoyed an edge in this category.

Table 3.3

Country	Japan		Japan	
Period	1960–1970		1970–1980	
Average growth rate	10.62%		4.84%	
Contribution	Absolute	Relative	Absolute	Relative
Labor	1.59	(15.0)	1.01	(20.9)
Employment	0.97	(9.1)	0.63	(13.0)
Hours	−0.06	(−0.6)	−0.26	(−5.3)
Sex, age composition	0.27	(2.5)	0.19	(3.9)
Education	0.41	(3.9)	0.45	(9.3)
Capital	3.40	(32.0)	1.29	(19.8)
Inventories	0.70	(6.6)	0.28	(5.8)
Nonres. struc. & equip.	1.47	(13.8)	0.83	(17.1)
Dwelling	0.27	(2.5)	0.13	(2.7)
Age of equipment	0.96	(6.6)	0.05	(5.8)
Technological progress	5.53	(53.0)	2.54	(52.5)
Knowledge	4.78	(45.0)	2.01	(41.5)
Improved res. alloc.	0.85	(8.0)	0.53	(11.0)
Total, allowing for rounding errors		(100.0)		(100.0)

Source: Shinohara 1986, p. 17.

The Cobb-Douglas Production Function

Suppose that the production function is of the Cobb-Douglas type, with disembodied technological progress:

$$Y = AK^a L^{1-a}, \quad \text{where } 0 < a < 1.$$

Then by defining $dY = Y(t+1) - Y(t)$, and likewise for dK, and dL, and dA, we can express the decomposition of growth as

$$\frac{dY}{Y} = a\frac{dK}{K} + (1-a)\frac{dL}{L} + \frac{dA}{A}.$$

It can be shown that when the factor market is competitive, parameter a is the capital share of output, namely rK/Y. Thus, $(1-a)$ is the labor share, wL/Y.

• Capital accumulation was more important than labor in Japan, in contrast to the US experience. The (absolute and relative) contribution of capital in Japan diminished significantly in the 1970s, however. In particular, the average age of structures and equipment rose.

• More than half of Japan's growth is attributed to "technological progress and residuals." Of the technological subcategories, "knowledge" represents (in the case of Japan) improvement in the average state of technology due to technology transfers from Western countries, better business organization, and improvements in management practice. US growth also received a strong contribution from advances in knowledge. The contribution of "scale economies" to growth was far greater in Japan, owing to the enlargement of the domestic and foreign markets.

Although the source approach demonstrates how the growth rate can be divided into contributions from various factors of production, it does not offer any explanation as to why those factors behaved as they did. In effect, this approach answers the question of why Japan grew so fast by raising other questions. For example, who financed the large increase in the capital stock in Japan? Was the much higher rate of technological progress in Japan due to "catching up" to the West? How much credit could the Japanese government claim for the achievement of rapid economic growth? The source approach also does not explain how the increased capacity was used, or whether the most efficient use was made of the increased capacity. If demand does not follow when supply is increased, economic growth stalls. We now turn to the question of how the components of aggregate demand grew.

GROWTH IN AGGREGATE DEMAND

As Japan's productive capacity expanded sharply, expenditures on the output it generated necessarily increased. Among the components of aggregate demand, investment and exports played key roles in the rapid expansion. The ratio of private fixed investment to GNP remained very high (sometimes topping 20 percent) from 1955 to 1975. Figure 3.3 shows the ratio of private fixed investment to GNP and that of exports to GNP in nominal terms. Note that the invest-

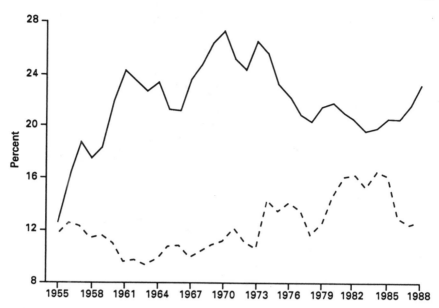

Figure 3.3
Nominal investment/GNP (solid line) and Exports/GNP (broken line).

ment ratio increased until 1973 but declined in the late 1970s, implying that investment was an engine of "high-speed" growth in the 1950s and 1960s. Note also that the export ratio does not seem to have increased during the 1950s and the 1960s.

Figure 3.4 shows the same ratios in real terms. Investment, exports, and GNP are each divided by the relevant price deflator; then investment and exports are divided by real GNP. In this figure, it is clear that the ratio of exports to GNP has been increasing continuously. Thus, in real (volume) terms, exports have contributed to absorption of output. The difference between figures 3.3 and 3.4 implies that export prices rose more slowly than the GNP deflator during the 1950s and the 1960s, so that Japanese goods became more and more competitive. (Note that the exchange rate was fixed at 360 yen per dollar from 1949 to 1971.)

The above analysis of the demand side suggests that the popular notion that Japan experienced investment-led growth and export-led growth is, in general, correct for the 1950s and the 1960s. The role of investment changed after the first oil crisis, however.

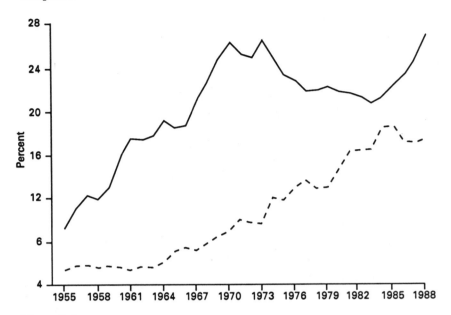

Figure 3.4
Real investment/GNP (solid line) and Exports/GNP (broken line).

REFORM AND THE BEGINNING OF STRONG GROWTH: 1945–1950[4]

The Second World War destroyed a fourth of Japan's national wealth and assets, a fourth of its structures, and 82 percent of its ships. The country was quickly repopulated as veterans returned home and started families. With little productive capacity, the Japanese population was near starvation. This section provides a description of how Japan brought itself from the aftermath of destruction to the starting point of strong economic growth. There were three stages to the transition: a period of high inflation, a recession due to an austerity plan, and a boom created by the Korean War.

As table 3.4 shows, inflation was rampant immediately after the war. This was a direct result of the monetization of government war bonds. The three-digit inflation was controlled only after a package of drastic emergency measures called the Dodge Plan was introduced in 1949. This austerity plan (explained in detail below) halted the increase in the monetary base, curbed the size of the government's budget, and fixed the exchange rate at 360 yen per dollar.

Table 3.4

	GNP growth rate (%)	Inflation rate (%)	Monetary base growth rate (%)	Gov't budget growth rate (%)	Trade balance to GNP ratio (%)	Major events
1945	...	51.1	148.2	9.0	...	Surrender of Japan (Aug.)
1946	...	364.5	67.5	418.3	...	Financial asset freeze (Feb.); price control (March); Zaibatsu dissolution
1947	8.4	195.9	132.9	75.9	−6.2	General strikes banned (Feb.); breakup of monopolies, land reform, labor reform
1948	13.0	165.6	61.5	135.1	−3.8	
1949	2.2	63.3	0.3	56.0	−2.0	Dodge Plan National railway labor problem
1950	11.0	18.2	18.9	1.2	0.3	Korean War (Oct.)
1951	13.0	38.8	19.9	24.0	−1.9	End of Korean War
1952	11.0	2.0	13.8	16.8	−2.3	
1953	5.7	5.0	10.8	16.6	−4.5	
1954	6.1	6.5	−0.9	2.3	−2.2	

Source: Toyo Keizai, Economics Statistics Annual, 1979.
Note: Monetary base is sum of currency and coin.

Three Economic Reforms Imposed by the Occupation Force

Soon after General Douglas MacArthur arrived in Japan as head of the Allied Occupation Force, he introduced several measures aimed at democratizing Japan politically and economically. Three major reforms imposed during the occupation—anti-trust measures, land reform, and labor democratization—affected the postwar Japanese economy significantly and are credited with promoting a higher rate of economic growth.

Anti-Trust Measures

The prewar *Zaibatsu* were groups of large companies across different industries controlled by family-owned holding companies. At the end of the war, major Zaibatsu groups held about 40 percent of equity (paid-in capital). The occupation force required the auctioning off of the shares owned by their holding companies, and thus the Zaibatsu groups were technically dissolved in 1946 and 1947. Furthermore, in 1947 the occupation force introduced a measure (called the Elimination of Excessive Concentration of Economic Power) intended to break up monopolistic companies. To maintain competition they also introduced the Anti-Monopoly Law. These policies made many markets more competitive, prompted vigorous investment demand, and enhanced consumer welfare.[5]

Land Reform

Also in 1946 and 1947, land was confiscated from absentee landlords with little compensation and resold to tenant farmers at bargain prices.[6] This drastic redistribution of wealth contributed to a considerable convergence in the standard of living. The percentage of farmland cultivated by tenant farmers declined from 46 percent in November 1946 to 10 percent in August 1950. On the one hand, the land reform created a middle class, thus contributing to income equity and political stability in the agricultural sector. The increase in agricultural production was rapid, and Japan's food supply was stable a few years after the land reform. On the other hand, the small lot size, partly a result of the land reform, has prevented farmers from taking advantage of scale economies. Agriculture has gradually become heavily subsidized and has been placed under numerous government controls.[7]

Labor Reform

Workers were granted the rights to organize in unions and to engage in collective bargaining by the Labor Union Law of 1946. The occupation force encouraged the organization of labor unions. Standards for the working environment and for compensation were established in the Labor Relations Adjustment Act of 1946 and the Labor Standards Law of 1947, respectively. As a result of these changes, labor unions spread quickly in every sector of the Japanese economy. The percentage of unionized workers jumped from 3.2 percent in 1945 to 41.5 percent in 1946, and then to 53.0 percent in 1948. In the midst of three-digit inflation and food shortages, unions and management clashed often. The labor unions planned a general strike for February 1, 1947; the occupation force, seeing that the labor movement was not moving along the course envisioned for it, banned that strike. Even after the occupation force withdrew its active support for labor unions, the number of strikes and labor-management conflicts continued to increase. In 1948 there were 913 strikes, involving more than 2.6 million workers. It was not until the 1960s that the cooperative labor-management relationship often cited in the Japanese management literature emerged nationwide.

In addition to the above-mentioned economic reforms, drastic social and political changes were implemented by the occupation force. The educational system was reformed on the American model, with all children required to attend elementary school for 6 years and junior high school for 3 years. High school (3 years) and college (4 years) are optional. Coeducation was introduced throughout the public schools.

The political system was also changed drastically by the occupation force. Under a new constitution drafted by the occupation force, the emperor became a "symbol" of the nation rather than the head of state. Military forces were permanently banned. Women were given voting rights, and elections for members of the House of Councilors were introduced. These reforms and social changes were carried out amid trials of war criminals, food shortages, runaway inflation followed by fiscal restraint, and political struggles between the right and the left. In order to prevent a total collapse of the economy, special aid and grants were extended to Japan by the United States and other Western countries.

The Education System

In Japan there are national guidelines for what should be taught in elementary schools and high schools. Textbooks for these schools must be approved by the Ministry of Education. There is no skipping of grades, however smart a student may be; therefore, anyone entering college is at least 18 years old.

Colleges and universities are classified as national, prefectural (or municipal), and private, depending on their major funding sources. Even private universities receive subsidies from the national government, amounting to as much as a third of a school's general budget.

The college entrance examination is one of the central events in a student's life, and sometimes it can affect a person's entire career. In addition to a nationally standardized test (like the SAT), there are university-specific exams. By the time he or she applies to a college or a university, the student must choose a major field, since the entrance exam is department-specific. Dates for university-specific exams are arranged so that a student can take exams for two different national universities. A student may take as many private-university entrance exams as he or she can handle in a year. (For about ten years prior to 1988, students had only one chance for admission to a national university.) Many universities, including most national universities, base their admission decisions solely on the student's performance on the entrance exam; a minority of schools consider high school grades, recommendations, or other information.

It is not uncommon for a student who fails the entrance exam to a good university to attend a "cram" school [yobikō] full-time for a year in order to prepare for another try, and many high school students attend cram schools in the evenings and on weekends. In fact, many junior-high students go to cram schools in order to get into good senior high schools.

The Japanese pre-college school systems are said to be stricter than their American counterparts. There are more school hours per week and more school days per year—on the average, 240 days in Japan, versus 180 in the United States.

The Political System

The Japanese political system resembles the British system. There are two houses in the Diet (parliament): the House of Representatives (Lower House) and the House of Councilors (Upper House). Although members of both houses are elected, the methods of election and the lengths of terms differ between the two houses.

The House of Representatives has more political power when the two houses are in conflict over a budget, a treaty, or the selection of a prime minister. The head of government, the prime minister, is elected in the Diet. The majority leader in the House of Representatives is the usual choice. According to the constitution, a majority of cabinet members must be members of the Diet. In practice, a great majority of cabinet members are chosen from the House of Representatives; the rest come from the House of Councilors and, on very rare occasions, from outside the Diet.

There are 512 seats in the House of Representatives and 252 in the House of Councilors. Japan is divided into 130 electoral districts for the House of Representatives. Each district elects from three to six representatives, and this improves the prospects of candidates from minority parties.

The redrawing of electoral districts in order to reflect changes in population distribution, which lags behind actual shifts in population, is always a hot political problem. Currently, the most underrepresented district has as much as three times the population of the most overrepresented district, per representative. Several lawsuits related to this issue have been tried before the Supreme Court. Voters who claimed that an election was unconstitutional lost the suit when the Supreme Court found that a ratio of less than 3 to 1 was within the bounds of tolerance. In some other cases of ratios *greater than* 3 to 1, the Supreme Court found elections unconstitutional but did not declare them void.

There are two ways to elect members of the House of Councilors: through electoral districts corresponding to prefectures, and through one national district. In the national district, voters vote for parties rather than for individuals, and the seats are given to individuals on the parties' lists (announced before the election) in proportion to the parties' earned votes.

Stabilization Efforts and Inflation

From 1946 to 1948 the Japanese government was trying to achieve two opposing goals: accelerating the recovery of productive capacity in major industries and taming inflation. On the inflation front, the government tried direct controls on prices and resource allocations. To rebuild productive capacity, the government pursued more traditional forms of fiscal and monetary policies.

The Japanese government directly planned the growth of the coal and steel industries. Its plan called for allocating domestically produced coal and imported coal preferentially to the steel industry, and domestically produced steel to the coal industry. The priority production plan [keisha seisan hōshiki] was very socialistic. The government also froze many consumer prices and rationed necessities such as rice.

Expansionary fiscal and monetary policies were adopted. The Reconstruction Bank, established in January 1947, became the primary machine for fiscal stimulation. The Reconstruction Bank issued bonds (most of which were bought by the Bank of Japan) and used the proceeds to subsidize key industries such as coal, fertilizers, electric power, and iron and machinery. The subsidies were used to keep the (controlled) producer prices higher than the (controlled) consumer prices. The Reconstruction Bank also made loans to public corporations. In essence, the arrangement was equivalent to government finance by the printing of money; in this respect, it was very Keynesian.[8] Of course, this type of Keynesian policy will cause inflation if the low production is due to a lack of productive capacity rather than a lack of aggregate demand; in such a case, the policy could exacerbate the problem of too much money chasing too few goods.

In an attempt to stop the momentum of inflation, the Japanese government took drastic action in February 1946, freezing assets and converting them into bank deposits, only a fraction of which were permitted to be withdrawn for living expenses.[9] In effect, the measure was equivalent to the confiscation of assets (and consequently of their purchasing power) through inflation. This measure was not successful in halting inflation, although it did succeed in bringing about greater income equity.

It is very difficult to evaluate Japan's economic policy of the years 1946–1948. Since the circumstances are extraordinary, standard economic theory may not be applicable. Although the policy failed to stop inflation, economic growth was strong during this period.

The Dodge Plan

The end to inflation did not come until drastic measures were taken to balance the budget. The American banker Joseph Dodge, already credited with ending Germany's postwar inflation, was appointed to work in Japan in 1948. The policy he initiated, which later became known as the Dodge Plan, was put into force in 1949. The main objective was to stop inflation by tightening the fiscal budget so that the government would not need to print money in order to finance its spending. The exchange rate was set at $1 = 360 yen, and various steps were taken to encourage exports.

Although the Public Finance Law of 1947 prohibited the government from issuing bonds, the Reconstruction Bank continued to issue bonds. For the fiscal year 1949, Dodge proceeded to balance the unified fiscal budget (which included special accounts and government agencies such as the Reconstruction Bank), in addition to the general budget. As the fiscal budget was tightened, the economy went into a severe deflationary spiral. Prices fell, and it became possible to lift price controls without great economic disruption.

The Dodge Plan successfully put out inflation, brought back the market economy, and reopened Japan to international trade. It was a classic example of breaking an inflation spiral.[10] The economy was, however, heading for a recession. The increase in production stalled, and the fear of job losses increased. A severe recession was averted only by the special export demand created by the Korean War.

The Early Days of the Cold War

In October 1947 the Cominform was organized by the Soviet Union and East European countries, and it became clear that the Communist Party was gaining power in China. In 1948 the blockade of Berlin by the Soviet Union was countered by a massive US airlift. As the world entered the Cold War period, the occupation policy changed. The most notable change was the creation of the "Self-Defense Forces." In addition, the policy of breaking up large companies was not fully carried through. The priority shifted to encourag-

Article 9 and the Self-Defense Forces

Japan's current constitution was drafted by the American occupation force in February 1946. After a little revision it was approved by the Diet (under the old constitution), and it became effective on May 3, 1947. A major thrust of the constitution is the establishment of a truly democratic state. It defines the emperor as the symbol of the unity of the state, without any real political power. All adults, male and female, received the right to vote for members of the Diet.

Article 9 of the constitution states that Japan renounces all military forces—explicitly including an air force, a navy, and an army—as means of resolving international conflicts. It is widely believed that at the time of the drafting of the constitution the United States wanted to keep Japan as non-militaristic as possible, but that the American policy shifted to encourage Japan to have some "self-defense" forces in order to counter the Communist threat during the Cold War. The Self-Defense Forces were established in 1954.

Some Japanese still interprete the constitution as not allowing *any* forces. The traditional line of the Socialist Party is that the Self-Defense Forces are unconstitutional. Many Japanese, however, believe that these forces are permissible under Article 9. Over the years, several Japanese governments have made interpretations and commitments with regard to the coexistence of the Self-Defense Forces and Article 9: not to possess any offensive capabilities, to keep the defense budget under 1 percent of the GNP, and to keep the Self-Defense Forces within the bounds of Japanese territory.

During the Persian Gulf Crisis of 1990–91, some members of the Liberal Democratic Party proposed to send Self-Defense Forces to the Gulf area in a support role (never in a combat role). This idea did not receive enough support, probably because many voters felt that it might lead to further stretching of the constitution.

ing greater production by existing companies rather than ensuring a competitive market by breaking up those companies. The aim of this policy was to strengthen Japan's productive capacity quickly.

The Korean War

After the outbreak of war in Korea (June 1950), Japan was used as a supply base for US and United Nations troops. This increased the demand for Japanese-manufactured goods and parts, and the economy grew quickly.

Summary

It is generally acknowledged that Japan owes much to the United States for helping, during the occupation, to create a foundation for postwar economic growth. The measures aimed at democratizing Japan, including the anti-monopoly policy, land reforms, and changes in labor relations, made the Japanese economy more competitive and dynamic. The Dodge Plan rescued Japan from runaway inflation, and a brisk rise in orders for Japanese manufactured goods due to the Korean War rescued Japan from a recession that the Dodge Plan might otherwise have caused.

RAPID GROWTH: 1950–1973

Japan's sovereignty was restored on April 28, 1952, when the San Francisco peace treaty, signed the preceding year, became effective.[11] Japan also resumed the independent formulation of economic policies after this date. The surge in orders for Japanese goods as a result of the Korean War continued until 1952. The increase in exports, through the multiplier effect, led to rapid expansion and provided much-needed foreign reserves. However, as production expanded, inflation resumed.

Table 3.5 summarizes the behavior of major economic variables in the late 1950s. In 1951, the lessening of the special demand for supplies for the Korean War left Japan in a difficult position. The balance of payments, which had been in surplus because of the extra demand, declined and became a major concern. From 1953 to 1957 Japan experienced trade deficits, although their magnitude declined over time.

Rapid economic growth in the 1960s is at the heart of the postwar Japanese economic "miracle." When Hayato Ikeda became prime minister in July 1960, his goal of "doubling income in ten years" became the focus of policy discussion and media attention.[12] Its adoption in December as the basic economic plan of the government indicated that strong growth-oriented economic policies would be coming. Critics initially argued that it was too optimistic to expect high growth rates for ten consecutive years, but the doubling of national income (measured by real GNP) was in fact achieved in seven years. (See table 3.6.)

Table 3.5

Calendar year	Real GNP growth rate (%)	CPI inflation rate (%)	Real domestic gross fixed investment (divided by GNP)	Real exports (divided by GNP)	Trade balance divided by nominal GNP[a]
1955	...	−1.0	9.3	5.4	−0.2
1956	7.3	0.0	11.0	5.8	−0.5
1957	8.1	3.2	12.2	5.8	−1.3
1958	6.7	−0.6	11.9	5.6	1.1
1959	9.3	1.3	12.9	5.8	1.0

Sources: nominal and real GNP, and investment: EPA, Choki Sokyu, 1988; CPI and trade balance: Toyo Keizai Tokei Nenpo, 1979.
a. ($million × 360)/Nominal GNP.

Table 3.6

Calendar year	Real GNP growth rate (%)	Inflation rates in WPI	in CPI	Real domestic gross fixed investment divided by real GNP	Real exports divided by real GNP
1960	13.6	1.1	3.8	15.9	5.7
1961	11.9	1.1	5.1	17.5	5.4
1962	8.9	−1.6	6.9	17.5	5.7
1963	8.4	1.6	7.5	17.9	5.7
1964	11.6	0.4	4.0	19.3	6.1
1965	5.9	0.7	6.7	18.7	7.1
1966	10.7	2.3	5.3	18.8	7.5
1967	11.1	1.8	3.7	21.2	7.2
1968	12.8	0.9	5.5	22.9	7.9
1969	12.5	2.2	5.5	25.0	8.6

Source: GNP, investment, export: EPA, Choki Sokyu, 1988; WPI, CPI: Toyo Keizai Tokei Nenpo, 1979 and 1989.

The high rate of growth was sustained for nearly 20 years. Over this period, every recession raised fears that the end of rapid growth had arrived; however, growth was soon renewed. The government's forecasts of economic growth in its "economic plans" consistently underestimated actual growth. The realized economic growth was clearly beyond even the most optimistic forecasts of the time.

There is a long list of reasons why Japan was able to sustain rapid growth up to 1973. Besides the competitive environment created by the changes implemented by the US occupation forces and the stimulation brought about by the increased demand for Japanese exports generated by the Korean War in 1950 and 1951, these reasons include

• a sustained period during which the prices of the raw materials and agricultural commodities which Japan had no choice but to import were relatively low,

• sound policy decisions by Japan's monetary and fiscal authorities through the 1950s and the 1960s, and

• a high saving rate, which provided sufficient funds to support a high investment rate.

The role of saving-*cum*-investment cannot be overemphasized. Wise investment in state-of-the-art machines made it possible to take advantage of the great technological progress that was occurring during this time. High investment, due to high potential growth, also increased aggregate demand, so that output and income grew faster. Finally, investment created the additional capacity to increase aggregate supply. Domestic investment (gross domestic fixed capital formation) accounted for 30–35 percent of Japan's GNP through the 1960s. In 1988 Japan still devoted 30 percent of its GNP to investment, while the United States committed only 17 percent of its GNP to investment.

Confidence among industrial leaders, capital controls against foreign investment, and a strong financial system that funneled money from domestic savers (households) to domestic investors (firms) worked to translate the high saving into high investment. It was truly fortunate that Japan could match a relatively high saving rate with a strong demand for domestic investment. Without its high saving rate, Japan would have had to borrow from abroad to maintain its high investment and its rapid growth. A large quantity of external, non-yen-denominated debt would have made Japan even more vulnerable to such external shocks as oil-price increases and worldwide interest-rate increases. If investment demand had been weak, or if Japanese capital had been attracted to foreign countries, or both, then rapid economic growth would not have been possible even with high domestic saving.

Balancing the budget was also essential to rapid growth. Because the government was prohibited by law from issuing deficit bonds (bonds to finance the deficit in the general budget, as opposed to special development projects) until 1965, government expenditures did not crowd out private investment. It should be noted, however, that the Fiscal Investment and Loan Program [Zaisei Tōyūshi], which came from the Postal Savings System, was utilized for government investment. Even after the law was changed, it was not until 1975—after the first OPEC shock—that the government deficit became large. Monetary policy was also conducted with the aim of financing Japan's strong investment needs. In sum, Japan's domestic fiscal and monetary policies were sound in the sense that they promoted rapid economic growth without disturbing the economy in the 1950s and the 1960s.

Since Japan lacks oil, iron, and many other important raw materials, it must generate considerable export revenue to pay for necessary imports. With the exchange rate fixed at 360 yen per dollar, constant productivity gains were made in order to make the costs of production cheaper, which in turn ensured international competitiveness.

How important a role did the Japanese government play in orchestrating economic growth? Since investment and exports were identified as the major components of demand growth, the government's role was concentrated in promoting investment and exports. There were two types of government plans in Japan: macroeconomic plans and microeconomic industrial policy.

Macroeconomic Planning

Japan's postwar economic plans started as rationing plans with a socialistic flavor, but soon there was a shift to "indicative" plans that emphasized the market. In 1955 the Economic Planning Agency (successor to the Economic Stabilization Bureau) began to announce five-year plans setting targets for the growth rate of the

---

The Economic Planning Agency

Japan's Economic Planning Agency (EPA) performs many tasks that are handled by several different agencies in the United States. It tabulates the national-income accounts (as the US Department of Commerce does), dates the economic peaks and troughs (as the National Bureau of Economic Research, a private research corporation, does in the United States), and prepares the White Paper on the Economy (which is comparable to the Economic Report of the President, prepared by the Council of Economic Advisors in the United States).

The Economic Planning Agency has created several long-term "economic plans" since the end of World War II. The word "plan" might give an incorrect impression that Japan has rigid economic planning. In fact, the long-term economic plan is closer to a forecast than to a plan. Since the EPA does not have any regulatory power, it has less influence on the course of economic policies than the Ministry of Finance or the Ministry of International Trade and Industry.

GNP and for its demand components. Those economic plans were more forecasts than directives, however. The EPA was not given authority to allocate funds or raw materials. (Those powers belong to the Ministry of Finance and the Ministry of International Trade and Industry.) Moreover, actual growth outpaced each of the EPA's plans until the first oil shock. Table 3.7 shows how the Japanese government underestimated the growth potential of the economy prior to the 1970s. A five-year plan was usually scrapped in two to three years when actual growth made it obsolete. During the 1970s, however, the economic plans *overestimated* the growth potential of the economy, partly because they could not anticipate the oil crises. In the 1980s, the growth rate was close to the target.

Those who find indicative plans effective emphasize the importance of the government's signal and its commitment to growth. It is often the case that investment in structures and equipment in a particular industry will not take place unless sales projections are favorable. Uncertainty might make investors pessimistic and keep the economy in a low-demand equilibrium. If an announcement by the government provides credible information on output projections for various industries and government expenditures, it stimulates investment decisions in the private sector. When the private sector believes the plan and behaves accordingly, the plan becomes self-fulfilling. Indicative planning can select a particular equilibrium

Table 3.7
Postwar economic plans in Japan.

Nickname	Cabinet decision date Name of prime minister	Planning horizon and plan survival	Growth	
			Planned	Actual
Five-year Economic Independence Plan[a]	December 23, 1955	FY 1956–1960	5.0	
	Hatoyama	FY 1961		6.1
		FY 1962		7.8
New Long-term Economic Plan	December 17, 1957	FY 1958–1962	5.8	
	Kishi	FY 1963		6.0
		FY 1964		11.2
		FY 1965		12.5
Doubling Income Plan	December 27, 1960	FY 1961–1970, ave.	7.8	
	Ikeda	FY 1961	9.0	13.5
		FY 1962	9.0	6.4
		FY 1963	9.0	12.5
Middle-term Economic Plan	January 22, 1965	FY 1964–1968	8.1	
	Sato	FY 1964		10.6
		FY 1965		5.7
		FY 1966		11.6
Economic and Social Development Plan	March 13, 1967	FY 1967–1971	8.2	
	Sato	FY 1967		13.1
		FY 1968		13.8
		FY 1969		12.3
New Economic and Social Development Plan	May 1, 1970	FY 1970–1975	10.6	
	Sato	FY 1970		10.2
		FY 1971		5.6
		FY 1972		10.4
Economic and Social Basic Plan	February 13, 1973	FY 1973–1977	9.4	
	Tanaka	FY 1973		6.5
		FY 1974		−0.0
		FY 1975		3.2
First Half of Showa 50s Economic Plan	May 14, 1976	FY 1976–1980	6.0+	
	Miki	FY 1976		5.1
		FY 1977		5.3
		FY 1978		5.1

Table 3.7
(continued)

Nickname	Cabinet decision date Name of prime minister	Planning horizon and plan survival	Growth	
			Planned	Actual
New Economic and Social 7-year Plan	August 10, 1979 Ōhira	FY 1979–1985 (midterm correction, 5.1)	5.7	
		FY 1979		5.3
		FY 1980		4.6
		FY 1981		3.5
		FY 1982		3.3
Outlook and Guide for the Economy and Society in the 1980s	August 12, 1983 Nakasone	FY 1983–1990 about 4.0		
		FY 1983		3.7
		FY 1984		5.1
		FY 1985		4.5
		FY 1986		2.7
		FY 1987		5.2
Japan Together with the World— Five-year Economic Plan	May 27, 1988 Takeshita	FY 1988–1993	3.75	
		FY 1988		4.9
		FY 1989		4.0?
		FY 1990		

a. This plan survived only two years and was replaced by the next plan.

among many possible equilibria.[13] This process works so long as the actual rate of economic growth exceeds the forecast, as it did in Japan for a long time. In sum, government planning solved the coordination failure that occurs in macroeconomic models in the Keynesian tradition.

Industrial Policy

In several instances specific industries were "targeted" (that is, identified to be full of growth potential) mainly because of their importance for Japan's overall economic activity. During the 1950s and the 1960s, targeted industries received favorable allocations of foreign exchange and subsidized loans through government agencies. The main purpose of industrial policy in those years was to identify "sunrise" industries and nurture them quickly. First, the government targeted industries with increasing-returns technologies (that is, industries in which the average cost of production becomes significantly lower when the scale of operation is expanded). Given a greater demand for the product created by export subsidies and import restrictions, a targeted industry could increase its capacity quickly, so that its average costs would go down. Thus, the industry could become cost-competitive by itself. This is a classic argument for "infant-industry protection."

Take, for example, the First Iron and Steel Rationalization Plan (1951–1954).[14] The plan called for the investment of 63 billion yen. The actual investment amounted to 120 billion yen. Government subsidies were provided, and the industry's outputs were used extensively in public works. During the Second Rationalization Plan, there was a fixed investment (over the eight years) of 500 billion yen. The demand for consumer durables had increased, and funds for investment were available though commercial loans from the private sector.

One of the major tools of Japanese industrial policy was the allocation of foreign reserves for the purchase of capital equipment and raw materials. Unless a firm was assigned foreign currency by the government, it could not carry out capacity expansion, since borrowing from abroad was essentially prohibited. Another tool was the subsidization of loans for investment in structures and equipment through government financial agencies such as the Development Bank.

The initial phase of industrial policy was easy for the government to undertake, since the allocation of funds or of foreign reserves automatically determined the investment plan. Through the 1960s, however, private domestic funds became abundant, and trade surpluses swelled foreign reserves. In this environment, the Ministry of International Trade and Industry (MITI) also supplied administrative guidance to regulate the speed of investment in order to avert excessive competition due to "overcapacity." The investment plans of firms were coordinated so that total capacity expansion fell within MITI's projections of demand expansion.

These policies were generally effective. Even administrative guidance had an impact on the behavior of the private sector. The final evaluation of industrial policy is mixed, however. It is true that some targeted industries (steel, shipbuilding, chemicals) blossomed.

But some of Japan's "star" industries, such as consumer electronics and precision optical products, were not targeted. The automobile companies refused to follow MITI's guidelines to reduce competition.

As was mentioned in chapter 2, Japan renounced military power. The budgets for the self-defense forces were kept very low—typically, below 1 percent of the GNP—relative to the defense budgets of other industrialized nations. Hence, a larger portion of the government's budget for industries was directed to improving social infrastructures and government investment projects. Although this aspect contributed to Japan's higher rate of economic growth, it would be difficult to quantify.

THE SLOWDOWN

Toward the end of the 1960s, Japan's economic growth accelerated and was accompanied by large trade surpluses. This was an indication that the yen, fixed at 360 per dollar since 1949, had become undervalued. Moreover, the problem was not limited to the yen. The United States was recording persistent trade deficits, while Germany sustained trade surpluses. A massive realignment of exchange rates was needed. Although the Bretton Woods regime of fixed exchange rates (in effect since 1944) had a mechanism for adjusting the exchange rate when a country's economy underwent significant structural change, it was rarely invoked. Devaluation was seen as a political embarassment by the devaluing country. It was also opposed by competing countries, who feared changes in price competitiveness.

The Bretton Woods fixed-exchange-rate regime gave way to floating exchange rates in the early 1970s. In August 1971, President Nixon suspended the gold convertibility of the dollar. After the adjustment period provided by the Smithsonian regime from December 1971 to February 1973, the major currencies began to float in the spring of 1973. Since Japan's government and private sector had been accustomed to the fixed exchange rate, the transition took some time.

The yen's revaluation (appreciation) was strongly opposed by business executives and politicians during the adjustment period. The opposition may have been due in part to fear of losing competitiveness in exporting industries. However, the accumulation of large trade surpluses made it clear that the yen should be revalued. Many Japanese and American economists argued for adjusting the exchange rate (opinions differed regarding how fast the adjustment should be), but political opinion went the other way. The Minister of International Trade and Industry hinted that moderate inflation in Japan would help. If adherence to the fixed-exchange-rate system had been considered the economic mandate, inflation to avoid revaluation would have been justified. However, the fixed-exchange-rate system was only a means to achieve other economic objectives, such as lower inflation and higher growth rates. Nevertheless, with an attitude more lenient toward inflation than revaluation and with the political goal of "transforming the Japanese archipelago," Prime Minister Tanaka's government increased the money supply and lowered the interest rate in 1972. Inflationary pressure built up throughout the spring of 1973.

When the oil embargo imposed by the OPEC countries was announced in October 1973, inflation took off. Inflationary expectations made the situation worse. "Wild inflation" [Kyōran Bukka] reached 30 percent in 1974. Wages increased more than 20 percent in that year, since prices were also rising, but in turn the increase in wages fueled inflation, resulting in a classic example of a price-wage spiral.[15]

It took at least several years for Japan to reallocate resources from unconditionally growth-oriented sectors to energy-conservation and pollution-control sectors.

The oil embargo of 1973 and the Nixon overture to China gave Japan a sense of fragility. Japan's lack of domestic energy sources had always been a fact of life, but it took the Kyōran Bukka for the Japanese to realize how crucial energy was. When Nixon suddenly visited China in February 1972, the shock to the Japanese public was comparable to that caused by the suspension of convertibility in the preceding year. The visit was an embarassment to the Japanese government, which had not been informed of Nixon's plans in advance. This incident also made the Japanese aware that they were not politically well-connected to Washington.

The global environmental problem, highlighted in the Club of Rome's 1972 report *The Limits to Growth*, also contributed to pessimism. This report had a strong impact in Japan, where the growth rate had been very high and where zero growth would mean substan-

Table 3.8
Japan during oil crises.

First oil crisis				Second oil crisis			
Calendar year	GNP growth[a]	Infla-tion[b]	Money supply[c]	Calendar year	GNP growth[a]	Infla-tion[b]	Money supply[c]
1971	4.3	−0.8	24.3	1977	5.3	1.9	11.1
1972	8.5	0.8	24.7	1978	5.2	−2.6	13.1
1973	7.9	15.7	16.8	1979	5.3	7.3	9.1
1974	−1.4	31.6	11.5	1980	4.3	17.8	7.2
1975	2.7	3.0	14.5	1981	3.7	1.4	11.0
1976	4.8	5.0	13.5	1982	3.1	1.8	7.9

a. Real GNP growth rate from previous year (%).
b. Rate of change in wholesale price index (%).
c. Growth rate of outstanding of M2 (or M2 + CD, after 1980) at end of year (%).

tial changes in the economy. Pollution in Japan was also reaching the point where many thought something had to be done. In four major court cases, companies that had carelessly polluted the environment were found guilty.

By the time of the second oil crisis (1979–1980), Japan's monetary policy was much more prudent, and the inflation rate was not greatly affected (see table 3.8).

The oil crises can be viewed as negative aggregate supply shocks that lowered the supply potential of the Japanese economy, at least in the intermediate run. A sudden downward shift in aggregate supply causes a decline in output (GNP) and an increase in inflation. If the downward adjustment of output is slowed, then inflation is aggravated, as in the 1973–74 episode; if a sharp increase in prices is to be avoided, a prolonged decline in output must be endured. In either case, the two oil crises decreased Japan's growth potential significantly.

Of course, the three major factors in the end of the postwar Japanese miracle—the oil crises, the decrease in investment, and the slowdown in technological progress[16]—were not independent of one another. The oil crises, which drew attention to Japan's heavy dependence on nonrenewable resources, gave many people a pessimistic outlook and caused downward shifts in expectations of future growth as well as in current growth potential. Japanese producers and investors suddenly became aware of the limits of the world's natural resources and of Japan's vulnerability as an importer of raw materials. Since expected future earnings fell, investment demand also fell. The decline in investment lowered current aggregate demand as well as future capacity, and slowed the adoption of advanced technology.

Moreover, it is possible to think that Japan finally caught up with the United States and the Western European countries technologically at some point in the mid 1970s. Since it is harder to develop a country's own new technology than to merely obtain licenses, Japan's growth rate then had to fall.

SUMMARY

Japan had sustained reasonably rapid growth from the 1880s to the beginning of the Second World War. That war devastated much of Japan's capital stock and was followed by high inflation; nonetheless, by the mid 1950s the Japanese economy was growing even faster. Investment was the key: the higher investment rate brought the higher rate of economic growth. Japan's high saving rate seems to have made investment easier. (In the 1940s and the 1950s, the worldwide capital market was not ready to finance capital expenditures in Japan.)

The exceptionally rapid growth of the Japanese economy came to an abrupt end in 1973–74, with the average growth rate dropping from about 10 percent to about 5 percent. Among the factors contributing to the lowering of the growth rate was the decrease in investment caused by the downward revision of the forecasts of future growth. Another factor was pessimism regarding the resources available to Japan, due to the monopolistic power of OPEC and to environmental concerns. Furthermore, by the mid 1970s Japan had caught up with the Western countries technologically.

Put differently, by the mid 1970s the major constraint on Japan's economic growth was no longer foreign-exchange reserves and aggregate demand; it was now aggregate supply potential.

Although investment is still higher in Japan than in other countries, Japan's growth potential is now only slightly higher than those of other advanced countries, such as Germany and the United States.

Table 3.9
Summary of real-GNP series.

Coverage:	1834–1940	1955–1970	1970–most current
yen units:	in millions	in billions	in billions
deflator:	1934–36 prices	1970 prices	1980 prices
Source:	*Patterns*	EPA *Choki Sokyu*, 1989	EPA Annual Report, 1989

APPENDIX: GUIDE TO GNP DATA

Prewar Data

See appendix to chapter 2.

Postwar Data

A report of national accounts is published by the Economic Planning Agency every March. Quarterly updates can be obtained from the agency or from any data service agency (for example, Nikkei NEEDS).

The national-income accounts, available at annual and quarterly frequencies, have often been revised. After Japan switched to a new System of National Accounts (SNA) basis, backdating with the new SNA measure took time. For several years, backdating with the consistent basis was available only from 1965. It was only in 1989 that the government completed backdating from 1955. The figures are compiled in the Economic Planning Agency's 1989 publication *Report on National Accounts from 1955 to 1969* [*Choki Sokyu Suikei*]. Newer data and revisions of the preceding few years become available every March in the EPA's *Annual Report on National Accounts*. In performing an analysis, one should make sure that one has the new backdated estimates.

Use of Data

Researchers performing econometric analyses involving postwar GNP data should be careful in handling the following points: The oil shock of 1973–74 caused a structural change in Japan, as is explained in chapter 4. The average rate of economic growth dropped from nearly 10 percent to about 5 percent. When the logarithm of the GNP series for the entire postwar period is analyzed, a linear trend term is not sufficient. Either a quadratic trend or a dummy variable for the post-oil-shock period is recommended.

NOTES

1. Denison and Chung (1976a, p. 81) estimate that it was in 1953 that "national income first exceeded the prewar peak." Ohkawa and Rosovsky (1973) estimate that the prewar peak in 1937 was surpassed around 1954, and the extrapolation of the prewar peaks in 1917 and 1937 was reached in 1962.

2. See Denison and Chung 1976b for a more detailed treatment of growth accounting.

3. Japan and Italy were the only exceptions among thirteen industrialized countries.

4. For a detailed discussion of the material covered in this section, see Nakamura 1981.

5. These policies are discussed in detail in chapter 7.

6. The holding of land by absentee landlords was banned; resident landlords were limited to 1 cho (2.45 acres), and land-owning tenants to 3 cho. The buying up and reselling of land was handled by a land committee. Tenant farmers paid 757 yen per tan (= 0.1 cho = 0.245 acres) of rice paddy and 446 yen per tan of any other kind of field; landlords received (in government bonds) 978 yen per tan of rice paddy and 577 yen per tan of other fields. The amount was no more than 7 percent of the annual crop value from the land. (Kosai 1986, p. 20)

7. Government intervention in rice distribution started in 1921, when the *Beikoku* act was enacted. In 1942 the food-control law was passed, and the government became the sole agent for purchasing rice and distributing (rationing) it to consumers. With modifications that allow some unregulated distribution, this law is still in effect.

Rice costs about 7 times as much to produce in Japan as in the United States. Rice imports are prohibited. The inventories of rice amount to more than a year's domestic consumption. The surplus of rice has prompted the government to order cutbacks in planting. Before the war, heavy taxation of the agricultural sector contributed to Japan's economic development by providing funds for investment in the manufacturing sector. Since the war, the agricultural sector has been increasingly subsidized rather than overtaxed.

8. Keynes' general theory was even cited in a speech to the Diet by Finance Minister Tanzan Ishibashi in July 1946.

9. In addition, there was a redenomination of the yen on March 3, 1946. A redenomination of the yen and a deposit freeze do not have to accompany each other. Another yen redenomination was proposed during the 1970s because the yen and the lira were the only currencies with three-digit exchange rates against the US dollar. Theoretically, making old 100-yen notes equivalent to a new one-yen would not change any real economic activity, aside from being a temporary boon for the printing business. However, the fear of inflation and the memory of the asset freeze and the subsequent confiscation produced opposition to the measure among the public.

10. The inflation in Japan was much smaller in magnitude than the famous German inflation of the 1920s or that in some of the Latin American countries during the 1980s. Therefore, a less drastic measure was necessary to curb it.

11. The peace treaty with the Soviet Union has not been signed yet, although diplomatic relations were established long ago. Japan has made it clear that the four islands off Hokkaido (the Northern Terriory) must be returned to Japan before the peace treaty can be signed. The four islands have been claimed by Japan since the Tokugawa period. Under the Yalta agreement in which the United States, the Soviet Union, and other countries agreed to limit Japan to the territory it had held before the start of its imperial aggression, these islands do belong to Japan. Soviet troops invaded and occupied them after Japan surrendered on August 15, 1945.

12. The forming of the Ikeda cabinet was preceded by a bitter clash between radical and moderate factions in the labor movement and by an argument between the Liberal Democratic Party and the opposition parties over the ratification of a revised US-Japan Security Treaty. After the Liberal Democratic Party voted for the treaty in the House of Representatives over strong (sometimes violent) opposition from other parties, the political conflict took to the streets. Prime Minister Kishi resigned in July to take responsibility for the "turmoil" and was replaced by Ikeda. The head of the Socialist Party was stabbed to death in October. One might suspect that Ikeda's income-doubling plan was intended to divert attention away from the confrontational political divisions and toward an economic target that all parties could agree with.

13. A macroeconomic equilibrium (in the simplest sense) means that aggregate demand equals aggregate supply. If aggregate demand equals aggregate supply at different levels, one says that there are multiple equilibria.

Suppose that a firm becomes optimistic about prospective sales, then hires more workers and produces more, thus increasing the aggregate supply. Since more workers are hired, more disposable income is generated, increasing the aggregate demand. If the workers' propensity for consumption and their marginal productivity satisfy a special relationship, the aggregate supply and the aggregate demand are equalized at a new level. This cyclical argument may work even with a constant price level.

14. "Rationalization" was a code word in Japan for capital-intensive investment in order to raise productivity, with implications of automation, state-of-the-art technology transfer, and streamlining of production and management. Moreover, it often meant that workers had to be transferred to other jobs, factories, or companies, if not laid off. Thus, labor unions often opposed "rationalization."

15. The cycle was interrupted in 1975; see chapter 8.

16. Kosai and Ogino (1984, p. 41) list two more factors: a falloff in the supply of labor and a slowdown in the expansion of exports. I do not consider those to have been very important, however. The labor supply (both in hours and in employment) indeed fell during the 1970s, but the decline in labor's contribution to growth from 1.59 percent during the 1960s to 1.01 percent in the 1970s was a relatively minor change. The export/GNP ratio increased during the 1970s.

BIBLIOGRAPHY

Denison, E. F., and W. K. Chung. 1976a. "Economic growth and its sources." In *Asia's New Giant*, ed. H. Patrick and H. Rosovsky. Brookings Institution.

Denison, E. F., and W. K. Chung. 1976b. *How Japan's Economy Grew So Fast*. Brookings Institution.

Kosai, Y. 1986. *The Era of High-Speed Growth*. University of Tokyo Press.

Kosai, Y., and Y. Ogino. 1974. *The Contemporary Japanese Economy*. M. E. Sharpe.

Nakamura, T. 1981. *The Postwar Japanese Economy: Its Development and Structure*. University of Tokyo Press.

Ohkawa, K., and H. Rosovsky. 1973. *The Economic Growth of Japan*. Stanford University Press.

Shinohara, M. 1986. *Nihon Keizai Kougi*. Toyo Keizai.

Chapter 4

BUSINESS CYCLES AND ECONOMIC POLICIES

Many key economic variables, such as GNP, industrial production, employment, and consumption, move together (i.e., grow at higher and lower rates together). Their fluctuations about their long-run trends have shown remarkable regularities for many decades. These co-movements characterize what is called the *business cycle*. To be precise, business cycles represent the deviation of major macroeconomic variables from their trends in a cyclical fashion for some duration. That is, there are pronounced co-movements and significant serial correlation among aggregate variables. A business cycle is divided into an expansion (boom) phase and a recession (contraction) phase. The former is the period from a trough (a low turning point) to a peak (a high turning point); the latter is the period from a peak to a trough. Business cycles have been observed in virtually all countries at various times, and their causes and possible cures have been popular topics in macroeconomics.

In this chapter, the short-run fluctuations of the Japanese economy are examined in connection with business cycles. The topic of business cycles is a good setting in which to think about the role of macroeconomic policy in the "stabilization" of the economy.

DATING OF BUSINESS CYCLES

In Japan, the Economic Planning Agency (a wing of the government) compiles a *diffusion index* (DI) and a *composite index* (CI) and uses these indices to identify business cycles.[1] Variables such as the industrial production index, the manufacturing shipping index, the manufacturers' raw material consumption index, and the import quantity index are checked every month. Conceptually, the DI is calculated by counting the number of indicators that show increases over their values of 3 months earlier and recording the percentage of such expansionary variables. If more than half of the indices are expanding, that month is judged to be in an expansionary phase; if fewer than half, a recessionary phase. (In the United States—where the reference dates of peaks and troughs are determined by the National Bureau of Economic Research, a nonprofit private organization—two consecutive quarters of negative growth in the GNP are considered evidence of a recession.) There are leading, contemporaneous, and lagging series of the DI. For the CI, each variable is weighted in a specific formula so that a quantitative measure of business cycles can be calculated.

REGULARITIES AMONG BUSINESS CYCLES

There are several regularities among business cycles. A 7–12-year cycle caused by fluctuations in fixed investments is sometimes called a *Juglar cycle*, a *medium-term cycle*, or a *major cycle*. A short-term cycle of 3–4 years, sometimes called a *Kitchin cycle*, corresponds to fluctuations in inventory investment.[2]

Empirical research into business cycles has produced a large body of literature. The main focus of business-cycle inquiry has been shifting toward theoretical studies accompanied by empirical analyses and away from simple dating and description of regularities. Economists are still debating what the initial shocks are that start a business-cycle fluctuation, how they propagate among sectors of an economy, and why their effects are prolonged. Some of the theories will be reviewed below.

POSTWAR BUSINESS CYCLES IN JAPAN

Between 1950 and 1970, most of Japan's economic fluctuations were triggered by fluctuations in the international balance of payments (discussed in chapter 3). When the Japanese economy was in a boom, imports rose faster than exports. (Imports to Japan rise with Japanese income; exports from Japan depend on foreign—particularly American—income.) With the exchange rate fixed at 360 yen per dollar under the Bretton Woods regime and with foreign reserves relatively scarce, there was no other option for the Japanese government but to try to slow growth when imports exceeded exports for an extended time. Interest rates were raised and government expenditures were cut until imports and investment slowed enough to bring the balance of payments back into line. (No capital-inflow balance was allowed before the mid 1970s.) In this sense, the international balance of payments acted as a check on economic booms.

Theoretically, inflation could have worked as a ceiling on economic activities in Japan, as it did in other countries during the 1950s and the 1960s. Because aggregate demand increases faster than aggregate supply, inflation would flare up to warn of the overheating of the economy. But the inflation rate in Japan stayed low and steady during the rapid-growth era of the 1950s and the 1960s. (We will see why shortly.)

Table 4.1 summarizes Japan's postwar business cycles. Growth rates during recessions were never negative, with the exceptions of the 1954 recession and the one that followed the first oil crisis. In that sense, a recession in Japan was largely a "slowdown" in growth (a *growth recession*) rather than a "contraction." Observe that expansionary periods were about three times as long as recessionary periods before the first oil crisis. One complete cycle from peak to peak (or trough to trough) lasted about 3 or 4 years. A notable exception was the very long expansion (57 months) from 1965 to 1970.

The two oil crises put strong contractionary pressures on the Japanese economy. The growth rate after the 1974 contraction was half that of the preceding expansionary phase, and after the second oil crisis Japan suffered an unusually long recession. That recession was not as acute as the one associated with the first oil crisis, but it was more prolonged, lasting 36 months. One reason for this difference is that monetary policies were conducted much more cautiously immediately after the second oil crisis. After the first oil crisis monetary restraint was applied too late, and inflation in the consumer-price index rose to 28 percent in 1974. After the second oil crisis the Bank of Japan moved quickly to restrain the economy and thereby avoided its earlier mistake.

THEORY AND ESTIMATION

Various schools of thought disagree over what causes business cycles and what economic policy could and should do to tame them. One camp believes that the market economy tends to be cyclical by nature, that this is due to private agents' making decisions that are

Table 4.1
Postwar business cycles in Japan. One complete cycle consists of a period of expansion (from a trough to a peak) and a period of contraction (from a peak to a trough of the next cycle).

Trough (month)	Expansion		Peak month	Recession	
	Length (months)	Average growth[b]		Length (months)	Average growth[b]
—	—	—	June 1951	4[a]	
Oct. 1951[a]	27	13.5%	Jan. 1954	10	−3.7%
Nov. 1954	31	10.1%	June 1957	12	5.0%
June 1958	42	14.0%	Dec. 1961	10	3.7%
Oct. 1962	24	13.3%	Oct. 1964	12	4.1%
Oct. 1965	57	14.4%	July 1970	17	3.9%
Dec. 1971	23	7.5%	Nov. 1973	16	−1.5%
Mar. 1975	22	5.9%	Jan. 1977	9	4.2%
Oct. 1977	28	5.6%	Feb. 1980	36	3.2%
Feb. 1983	28	6.3%	June 1985	17	4.2%
Nov. 1986	46	(as of August 1990)			

a. Dates for peaks and troughs are by EPA. Some argue that the trough of the first cycle should instead be April of 1952 (see Shinohara 1986, p. 25).
b. The average growth rate is calculated as the simple (straight-line) annualized growth rate from peak (quarter) to trough (quarter) or from trough (quarter) to peak (quarter). Thus, the rate reported here overstates the growth rate of an expansion that lasts for significantly longer than a year, in comparison with a calculation in which the compounding annual rate is used.
Sources: Economic Planning Agency, Japan Economic Indicators, 1986; Economic Planning Agency, Annual Report on National Income Statistics, 1975; Economic Planning Agency, Annual Report on National Account, 1986; Toyo Keizai Shinpo, Economic Statistics Annual, 1986.

inconsistent in the aggregate as well as to exogenous shocks such as droughts, floods, and oil crises, and that the role of economic policy is to alleviate inefficiencies caused by business cycles. On this Keynesian view, demand shocks are preeminent. For example, in a very simplified model, when demand is overstimulated for some reason, inflation flares up. In order to curb inflation, fiscal and monetary policies would be tightened, which would contract the economy. After a recession brings down the inflation rate, the economy can resume its growth. The theory contends that without policy intervention the amplitude of the cycle would be greater. Another camp believes that the market economy, left alone, is reasonably stable and without substantial fluctuations. This school believes that policy interventions worsen the amplitude of cycles. A third camp believes that whether or not government policy is capable of lessenening the economic fluctuations, it is not desirable anyway.

In this section, the Keynesian approach will be introduced to explain Japan's experience with business cycles. Other theories of business cycles are surveyed in an appendix at the end of the chapter.

The Keynesian Approach to Business Cycles

Keynesians believe that major disturbances which affect aggregate demand are the sources of business cycles. There are many ideas about the major source of these shocks and about the nature of the mechanisms that prolong their effects. Keynesians also tend to believe that prices and wages are sluggish—that is, that prices and wages do not change quickly enough to equate demand and supply.

Keynes (1936) originally postulated that investment was governed by the "animal spirits" of entrepreneurs. Thus, investment was regarded as an exogenous source of fluctuations in an economy. It is not essential to Keynesian theory whether a shock is in consumption, in investment, or in exports, as long as it originates on the demand side and as long as the Keynesian propagation mechanism explained below is correct.

Once an unexpected increase occurs in consumption, investment, or exports, an "accelerator-multiplier" process works to propagate and prolong the shocks. A surge in demand (sales) represented by a sudden decrease in inventories will stimulate producers to produce more by hiring more workers, and to expand productive capacity by investing more. There will be increased employment, which results in increased consumption and investment. Both will create more demand for products. Thus, an increase in demand tends to reinforce and prolong itself, creating a sustained boom. This process, however, cannot continue forever. Economic growth will hit a ceiling formed by the limit of production capacity on the supply side. If aggregate demand exceeds aggregate supply, prices will go up. A price increase will reduce the real money supply, which in turn bids up interest rates (the intertemporal prices of money). Higher interest rates discourage investment, thereby dampening growth. Inflation will also prompt the government to put a discretionary restraint on the economy. Once the economy hits a downturn, the whole process will be reversed.

It is common among Keynesians to believe that the government has the ability to correct deviations of demand from supply, whereas the market economy left alone is either downright unstable or else too slow in adjusting to equilibrium after a shock hits the economy. The government, it is said, can offset various shocks by "fine-tuning" monetary and fiscal policies.

Applications to the Japanese Economy

Applying the Keynesian story to the Japanese experience of 1955–1970 requires a slight modification. Until the mid 1960s, Japan had strict capital controls: Any foreign investment in Japan and any Japanese investment were subject to government approval. Foreign currencies earned by exporters had to be converted into yen, and any importers who needed foreign currency had to apply to the government for it. Any claims against foreign countries were thus maintained as foreign reserves held in the Foreign Exchange Fund Special Account. To prevent the loss of its foreign reserves, Japan had to maintain a trade balance of zero over each business cycle.

Until August 1971, Japan maintained a fixed exchange rate of 360 yen to the dollar. In order to maintain a trade balance without altering the exchange rate (or the domestic price level), imports had to be managed. Exports could not be managed, since they depended mostly on foreign income, which was beyond the Japanese government's control.

One determinant of imports is domestic income. A large component of Japan's imports is raw materials to be used in production, and these are very sensitive to the domestic production level. Whenever the Japanese economy sustained an expansion, imports increased faster than exports and the trade balance moved into deficit. Accordingly, the government had to prevent a sharp increase in imports in order to maintain its foreign-exchange reserves. The reduction in imports was achieved by applying the brakes to the overall economy. Interest rates were raised, and lending from banks and government expenditures was slowed down. Policy restraints were maintained until the balance of trade was restored. In other words, in order for the trade balance to be maintained it was necessary to adjust domestic income via government policy.

Apparently the government's policies were causing recessions and booms in Japan during this period. Every postwar recession was preceded by a period of policy restraint, and each period of restraint (with two exceptions) was followed by a recession. The beginning of each period of expansion was either closely preceded by or simultaneous with the relaxation of policy restraints.

This should not be confused with the idea that cycles were "caused" by economic policies, however. Pursuing a goal other than economic growth—namely the maintainance of the balance of payments—made it necessary to restrain growth. Thus, it is not necessarily correct to argue that without those restraints the Japanese economy would not have had business cycles.

Trade balances, not inflation, acted as the ceiling for Japan's booms before the mid 1960s. The balance of trade effectively determined the upper limit on the growth of demand. In other words, the income level that caused imports to exceed exports was lower than the potential maximum level of supply. Thus, the demand side of the economy was restrained before it exceeded the aggregate supply. Inflation was mild and steady throughout the 1960s.

After 1971, the story is different.[3] First, the exchange rate became flexible and capital controls were relaxed. Second, the oil crises were a source of major supply-side shocks in the 1970s. In 1971 the government revalued the exchange rate, and between 1971 and 1973 the yen-dollar rate was unsuccessfully varied in search of a new, stable level. Finally, in February 1973, all efforts to fix the exchange rate were abandoned. The yen-dollar exchange rate has been floating "cleanly" (that is, without major intervention from monetary authorities) during most of the period since February 1973.[4] These changes in the early 1970s created a new situation as far as the growth ceiling was concerned. As early as the late 1960s trade surpluses were being maintained for long periods of time, even during expansionary periods. This means that the ceiling on demand growth due to the balance of payments was raised, and the aggregate-supply ceiling was soon to become lower than the balance-of-payments ceiling.

The oil crisis of 1973–74 caused a sharp decrease in productivity, which corresponded to a sudden lowering of the aggregate-supply

> **Keynesian Macroeconomic Equilibrium**
> Consider a simple Keynesian macroeconomic equilibrium at a fixed aggregate price. Recall that aggregate demand can be understood as the definition of GNP:
>
> $$Y^d = C + I + G + (EX - IM).$$
>
> In the simplest macroeconomic model, consumption is assumed to be a function of current disposable income, Y: $C = cY$. Suppose that I and G are determined exogenously. Exports (EX) are determined by foreign demand, and are thus exogenous to Japan's economy. Imports (IM) depend on domestic disposable income: $IM = mY$.
>
>   Suppose that aggregate supply, Y^s, is fixed in the short run, and that an equilibrium is attained, $Y^d = Y^s$, at Y. Substituting all the assumed relationships into the equation above, we obtain
>
> $$Y = cY + I + G + (EX - mY).$$
>
> That is, $(1 - c - m)Y = (I + G + EX)$, or
>
> $$Y^* = (I + G + EX)/(1 - c - m).$$
>
> At the equilibrium level of income, Y^*, there is no guarantee that the trade balance (balance of payments), $EX - IM$, is kept to zero. If domestic prices, foreign prices, and the exchange rate all remain constant (e.g., if we are living in a fixed-exchange-rate regime), the price mechanism is inoperative, so there is no mechanism to restore the balance of payments. Given $IM = mY$, restraining the economy (say, by reducing G) would restore the balance of payments. But then the aggregate demand would be less than the potential output level—that is, a macro disequilibrium, or a recession, would result.

ceiling. Japan could either keep fewer products for domestic use (because it had to pay more for imported crude oil) or else reduce aggregate supply in order to reduce the use of oil, provided that the level of oil used in production was fixed in the short run. In other words, sharp oil-price increases represented "adverse" technological progress for Japan: Producers received less output from the same inputs of labor and capital. (In the long run, however, the average amount of oil necessary to produce a certain amount of output dropped, because of the adoption of energy-saving technologies, so less oil was needed to produce and consume the same amount of domestic output.)

  A delay in the restraining of demand created the "wild" inflation of 1973–74, which was brought down by the creation one of Japan's

Table 4.2
Comparison of GNP volatility: standard deviation (prewar)/standard deviation (postwar).

Prewar period	Postwar period	Japan	United States
1885–1940	1955–1985	1.31[a]	3.40[a]
1901–1928[b]	1955–1973[b]	1.77	1.79
1869–1940	1950–1985	—	3.00[c]

a. Full samples for Japan and corresponding samples for US.
b. Ignores Great Depression and oil crises.
c. Full samples for US.
Source: Author's calculations.

worst postwar recessions. It was unfortunate that the 1973 oil crisis occurred at a time when Japan was experiencing inflationary pressure from the higher balance-of-trade ceiling and a delay in the appreciation of the yen against the dollar.

Have the Postwar Business Cycles Been Less Volatile than the Prewar Ones?

On casual observation, Japan's post-World War II economy is more stable, thanks to wise macroeconomic policies, than the prewar economy. Recently there has been renewed interest in this subject. One way to evaluate whether the postwar business cycles have been less volatile[5] than the prewar ones is to create time series of deviations of the GNP from its quadratic trend for the prewar and postwar periods, and to measure the standard deviation of the time series of the GNP for each period and then compare the prewar standard deviation with the postwar standard deviation. From table 4.2, which summarizes the results of this evaluation, we can conclude that

• the postwar business cycles are less volatile than the prewar ones,

• Japanese business cycles are more similar before and after the war than are US business cycles, and

• if we ignore the Great Depression during the prewar era and the oil crises during the postwar era, the prewar-postwar volatility ratio is much smaller and is comparable between the two countries.

There are several possible interpretations of these results. First, postwar "stabilization policy" simply may have been successful.

Vector Autoregressions

It is very difficult to determine empirically what are exogenous shocks and what are policy-induced shocks to the economy. So far, there is no conclusive evidence for or against the conventional views on the causes of Japanese business cycles. Many researchers are trying to develop effective methods to this end, and are testing various models on postwar data. One such attempt is in the use of *vector autoregressions*.

Sims (1980) constructed a system of vector autoregressions with variables including the interest rate (R), output measured by the industrial production index (IP), money (M), and prices (P). A vector of the current variables,

$$x(t) = \{R(t), IP(t), M(t), P(t)\},$$

is explained by the effects of past variables, $x(t-1)$, $x(t-2)$, . . . , and a disturbance term, $e(t)$. A disturbance term can be interpreted as a shock (unexpected change) to that variable.

By tracing the effects of a particular disturbance on its own and other variables in the system over time, we can determine the relative explanatory power of the disturbance.

Sims found that the interest rate was more powerful than money in explaining fluctuations in output, while monetary disturbances, such as money-supply increases, explained price fluctuations in the long run. Sims argued that this finding was consistent with the Keynesian theory of business fluctuations (as opposed to the monetarist explanation or the new classical explanation).

A similar analysis was conducted for Japan. It was found that neither money nor interest rates explain fluctuations in output and prices (Hayashi and Ito 1981). Output and prices are fluctuating, apparently independent of monetary shocks. These findings are more consistent with the interpretation that real shocks are responsible for economic fluctuations in Japan. It may appear that this interpretation is inconsistent with the Keynesian version of business cycles. The observed interest-rate variable may not have been fluctuating enough to reflect the true conditions of the money market, however. (See the discussion of disequilibrium analysis in chapter 5.) Monetary policy was influential in causing recessions under the Bretton Woods system (in order to maintain the balance of payments), and the policy relied on tools such as window guidance (see chapter 5), which were not a part of the market mechanism. More empirical research is needed.

Eichenbaum and Singleton (1986) used similar techniques to investigate whether the real-business-cycle theory is supported by US data.

Another possible interpretation is that Japan's industrial structure became much more diversified and robust after the war, when many new industries emerged (including service industries, which tend to be relatively free from severe cycles). A final possibility is that external shocks were smaller after the war than before. The Keynesian viewpoint favors the first interpretation, but without further econometric investigation it is impossible to eliminate the other possibilities.[6] This kind of analysis is very intricate. In order to study the exact nature of declining fluctuations, for example, it is necessary to apply the technique of vector autoregressions, an advanced technique of econometrics. (The flavor of such analysis, which is beyond the scope of this book, is suggested by the accompanying box.)

Are Economic Fluctuations Diminishing in Amplitude?

Since the mid 1970s, the amplitude of Japan's economic growth appears to have declined. This is clear from table 4.3, which gives comparative summary statistics for growth rates of real GNP for the 15 years prior to 1975 and the 15 years after 1975 for Japan and the United States. In Japan, although the average growth rate declined by half, the volatility of growth declined significantly during the second 15-year period. This is evident either from the standard deviation or from the range (the difference between the maximum and minimum growth rates). The coefficient of variation (that is, the standard deviation divided by the mean) decreased by half in Japan.[7] A similar decrease in the amplitudes of fluctuations was not observed in the United States.

Why have the amplitudes of economic fluctuations decreased in Japan? First of all, a close examination of the composition of aggregate demand reveals that investment became less volatile. To be precise, the weight of inventory investment is declining, and the volatility of inventory and fixed investment has declined. Since investment fluctuations are a major source of economic fluctuations according to both Keynesian and non-Keynesian stories (recall the brief section on regularities), the declining weight of investment contributes to the decline in overall economic fluctuations.

The average share of inventory investment in Japan's GNP (in real terms) for the years 1975–1989 is 0.6 percent, versus 2.0 percent for 1960–1974. The standard deviation of the share declined from 0.63

Table 4.3
Growth rates.

	Japan					United States				
	AVE	MAX	MIN	SD	SD/AVE	AVE	MAX	MIN	SD	SD/AVE
1960–1974	9.2	13.6	−1.4	3.91	0.43	3.5	5.8	−0.5	2.03	0.58
1975–1989	4.4	5.7	2.5	1.04	0.24	2.9	6.8	−2.5	2.52	0.88

Source: Author's calculations.
Data source: See appendix to chapter 3.

for 1960–1974 to 0.22 for 1975–1989. The average share of "fixed" investment in GNP did not decline during 1975–1989 in comparison with 1960–1974. In fact, it rose slightly, from 30.3 to 32.1. The standard deviation of the fixed-investment share, however, declined from 4.81 to 1.91. This undoubtedly contributed to the considerable decline in overall economic fluctuations.

There are three possible reasons behind the decline in inventory fluctuations. First, the industrial structure shifted toward a larger service sector, so inventories could be smaller in proportion to output. (This factor is more intense for the United States, yet a similar decline in economic fluctuations was not observed there.) Second, the inventory-management system used in Japan became so advanced that the inventory ratio declined in the manufacturing sector. Third, monetary policy became steadier after 1975. The average growth rate of the money supply has been brought down gradually since 1975, and its fluctuations have also lessened.[8]

In the second half of the 1980s, both the United States and Japan sustained steady growth without recessions.[9] Japan has not experienced negative growth since 1974. As expansionary phases become longer and recessionary declines become shallower, the interest in business cycles in Japan seems to fade away.

POLITICAL BUSINESS CYCLES

A new theory of political business cycles has recently become popular among political scientists and economists. This theory emphasizes the role of political motivations in causing business cycles. Two versions of the theory have become popular with respect to American history. The *manipulative model* emphasizes the incumbent party's attempts to be reelected; the *partisan model* supposes that a party forces its philosophical agenda on the economy.[10]

In the United States, according to Nordhaus (1975), the four-year interval between presidential elections causes a four-year business cycle. The incumbent's desire to win another term or to maintain his party's hold on the White House provides an incentive to manipulate the economy. Toward the end of its term, the administration stimulates the economy in order to lower unemployment and hands out federal grants and subsidies to various political interest groups. The election thus takes place in an expansionary phase. After the election is over, inflation might flare up as a result of overstimula-

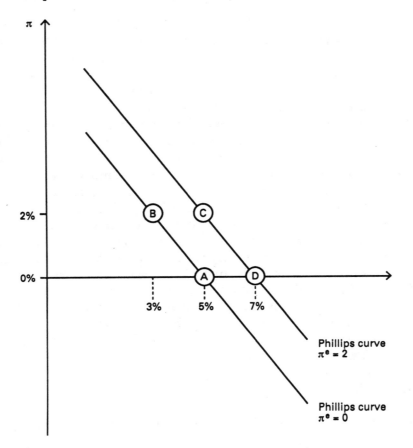

Figure 4.1
The Phillips curve and political business cycles.

tion of demand prior to the election. Monetary and fiscal restraints are applied to bring down inflation during the first year of the next presidential term, and this initiates the downward phase of the cycle.

With the help of an expectation-augmented Phillips-curve diagram, such as figure 4.1, the Nordhaus argument can be understood as follows. Suppose that the initial position is state A, where zero inflation is accompanied by the natural rate of unemployment (say, 5 percent). The incumbent administration stimulates the economy in the election year and brings the economy to state B, where the lower unemployment rate is achieved at the expense of higher inflation. It is assumed that providing more jobs makes voters happier even if the inflation rate is unexpectedly increased. The incumbent wins the election. The voters realize that inflation is higher than expected, so the expected inflation rate is adjusted upward. This causes the expectations-augmented Phillips curve to shift upward, which causes more unemployment at the same inflation rate (state C). Next, policy makers bring down the inflation by causing a recession. The economy moves to state D. This eradicates inflation. Then inflationary expectations bring the economy back to state A. But wait, there's another election coming up. . . .

In order to verify this hypothesis, let us compare the unemployment rates for election years with those of the preceding years. Out of the ten presidential elections from 1952 through 1988, the unemployment rate dropped eight times in the election year from what it had been the year before. The two exceptions were 1960, when Kennedy won unexpectedly, and 1980, when the incumbent, Carter, was defeated.

The partisan model, emphasized by Hibbs (1977, 1987), supposes that parties with different core constituencies pursue different economic policies. The change in parties causes a change in social

---

General Elections

On occasions when the two houses are in conflict, the Lower House (the House of Representatives) usually commands more power. Therefore, the election of the members of that house—the general election—is the most important political event in Japan. A general election must be held at or before the end of a four-year term of the Lower House. The prime minister can call a general election by dissolving the Lower House, which he may find an excuse to do if he thinks the timing is politically advantageous. This provides the opportunity to call an election when the economy is performing well, so that the voters can be expected to respond favorably to the incumbent. If the Lower House passes a no-confidence resolution against the cabinet, the prime minister must either dissolve the Lower House or resign; if he resigns, the Lower House elects a new prime minister without a general election.

Only once in postwar history has the Lower House lasted a full term. On two occasions (and only once after 1955), no-confidence votes triggered its dissolution. Thus, most general elections have been called for the convenience of the prime minister and his party.

Table 4.4
Average growth and inflation rates of nth years of US presidential terms, 1949–1988.

	Democratic Party				Republican Party			
	1st	2nd	3rd	4th	1st	2nd	3rd	4th
Growth rate	3.3	6.2	4.9	3.3	3.1	−0.5	3.4	4.2
Inflation rate	1.8	4.9	6.0	4.8	5.2	4.0	3.4	3.5

Source: Author's calculations.
Data source: See appendix to chapter 3.

priorities. In particular, the Democratic party is assumed to tolerate moderate inflation in exchange for lower unemployment, and the Republican party is assumed to seek lower inflation even at the expense of higher unemployment. This hypothesis predicts that a Democratic administration will accelerate the economy early on (bringing the economy from A to B in figure 4.1), which may cause inflation to flare up the following year, and that the growth will slow down without lowering the inflation rate (B to C). It also predicts that a Republican administration will cause a recession early on, so that inflation will come down (C to D) and then a recovery of growth will be attained without inflation (D to A). Some evidence for this hypothesis can be found in the patterns of growth and inflation rates through four-year presidential terms, as table 4.4 shows.

These models cannot be applied to Japan without major modification. The timing of general elections in Japan is an endogenous policy variable of the parliamentary system. The prime minister may dissolve the House of Representatives at any time during his four-year term. Thus, it is an interesting question whether elections cause business cycles or whether economic expansions trigger general elections.

Inoguchi (1983) and Ito (1990), among others, have modeled political business cycles in the parliamentary system. Inoguchi concluded that it was more likely that the Japanese government seized the opportunity created by good economic performance to call a general election. He attributed his finding in part to Japan's strong bureaucratic system, which is independent of political influences. His conclusion was not based on rigorous estimation procedures and hypothesis testing, however.

Ito's (1990) hypothesis was that the probability of an election tends to increase with the growth rate, to decrease with the inflation rate, and to increase as the number of quarters since the last election increases. In particular, an election called relatively early in the term is accompanied by a very high economic growth rate, and an election called near the end of the term may be accompanied by a moderately high economic growth rate (since time is running out). Hence, when we plot the growth rate of each election cycle (on the y axis) against the number of quarters elapsed (on the x axis), the curve representing the length of the election cycle (called the *election timing curve*) tends to be downward-sloping.

Figures 4.2 and 4.3 show the relationship between election timing as a function of the number of quarters since the last election and

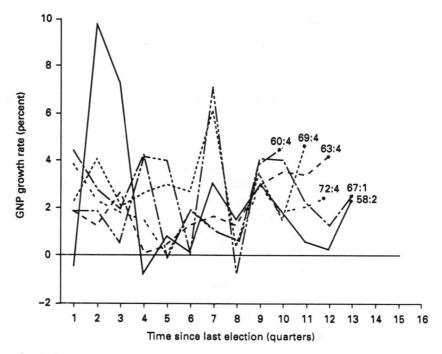

Figure 4.2
Election cycles before the first oil-price crisis. ———: quarters 1955:2–1958:2. —— ——: 1958:3–1960:4. ————: 1961:1–1963:4. ————: 1964:1–1967:1. –––––: 1967:2–1969:4. –————: 1970:1–1972:4.

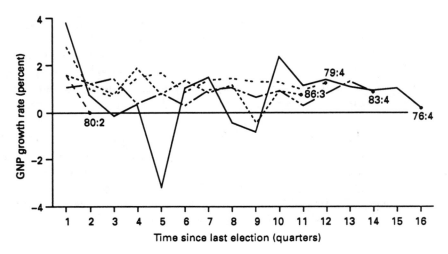

Figure 4.3
Election cycles after the first oil-price crisis. ———: quarters 1973:1–
1976:4. — — —: 1977:1–1979:4. — — –: 1980:1–1980:2. — — — —: 1980:3–
1983:4. – – – – –: 1984:1–1986:3.

the growth rate. The sample period, 1955–1986,[11] is divided into the
years before (figure 4.2) and after (figure 4.3) the first oil crisis.

In figure 4.2, the downward-sloping election threshold is evident.
Elections called between the tenth and eleventh quarters after the
last election were accompanied by growth rates exceeding 4 percent.
When the term went into the fourth year (the thirteenth quarter),
elections were called with the growth rate as low as 2 percent. In
each case, however, the growth rate for each election quarter is higher than that for the preceding quarter. Moreover, the plot of election
quarters (marked by dots and quarter identifications) shows the
downward-sloping property predicted earlier in this section.

In figure 4.3 the downward-sloping property is not evident. The
first election cycle after the first oil crisis went the full four-year
term for the first time. It is likely that the government did not realize that a structural change had permanently lowered the growth
rate. The government waited and waited for a high-growth quarter,
but it never came. The election cycle that started in the first quarter
of 1980 lasted half a year. This early dissolution of the government
was due to the "accidental"[12] passage of a no-confidence vote.

Hence, this election cycle is an outlier from our view of political business cycles.

More sophisticated empirical analyses of the postwar Japanese experience strongly indicate that the Japanese government did not manipulate policies in anticipation of approaching elections, as political business-cycle theories made for a presidential system might indicate.[13] Instead, general elections were usually held during times of autonomous economic expansion. In other words, the Japanese government opportunistically manipulated the timing of elections rather than the economy.

A few caveats are in order before we conclude this section. Although some evidence for political business cycles has been presented here, that evidence is not conclusive or definitive. Some readers may feel that economic performance cannot be the only factor determining the results of an election. Political stances as well as individual popularity may prove to be more important. The number of observations is small (only ten presidential cycles for the postwar United States), and political priorities have been changing with time. More research will be needed on political business-cycle theories. Research in which political factors are explicitly considered will be very important.

SUMMARY

The Japanese experience prior to 1973 is best understood in terms of the traditional Keynesian model with a balance-of-payments constraint. When an economic expansion continued for a while and foreign reserves declined, monetary and fiscal policies were used to cause a recession in order to reduce imports. After 1973, two oil crises (which were essentially adverse supply shocks) were major causes of business fluctuations in Japan.

The volatility of Japan's business cycles is similar for the prewar and postwar periods—much more so than in the case of the United States. But within Japan's postwar experience the amplitude of fluctuations became much smaller after 1975. This may be attributed to several factors, including the lifting of the balance-of-payments constraint through the adoption of flexible exchange rates and the move toward better monetary policies in order to prevent inflation.

The study of business cycles is related to the question of the role of macroeconomic policies in "stabilization." The facts introduced in this chapter are not conclusive regarding whether the government should intervene in order to achieve economic stabilization.

APPENDIX: THEORIES OF BUSINESS CYCLES

A MACRO MODEL

A simple macroeconomic model, the IS-LM model (presented in table 4.5), outlines the differences among theories of business cycles.

Suppose that aggregate demand is determined by the IS-LM model. If the aggregate demand is greater than the aggregate supply (that is, if there is excess demand), then the price level will rise (slowly) over time, and *vice versa*.

Keynesians

A Keynesian economist assumes that prices are rigid in the short run. This means that there is no guarantee that aggregate demand, Y^d, becomes equal to aggregate supply, Y^s. If investment demand (I) fluctuates with investors' moods ("animal spirits"), then it becomes a disturbance to the economy. Alternatively, fluctuations in the income (Y^*) of foreign countries would affect exports from this country. Fluctuations in the components of aggregate demand I and EX cause the aggregate demand to fluctuate. The aggregate supply, on the other hand, is relatively constant over the short run. Therefore, aggregate-demand fluctuations result in periods of inflation and recession—that is, business cycles.

In order to curb the cycles, the government makes use of monetary and fiscal policies. When the autonomous part of aggregate demand (C + I + X − M) is high, which implies that the economy is overheating (i.e., inflation is coming), the government will reduce its expeditures (reducing G) and the central bank will contract the money supply so that the interest rate rises (which induces I to decline). When the autonomous part of aggregate demand is low, the government will stimulate the economy by raising G and M. In this way, aggregate demand is "stabilized," and the volatility (amplitude) of business cycles will be mitigated by the government's policy actions. Variants of this line of thinking have often

Table 4.5

Equations	Interpretations
$Y^d = C + I + G + (EX - IM)$	Aggregate demand = Consumption + Investment + Gov. Expenditure + Exports − Imports.
$C = c(Y - T)$	Consumption is a function of disposable income—that is, income less tax.
$I = I(Y(t - 1), Y(t - 2), r)$	Investment is a function of past income and the real interest rate.
$G = \bar{G}$	Government expenditure is constant.
$EX = EX(YF, ep^*/p)$	Exports are a function of the income of foreign countries and the terms of trade.
$IM = IM(Y, ep^*/p)$	Imports are a function of income and the terms of trade.
ep^*/p	the terms of trade—that is, the relative price of imports and exports
$M/P = L(Y, r)$	The real balance of the money supply is equal to money demand, which is a function of income and interest rates.

Constraints (applicable in Japan until late 1960s)

$G = T$	Government Expenditure = Tax over the business cycle.
$EX = IM$	Trade balance = 0 over the business cycle.
$e = \bar{e}$	The exchange rate is fixed.
$Y^s = F(K, L, A)$	Aggregate supply is determined by a function of capital, labor, and technological level.

been called "activism," "fine tuning," or "discretionary policy" in the literature.

Monetarists

Monetarists believe that an economy is essentially very stable even without government action. Flexible prices are assumed to bring the economy to equilibrium quickly, so that aggregate demand usually equals aggregate supply. Although there may be an occasional deviation of actual output from potential output, the government should not attempt fine tuning. Monetarists argue that the money supply is a powerful policy tool. Since they believe there is a long and unpredictable lag before an increase in the money supply affects the economy, they think the best the government can do is hold the money supply steady. Since the private sector of the economy is thought to be stable, monetarists believe that government intervention (particularly changes in monetary policy) is a major source of disturbances in the economy.

In the IS-LM framework, monetarists assume that the money-demand function $L(Y, i)$ is stable; that prices are flexible enough to bring Y to the level of aggregate supply, $F(K, L, A)$; and that the money supply, M, is a major source of disturbances. Monetarists would recommend that the government maintain stable growth in the money supply and refrain from "discretionary" policies or "fine tuning."

The monetarist view gained popularity during the 1970s, when it was apparent that the Keynesian policies of the late 1960s had failed and when worldwide stagflation (high inflation with low output) contradicted the traditional view of Keynesian business cycles.

Equilibrium Business-Cycle Theories

In the late 1970s, a new theory of business cycles emerged when microeconomic tools were applied to the macroeconomic framework—in particular, to the assumption that aggregate demand and aggregate supply are always equal.

The monetary version of equilibrium business-cycle theory assumes that the money supply is the source of disturbances. The theory relies on informational difficulties to cause propagation and serial correlation in the deviations of output from its trend. Real

Table 4.6
Summary of competing theories of business cycles.

	Keynesians	Monetaries	Equilibrium theorists (a) Monetary version (b) Real version
Source	External animal spirits; the accelerator	Monetary policy	(a) Asymmetric information (b) Time to build new capital
Key assumption	Prices rigid in the long run	Prices relatively flexible	Agg. D = Agg. S always
Fluctuation	Agg. demand (IS) fluctuates	Agg. demand (LM) fluctuates	(a) Agg. demand (LM) fluctuates (b) Agg. supply fluctuates (IS–LM framework rejected.)
Political recommendation	Stabilization policy (fine tuning)	Steady money-supply growth (Lags prohibit fine tuning.)	Policies do not matter (Sargent-Wallace proposition.); or policies are ineffective or destructive.

business-cycle theory relies on particular production technologies to propagate random shocks which may occur in one sector to other sectors, and to cause sustained effects over time in the aggregate economy.

Summary

Table 4.6 summarizes the three theories discussed above.

NOTES

1. For detailed accounts of business cycles during the prewar and postwar periods in Japan, see Fujino 1965. On more recent changes in business cycles in the United States and in Japan, see Garner et al. 1990, Gordon 1986, and Horiye et al. 1987.

2. Although it is not well established, some believe that there are long swings in the economy (the Kondratief cycle) and that these have been triggered by major scientific discoveries and applications, such as the railroad boom, the automobile revolution, and computerization.

3. Kosai and Ogino (1984, pp. 25–32) give an excellent account of this transformation in the growth ceiling of the economy.

4. The political pendulum started to swing back toward the management of exchange rates after the Plaza Agreement of September 1985. This experience will be described and analyzed in detail in chapter 11.

5. A time series is "volatile" if it often deviates, either upward or downward, from a normal level—that is, a long-run average (or trend) of the variable.

6. Some qualifications to this analysis: there are other ways to construct a "trend"; the prewar GNP estimates for the US may be biased in such a way that they look more volatile than they actually were; the result is sensitive to the choice of sample periods.

7. Garner and Wurtz (1990) make similar points about US business cycles.

8. This point will be elaborated in chapter 8.

9. As of this writing, the United States had sustained the longest peacetime expansion (1982–1990) and Japan has sustained the second-longest expansionary phase in its postwar history. If a third oil crisis does not occur soon, the current Japanese expansionary phase is expected to become the longest.

10. An excellent survey of the literature on the political business cycle is Alesina 1988. The two versions explained in this section correspond to Alesina's versions with "irrational voters." See his book for models in the two versions with "rational voters," which are not discussed here.

11. Years before 1955 are excluded because in that year the political structure was changed by the merger of two parties to form the Liberal Democratic Party.

12. Some LDP members were absent from the Diet floor when the no-confidence vote was taken. Some observers contend that they were "accidentally" absent, and some observers think that the absence was deliberate.

13. See Ito and Park 1988 and Ito 1990 for evidence. See Cargill and Hutchison 1990 for opposing views.

BIBLIOGRAPHY

Alesina, A. 1988. "Macroeconomic and politics." In *NBER Macroeconomics Annual 1988*, ed. S. Fischer. MIT Press.

Cargill, T. F., and M. M. Hutchison. 1990. "Political business cycles in a parliamentary setting: The case of Japan." Working paper 88-08, Federal Reserve Bank of San Francisco; revised 1990.

Eichenbaum, M., and K. J. Singleton. 1986. "Do equilibrium real business cycles theories explain postwar US business cycles?" In *Macroeconomics Annual 1986*. National Bureau of Economic Research.

Fujino, S. 1965. *Nihon no Keiki Junkan [Business Cycles in Japan]*. Keiso Shobo.

Garner, C. A., and R. E. Wurtz. 1990. "Is the business cycle disappearing?" Federal Reserve Bank of Kansas City *Economic Review*, May–June: 25–39.

Gordon, R. J. 1986. *The American Business Cycle: Continuity and Change*. University of Chicago Press.

Hayashi, F., and T. Ito. 1983. "Goriteki kitai kaisei to macro model." In *Macro Keizai Gaku to Keizai Seisaku*, ed. K. Kaizuka et al. University of Tokyo Press.

Hibbs, D. A., Jr. 1977. "Political parties and macroeconomic policy." *American Political Science Review* (December): 1467–1487.

Hibbs, D. A., Jr. 1987. *The American Political Economy: Macroeconomics and Electoral Politics in the United States*. Harvard University Press.

Horiye, Y., S. Naniwa, and S. Ishihara. 1987. "The changes in Japanese business cycles." Bank of Japan *Monetary and Economic Studies* 5, no. 3: 49–100.

Inoguchi, T. 1983. *Gendai no Nihon Seiji Keizai no Kozu [Contemporary Political Economy in Japan]*. Toyo Keizai Shinposha.

Ito, T., and J. H. Park. 1988. "Political business cycles in the parliamentary system." *Economics Letters* 27: 233–238.

Ito, T. 1990. "The timing of elections and political business cycles in Japan". *Journal of Asian Economics* 1: 135–156.

Keynes, J. M. 1936. *The General Theory of Employment, Interest and Money*. Macmillan.

Kosai, Y., and Y. Ogino. 1984. *The Contemporary Japanese Economy*. M. E. Sharpe.

Nordhaus, W. 1975. "The political business cycle." *Review of Economic Studies* 42 (April): 169–190.

Chapter 5

FINANCIAL MARKETS AND MONETARY POLICY

The conduct and the effectiveness of a country's monetary policy depend on the structure of its financial markets, which funnel the surplus funds of economic agents (mainly households) to those who need them (mainly corporations, and more recently the government). There are long-term and short-term financial markets. In the long-term market, young households save for retirement and pension funds manage their assets; corporations borrow from these funds in order to make fixed investments. The short-term market, via various instruments, transfers the temporary surpluses of some agents to cover other agents' temporary shortages of funds.

Traditionally, governments have regulated the financial markets heavily. This has been done by means of price controls (for example, deposit interest-rate ceilings and usury ceilings) and by means of entry restrictions. In the United States, the Glass-Steagel Act separates banks and securities companies. In Japan, a similar regulation (the Securities Transaction Law, article 65) creates barriers between banking and securities dealings. Even within the banking sector, regulations create barriers. There are legally mandated specializations in Japan between trust banking and commercial banking, as well as between long-term, bond-financed banking and versatile, deposit-financed commercial banking. In the United States there has traditionally been a separation of business between long-term financial markets (thrift institutions) and short-term ones (commercial banks). In addition, the United States limits interstate banking.

The international aspect of financial markets has recently become very important, for several reasons. First, the differences among financial institutions and organizations give us important insights into the feasibility of alternative systems of financial organization. In a sense, different countries are conducting experiments with alternative financial systems. Second, the domestic financial markets of any one country have become increasingly integrated into the world market. Corporations borrow from domestic sources or from abroad, depending on the prevailing interest rate and other conditions on loans, if there are no other restrictions on international borrowing and lending. In this age of international finance, fund managers have to be extremely well informed about the financial markets of other countries. A government cannot efficiently manage monetary policy without thinking of influences from other countries and of the policy's effects on other countries. Third, the differences among financial organizations and the restrictions on financial transactions between countries have caused some friction when these markets have been opened internationally. Therefore, financial organizations and restrictions have been an important subject of international negotiations.

Recently both the United States and Japan have moved to deregulate and liberalize financial markets. (The United States calls the movement toward fewer restrictions "deregulation"; the Japanese term is "liberalization" [jiyūka].[1]) Reforms sometimes only serve to make regulation conform to what has already happened in the market. For example, in the United States in the late 1970s, high inflation and high money-market interest rates led small depositors to pressure financial institutions to provide ways to evade deposit-rate ceilings. The creation of accounts that allowed the transfer of funds between checking and savings effectively permitted banks to pay savings-account interest on checking accounts. This prompted the regulatory authorities to allow NOW (negotiable order of withdrawal, or interest-paying checking) accounts.

Also in the United States, money-market mutual funds (MMMFs), managed by securities firms, are invested mainly in corporate bonds and large-denomination certificates of deposits. The MMMFs avoid the interest-rate restrictions because the securities firms are not banks. A commercial bank is defined as a financial institution that takes deposits and makes commercial loans. A firm that takes deposits, but does not make loans, and instead manages the fund in the money market, is not subject to the banking regulations. In the late 1970s the MMMFs grew very quickly and started to take customers away from banks. Threatened by

their success, the banking community welcomed the Depository Institutions Deregulation and Monetary Control Act of 1980. This reform, among other things, created Money Market Deposit Accounts
(MMDAs), which are not subject to regulation of their interest yield.

Recent liberalizations of the Japanese financial markets have been
due in part to US-Japan negotiations on financial matters. The
United States proposed the so-called Yen/Dollar Group Meeting
when President Reagan visited Prime Minister Nakasone in Tokyo
in November 1983. This resulted in the report of May 29, 1984, and
in the regular follow-up meetings that have been held since then.
The United States requested aggressive deregulation of Japanese
financial markets, not only with respect to international transactions but also including domestic organizations. At the time the
United States hoped that a reduction of barriers in Japanese financial markets would cause the demand for the yen and for yen-
denominated assets to rise, which would help reduce the value of
the dollar (or raise the value of the yen).[2]

After the deregulation of the 1980s, Japan's financial institutions
became quite similar in organization and functions to their American counterparts. The banking and securities businesses are still
rigorously separated in both countries. Certificates of deposit, short-
term financial markets, and business-loan markets perform similar
functions in the two countries. There remain four notable differences between the Japanese and American financial markets,
however.

First, the markets for corporate bonds and "commercial paper" are
underdeveloped in Japan, mainly because until the 1980s a firm de-
siring to issue corporate bonds was first required to comply with
certain regulations[3]—for example, bonds had to be collateralized.
(Since these requirements were deregulated, many convertible
bonds and bonds with warrants have been issued, particularly for
the "Euro-market"; however, straight corporate bonds without
collateral are still rare in Japan.)

Second, the interest rate on consumer deposits is still regulated in
Japan, whereas it has been completely deregulated in the United
States. In Japan, the government strictly regulates interest-rate
ceilings as well as the yield structure among different deposit instruments. The yields on many deposit instruments are tied to the
official discount rate.

Third, in Japan a market for treasury bills—an important short-term financial market in the United States—is virtually non-existent. There are indeed two types of short-term government securities: Financial Bills (FBs), which have been used to smooth out financing, and Treasury Bills (TBs). However, Financial Bills are not intended to be traded in the market (the central bank holds most of them, and their yield is fixed at a low level), and the Ministry of Finance has been reluctant to issue a large number of Treasury Bills (short-term government securities).[4] The ministry first issued 6-month TBs in 1986; 3-month TBs were issued in September 1989. The TB market is still much too small to produce a benchmark interest rate. As of April 1990 the outstanding amount of TBs was 6.5 trillion yen (up from 2.4 trillion a year earlier), versus 26 trillion yen outstanding at the end of the month in the call market.

Fourth, the market for long-term government bonds in Japan has some peculiar characteristics. Ten-year bonds, which are the typical long-term bonds held in Japan, are issued after negotiations between the Ministry of Finance and a syndicate of financial institutions; medium-term bonds (maturing in 2–4 years) are issued by auction. Some particular issues of the 10-year bonds are designated by market participants as "bellwether" bonds and are traded actively. As a result, these benchmark bonds yield significantly less than other comparable bonds, because of the liquidity premium that buyers are willing to pay (Sargen et al. 1986). This also shows how thin the market is for government bonds other than "bellwether" bonds.

Can these differences be expected to vanish soon? The establishment of a market in short-term government securities would enable the Bank of Japan to conduct open-market operations. (The traditional means of monetary control in Japan, such as controls on the increment to total loans, have grown weak and ineffective.) The TB market would also create short-term, risk-free instruments for portfolio management. Consequently, it would pioneer the deregulation of consumer-deposit rates, since consumer deposits must compete with other risk-free assets. In addition, the short-term, risk-free TB market would make the yen more attractive to the portfolio managers of foreign institutional investors and foreign central banks.

Deregulation of deposit interest rates has advanced steadily in Japan. As of the spring of 1991, the minimum amount for a "money-market" certificate of deposit is 1 million yen, although the interest rate is regulated with a predetermined formula indexed to some money-market rates (different rates, depending on the maturity and the balance). It is expected that the minimum will be lowered further, and that the restriction on the interest rate will be phased out in the near future.

INSTITUTIONAL CHARACTERISTICS

Commercial (City and Regional) Banks

In Japan there are two kinds of commercial banks: city banks [toshi ginkō] and regional banks [chihō ginkō]. As of April 1991 there are eleven city banks. Each of them has its headquarters in a large city and operates a nationwide network of branches. Their liabilities consist largely of deposits, both from corporations (55–60 percent) and from individuals. A larger city bank acts as the core of an enterprise group by meeting the financial needs of the individual firms. Lending to large firms (firms whose capital totals more than 100 million yen) accounts for more than 30 percent of their assets. Recently there has been an increase in lending to medium-size and small firms (which now accounts for 35–40 percent of the city banks' assets) and to individuals (currently 8 percent of the city banks' asset portfolios) by city banks. City banks are now aggressively lending to small and medium-size corporations and to individuals (mostly through housing loans), thus operating in the traditional territory of regional, long-term, and trust banks. City banks are also a developing force in the area of international finance.

A regional bank is strong only in a specific city or prefecture, although the area it may serve is not legally restricted. More than half of its lending is typically directed to medium-size and small firms (firms with capital of under 100 million yen) in the prefecture. More than half of its liabilities take the form of time deposits (certificates of deposit) from individuals.

In April 1989 almost all of the mutual banks converted themselves into regional banks, forming the Second Association of Regional Banks.

Japanese city and regional banks are allowed to have branches nationwide, but the total number of branches and their locations are subject to the approval of the Ministry of Finance. In the United

> **Money**
> The Japanese do not use personal or traveler's checks. Most transactions are carried out in cold cash. The use of credit cards (much less frequent than in the United States) and of electronic transfers between bank accounts (much more frequent) supplement currency as means of payment. Because people carry currency around instead of personal checks, the transaction demand for currency should be higher in Japan. This conjecture is confirmed by the fact that the currency outstanding, measured as a fraction of final private consumption in 1985, is 12.7 percent in Japan and 6.7 percent in the United States. In a ratio of 1985 GNP, the currency outstanding is 7.4 percent in Japan versus 4.3 percent in the United States.

States there are regulations on interstate banking, and many states have adopted "unit banking[5]"; as a result, a Japanese bank tends to be larger in size than an American commercial bank and more stable in its management. In Japan there are only 11 city banks (after a merger of two city banks in April 1991), 64 first-group regional banks, and about 60 second-group regional banks, whereas there are more than 15,000 commercial banks in the United States.

No commercial bank has failed in postwar Japan. In terms of assets, the top ten banks in the world are Japanese banks.

Long-Term Credit Banks

Three Japanese banks specialize in issuing long-term bonds instead of taking deposits to finance their long-term lending. Each of these banks is allowed to issue bonds worth up to 300 times its equities. These banks, called *long-term credit banks*, are distinguished from city and regional banks by their long-term nature of both sides of the balance sheet. The majority of the loans these banks make are for fixed capital investments. The Industrial Bank of Japan [Nihon Kōgyō Ginkō] and the Long-Term Credit Bank of Japan [Nihon Chōki Shinyō Ginkō] are large and especially important; the Nippon Credit Bank [Nihon Saiken Sinyo Ginko] is smaller. Long-term credit banks are leaders in the business of underwriting the securities of large corporations and local governments. In terms of function, the closest American analogue to these banks is "investment banking."

Trust Banks

Trust banks receive and manage funds on behalf of the money's owners. Postwar trust banking, however, is an intermediary of long-term financing, in the sense that a major function of postwar Japanese trust banking has been to sell small "trust deposits" to households, make long-term loans or long-term financial investments, and pay dividends on the trust deposits. In a sense, "trust deposits" are much like mutual funds made up of stocks and bonds. Lending from trust banks represents the major competition to lending by long-term credit banks.

Only recently have pension funds become a significant portion of trust banks' total liabilities. A rapid growth in pension funds, however, is expected in the near future, as corporations are accumulating pension funds at a fast pace. Partly because of this growth potential, and partly because of their longer experience, non-Japanese trust banks are trying hard to enter the Japanese trust-banking market. There are only seven Japanese trust banks (plus one city bank and two regional banks that are allowed to operate trust businesses along with regular commercial bank businesses); there are already nine foreign trust banks in Japan.

Three major differences distinguish Japanese trust banks from American ones. First, Japanese trust banks have significant operations in the business of "financial trusts," which are rather similar to mutual funds. Small trust funds are collected and merged into a large fund for investment or lending. Second, Japanese trust banks direct about 30 percent of their funds to loans, investing the rest in securities and equities. Third, when a Japanese bank handles trust business, the separation in organization and human resources of the banking business from the trust business is weaker than it would be in the United States (Suzuki 1987, pp. 206–215).

Securities Companies

Four securities companies—Nomura, Nikkō, Daiwa, and Yamai-chi—account for 70 percent of the securities dealings (buying and selling in the market) in Japan. As the Tokyo securities market has become one of the largest in the world, Japan's securities business has been growing rapidly.

Japanese securities companies became important players in world markets in the 1980s, especially by mediating Japanese purchases of US government bonds. The road to prosperity, however, was not smooth. In 1965 the Japanese economy was in recession, and the Yamaichi Securities Company made a mistake in its dealings which nearly caused it to go bankrupt. The Bank of Japan made emergency loans to Yamaichi, via city banks, in order to avert a general financial crisis. The securities laws were amended in May 1965 in order to more tightly regulate securities companies; among other regulations, operating a securities company now required a license from the government.

The recession of 1965 also forced the Japanese government to start issuing bonds to finance its deficits. (The principle of maintaining a balanced budget had been adhered to since the end of the occupation, in 1952.) Ironically, the securities companies suffered a setback at the time government bonds became available in the market. The weak, unstable condition of the securities companies at the time might be partially responsible for the unusual way Japanese government bonds are floated: Long-term government bonds are sold by the Ministry of Finance to a syndicate of financial institutions (including securities companies and city banks) after the term and the market shares of the firms have been negotiated.

Insurance Companies

In Japan, life-insurance and non-life-insurance companies are strictly segmented. Most large life-insurance companies, such as Nissay (Nihon Seimei) and Asahi Seimei, are mutual rather than incorporated companies. Insurance premiums have been subject to strict control by the Ministry of Finance. During the late 1970s and the 1980s life-insurance companies grew rapidly, partly because of their huge success in marketing single-premium life-insurance (endowment) policies. These policies were used as a substitute for bank deposits and bond holdings by ordinary savers. The returns on such policies over several years were unrivaled by the returns on any bank deposits or bonds, since bank deposits were subject to interest-rate ceilings and the bond market was restricted to big companies.

In the 1980s, Japanese life-insurance companies became important in the market for US government bonds. The Ministry of Finance deregulated how much they could invest in foreign securities. The limit was changed from 10 to 25 percent of total assets in March 1986, and to 30 percent in August. (There was another limit on the increase of foreign securities. It was 10 percent of an increase in assets from May 1982, 20 percent from April 1983, and 40 percent from April 1986; it was deregulated completely after August.)

Other Private Financial Institutions

Japan's financial institutions include mutual banks [sōgo ginkō] (a majority of which became regional banks in April 1989), credit banks [shinyō kinko], credit unions [shinyō kumiai], and labor credit unions [rōdō kinko]. These are rather small depository institutions which lend to small and medium-size firms. The much larger Agri-Forest Central Bank [Nōrin Chuō Kinko] acts as a manager of funds by centralizing the investments of all the agricultural, forest, and fishery credit unions; its assets rival those of a large city bank. Since the mid 1980s, the Nōrin Chuō Kinko has invested in foreign securities.

Government Institutions

Postal savings accounts are much like bank depository accounts. With the intention that the government provide a fair opportunity to depositors in every town and village, about 24,000 Japanese post offices offer these accounts. Individuals may open various types of postal savings accounts, and may deposit up to 10 million yen ($33,000, at 150 yen/$). As in banks, ordinary savings deposits and savings with fixed maturity are available. Savings with indefinite maturity (up to 10 years) are also available.

Deposits in postal savings accounts become funds for the Fiscal Investment and Loan Program, which is governed by the Ministry of Finance. The FILP allows the government to invest in infrastructure and public works without increasing taxes directly. Since it is a kind of "capital budget" and not part of the government's general budget, the size of the Japanese government, measured by the general budget, appears to be small. If the FILP were included in the general budget, the Japanese government would look about 50 percent larger.

The interest rates on postal savings accounts are regulated by the Ministry of Posts and Communications, whereas the interest rates for bank deposits (except those which are deregulated) are regulated by the Ministry of Finance. After a change in the official discount rate of the central bank, a change in interest yields is often delayed to allow consultation between the two ministries.

The Central Bank

Both the Bank of Japan and the US Federal Reserve System are independent of their respective governments and have their own policy tools and objectives. In principle, either of these central banks could act quite independently from the country's fiscal authority (in the United States, the Treasury; in Japan, the Ministry of Finance). In normal circumstances, however, the central bank consults with the fiscal authority in order to coordinate policy.

Some argue that the Bank of Japan decreased the official discount rate in 1972 because of pressure from the government. Many in the central bank felt it necessary at the time to *raise* the discount rate, because the economy was overheating rather than stagnating, but the pressure from the fiscal authority was too great. The consequence was high inflation in 1973–74, although some of the blame must go to the oil crisis.

After the inflation of 1973–74, the Bank of Japan seemed to have increased its autonomy and power in conducting monetary policy. In 1975 the bank introduced a new monetary policy which included a "forecast" (soft target) of monetary growth. It has successfully implemented the independent policy since 1975. The monetary target may be a tool with which the bank maintains its "independence" from the fiscal authorities.

The highest decision-making body within the Bank of Japan is the Policy Board [Nihon Ginkō Seisaku Iinkai], which consists of the bank's governor, four appointed members from the private sector, and two government representatives, one from the Ministry of Finance and one from the Economic Planning Agency. The members from the private sector have most often been chosen from the city and regional banking community, the manufacturing industry, and the distribution industry. The two government representatives do not vote. The Policy Board is comparable in function to the Board of Governors in the US Federal Reserve System. In the United States, a

Table 5.1

	Japan	United States
Central bank	Bank of Japan	Federal Reserve System
Commercial banks	11 city banks (branch banking)	15,300 commercial banks (units banking in many states)
	64 (1st group) regional	
	60 (2nd group) regional	
	7 trust banks	3833 savings and loans
	3 long-term credit banks plus foreign banks	386 mutual savings
Interbank market (only banks)	Call market	Federal funds market
(plus financial institutions)	Tegata (bill discount) market	
Open market	Fiscal bills (FB) and Treasury bills (TB)	Treasury bills (TB)
(open to non-financial)	CD market	CD market
	Gensaki market	Repurchase agreements
	Bankers' acceptances	Bankers' acceptances (BA)
		Commercial paper (CP)
Long-term gov't security	Government bonds[a]	Government bonds
Consumer deposits instruments	Ordinary deposits	Checking accounts,
	No personal checks[b]	NOW, superNOW,
	Time deposits[c]	MMDA
Money-market funds	Chūkoku funds	MMMF[d]
Government deposit	Postal saving	Not available

a. Government bonds in Japan are not completely free from regulation. They are issued to a syndicate of financial institutions at a negotiated yield, rather than at an auction open to the public.

b. Since personal checks are not used in Japan, it is inappropriate to compare consumer deposit instruments.

c. Traditional time deposits have regulated interest rates. New types of deposits with "liberalized" interest started in 1985.

d. MMMFs (money-market mutual funds) are offered by securities companies which collect small funds and invest them in money-market instruments such as CDs, CP, and BAs. Chūkoku funds are close substitutes for MMMFs. The portfolios of Chūkoku funds are limited to government bonds which yield less than large CDs, however.

change in the discount rate is decided upon by the Federal Open Market Committee of the Federal Reserve; in Japan it is decided upon by the Executive Committee [Yakuinkai], which includes other high-ranking Bank of Japan officials. The FOMC is composed of seven members from the "Fed's" board of governors and five presidents of District Reserve Banks.

Table 5.1 compares the various financial markets and institutions in the United States and in Japan.

JAPAN'S FINANCIAL MARKETS IN THE 1950s AND THE 1960s

During the 1950s and the 1960s, the Japanese financial markets were heavily regulated and isolated from the world financial market. The government virtually prohibited flows of capital into or out of Japan. The monetary authorities explicitly or implicitly fixed most interest rates at low levels. Lending from banks was often rationed. Consumers and small businesses often had difficulties obtaining mortgages and business loans.

The conventional view is that the low-interest-rate policy was designed to stimulate investment in targeted industries. In addition to controlling interest rates, the Bank of Japan regulated the amount by which banks could increase loans in a month. To restrict monetary growth, the Bank of Japan would simply direct city banks not to increase their loans to business by altering the lending limit. To encourage monetary growth, the Bank of Japan would ease the lending limit. These monetary policies are sometimes credited for the export-led, investment-led growth of the 1950s and the 1960s.

During this period the Bank of Japan did not use open-market operations, a major tool of the Federal Reserve. The Bank of Japan's policy tools consisted solely of interest-rate controls, lending-limit controls, and "window guidance" for direct lending by the central bank to city banks.[6]

Suzuki (1980) summarized the characteristics of the Japanese financial markets in the 1950s and the 1960s in terms of four phenomena: "overloan" (a "Japanese-English" term), overborrowing, the imbalance of bank liquidity, and the predominance of indirect financing.

"Overloan" refers to the unusually high level of direct lending from the Bank of Japan (BoJ) to the city banks. Of course, banks are

Table 5.2
Corporate finance (percentage in asset liabilities).[a]

	Japan		United States		West Germany	
	Internal	External	Internal	External	Internal	External
1965	24.9	75.1	61.6	38.4	41.0	59.0
1970	19.4	80.6	53.8	46.2	38.2	61.8
1975	20.9	79.1	51.5	48.5	29.1	70.9
1980	20.4	78.5	45.7	53.6	25.1	73.1

a. "Internal" funds include retained earnings and equities; "external" funds
   include bank loans and corporate bonds.
Source: Toyo Keizai Shinpo *Economic Statistics Annual*, various issues.

entitled to borrow from the central bank when there is an urgent
need for liquidity; this is a central bank's function as the lender of
last resort. What was unusual in Japan was the chronic nature and
the relatively large magnitude of such lending. In fact, during the
1950s and the 1960s lending from the BoJ to city banks functioned
as one important channel to control the monetary base. Since there
were few qualified securities, the Bank of Japan could not control
the monetary base by the more traditional means of open-market
operations; however, it could use loans for the same purpose.

The ratio of the BoJ's lending to the total liability of the city banks
averaged around 7–8 percent in the 1950s and 6 percent in the
1960s. It dropped to around 2 percent in the 1970s and remained at
that level in the 1980s. Since loans are made at the official discount
rate, which is typically lower than the market (lending) rate, city
banks make profits without risk by borrowing from the BoJ and
lending to the private sector. Hence, the BoJ must ration such loans,
and those that it does make function as subsidies to city banks.[7]

"Overborrowing" describes the corporate sector's dependence on
bank loans rather than on equity to raise funds. Table 5.2 compares
Japan, the United States, and West Germany in terms of bank liabilities for the years 1965–1980. According to Suzuki, this is a postwar
phenomenon. He reports that internal financing supplied 70.9 percent of the Japanese corporate sector's funds between 1914 and 1920
and 57.7 percent between 1935 and 1940. The percentage dropped to
37.7 between 1950 and 1954 and then declined further, as the table
shows.

Main Banks

The "main bank" [*mein banku*, in "Japanese English"] for a company is usually a leading lender to the company, a top-ranked shareholder (among the financial institutions), or both. A firm and its main bank have a long-term relationship; that is, a change of top lenders or of top shareholders is rare. The firm receives help from the main bank with its finances and management (including a kind of consulting service) regularly, but especially when the firm is in financial trouble. The main bank even sends a person to the board of the company when the company's financial trouble becomes serious.

The bank of a narrowly defined enterprise group (to be explained in chapter 7) is naturally the main bank to each of the member firms, but a bank at the center of an enterprise group also serves as the main bank for many other firms loosely affiliated with the group. Banks other than the Big Six enterprise group banks are also main banks of their respective clients. The function of this main bank–firm relationship is a popular topic of academic investigations. See, for example, Horiuchi et al. 1988.

Overborrowing still characterizes the Japanese financial markets, despite the downward trend in external financing. There are several reasons for this: Banks are the centers of enterprise groups. (Many argue that banks play roles other than that of a lender. The bank from which a firm borrows most is usually called its "main bank.") Overborrowing, a characteristic of the financial market, derives from this organizational structure. Lending by banks to firms in their groups is one of the characteristics of the enterprise-group relationship.

An imbalance of funds exists within the Japanese banking system. Roughly speaking, city banks and regional banks operate in different markets. As described above, city banks generally lend to big businesses and regional banks generally lend to small and medium-size businesses in the region. Historically, city banks have lent more funds than they could raise through deposits, while regional banks have found themselves with surplus funds.

In the 1950s and the 1960s, because short-term financial markets (such as those for treasury bills and certificates of deposit) were not well established, funds were channeled from institutions with excess funds to institutions without enough funds for their lendings through the call market (which then did not differentiate between

Table 5.3
Call-market lending and borrowing (percentage of total assets and liabilities).

	City banks		Regional banks	
	Lending	Borrowing	Lending	Borrowing
1950	0.4	0.3	0.3	0.3
1955	0.3	2.3	2.9	0.3
1960	0.0	3.0	3.5	0.2
1965	0.0	4.9	3.2	0.2
1970	0.0	5.5	3.3	0.1
1975	0.2	2.9	2.3	0.2
1980	1.7	3.7	1.5	0.4
1984	2.9	4.7	2.9	1.0

Source: *Economic Statistics Annual*, March 1985.

overnight loans and over-the-month loans). The call market, supposedly an interbank market for short-term lending and borrowing, was actually functioning to correct the structural imbalance of funds. Table 5.3 illustrates the imbalances of bank liquidity. The phenomenon more or less disappeared during the 1970s, after the establishment of other financial markets.

Kansetsu Kinyū no Yūi, the Japanese term for "predominance of financial intermediaries," is sometimes translated as "indirect financing." In the 1950s and the 1960s, the banking sector mediated almost all financial flows from the household sector to the corporate sector. This characteristic is related to the overborrowing of the corporate sector. Both characteristics point to the possibility of some barriers in the securities market. For some reason, the Japanese household sector prefers to hold its savings in the form of bank deposits rather than in equities or bonds. (See table 5.4.) In addition, corporations have borrowed from banks rather than raise funds in the corporate-bond market. The reasons for this preference include institutional costs, such as the regulation that corporate bonds must be backed by collateralized assets.

Figure 5.1 summarizes the four characteristics of the Japanese financial markets of the 1950s and the 1960s in a flow-of-funds diagram.

Table 5.4
Households' holdings of financial assets (percentage of total financial assets).

	Japan					United States				
	C	D	I	S	(E)	C	D	I	S	(E)
1973	20.5	54.7	12.8	12.0	(3.7)	6.8	27.5	20.1	43.9	(31.0)
1978	15.8	58.5	13.0	12.7	(2.3)	6.5	32.0	21.3	37.8	(23.6)
1983	11.2	60.5	15.1	12.7	(1.6)	5.9	30.1	25.8	36.4	(24.2)
1987	12.1	43.7	33.8	24.4		5.6	33.0	44.9	25.7	

C: cash and transactions accounts
D: savings accounts
I: insurance and pension funds
S: securities
E: equities (as a subcategory of securities)
Source: Bank of Japan, *International Comparative Statistics*, various issues.

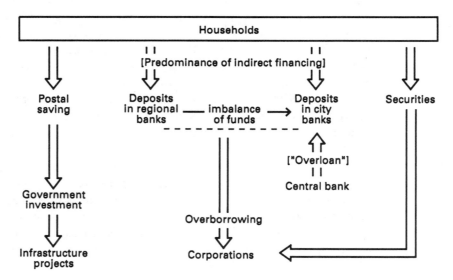

Figure 5.1
Schematic diagram of the flow of funds.

DISEQUILIBRIUM IN FINANCIAL MARKETS

With interest rates regulated both on the deposit side and on the business-loan side, it is natural to suspect the existence of credit rationing. Casual observations made during the 1950s and the 1960s provide much circumstantial evidence of credit rationing.[8] The business-loan rate did not fluctuate much. What happened was that the monetary authorities imposed credit constraints. The regulation of the total monthly increase in the loans of each bank proved to be a binding constraint on bank lending. Corporations did not have alternative sources of funding until the mid 1970s; the domestic securities market was underdeveloped, and loans from abroad were not allowed.

Ito and Ueda (1981) conducted an econometric test of credit rationing in the American and Japanese business-loan markets. They specified and estimated the demand function and the supply function of business loans in each country. For each quarter, the business-loan interest rate was assumed to be constant (owing to explicit or implicit regulation), so that excess demand or excess supply could exist. If there was excess demand in that market, the transaction would take place on the supply curve; if there was excess supply, the transaction would take place on the demand curve. The interest rate would be adjusted from one period to the next. The rate would go up if there had been excess demand and down for excess supply. Specifying how the interest rate would adjust over time, and estimating it along with the demand and supply functions, would yield the adjustment speed of the interest rate. US and Japanese business-loan demand and supply were estimated for the period from the second quarter of 1968 to the first quarter of 1977. The estimated adjustment speeds implied that the interest-rate adjustment speed was much lower in Japan. The Japanese business-loan market was judged to be in disequilibrium more often than its US counterpart because of its sticky interest rate.

CHANGES IN THE 1970s

After 1973, when oil prices went up significantly, the economies of the major industrialized countries operated under floating exchange rates. This had various structural implications for the

Japanese financial markets. The following characteristics emerged in the 1970s:

• As expectations of future growth diminished, largely because of the first oil crisis, private investment slowed. This, in turn, caused corporations to reduce their rates of borrowing. Some corporations started channeling their surplus funds into the newly created short-term open market and started demanding higher interest rates on deposits. Managers of corporate funds thus created a need for financial deregulation.

• The city banks' need to raise funds shrank as the demand for business loans declined. City banks reduced their reliance on loans from the Bank of Japan. Thus, the share of "overloans" in total liabilities dropped by more than half, and the "imbalance of funds" virtually disappeared.

• The Japanese government emerged as a large borrower in the financial market after 1975. The government created a large deficit to stimulate the economy after the first oil crisis. This happened concurrently with the reduction in private borrowing. As a result, despite the large increase in government borrowing, interest rates did not soar and credit rationing did not worsen. In fact, most interest rates were still regulated.

• International capital flows were deregulated. With a floating exchange rate, there was no need for the central bank to buy foreign exchange. The private sector could now accumulate foreign claims or borrow from abroad. There was pressure from abroad for Japan to open up its financial markets, too; a country with such a high rate of growth looked attractive to foreign investors.

• There was an implicit change in Japan's economic policy. The oil crises had made it clear that a high rate of economic growth would run the economy into the resource constraint. The government felt that export-oriented and investment-oriented growth financed through overborrowing and indirect financing had to be modified. New policy targets, such as the conservation of energy and the controlling of pollution, emerged. It is ironic that export growth was what halted the Japanese recessions caused by the two oil crises.

• The government deficit became worse after 1975. (See chapter 6.) A large quantity of government bonds were issued after negotiations between the Ministry of Finance and a syndicate of private financial institutions. The yield on government bonds was well below the market rate (even when adjusted for risk), so the portfolios of city banks decreased in value. Financial institutions rallied for deregulation of the bond markets, for the establishment of an auction for medium-term government bonds, and for less regulation of the resale of government bonds to the public.

THE SHORT-TERM FINANCIAL MARKET

The short-term financial market is the one segment of the Japanese financial market that is free from strict regulation. The call market, which can be thought of as the interbank market, is quite comparable to the Federal Funds market in the United States.

The *Tegata* (bill discount) market is a representative short-term financial market. It is the market for short-term financing, from two weeks to six months. (Until November 1988, maturities were limited to between one month and three months.) The Tegata market was spun off from the call market in 1971. Until then the call market handled everything from overnight money to over-month-end funds, the latter accounting for more than half of the volume. Implicit interest regulations were imposed on the call and Tegata markets until the late 1970s.

The *Gensaki* (repurchase agreement) market, organized by securities houses in 1949, became important when all financial institutions and large corporations began to participate in it, in the mid 1970s. In March 1976, a directive from the Securities Bureau of the Ministry of Finance set rules for the trading of repurchase agreements. For example, they defined qualifying securities and required written contracts. Between October 1978 and April 1981 the Bank of Japan gradually relaxed its regulations on the extent of city and local banks' participation in the market. Non-resident institutions have been allowed to participate in the Gensaki market since May 1979. Since it is not a deposit instrument but a security-transaction agreement, the Gensaki has been always free of interest-rate regulations. This is an open market—that is, nonfinancial organizations can participate in it for short-term lending and borrowing purposes.

The main sellers of Gensaki are securities houses, although the share of city banks grew in the 1980s. Large corporations purchase most of the agreements, but nonresident institutions have become increasingly important since their entry in May 1979. In the absence of an active market for treasury bills or commercial paper, the Gensaki market has been the main place in which temporary surplus funds of large corporations can be directed to other uses.

In Japan, the tax rates on securities transactions are lower for government bonds than for other bonds. The government also levies taxes on Gensaki, with a few exceptions.[9] Since the tax is independent of the maturity of the repurchase agreement, the cost of the tax rises as the maturity shortens. This makes short-term (especially one month or shorter) repurchase agreements less attractive, and consequently they are not widely used. Since certificates of deposit (CDs) became available, in May 1979,[10] Gensaki transactions with CDs as instruments have become increasingly popular. There are no transaction taxes on CD Gensakis.

There is no regulation of interest rates on CDs, but there are several regulations regarding the terms of CD issues. Initially, the minimum denomination was a half-billion yen ($2.5 million); it has been lowered in steps to 50 million yen. Any depository institution can issue a CD, although city banks currently issue most of them, followed by local and nonresident banks. The size of the CD market grew to equal that of the Gensaki market by 1982, and by 1985 it was twice as large as the Gensaki market.

A comparison of the size and growth of different money markets (table 5.5) indicates how regulations have affected them. The growth of the Gensaki market from 1970 to 1980 was due to the fact that it was the only market with unregulated interest rates throughout the decade. After the introduction of CDs (a close substitute for Gensakis), the Gensaki lost its magic because CD interest rates were also unregulated. The transactions tax (on securities) made the Gensaki less attractive than the CD for many customers. In the 1980s the CD market grew quickly. The Tegata market, freed from interest-rate regulation in the late 1970s, also grew in the 1980s.

Government securities are conspicuously absent from the short-term financial market in Japan. (In the United States, the Treasury Bill market sets the benchmark short-term interest rate.) The creation of a risk-free, short-term asset is considered to be essential in making the yen a part of the portfolios of foreign investors and in making it more attractive as a reserve asset for other central banks. The risk-free rate is also important in arbitrage between yen-denominated assets in Japan and outside Japan, and in arbitrage be-

Table 5.5
Average of the twelve monthly average balances of call and Tegata instruments (end-of-year balances for Gensaki and CDs), in billions of yen.

	1970	1975	1980	1981	1982	1983	1984	1985	1986	1987	1988	1989
Call	1,693	1,968	3,258	4,459	4,528	3,836	4,544	5,046	7,957	14,564	16,642	22,300
Tegata	*	5,193	6,120	3,989	3,867	5,682	6,667	9,440	13,255	13,982	11,972	18,024
Gensaki	619	1,679	4,507	4,481	4,304	4,288	3,562	4,642	7,117	6,922	7,350	6,304
CD	na	na	2,323	3,291	4,342	5,665	8,461	9,657	9,926	10,833	15,973	21,086

* In 1971 the call market was split into the (new) call market, with short maturity, and the Tegata market, with maturities longer than one month.
Source: Bank of Japan

tween short-term and long-term assets. Although efforts have been made to create such a market for such securities in Japan, progress has been slow. Six-month government bonds were first issued in 1986 in Japan, but the outstanding amount has been so low that this cannot be called a major market. Three-month bonds were first auctioned in September 1989. Although near-maturity long-term bonds are available, transaction costs due to taxes become prohibitively high as the maturity date approaches.

DEREGULATION

Japan's financial markets have been changing quickly partly because of pressure from the United States (through the Yen/Dollar Working Group and its follow-up meetings) and partly because of internal needs, such as the need to prevent disintermediation caused by competition from high-yielding trust funds and insurance policies. The recent financial deregulation in Japan has had many interesting ramifications,[11] but we will focus on the deregulation of deposit interest rates and on its impact on monetary policy since 1985. There are two reasons for this focus: First, Japanese households prefer (as has been mentioned) to hold cash and bank deposits. As table 5.6 shows, more cash and demand deposits exist for economic activities (GNP), and cash and demand deposits command larger shares of the household-asset portfolio. Hence, any change in deposit behavior in Japan would have a large impact on the financial market. Second, the behavior of the money stock has a direct implication for monetary policy. Since the money supply is emphasized as the intermediate target of Japanese monetary policy, the change in the course of the money supply brought about by deregulation has a profound implication for monetary policy.

The interest rates for large-amount time deposits (LTDs) were deregulated in 1985, and the share of these deposits in the money supply has skyrocketed. Most of the depositors are corporate customers. The lowering of the minimum deposit amount for money-market certificates (MMCs) to 10 million yen in October 1987 made those certificates more popular among households. The shares of LTDs and MMCs in the money supply are plotted in figure 5.2, which clearly shows that each step of deregulation was matched by a surge in shares. The share of LTDs in the monetary stock rose

Table 5.6
Currency and demand deposits.

	Japan	United States	West Germany
Currency/GNP (1987)	8.3%	6.4%	6.2%
(1989)	9.4%	6.1%	6.6%
Demand deposits/GNP (1987)	21.5%	10.6%	11.9%
(1989)	19.9%	9.4%	12.5%
Household-sector financial portfolios (% of financial assets), 1988[a]			
Currency & demand dep.	9.7	4.9	8.2
Time & saving deposits	47.7	25.7	44.1
Insurance & pension fund	19.0	29.2	21.5
Securities	22.5	37.6	18.3
(stocks, market value)	(13.8)	(22.5)	(2.8)

a. Japanese households include nonprofit organizations.
Source: Bank of Japan, Comparative Economic and Financial Statistics, 1987 and 1990.

from nil in 1985 to 25 percent in 1990. This suggests a significant structural change in the money demand function and a significant increase in the cost of funds for banks.

THE "MISTAKE" OF JAPANESE MONETARY POLICY, 1971–1975

Around the middle of the 1970s, Japan experienced a significant decline in economic growth. The transition from the high growth of the 1960s to the low growth of the 1970s was not smooth. The monetary authorities made a few obvious mistakes.

As was discussed in chapter 3, Japan sustained current-account surpluses in the late 1960s despite its strong growth. During the 1950s and the 1960s, the balance of payments acted as a check against overheating. Monetary policy, responding to the balance-of-payments signal, automatically prevented inflation. But around 1970 the structure seemed to change. The balance-of-payments ceiling on economic growth became higher than the inflation ceiling on economic growth. Thus, monetary policy entered a new phase.

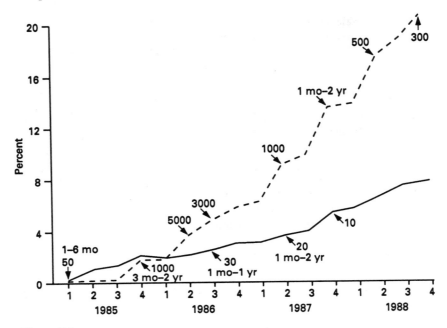

Figure 5.2
Shares in the money stock of money-market certificates (solid line) and large-amount time deposits (broken line) and timing of deregulation. Numbers represent minimum anounts for deposits, in millions of yen; months and years represent allowed maturity for deposits.

In 1968 and 1969 the Japanese economy was in a boom—the GNP was growing at a rate in excess of 12 percent. But the current-account surplus was more than $2 billion, an amount then considered large. The inflation rate (measured in terms of increase in the consumer-price index) was hovering at 5.5 percent. The correct approach to macroeconomic adjustment would have been to start revaluing the yen; however, the Japanese government resisted revaluation—partly because it regarded the Bretton Woods system as an unbreakable promise and partly because it wanted to protect export-based industries. In 1970 Japan's GNP was still growing at a rate of 10 percent, and the current-account surplus was still $2 billion, but the inflation rate worsened to 7.7 percent. The United States was running current-account deficits, shaking world confidence in the key currency of the fixed-exchange-rate system. It became clear that the fixed exchange rates could not be maintained and that a sharp adjustment was needed.

The fixed-exchange-rate system, which had maintained the exchange rate of 360 yen per dollar, was essentially abandoned on August 15, 1971, when President Nixon took the dollar off the gold standard.[12] After a short period of floating exchange rates, the Smithsonian Agreement of December 1971 was reached in an attempt to restore the fixed-exchange-rate regime. The Smithsonian Agreement set the exchange rate at 308 yen per dollar. In February 1973, the world sailed into the age of floating exchange rates.

Between 1971 and 1973, the Japanese current-account surplus grew despite efforts to keep it down. At the same time, the "adjustment inflation" argument—that in order to avert further appreciation of the yen (from the Smithsonian rate) inflation should be tolerated, if not caused—gained support in Japan. The government planned deliberate inflation for 1972. The money supply was increased very rapidly in 1971 and 1972; however, prices were stable, because the reduction in import prices caused by the revaluation of the yen masked domestic inflationary pressure.

The Bank of Japan maintained high monetary growth in 1972–73 in order to keep the yen from appreciating further from the Smithsonian rate. This attempt to keep the yen undervalued created substantial inflationary pressure. Another factor was the 1972 lowering of the discount rate in order to push the "Reconstruct the Japanese Archipelago Plan" being promoted by Prime Minister Tanaka; this adjustment added fuel to the monetary increase of 1971–72.

Prices started to rise in 1973. The CPI inflation rate was increasing, registering annual rates of 7.5, 10.5, and 12.5 percent during the first three quarters. Prices were already rising rapidly when OPEC announced the oil embargo and the sharp oil-price increase on October 16. The first oil crisis further accelerated inflation. Inflation and a sharp drop in the GNP marked the end of Japan's rapid economic growth.

In retrospect, it was a mistake to put forward a particular exchange rate as an absolute target with priority over considerations of inflation and growth. The high inflation of 1973–74 in Japan was the result of efforts to maintain the overvalued yen (that is, 360 yen/$ before August 1971 and 308 yen/$ between December 1971 and February 1973).

A COMPARISON OF JAPANESE AND AMERICAN MONETARY POLICIES, 1975–1989

The debate between the Keynesians and the monetarists was most intense from the mid 1960s to the mid 1970s. The two camps argued whether monetary policy could be used to stabilize economic fluctuations. Later, this debate yielded center stage to a dispute between New Classical Macroeconomists and New Keynesians.

What appears below is only a brief description of the early debate. See appendix B to this chapter for details of the three different theories: traditional Keynesian, monetarist, and New Classical Macroeconomic. The appendix to chapter 4 should also be consulted, because much of the debate concerned stabilizing economic fluctuations.

The role of monetary policy in stabilization had been debated by traditional Keynesians and monetarists since the 1950s. The Keynesians asserted that monetary policy could be used to stabilize an economy; they claimed that as components of the aggregate demand (in particular, investment) fluctuated, the money supply could be fine-tuned to keep aggregate demand equal to potential output.

The monetarists asserted that monetary policy should not be used to fine-tune the economy. Because of various lags in policy decisions and in the private sector's response to policy actions, the actual effects of monetary-policy measures often come at a time when the policy action is no longer needed. Therefore, monetary-policy actions may often aggravate fluctuations. Hence, monetarists recommend leaving the private sector alone by keeping the rate of monetary growth constant.

The US Experiment with Monetarism: 1979–1984

The United States conducted monetary policy in a more or less Keynesian manner throughout the 1960s and the 1970s. After a sharp increase in the inflation rate in the 1970s, the Federal Reserve announced a new policy rule that sounded like an implementation of monetarism. The Federal Reserve Board instituted its "new operating procedures" on October 6, 1979. Paul Volker, the chairman of the "Fed," announced a major change in monetary policy "to support the objective of containing growth in the monetary aggregates

... by placing greater emphasis on the supply of bank reserves and less emphasis on confining short-term fluctuations in the Federal Funds rates." Wide fluctuations in the monetary supply (M1), in real output, in interest rates, and in inflation followed the policy announcement. Inflation fell, but only after the United States experienced its worst postwar recession (during 1981 and 1982). The Fed permitted the money supply to increase beyond its target after the summer of 1982, and the policy implemented in October 1979 was formally abandoned on October 5, 1982. After the monetary target was abandoned, the money supply increased at a faster pace. M1 increased at only a 6.5 percent rate in 1981, but it grew 8.8 percent in 1982 and 9.7 percent in 1983. Despite repeated warnings from monetarists, these increases did not cause inflation.

Milton Friedman, skeptical about the prospect of practicing monetarist policy in October 1979, quickly disinherited the Fed from monetarism. As early as December 1980, Friedman complained that the Federal Reserve had failed to keep its promise of October 6, 1979. Monetarists claim that the Fed, despite its rhetoric, failed to implement a monetarist policy. The Fed permitted M1 to fluctuate widely and even allowed it to swing outside the target range.

Keynesians conclude that the experiment showed that it is neither possible to control the money supply as targeted nor desirable to attempt to target the money supply. The monetary tightening of 1981, which was due to an unrealistic goal for M1 growth, hurt the economy. Moreover, Keynesians argue that the occurrence of no inflation despite a high monetary growth rate after 1982 is solid evidence that monetarists are wrong.[13]

Is the Bank of Japan Quietly Monetarist?

Between 1956 and 1973, the Bank of Japan permitted monetary growth to fluctuate between 15 and 20 percent per annum, curtailing monetary growth when the international balance of payments became a binding constraint but otherwise relaxing monetary growth to finance economic growth. In Japan, the growth rate of the nominal GNP closely follows the growth rate of the money supply (M2 + CD). If one believes in unilateral causality from money to nominal GNP, then one may conclude that fluctuations in nominal GNP will follow fluctuations in monetary growth by several quarters.

After the mistake of creating high inflation in 1973–74, the Bank of Japan announced a new monetary policy procedure in 1975, emphasizing the importance of the money supply. Since 1975 the BoJ has used the money supply as an intermediate target. The Japanese implementation of monetary targeting differs from its American counterpart in a few technical ways. For example, the monetary target (the BoJ calls it a "forecast") is expressed quarterly in terms of annual changes in M2 + CD.[14] Fluctuations in the money supply have decreased. Both trend growth and fluctuations around the trend are smaller. It is apparent from figure 5.2 that as the money-supply growth rate is gradually reduced, so is the nominal-GNP growth rate—but without interfering with the real-GNP growth rate. This means that the gradual decrease in the money-supply growth rate reduced inflation without reducing economic growth. Figure 5.3 illustrates, according to monetarists, that as the amplitude of monetary fluctuations became smaller, so did the amplitude of nominal GNP fluctuations, and that inflation slowed as monetary growth slowed.

The Bank of Japan must think that there is a high correlation between M2 + CD and future (but not current) nominal GNP. Perhaps the reasoning is that M2 + CD is more stable than M1, and thus more suitable for gradual adjustment. In addition, the BoJ may believe that it can control M2 + CD in the intermediate run. The BoJ also emphasizes that it is merely stating its forecast and not announcing a target, thus avoiding a jittery response from the private sector.

Suzuki (1985) calls Japanese monetary policy "eclectic gradualism," which is a position between Keynesian fine tuning and a monetarist $k\%$-growth rule. Although he hedges his conclusion, his analysis (especially his observation about the experience after 1975) conforms with what a monetarist would preach. Is the Bank of Japan in fact monetarist? Milton Friedman, a founding father of monetarism, thinks so. In his writings, Friedman praises the BoJ for "practicing" monetarism without vocalizing it:

Japan illustrates a policy that is less monetarist in rhetoric than the policies followed by the United States and Great Britain but far more monetarist in practice. (1985a, p. 27)

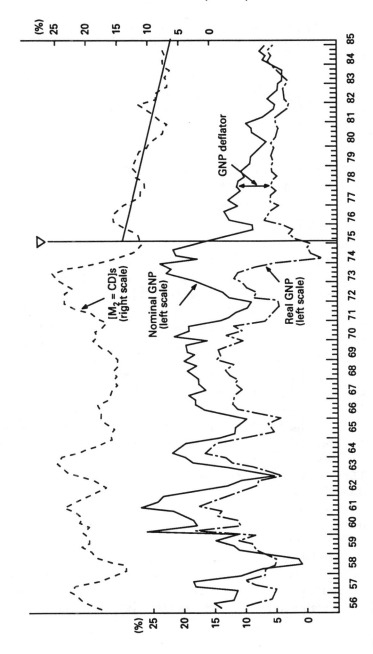

Figure 5.3
Growth rates of money stock and GNP, calculated against same quarter of previous year. "M_2 + CDs" data (before 1979:1, "M_2" data) are averages of end-of-month observations; e.g., the first quarter is an average of the data at the ends of January, February, and March. Source: Suzuki 1985.

The Bank of Japan has been the least monetarist central bank in its rhetoric, the most monetarist in its policy. It has also achieved the best results. (1985b)

Before we accept Friedman's assertions, we should carefully compare the monetary policy pursued by the Federal Reserve during 1979–1982 with that followed by the Bank of Japan during 1975–1985:

• The BoJ targeted M2 + CD; the Fed targeted M1.

• The Fed announced its statistics every week; the Japanese monetary authority announced monetary statistics monthly.

• The BoJ announced its statistics in terms of annual increases instead of week-to-week changes.

According to Ito (1989), the Bank of Japan did not practice the $k\%$-growth rule preached by monetarists. That study reveals that when the actual monetary growth rate deviated from its target ("forecast") rate, the target rate of the following period (quarter) was most likely to be adjusted toward the actual growth rate. That is, if the actual growth rate was higher than the target rate in quarter T, the target rate of quarter $T + 1$ was higher than the target rate in quarter T. Hence, it was more than just a base drift. In addition, the target was unbiased in the sense that the mean of the forecast error was zero—the "forecasts" were rational expectations.

The observed facts are not consistent with monetarist practice. If the $k\%$ rule had been taken seriously, the target rate for quarter $T + 1$ should move in the opposite direction of the deviation so that $k\%$ growth in the money stock could be maintained in the long run. That is, if the actual rate was higher than the target rate in quarter T, then the target rate of quarter $T + 1$ should be *lower* than the target rate in quarter T, in order to compensate for the unexpected increase.

Thus, despite praise from monetarists, the monetary policy of the Bank of Japan cannot be judged to have been practicing monetarism as defined by the $k\%$ rule. Moreover, the monetary growth rate rose beyond the "forecasts" in 1987 and 1990 to an extent that would be inexplicable if the $k\%$ rule had actually been pursued.

Recent Developments

American monetary policy in the second half of the 1980s succeeded in supporting an economic expansion without producing strong inflationary pressure. The M1-growth-rate target was dropped, because financial deregulation had blurred the distinction between transactions and savings deposit instruments.

From September 1985 to the summer of 1987, the United States (along with Japan and the major European countries) used monetary policy to ensure that the dollar would depreciate enough to reverse the trend toward deeper US trade deficits. After US monetary policy was slightly tightened out of fear of inflation, the New York stock market suddenly experienced a huge drop (on October 19, 1987, now known as Black Monday). Monetary policy was then relaxed in order to keep the Black Monday crash from having serious financial consequences. American monetary policy from 1987 to 1990 tried to balance the goals of maintaining economic expansion and preventing inflation. However, by the summer of 1990 (when the Iraqi invasion of Kuwait occurred) the inflation rate of the CPI was nearly 5 percent and growing.

Japan used monetary policy from 1985 to 1987 to ensure an appreciation of the yen (a depreciation of the dollar) in order to prevent its trade surpluses from soaring. The official discount rate was lowered from 5 to 2.5 percent, and the market interest rates declined accordingly. The M2 + CD growth rate, which has been declining since 1975, was down to 7.3 percent in 1983, but then it started to rise; it climbed to 10.8 percent in 1987. In 1987 the rate of monetary growth continually surpassed the Bank of Japan's monetary "forecasts." Relaxed monetary policy also produced asset inflation; stock prices and land prices soared in 1986–1988.

In Japan the official discount rate was as low as 2.5 percent in 1987–88. Raised five times between May 1989 and August 1990, it reached 6 percent on August 30, 1990. The rate of monetary growth continued to rise, however, reaching 12.0 percent in 1989. The acceleration in monetary growth from 1987 to 1989, which took place despite increases in interest rates, may have been due to financial deregulation, which can cause the money demand function to shift. When financial deregulation is occurring, therefore, the growth rate of the money supply may be a misleading signal. This effect is clearly evident in the United States' experience with financial deregulation during the first half of the 1980s.

SUMMARY

Some of the unique characteristics of Japanese financial institutions, markets, and monetary policy have been disappearing in the wake of deregulation. In terms of monetary policy and the functions of financial markets, Japan is quite comparable to the United States; however, a few surviving differences, including Japan's system of postal saving, continuation of deposit-interest-rate regulations, "main banks," and lack of a mature treasury-bill market, are worthy of note. Japan's monetary policy has sometimes been praised by monetarists as an example of actual monetarist practice, but a closer investigation reveals that there is no such evidence to support the claim that Japan pursued monetarist policies.

APPENDIX A: GUIDE TO FINANCIAL DATA

One should take great care when using Japanese data, especially for econometric analysis. For one thing, some of the data available in English are inaccurately described. For example, the Main Economic Indicators table of the Organization for Economic Cooperation and Development lists the Gensaki rate as the short-term interest rate for Japan (which is correct), but incorrectly labels it as an end-of-the-month rate when it is in fact a monthly average rate. Furthermore, since many regulations in Japan are different from those in the United States, two interest rates with the same name do not necessarily perform the same function. For example, the Treasury Bill rate, which is used widely in the United States as a representative short-term rate, is not a market rate in Japan. The Japanese FB rate is tied to the official discount rate and changes only when the official discount rate changes. It makes no sense to use the FB rate (which was sometimes called the TB rate in the English data documentation before the current 6-month and 3-month TBs were issued) in testing hypotheses concerning the Japanese term structure, or covered and uncovered interest parity. The history of the (6-month and 3-month) TB rate is still too short to be useful for most analyses.

Japanese money-supply data are available in two configurations: the monthly average series and the end-of-the-month series. In the case of interest-rate data, one should note whether or not the interest rate of the particular instrument was regulated (explicitly or implicitly). A regulated interest rate is not suitable for standard econometric work or economic analysis.

In the analysis of monetary policy, a measure of money—a *monetary aggregate*—is a necessary tool. Fortunately, the definitions of the monetary aggregates M1, M2, and M3 are currently comparable between the United States and Japan, although the US definitions of these aggregates have been changing to reflect financial innovations.

In both countries, the narrowly defined monetary aggregate M1 includes currency in circulation and "demand or checkable deposits," although the precise definitions, availabilities, and natures of various demand deposits vary over time and between the two countries. Since the Japanese do not use personal or traveler's checks, a major component of "demand deposits" has been "ordinary deposits," which yield a regulated, low rate of interest and pay out cash on demand. But one cannot write checks on "ordinary deposits." In the United States, the term "demand deposits" used to designate checking accounts, which under Regulation Q could not bear interest. As a consequence of the financial reform law of 1980, the NOW (negotiable order of withdrawal) account appeared nationwide. (It was available in some New England states earlier.) A NOW account is simply an interest-bearing checking account. Thus, Japanese "ordinary deposits" are similar to American NOW accounts in that both yield a regulated interest rate and convert to cash on demand at the teller or the cash machine.

After a significant adjustment of definitions and statistics in the early 1980s, M1 in the United States now comprises "checkable accounts," including NOW accounts and money-market checking accounts. Money-market accounts are not included in Japan's M1. Deposit interest rates for accounts included in M1 in Japan are regulated and are tied to the BoJ's official discount rate.

The money measure M2 includes M1 plus some accounts that share with savings accounts the characteristics of less-frequent transactions and (consequently) higher interest rates. In Japan, non-transferable "time deposits" [teiki yokin] are popular among small investors. The interest rates on time deposits (other than "large time deposits" [ohguchi teiki yokin] and money-market certificates) are regulated. Negotiable certificates of deposit (CDs) are also included in M2. The Bank of Japan announces both the straight M2 (without CD) and the "M2 + CD" as official statistics. The series most relevant to economists would be "M2 + CD," which corresponds to the US definition of M2. In the United States, M2 includes passbook savings, small-denomination CDs, and Money Market Deposit Accounts, individual money-market mutual funds (MMMFs), certain types of overnight repurchase agreements (RPs), and Euro-market deposits.

M1 and M2 + CD are the most frequently used monetary-supply concepts. The broader concept M3 is also sometimes used; in Japan this includes M2 + CD plus the balances in postal savings accounts, the principal of trust accounts [Kinsen shintaku and Kashitsuke shinkaku], and other deposits in the credit-union-type institutions that exist in agriculture, fishing, and other industries. Postal savings in Japan command a large quantity of balances, rivaling the deposits in commercial banks. In the United States, M3 includes M2 plus large-denomination CDs, RPs, and MMMFs held by institutions. These monetary aggregates are important when one is analyzing monetary policies. Tables 5.7 and 5.8 summarize the characteristics of the data.

In Japan the call market (overnight or seven-day borrowing) and the Tegata market (borrowing for up to three months) were not separated until 1971. The distinction in maturity was not made until 1978, and the distinction was "over one month" and "over two months" instead of "one month" and "two months" between 1978 and October 1980.

The Gensaki rates were originally compiled by the Japan Association of Securities Business. The Bank of Japan did not start carrying data on them in its *Economic Statistics Annual* until 1979. This shows that the Gensaki market, which had been free from regulation, was not considered important by the Bank of Japan until the end of the 1970s.[15] Many economists consider the Gensaki rate, which is observed regularly and which is available from the research department of any large securities house in Japan, to be the best economic series as a regulation-free interest rate in the 1970s.

Although the OECD data book indicates that the data on Gensaki

Table 5.7
Monetary aggregates.

		Available
M1	End of month	
M1	Monthly average	
M2	End of month	
M2	Monthly average	
M2 + CD	End of month	May 1979
M2 + CD	Monthly average	May 1979
M3	End of month	1971

Table 5.8

	Maturity	Conversion	Available since	Sources[b]	Date of interest-rate deregulation
FB [Seifu Tanki Shoken]	60 days	end of month	1971:1	BoJ, OECD	Not yet
Call[a]	unconditional	average of daily	1955:1	BoJ, OECD	1979:4
Bill Discount [Tegata][a]	2 months	average of daily	1971	BoJ	1979:10
	3 months	highest & lowest	1971	BoJ	1978:11
	1 month	highest & lowest	1971	BoJ	1978:11
Repurchase Agreement [Gensaki][a]	3 months	average	1977:2	BoJ	always
		end of month	1977:2	BoJ	always
		end of month	1975:1	MG	always
	2 months	end of month	1977:2	BoJ	always
	1 month	end of month	1977:2	BoJ	always
CD market	120 days	average of new issues	1979:5	BoJ	always

a. See discussion in text near end of appendix A.
b. BoJ: Bank of Japan, *Economic Statistics Annual*, published at end of March every year. OECD: Organization for Economic Cooperation and Development, *Main Economic Indicators*, various issues. MG: Morgan Guarantee Trust, *World Financial Markets*, various issues.

are taken at the "end of period," cross-checking reveals that they are the simple "average of daily figures" over the month.

The Morgan Guarantee Trust Data Bank treats the Gensaki series since 1975 as the "representative money-market rate" for Japan. *World Financial Markets* did not employ the Gensaki as the "representative money-market rate" until 1979, however. Therefore, copying the numbers from back issues of *World Financial Markets* does not retrieve the Gensaki rate. See the footnote in the December 1978 *WFM* for an old series.

APPENDIX B: THEORIES OF MONETARY POLICY

Traditional (Keynesian) Views

Keynesians use the IS-LM approach to explain the use of monetary policy. The IS-LM framework comes with the assumption that prices and wages are inflexible. Under this assumption, changes in the money supply can lessen fluctuations in aggregate demand. In the IS-LM framework, aggregate demand is determined by money demand, money supply, and the investment-saving relationship. Money demand depends on many factors, including the interest rate; thus, when the interest rate fluctuates, the relationship between money and income also fluctuates. If for some reason money demand shifts up, so that people are willing to hold more money at each level of aggregate income, the LM curve shifts to the left, income decreases, and the interest rate goes up. Such changes in money demand can be offset by "fine-tuning" the money supply to shift the LM curve back to its original position, thus maintaining the desired level of aggregate income. Similarly, the monetary authority can fine-tune the money supply to offset fluctuations in the IS curve. Keynesians assert that the money supply can and should be used to smooth short-run economic fluctuations.

Monetarist Views

Monetarists argue that an economy will always move to its full-employment level of output even if it is disturbed. That is, real GNP will be stable if not disturbed by policy. This means that there is a stable relationship between the money stock and the nominal GNP.

Therefore, if the money stock is kept stable the price level should remain stable. Monetarist arguments rest on the following major assumptions:

• The money demand function is stable.

• The economy functions as a "classical" economist would predict: prices and wages are flexible, so aggregate supply and aggregate demand are always in balance (there is no chronic underutilization of capital or involuntary unemployment).

• The money supply can be controlled by the monetary authority.

• Fiscal policy has no effect on nominal GNP unless it is accompanied by changes in the money supply.

• The real interest rate is constant, so a change in nominal interest rates reflects a change in the expected inflation rate.

In addition, Milton Friedman has presented evidence in various volumes of his work that the nominal GNP lags 6 months to 2 years behind the money supply in terms of its fluctuation pattern (the occurrence of peaks and troughs), that nominal spending lags about 6–9 months behind the money supply, and that the price level lags by 18–24 months (see Friedman 1985a, p. 16).

Based on their assumptions and arguments, monetarists conclude that the money supply should be increased at a constant rate forever, and that any money-supply fluctuations are harmful. In other words, money should not respond to output or interest-rate fluctuations. This is what Friedman means when he writes "All monetarists, I believe, favor steadiness." (1985a, p. 17) In other words, if the central bank keeps monetary growth steady, the economy will stabilize itself. As Friedman admits, there is no consensus among monetarists as to which monetary aggregate (M1, M2, or something else) should be targeted, or as to what the appropriate growth rate, k, is.

Keynesians criticized monetarism on the grounds that stabilizing monetary growth need not necessarily stabilize the economy, whereas flexible policy responses would enhance the stability of the economy. In addition, the money demand function, or monetary velocity, is highly unstable, and the level of real interest rates varies according to conditions in the financial market. In particular, changes in the institutional environment, such as financial innovations, shift the money demand function and the real interest rates.

Views of New Classical Macroeconomists

There are other economists who believe that the money supply should not be used to try to smooth economic fluctuations. Their conclusion is similar to that of the monetarists, but their logic is quite different. These "new classical macroeconomists" think that economic fluctuations should not necessarily be regarded as a bad thing. If fluctuations, or business cycles, emerge even when economic agents are optimizing, then they should not be stabilized. The new classical macroeconomists criticize the Keynesians for their very use of the IS-LM framework (which assumes inflexibility of prices and wages), and assert that prices and wages in the market economy should, and do, adjust to the equilibrium level fast enough. Monetarists and new classical macroeconomists agree that money should not be accommodative or used for "fine tuning," but the new classical macroeconomists criticize the monetarists for their theory's lack of a microeconomic foundation.

The new classical macroeconomists are, in fact, microeconomists in disguise. Their arguments rest on the proposition known as the first theorem of welfare economics: that a competitive equilibrium is Pareto optimal, and that hence no government interventions would improve everybody's economic welfare simultaneously, because at an equilibrium the efficient use of resource allocations is achieved. Critics of the new classical macroeconomists attack the many assumptions needed to guarantee their proposition. The frequently attacked assumptions include perfect information, complete markets for contingent commodities, no externalities, and no oligopolies. The real macroeconomy does not satisfy these assumptions.

NOTES

1. For differences in deregulation in the two countries, see Cargill 1985.

2. One might wonder why some of the deregulation of Japanese domestic financial institutions has resulted from "foreign pressure" rather than internal pressure arising from domestic needs. I will present one theory explaining this in chapter 12.

3. Another impediment to bond issues is that the amount of bond issues has been controlled by banks as well as securities companies. See Hamada and Horiuchi 1987.

4. Many people, including the authors of the 1984 report of the US-Japan Yen/Dollar Working Group, have stressed the need for a short-term safe asset, denominated in yen, that would be available to foreign investors.

5. Unit banking is a system that does not allow a bank to have branch offices, or that allows only one branch (which must be near the headquarters). New York and California are two prominent states that had long allowed branch banking. In the wake of financial deregulation, unit banking has essentially been replaced by branch banking.

6. The reserve ratio policy was attempted for a brief period in 1957.

7. This was said to have lowered the cost of capital in Japan. It was criticized by the United States in the discussion of the follow-up meeting of the Yen/Dollar Working Group. Responding to the criticism, the BoJ broadened the base of institutions by including foreign institutions in Japan.

8. See, for example, page 314 of Patrick and Rosovsky 1976.

9. The transaction tax is set at 3/10,000 of the selling price of a government bond, and at 4.5/10,000 for other securities. When the seller is a securities company the rates are respectively 1/10,000 and 1.5/10,000. The transaction is tax-exempt if the seller is the central government or the local government, or if the instrument is a FB with a maturity of less than one year, or if an institution is selling a government or government-agency bond which was purchased by that institution at the time of new issue and the bond is sold within one year of its issuance at the time of the Gensaki sales, or if the Bank of Japan is purchasing the instrument in an open-market operation. Note that each repurchase agreement is subject to this tax twice: once at the "start" and once at the "end" of the agreement.

10. In Japan the term CD is sometimes used for "cash dispenser," and NCD is used for "negotiable certificate of deposit." Certificates of Deposit, commonly known as CDs in the United States, were first issued in the United States by the First National City Bank (Citibank) in February 1962. After May 1973, the interest-rate ceiling (Regulation Q) ceased to apply to large CDs (over $100,000). Currently there are no binding interest-rate regulations on short-term financial instruments in the United States.

11. Among these are the development of the Euroyen market, the increase in the number of foreign financial institutions in Japan, the creation of the Japan Offshore Market, and the development of a futures market.

12. Even after the Nixon announcement, Japan was the last among the OECD countries to realize that major exchange-rate adjustment was necessary. The Tokyo market stayed open for three days after the major European markets were closed for adjustment of the exchange rate. Consequently, in the wake of speculation, the Bank of Japan quickly accumulated dollars in order to maintain the rate of 360 yen/$.

Although in Japan the term "Nixon shock" usually refers to the abandonment of the gold standard, the shock was in fact twofold; its other aspect was the opening of diplomatic relations between the United States and mainland China.

13. See B. Friedman 1984 and other articles in the same issue of *American Economic Review*. See also McCallum 1985.

14. When the target was taken seriously in the United States, the Federal Reserve set upper and lower bounds for M1 growth as its announced target. Whereas Japan announces actual M2 + CD monthly, the US announced actual M1 weekly. The US announcement policy drew a jittery response from participants in the financial market.

15. Some BoJ officials might dispute the accuracy of data collected by the association.

BIBLIOGRAPHY

Cargill, T. F. 1985. "A US perspective on Japanese financial liberalization." *Monetary and Economic Studies* 3, no. 1: 115–149.

Friedman, B. M. 1984. "Lessons from the 1979–82 monetary policy experiment." *American Economic Review* 74, no. 2: 382–387.

Friedman, M. 1985a. "Monetarism in rhetoric and in practice." In *Monetary Policy in Our Times*, ed. A. Ando et al. MIT Press.

Friedman, M. 1985b. "The Fed's monetarism was never anything but rhetoric." Letter to the editor, *Wall Street Journal*, December 18, 1985.

Hamada, K., and A. Horiuchi. 1987. "The political economy of the financial market." In *The Political Economy of Japan*, Volume 1: *The Domestic Transformation*, ed. K. Yamamura and Y. Yasuba. Stanford University Press.

Horiuchi, A., F. Packer, and Shin'ichi Fukuda. 1988. "What role has the 'main bank' played in Japan?" *Journal of the Japanese and International Economies* 2: 159–180.

Ito, T. 1989. Is the Bank of Japan a Closet Monetarist? Monetary Targeting in Japan, 1978–1988. NBER working paper 2874.

Ito, T., and K. Ueda. 1981. "Tests of the equilibrium hypothesis in disequilibrium econometrics: An international comparison of credit rationing in business loans." *International Economic Review* 22: 691–708.

McCallum, B. T. 1985. "On consequences and criticisms of monetary targeting." *Journal of Money, Credit, and Banking* 17, no. 4: 570–597.

Patrick, H., and H. Rosovsky, eds. 1976. *Asia's New Giant*. Brookings Institution.

Sargen, N., K. Schoenholtz, S. Blitz, and S. Elhabashi. 1986. Trading Patterns in the Japanese Government Bond Market. Bond Market Research, Salomon Brothers, Inc.

Suzuki, Y. 1980. *Money and Banking in Contemporary Japan.* Yale University Press.

Suzuki, Y. 1985. "Japan's monetary policy over the past 10 years." *Bank of Japan Monetary and Economic Studies* 3, no. 2: 1–10.

Suzuki, Y., ed. 1987. *The Japanese Financial System.* Clarendon.

Chapter 6

PUBLIC FINANCE AND FISCAL POLICIES

Fiscal and monetary policy are important instruments by which a government exerts influence on the course of an economy. Tax policy has both macroeconomic and microeconomic aspects. The overall size of the government has important macroeconomic implications. Government expenditures, G, and tax revenues, T, are included in any simple macroeconomic model. However, the same level of revenues may be achieved by different kinds of taxes and different tax-rate schedules, or even by borrowing. A choice of a particular mix of taxes gives an incentive or a disincentive for particular types of consumption and investment. Government spending finances many public goods, many of which are elements of the infrastructure (such as roads, railroads, sewerage, parks, and utilities). Allocations among the possible funding projects reveal political priorities of the government and may affect the productivity of the private sector.

Japan's national [chuō], prefectural, and municipal governments roughly correspond to the federal, state, and municipal governments in the United States. Prefectural and municipal governments in Japan sometimes are aggregated into "local" [chihō] governments, whereas in the United States the term "local" is usually reserved for "municipal" governments. In this chapter, the revenue and spending policies of the national government of Japan are the major targets of investigation.

Technically, the Japanese national government has three types of budgets: a general-account budget [ippan kaikei], a special-account budget [tokubetsu kaikei], and a government-agencies budget [seifu kankei kikan]. However, the term "government budget" usually refers to the general account only.

Table 6.1
Data on three accounts of the Japanese national government (billion yen, nominal).

| FY | Account | | | |
	General	Special	Net[a]	Gov't agencies
1981	46,921.2	92,321.0	80,212.4	22,171.5
1988	61,471.1	147,492.2	115,623.1	5,062.2[b]

a. General + Special − adjustment.
b. Some government agencies, most notably National Railways and Nippon Telephone and Telegram, were privatized in 1987, so the budget of government agencies was reduced significantly.

In association with the three budgets, the FILP (Fiscal Investments and Loans Program) plays an important role. The FILP may be understood as a capital budget of the national government, and it is overlaid on the three types of accounts, especially the latter two. Typically, the FILP draws on funds from postal savings and makes loans to special accounts and government agencies.

Special accounts are set up for various reasons. Some are for specific projects, such as highway and airport construction; others are set up to fund specific purposes with specific revenues, such as social security accounts. There were 38 special accounts in 1990. The total size of the special-accounts budget is about three times that of the general account. However, there are significant flows between general accounts and special accounts, such as subsidies from taxes to social security accounts, so the aggregate size of the general and special accounts, net of internal flows, is about twice the size of the general account. This implies that special accounts have independent revenue sources as large as those of general accounts.

Government agencies, including the Development Bank, the Export-Import Bank, and other smaller financial agencies, have a total budget equal to approximately 10 percent of the general budget and receive major portions of their funding from the FILP.

The ratio of a government's expenditures to the country's GNP is often a measure of how big the government is. The ratio is about 15 percent in Japan and 22 percent in the United States. The same ratio exceeds 25 percent in the United Kingdom, 30 percent in Italy, and 50 percent in Sweden. Citing this ratio, conservative politicians and economists in the United States sometimes praise Japan for its

The Fiscal Year

The fiscal year in Japan runs from April 1 to March 31, as does the school year. In the United States, the fiscal year runs from October 1 to September 30. Before 1977, the US fiscal year started July 1. The period from July 1, 1976, through September 30, 1976, is a separate fiscal period known as the *transition quarter*.

Most data on taxation and government spending are available only on a fiscal-year basis. When these data are matched or compared with other statistics kept on the calendar-year basis, careful adjustments are sometimes required.

In Japan, GNP and other major macro statistics are published both on a calendar-year and on a fiscal-year basis.

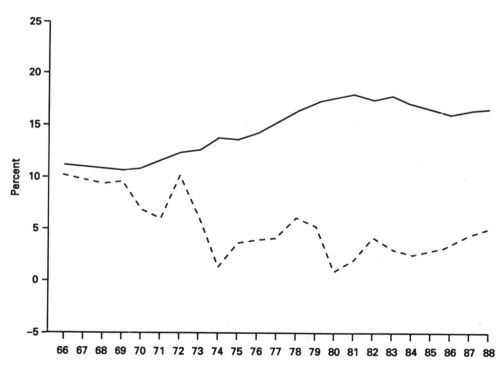

Figure 6.1
Real GNP growth rate (broken line) and ratio of government spending to GNP (solid line) for Japan.

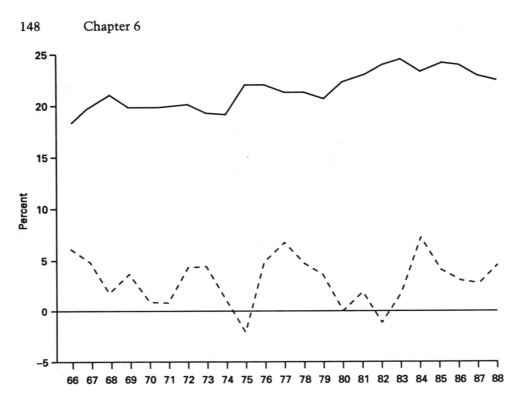

Figure 6.2
Real GNP growth rate (broken line) and ratio of government spending to
GNP (solid line) for United States.

"small government," which has a high priority on the conservative
agenda. This, however, may be an incorrect interpretation of the
spending/GNP ratio, because in the case of Japan "government expenditures" refers to the general account only. There is a capital
budget in Japan. If the revenues of the FILP (and expenditures
through special accounts and other channels) are added to the
general account, adjusting for double-counting, the government
expenditures/GNP ratio of Japan is quite close to that of the United
States. (Moreover, if special accounts are counted it is much larger
than the combined US federal budget, which counts both on-budget
and off-budget expenditures.)

The Japanese local governments are often said to be less "autonomous" from the national government than their US counterparts.
In Japan, independent revenue sources are limited, and more regulatory details are controlled by the national government. (For example,

The Japanese Budget Process

In July of year $T - 1$, the Ministry of Finance issues a ceiling for the total budget of each ministry or government agency. Subject to this ceiling, the ministries and agencies submit their budget requests to the Minister of Finance by the end of August. Then, the Ministry of Finance and other ministries and government agencies negotiate a budget plan during the fall of year $T - 1$. At the end of December of year $T - 1$, or at the beginning of January of year T, the cabinet approves the tentative government budget "plan" (Fiscal Law, Article 18). Although the details of the plan have to be worked out and then submitted to the Diet for approval, the total amount budgeted seldom changes after the cabinet has approved the plan. The plan incorporates the "government forecast" of economic growth and inflation for fiscal year T, usually announced at the end of January or the beginning of February of calendar year T. The Diet approves the cabinet plan around the beginning of the fiscal year (April 1). There is rarely a conflict between the Diet and the Cabinet. During the fiscal year, the budget may be revised to reflect evolving economic conditions. Since 1965 the budget has often been revised at least once in the fall or winter, and in fiscal years 1965, 1977, and 1987 it was revised twice. A first revision has been approved as early as August (e.g. FY 1965), and a second revision as late as the first week of March (e.g. FY 1969 and FY 1988). The actual (*ex post*) government expenditures are determined on March 31 of year $T + 1$.

local tax law is under the supervision of the Ministry of Finance, and there is a "standard" property-tax rate of 1.4 percent nationwide.) Of the taxes and social security contributions that citizens pay, about 64 percent was collected as national taxes and 36 percent as local taxes in 1987. The percentages in the United States are 57 and 43, respectively. Grants to local government constitute close to 20 percent of the national government's budget in Japan, versus about 12 percent in the United States. Aside from social security contributions, the individual income tax and the corporate income tax are the dominant national revenue sources in Japan (70–75 percent) and the United States (90 percent). The share of corporate income tax revenues relative to individual income tax revenues is higher in Japan than in the United States. In Japan, the percentage of revenues from indirect taxes in the national government budget is as large as 29 percent. The ratio is larger than that of the United States, but less than those of European countries.

The budget deficit (i.e., the issues of government bonds) reached 5.5 percent of Japan's GNP in 1979 and 1980—higher than the comparable ratio in the United States in any year of the 1980s except 1983 (when the US ratio was 6.3 percent). When financing deficits, the Japanese government has used two types of government bonds: construction bonds and deficit bonds. Before 1965, the Japanese government did not borrow. In 1965, a large unexpected shortfall in revenues caused the government to issue construction bonds earmarked for public construction. The downturn that followed the first oil crisis led the Japanese government to issue deficit-financing bonds in 1975. No deficit bond (except for rollovers) was issued by the Japanese government in the fiscal year 1990. This means that, after fifteen years of large deficits, the government budget was finally brought back to a balance in FY 1990.

THE TAX STRUCTURE

The individual income tax and the corporate income tax are major sources of revenue for the Japanese national government. Each of these two taxes accounted for about 35 percent of the total tax and other revenues of the national government in 1988. Other national revenue sources include an inheritance tax (3 percent of revenues), a liquor tax (4 percent), a gasoline tax (3 percent), a security-transactions tax (4 percent), a commodity tax (4 percent), stamp revenues (4 percent), and customs duties (1 percent). The commodity tax (on luxury goods) was replaced by an across-the-board consumption tax (a kind of value-added tax) in April 1989.[1] In the United States, revenues from the corporate income tax are outweighed 4 to 1 by those from the individual income tax, whereas the two are about the same in Japan. The Japanese prefectural governments raise revenues mainly from an inhabitants' tax and an enterprise tax; the municipal governments raise most of their revenues from an inhabitants' tax and a property tax. Inhabitants' taxes, imposed both on a per-capita basis and on an income basis, correspond to state and local income taxes in the United States. In the United States, the state income tax is deductible from the federal income tax, and vice versa; this kind of deductibility is absent in Japan.

Table 6.2
National (federal) receipts.

	United States, 1989 ($ billion)		Japan, 1988 (100 billion yen)
Individual	445.7	Individual	179.5
withheld	361.3	withheld	129.9
others[a]	84.4	others[a]	49.7
Corporation	103.6	Corporation	184.4
Social insurance tax and contributions	359.4	Social insurance special accounts[b]	112.1
on-budget	99.9		
off-budget	163.7		
Excise	34.1	Commodity	20.4
		Liquor	22.0
Estate & gift	8.7	Inheritance	18.3
Customs duties	16.3	Customs duties	7.4
Miscellaneous[c]	21.8	Miscellaneous[d]	89.9
Total	990.7		634.0
on-budget	827.0		521.9

a. Includes a subtraction of "refunds" ($70.5 billion).
b. Annuities and pension premiums in special accounts of Kokumin nenkin, Kosei nenkin, and Kanpo.
c. The only major "miscellaneous" item in the US is "Deposit of earnings, Federal Reserve System."
d. Includes Motor Vehicle Tonnage Tax, Securities Transactions Tax, Gasoline Tax, and other taxes.
Sources: (US) Economic Report of the President, 1990, p. 385; Budget of the United States Government, Fiscal Year 1991. (Japan) Ministry of Finance, Fiscal Statistics Annual, 1990.

The Individual Income Tax

One major difference between the Japanese and American tax systems is that Japan does not have a tax identification number comparable to the social security number used in the United States. Hence, in Japan it sometimes is difficult to tax the sum of an individual's various incomes in a progressive manner. As a result, horizontal equity—the principle of equal taxation for the same amount of income, regardless of sources—is widely violated in Japan.

Interest and dividend income had enjoyed broad exemptions in Japan until April 1, 1988. Now, the 20 percent uniform rate is applied to all interest income other than that earned by "special maruyu" accounts reserved for the elderly, the handicapped, and single parents. (For discount bonds, the rate is 18 percent and the tax is collected at the time of purchase.) The income tax on interest is withheld at the time of payment. Capital gains are also taxed separately. Before January 1989, capital gains from securities transactions (typically stock transactions) were tax-free unless the individual traded more than 30 transactions, each involving more than 120,000 shares, in a year. Since January 1989, the tax on capital gains has been 1 percent of the proceeds: capital gains are presumed to constitute 5 percent of proceeds, and 20 percent is the tax rate for capital gains. (One may elect to have capital gains treated as regular income; however, 1 percent of sales is more economical for large investors.) For investors with long holding periods, stock transactions typically yields capital gains of more than 5 percent of value. In this sense, capital gains are still taxed lightly.

Retirement, timber, occasional, and miscellaneous incomes have separate deductible amounts. Japanese workers receive a sizable retirement severance payment. If it were subject to the usual income-tax scheme, the typical retirement severance payment would put the worker in the top bracket of the progressive schedule. Hence, there is a special deduction for retirement income. Occasional income is formally defined as income deemed to be temporary and particular to one year; this may be considered to be a substitute for income averaging. Miscellaneous income includes all other types of income, such as honoraria.

A major part of the individual income tax is collected by withholding of employment income. Withholding is adjusted at the end of the year at the source for various kinds of deductions, and for changes in salary level, in tax law, and in family composition that may have occurred during the year. As a result, Japanese employees are subject to a lump-sum adjustment in the last paycheck of the year. Those who have only employment income (under 15 million yen) and interest income (both withheld automatically), plus limited amounts of some other kinds of income, are not required to file a tax return at all. Those who have some other kinds of income (for example, real estate, miscellaneous, and occasional income above a certain threshold) have to file a final return between mid February and mid March.

In 1989, the top marginal rate for individual taxable income (after deductions) was 50 percent in Japan (for income more than 20 million yen) and 33 percent in the United States (for a joint return with taxable income between $74,850 and $177,720).[2]

Many employees in Japan have expressed frustration with how heavily they are taxed. The frustration is twofold. First, self-employed businesspeople, doctors, and farmers enjoy generous deductibility of expenses. Second, it is widely known that tax compliance is highest for employees, since their taxes are withheld at the source. Regarding deductibility, the Ministry of Finance would point out that the basic deduction for employees is relatively high.[3] Some of the deductibility allowed for other types of income is so outrageously generous, however, that many employees are not convinced by this argument. For example, doctors may write off as expenses 72 percent of their income from treating patients under social health insurance. (The recent tax reform capped this deductibility at 50 million yen.) Also, family businesses can pay "salaries" to family members, who enjoy the basic deduction for employees, while the entire salaries are deducted as expenses from the income of the head of the household. Regarding compliance, the ratio of compliance relative to income is said to be 90 percent for employees, 60 percent for the self-employed, and 40 percent for farmers. This rule of thumb [koroyon] can be verified by comparing the different kinds of income reported to the tax authority against the corresponding kinds of income found in national income statistics (Ishi 1989, pp. 80–81). The issue of compliance with the income tax was one of strong driving forces behind the introduction of a consumption tax.

The Consumption Tax of 1989

The so-called consumption tax [Shohi zei] is in fact a value-added tax (VAT). The 3 percent assessment is based on the value added—that is, the difference between the sale price and the cost at each stage in the production of every good or service. In contrast with the sales taxes in many states of the United States and the VATs in Europe, no exemption is made for food or clothing in Japan.

A VAT was first proposed by the Ōhira government in 1978, but the proposal disappeared when the Liberal Democratic Party was defeated in the election of 1979. A second drive, led by the Nakasone government in 1987, failed partly because of opposition from small and medium-size businesses, a traditional constituency of the LDP. Finally, the Takeshita government succeeded in introducing the tax. The bill was passed in the Diet on December 24, 1988, and the tax was introduced in April 1989.

There were three major reasons for the introduction of a value-added tax in Japan. First, as mentioned above, the income tax had many loopholes. Even if some types of income escaped taxation, taxing consumption would partially rectify the inequality. Second, the anticipated heavy burden of social security outlays in the 21st century called for an instrument that would make it easy to increase revenues. Third, the commodity tax, whose purpose was to tax luxury goods, had become outdated. For example, cameras were subject to the commodity tax, but personal computers were exempt because they were new commodities. The new consumption tax was intended to cover all commodities, without differentiating "ordinary" and "luxury," thereby eliminating the distortion of the commodity tax.

Once the consumption tax was introduced, people became furious. The new tax was said to be responsible for the defeat of the Liberal Democratic Party in the election of the House of Councilors in July 1989. Voters' furor over the consumption tax can be classified in three categories: naive resentment against a new tax, resentment against the regressive nature of the new tax, and resentment against the loopholes in the implementation of the tax. Let us examine these factors in order.

In introducing the new tax, the Ministy of Finance advised wholesalers and retailers that the 3 percent tax should explicitly be added to the existing price. For example, 200-yen milk should become 206 yen, and a 1000-yen book should become 1030 yen. This advice was based on two apparently conflicting concerns: the government was concerned that some businesses would round off their prices to (for example) 210 yen instead of 206, or 1050 instead of 1030, and some businesses were worried that they might have to absorb the 3 percent in their profit margin because their customers would not be willing to pay higher prices. Consumers became quite aware of the new tax when they began to be charged odd amounts at the checkout and when they starting receiving change in one-yen coins, which had been out of circulation of a long time. Although consumers became accustomed to the new institution, eventually the prices of many goods and services were rounded up or down, without objections from the Ministry of Finance.

Some critics, including opposition parties, opposed the consumption tax because, they charged, the wealthy and the poor were required to pay the same percentage. The Ministry of Finance quickly pointed out that a reduction in income tax would accompany the introduction of the consumption tax, and that the package as a whole would be revenue-neutral. Revenue-neutrality in this sense does not necessarily imply distributional neutrality, however. Obviously, for the poorest, who had not been paying income taxes, the new tax was a pure increase. In order to meet this criticism, a one-time payment for the poorest families was included in the tax-reform package. Several simulations showed that the middle-income families lost and the upper-income families gained in the tax reform.[4] Some critics pressed for the exemption of food and other necessities from the new tax, and in 1990 the Ministry of Finance proposed reducing the rate for food to 1.5 percent.

A third major shortcoming of the consumption tax arises from the fact that small businesses that have annual sales under 30 million yen ($200,000 at 150 yen/dollar) are exempt from paying consumption taxes to the authority, and from the fact that a company whose annual sales are under 500 million yen ($3.3 million) may use a simplified formula for calculating value added (a fixed rate of value added—20 percent for retailers and 10 percent for wholesalers—may be presumed, without recordkeeping). These exemptions are seen as loopholes by opponents of the tax.

On the revised budget of fiscal year 1989, the revenue from the consumption tax is 3.6 trillion yen (that is, 6 percent of the total tax revenue); on the initial budget of fiscal year 1990, the amount is 5.3 trillion yen (8.7 percent of the total tax revenue).

As of April 1991, a proposal of alleviating shortcomings of the consumption tax, described above, is under discussion in the Diet. According to the proposal, some commodities and services (including rents, textbooks, baby deliveries, and funerals) would be exempted from the consumption tax, and the ceiling for a company with a simplified formula would be reduced to 400 million yen. In addition, small companies in manufacturing, construction, mining, agriculture, and fisheries are presumed to have value added as 30 percent of sales, and small companies in transportation, communication, and real estate are presumed to have value added as 40 percent of sales.

The Corporate Income Tax

The taxation of corporate income comes up often in discussions between the United States and Japan, and in debates between the business community and the taxation authority in both countries.

Table 6.3 shows how the effective burden of the corporate income tax has declined in the United States and the United Kingdom as a

Table 6.3
Corporate tax burden.

		Japan	US	UK
Effective tax rate	1984	52.92[a]	51.18[b]	52.00
	1987	51.55[a]	40.34[b]	40.00
Real tax burden[c]	1984	51.57	32.28	18.06
	1987	50.05	31.28	23.49

a. Sum of corporate tax rate, municipal corporate inhabitant tax rate, and prefectural enterprise tax rate, calculated with adjustment for the fact that the enterprise tax is deductible in calculating income for the corporate inhabitant tax rate and enterprise tax in the following year.
b. In the United States, state tax is deductible in calculating income for federal tax.
c. Adjusted for difference in (accelerated) depreciation schedule, expensing, investment tax credit, and other investment inducement measures, when available.
Source: Homma 1990, p. 284.

result of a series of tax reforms in those countries in the 1980s. American readers may be surprised to see that the corporate tax burden is much higher in Japan than in the United States, since they may often have heard the argument that the cost of capital is lower in Japan than in the United States. That argument is incomplete if the comparison is done on a before-tax basis. For Japanese corporations, any advantage due to a lower cost of capital (through the issuing of bonds and equities) may be canceled out by higher taxes.

And there are other, broader topics related to corporate income taxation. With the easing of regulations and technological advances in communication and transportation, capital became highly mobile in the 1980s. When one country (or US state) tries to impose a higher tax rate on corporations, it may induce some of them to move their headquarters or their production operations to another country or state. Hence, the corporate tax rate influences business strategy. Consider these two episodes:

• In the mid 1980s, legislators in several states in the western US attempted to introduce a "unitary tax" system under which *worldwide* income would be used as a base for the taxation of a multinational corporation's factory or subsidiary. Several Japanese companies campaigned against these attempts, which were defeated in the state legislatures.

• Yaohan, one of the largest retail chains in western Japan and southeast Asia, announced in 1990 that it would move its headquarters to Hong Kong. Many suspected that one of the reasons for the move was to save tax payments on worldwide income. (Another reason, which was given in Yaohan's official announcement, was that it would be difficult for Yaohan to expand its network within Japan because of the Large Retail Store Law.)

In calculating corporate income, the Japanese law allows some deductions for dividend payments; the current US law does not. Since dividend income is subject to the individual income tax, giving dividend relief makes sense to avoid double taxation. This, however, does not seem to encourage Japanese firms to pay out more dividends. Japanese companies are known to keep their income for reinvestment. The annual dividend returns on investment in companies listed on the Tokyo stock market typically range between 1 and 2 percent.

The Inheritance Tax

In Japan all of a decedent's property is subject to the inheritance tax, which differs from the US estate tax in that it is imposed on the recipients (beneficiaries) rather than on the estate. The structure of bequest taxation is affected significantly by this philosophical difference, which is not as superficial as it may seem.

In Japan, a progressive rate schedule is applied to each "statutory heir" and then aggregated to calculate the total tax liability. More statutory heirs for a given estate would lessen the total tax liability on the estate. (This was a known loophole for millionaires in Japan prior to 1988. The definition of statutory heirs and the tax-saving scheme will be explained below.) In the United States, the number of heirs is irrelevant in the calculation of the estate tax; the tax is assessed progressively on the value of the estate, regardless of its distribution. In both countries, agricultural land and family business properties benefit from special provisions that lessen their assessment value. In Japan, land for other purposes is also assessed significantly below the market value. Bequeathed residential land is assessed at around 30–50 percent of market value. There is no such provision in the United States.

In Japan land and structures account for more than 60 percent of bequeathed assets; in the United States the share of real estate is only about 25 percent. This reflects the fact that the price of a unit of land is much higher in Japan and the fact that land is taxed lightly (Homma and Atoda 1989; Barthold and Ito 1991). In the United States, land is cheaper and is assessed at its market value for estate-tax purposes. The light taxation on land in Japan encourages the bequest-minded elderly to purchase real estate with debt, since the liability is deductible in full from the bequeathed asset value. Since land is typically a nondivisible property, aged parents holding onto property may depress their consumption relative to their assets. That is why light land taxation is sometimes mentioned as a reason for the high saving rate in Japan. In both countries, the bequest (estate) and gift taxes are, in principle, taxed on all intergenerational transfers. There are various deductions and credits on transfers within a generation, and penalties on transfers to recipients other than lineal descendants. However, how this principle is reflected in the tax code differs in the two countries. In Japan, the Civil Code guarantees a spouse, a son, or a daughter a minimum share of bequest (50 percent of the "statutory" share). Rather than a tax incentive, this is a direct intervention in intergenerational transfers. From the principle of taxing intergenerational transfers, the US estate and gift tax systems exempt any transfers, *inter vivos* or upon death, to a spouse. In Japan there is a limit on tax-free bequests or gifts to a spouse, although a relatively large amount of tax credit is available for a bequest to a spouse.[5]

The Japanese civil-law concept of "statutory heir" is crucial to an understanding of the Japanese inheritance tax. It is presumed in civil law that, unless otherwise designated, half of an estate goes to a spouse, and each child receives an equal share of the remainder. Take, for example, the case where a spouse and two children survive the decedent. They constitute three statutory heirs. The spouse has a statutory share of 1/2, and each child has a statutory share of 1/4. In the case of a spouse and three children (that is, four statutory heirs), each child has a statutory share of 1/6. If the spouse predeceased and three children are alive, each child has a statutory share of 1/3.

Moreover, the half of statutory share is a guaranteed bequest. For example, if a spouse and two children survive the decedent, the spouse is entitled to no less than 1/4 and each child to no less than 1/8 of the property. Even if the decedent leaves a will designating a sole recipient of an entire estate, statutory heirs may sue for their automatic entitlement. More important, regardless of the actual distribution of property, the number of statutory heirs and statutory shares determine the total inheritance-tax liability.[6]

A new direction for research concerning Japan's high saving rate is the link between the bequest behavior and the aggregate household saving rate. In this regard, the effect of bequest taxation on bequest behavior is important.

GOVERNMENT SPENDING

The most salient aspect of the Japanese national budget is the relatively small expenditure for national defense—only 6 percent (in 1988) of the general account, versus about 25 percent of federal expenditures in the United States.

Interest payments on government bonds reached about 20 percent of the 1988 budget in Japan, versus about 15 percent in the United States.

Table 6.4
Expenditures of national governments.

Japan, 1988 (100 billion yen)		United States, 1989 ($ billion)	
Social programs and securities	103.8	Social programs	306.1
		Social Security	232.5
		on-budget	5.1
		off-budget	277.5
Education and science promotion	48.6	Science, space, and technology	12.8
Interest payments	115.1	Net interest	169.2
		on-budget	180.5
		off-budget	−11.4
Grants to local governments	109.1	Commerce and housing credit	28.0
National defense	37.0	National defense	303.6
Public works	60.8	Public goods[b]	33.0
Economic cooperation	6.8	International affairs	9.6
Energy	4.6	Energy	3.7
		Natural resources and environment	16.2
Food control	4.5	Agriculture	16.9
Veterans benefits, etc.	18.8	Veterans benefits and services	30.1
Others[a]		Others[a]	
Total	567.0	Total on-budget	1,142.6

a. Includes expenditure items related to pensions (old system), medium-and-small-enterprise assistance, industry investment, and miscellaneous expenditures.
b. Includes "transportation" and "community and regional development."
Sources: (US) Economic Report of the President, February 1990; (Japan) Ministry of Finance, Fiscal Statistics, 1990.

Table 6.5
Shares of public works in Japan's general account, by objectives.

	1975	1985	1990
Flood prevention and irrigation	16.0	15.7	17.5
Road	32.0	26.8	28.8
Ports, fishery ports, and airports	7.8	7.4	8.3
Housing	9.1	13.6	12.3
Sewerage	9.5	14.1	15.4
Infrastructure for agriculture	12.2	12.8	14.0
Forestry roads	2.5	2.4	2.5
Other	10.9	7.2	1.2

Source: Toyo Keizai, *Keizai Tokei Nenpo,* various issues.

The relationship between national and local governments is different in Japan. Twenty percent of the Japanese national budget is directed to local governments as grants.

About 10 percent of the Japanese budget goes to the public works, including road construction, irrigation, and sewer facilities. This, however, does not mean that only a small share of the Japanese budget goes to public works; more is done in this area with the FILP (see below).

Spending on public works in the general-account budget of Japan can be further classified in terms of objectives (table 6.5). Public works related to agriculture, infrastructure, and irrigation have predominated for a long time. This does not reflect the actual needs of Japanese society. Many economists and policy makers would agree that improvements to sewers, highways, and airports have been needed for a decade and will continue to be needed in the coming decade. Why doesn't the general-account budget respond to the needs of Japanese society? Sakakibara (1990) attributes this to the political clout of the Ministry of Agriculture, Forestry, and Fisheries.

Fiscal Policy as a Tool for Macroeconomic Stabilization

Traditional Keynesian macroeconomic policy recommends an increase in the share of government expenditures in the GNP during a recession and a decrease during a boom. This kind of "leaning against the wind," if implemented correctly, will lessen the magnitude of economic fluctuations. To some extent, a constant growth of expenditures and a progressive income tax will serve as an "automatic stabilizer." An interesting question is whether such a stabilization policy have been actively (or "discretionarily") pursued in Japan and in the United States.

One way to test the "leaning against the wind" hypothesis is to compare the economic growth rate and the ratio of fiscal expenditures (general accounts) against the GNP. A low economic growth rate accompanied (or immediately followed by) a high fiscal/GNP ratio is an indication of Keynesian policy. The expenditure/GNP ratio is plotted against the GNP growth rate in figures 6.1 (for Japan) and 6.2 (for the US). The expenditure/GNP ratio has a long-run trend and some fluctuations around it. The fluctuations are small because most items in the budget are committed for nondiscretionary components. Even so, a careful examination reveals that in both countries a sharp decrease in the growth rate of the GNP is accompanied or immediately followed by a rise in government expenditures as a share of GNP. For Japan this tendency is clearly evident in 1974 and 1980. This examination, however, is insufficient, for several reasons. First, effects of the automatic stabilizer and effects of the discretionary policy may not be differentiable. Second, the fiscal budget is planned many months ahead of actual revenues and expenditures. Although the budget can be revised within the fiscal year, there is a limit to how much revision can be made. Hence, the government's intentions may appear in the statistics to lag the actual developments of the economy by up to a year. Third, there are several ways to stimulate the economy other than by inflating general (on-budget) accounts. In Japan, public works done through the FILP are said to be used more as a discretionary fiscal policy tool than those in the general budget. There is a way to correct for the first and second problems: The discretionary policy can be measured if one can infer how the fiscal authority reacts to deviations between the plan and the actual performance of the economy during the fiscal year. If the economy is weaker than anticipated, a Keynesian government will increase deficits to keep expenditures high to stimulate the economy.

For Japan, the "cabinet budget plan" for fiscal year T can be regarded as the government's intention with information as of January of year T. The difference between the plan (January, year T) and actual expenditures (March, year $T + 1$) reflects the concurrent revisions of the government's intentions and its views on economic conditions during the budget period. When the government uses a Keynesian discretionary policy for stabilization of income, we should detect a change in this year's budget from last year's budget in reaction to the "forecast" errors in the growth rate—that is, the deviation of actual outcome from the government's forecast. This can be checked by regressing the budget increase on the errors in government forecast about economic growth, with the hypothesis indicating a negative coefficient. Asako, Ito, and Sakamoto (1991) indeed found such a result. They tested other specifications with the same spirit, and found evidence that is consistent with a notion that the Japanese government has engaged in Keynesian discretionary policy.

The FILP

Most of the 18,000 post offices in Japan have a counter for deposits and withdrawals. They offer a wide range of deposit instruments: demand deposits, time deposits, and saving certificates with interest compounding for up to 10 years. They also offer annuity and insurance policies. The household sector hold roughly a fifth of its financial wealth in post-office deposits and insurance policies.

Most of the funds deposited in post offices are transferred by the Ministry of Post and Communications to a special account in the Ministry of Finance. (Some of the fund is now managed in the securities market directly by the Ministry of Post and Communications.) Through this special account, the fund is distributed as capital funds and loans to government agencies and invested into projects managed in other special accounts. The government's decisions on the collection and distribution of these funds constitute the Fiscal Investments and Loans Program (FILP), which is planned in parallel with the general-account budget and which is just as important.

The FILP has grown to more than half the size of the general-account budget. The FILP obtains most of its funds from postal saving and government annuity and pension plans. Additional funds come from the general budget through the industrial investment special account. In the late 1970s, from 50 to 60 percent of the FILP funding came from postal savings. Recently the weight of returned funds from previous loans has become large; it reached 50 percent in

Table 6.6
Budget shares (percentages) of FILP, by objectives.

	1955	1965	1975	1985	1990
Housing	13.8	13.9	21.4	25.4	30.3
Infrastructure for home environment	7.7	12.4	16.7	15.7	15.3
Social welfare	2.1	3.6	3.4	2.8	3.1
Education	4.5	3.1	2.9	3.6	2.0
Medium and small businesses	8.1	12.6	15.6	18.0	15.7
Agriculture, forests, fishing	8.9	7.2	4.1	4.3	3.1
Natural disasters (prevention and restoration)	7.7	3.1	1.2	2.3	1.2
Roads and highways	3.7	7.9	8.0	8.8	9.8
Transportation and communication	12.2	13.9	12.7	8.4	8.3
Regional development	8.5	7.0	3.3	2.4	2.5
Industries and technology	15.8	7.8	3.0	2.9	2.9
International trade and cooperation	7.0	7.5	7.7	5.4	5.8

1988. However, it is fair to say that the FILP is funded mostly by current and previous postal savings.

In 1988, the FILP distributed funds to, among others, nine special accounts, eleven government-funded corporations, 36 government agencies, and nine partially government-owned corporations. During the 1950s and the early 1960s, the funds went to the industrial infrastructure and to industrial development projects through the Development Bank of Japan, the Electricity Development Corporation, and the National Railway. In 1965, the National Railway, the Export-Import Bank of Japan, the Development Bank of Japan, the Medium and Small-size Business Corporations, and the Housing Corporation were the top five recipients of FILP funds. In 1988, the top five were the Housing Finance Corporation, the Postal Saving Special Account, the Pension and Welfare Corporation, the Highway Corporation, and the Public Finance Corporation. This indicates a change in political priorities. Typically, these special accounts and government corporations receive loans from the FILP and then give out subsidized loans to various projects, to private businesses, and to households, with interest subsidies coming from the general account (that is, taxes). For example, the Housing Finance Corporation gives out low-interest-rate loans to qualified households, with a cap on the amount and with conditions on the type of a home which can be financed. Clearly the priority has shifted from the industrial infrastructure to housing and other home-related objectives.

The role of the FILP has been a topic of intensive study. Some think the FILP is a public financial intermediary; others think it represents a disguised government debt. Many researchers point out that in the 1950s and 1960s the Development Bank played a key role in identifying and helping to finance rising industries. This was done mostly by means of the FILP, and not by means of the general account.

In the coming years, the debate over the role of postal saving and the FILP will intensify as the traditional role of the FILP becomes less important. Some argue that postal saving should be separated from the usual business of the post office and privatized, but they are still in the minority.

THE RISE AND FALL OF THE GOVERNMENT DEFICIT, 1975–1989

The unfortunate experience of monetizing debts before and during the Second World War must have had an important influence on the Finance Act of 1947, according to which the Japanese government could issue bonds only if the funds were to be used for public construction, capital contribution (for international organizations and government agencies), or loans.[7] Government bonds issued on the basis of Article 4 of this law are called "construction bonds" [Kensetsu Kōsai]. These bonds, which could have been legally issued earlier, were not issued until 1965, when Japan was in the midst of a particularly severe economic slowdown. Once construction bonds had been issued, they were issued regularly thereafter.

In the supplementary budget of FY 1975, government bonds that were not based on the Finance Act were first issued. These are called "deficit-financing bonds" [Tokurei Kōsai, or Akaji Kōsai]; they will be referred to below as "deficit bonds." These bonds are issued as an "exception" to the rule. Although it is not clear how construction bonds and deficit bonds are distinguishable from the economist's point of view, it is convenient to differentiate them in judging the fiscal stance of the Japanese government. Thus, we will follow the legal tradition and exclusively examine "deficit bonds." We will also limit our discussion to the national government's general budget.

Since deficit bonds were issued as a temporary, exceptional measure, the Japanese government aimed at bringing the government budget back into balance as soon as possible. In January 1976, the government plan set FY 1980 as a target date for the elimination of government deficits (as defined by the deficit bonds). However, by 1979 it was clear that it would not be possible to balance the budget by 1980. In fact, the deficit/GNP ratio has climbed rapidly from 1975 to 1979. A new plan put forth January 1979 stated that deficits would be eliminated by FY 1984. In 1983, although the deficit/GNP ratio had started to decline, the debt/GNP ratio was still increasing. The target date was again pushed back. In August 1983 the government announced that deficits would be eliminated by FY 1990; this revised goal was achieved.

The rise and fall of the government deficit relative to the general budget completed a fifteen-year cycle in 1990, as figure 6.3 shows. Although there was an outstanding stock of government debt at the

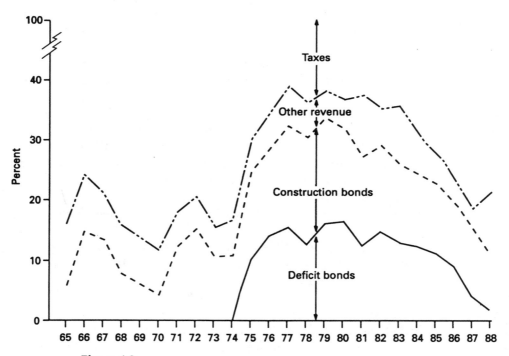

Figure 6.3
Revenue components, Japan.

end of this cycle, the year 1990 marks the end of an epoch in the postwar fiscal policy of Japan.

Table 6.7 compares the Japanese and US budgets in terms of expenditures and bonds relative to GNP. In Japan, the ratio of deficits (measured by issues of construction and deficit bonds) to GNP peaked in 1979 at 6.0 percent; in the United States, the deficit ratio peaked at 6.3 percent in 1983. Before 1982 the deficit/GNP ratio was constantly higher in Japan than in the United States.

How did Japan manage to run up deficits in the second half of the 1970s and then reduce their burden in the 1980s without a major disaster? According to Asako et al. (1991), three things caused the large increase in deficits from 1975 to 1980. First, the government probably did not realize that the potential growth rate of the economy had decreased dramatically after the first oil crisis. Thus, the government tried in vain to stimulate the seemingly depressed economy—which was, in hindsight, close to full capacity—by deficit financing. The government did not realize this until 1977 or 1978. Second, social security benefits were increased dramatically (probably too much) in 1973, and they were indexed. Hence, as severe stagflation took hold in 1974–75, benefits soared while revenue was suppressed. (See Noguchi 1987 for details of this argument.) Third, the Ministry of Finance may have been overoptimistic about the prospect of a value-added tax (or some form of sales tax) being instituted toward the end of the 1970s.

After 1978, the government tried to contain the mounting deficits. However, it had to allow more deficits to combat the recessionary effect of the second oil crisis (1979–80). Hence, the real effort came in the first half of the 1980s. An across-the-board freeze on increases of spending was imposed. Hence, as real growth and inflationary "bracket creep" increased revenues, the deficit ratio dropped. The rate schedule of the income tax was not revised for several years, and that of the inheritance tax was not revised for more than thirteen years. This austerity plan finally worked, and the issuing of deficit bonds ceased with the budget plan of 1990.

RICARDIAN NEUTRALITY

In the analysis of fiscal and tax policy, one important research topic is the macroeconomic impact of government deficits. There are several ways to pose the same question: When a given amount of

Table 6.7
Deficit and budget relative to GNP.

FY[a]	General account, Japan				Federal budget, United States[b]			
	Expenditures[c]	Deficit[c]	Expenditures[f] / GNP[d]	Deficit / GNP[d]	Outlays[e]	Deficit[e]	Outlays[f] / GNP[d]	Deficit / GNP[d]
1970	81.9	3.4	10.9%	0.5%	195.6	2.8	19.8%	0.3%
1971	95.6	11.9	11.5	1.4	210.2	23.0	19.9	2.2
1972	119.3	19.5	12.4	2.0	230.7	23.4	20.0	2.0
1973	147.8	17.7	12.7	1.5	245.7	14.9	19.2	1.2
1974	191.0	21.6	13.8	1.6	269.4	6.1	19.0	0.4
1975	208.6	52.8	13.7	3.5	332.3	53.2	21.8	3.5
1976	244.7	72.0	14.3	4.2	371.8	73.7	21.9	4.3
1977	294.9	95.6	15.3	5.0	409.2	14.7	21.2	2.8
1978	341.0	106.7	16.3	5.1	458.7	53.6	21.1	2.5
1979	387.9	134.7	17.2	6.0	503.5	59.2	20.6	2.4
1980	434.1	141.7	17.7	5.8	590.9	73.8	22.1	2.8
1981	469.2	129.0	18.1	5.0	678.2	78.9	22.7	2.6
1982	472.5	140.4	17.3	5.0	745.7	127.9	23.8	4.1
1983	506.4	134.9	17.8	5.2	808.3	207.8	24.3	6.3
1984	514.8	127.8	17.0	4.2	851.8	185.3	23.1	5.0
1985	530.0	123.1	16.5	3.8	946.3	212.3	23.9	5.4
1986	536.4	112.5	16.0	3.4	990.3	221.2	23.7	5.3

1987	577.3	94.2	16.4	2.7	1,003.8	149.7	22.7	3.4
1988	614.7	71.5	16.5	1.9	1,064.0	155.1	22.2	3.2
1989	663.1	71.1	16.7	1.8	1,142.6	152.0	22.2	3.0
1990	662.4	55.9	15.9	1.3	1,197.2	−123.8	21.8	2.3

a. Fiscal years of the US and of Japan do not coincide. Fiscal year periods for 1970 and 1975, 1976 in the US were different from the following years in this table. The "transition quarter" for the US is not shown. (See box inset on "fiscal year.")
b. US federal budget includes on-budget and off-budget.
c. 100 billion yen.
d. GNP on fiscal-year basis.
e. $ billion.
f. Expenditures and outlays are on "actual" basis for 1975–1988. Numbers for 1990 are "estimates" for US and "plan" for Japan.

Sources: (US) Economic Report to President, 1990; (Japan) Zaisei Tokei [Fiscal Statistics], 1990.

> **Social Security Reform**
> According to Noguchi (1987, pp. 205–208), the social security reform of 1973 made the system too generous. Free medical care for the aged and subsidies for expensive medical treatments were introduced, and the rate of the government's contribution to health insurance for the self-employed was raised from 50 percent to 70 percent. Benefits of public pension programs were enhanced. The ratio of the old-age benefits was raised from 20 percent of the average salary to 43 percent. Noguchi contends that these reforms took place without sound fiscal calculation. The reform was responsible for increasing expenditures in the second half of 1970s, since most benefits were indexed to inflation. Noguchi also argues that the Ministry of Welfare grossly miscalculated the rate of return for social security contributions, so that when the demographic structure becomes more normal in the twenty-first century the social security account will experience large deficits (to be subsidized by the general account—that is, taxes), unless benefits to the retiring generations are cut and/or the contributions of the future working generations increase dramatically.

government expenditure has to be financed, does it make a difference whether it is financed by taxes or by bonds? Does the private sector regard government bonds as net wealth? Do government bonds crowd out private investment? These questions are particularly relevant in view of the rise and fall of government deficits in Japan and the increasing federal deficits in the United States.

In the traditional Keynesian macroeconomic model, a substitution of government bonds for taxes would increase the disposable income of households, so that both aggregate consumption and income would rise (that is, shift the IS curve to the right). This, however, would raise the real interest rate and crowd out private investment.

In another school of thought, government bonds are regarded by rational consumers as future obligations in the form of increased taxes. Thus, bond-financed expenditures (as opposed to tax-financed expenditures) will fail to stimulate an economy if the current tax burden and the future tax burden (implied by the bonds which substitute for the current tax burden) are regarded as equivalent in consumers' intertemporal budget constraints. This equivalence, known as *Ricardian equivalence*, can be proved under several assumptions (discussed below). In summary: In the presence of deficits, consumers see through the veil of deficits and realize the necessity of a future increase in taxes, so they increase their saving by the amount of the current tax reduction; that is, they keep their level of consumption unchanged. It is central to Ricardian equivalence that the current tax burden and the future tax burden are completely substitutable in the budget constraint. However, if the generation that bears current taxes in tax-financed expenditures and the one that will pay future taxes are different, the proposition may fail. Barro (1974) showed that even if two generations are involved, they can be connected through altruistic bequests to make the equivalence hold.

There is a vast literature identifying which assumptions are central to Ricardian equivalence and whether they are plausible. The major criticisms of the equivalence proposition can be summarized as follows:

• If some of the currently living generations suffer from liquidity constraints (saving is zero and consumers' borrowing from future income is prohibited), then a substitution of taxes by debts will stimulate consumption, because a better (utility-increasing) consumption pattern for those liquidity-constrained generations is achieved by increasing the current disposable income.

• If bequests are zero, then increasing taxes may not be contractionary, since altruistic saving for bequests cannot be decreased further.

• Suppose that bequests are planned as deferred payments in return for care provided by children and others rather than motivated by pure altruism, that is to enhance children's welfare. Then the existence of bequests does not restore the equivalence proposition. (See Bernheim, Schleifer, and Summers 1985.)

• If taxes are distortionary (that is, if there are different marginal rates for different kinds of income or consumption), the equivalence proposition will not hold. For example, if the current tax reduction is concentrated on marginal capital income, saving will be encouraged and consumption discouraged.[8]

In summary: It is widely believed that it is unlikely that the real world satisfies all the assumptions required for the equivalence proposition, but that the proposition establishes a good benchmark from which the reasons for and the magnitude of deviations can be discussed.

Implications of Ricardian equivalence are very much relevant to the real world. For example, if equivalence holds, the dollar appreciation in the first half of the 1980s cannot be attributed to US federal deficits. The popular belief is that federal deficits raised the real interest rate, which in turn attracted foreign (especially Japanese) capital flows and appreciated the dollar. The link from federal deficits to the real interest rate would not hold under Ricardian equivalence.

Methodology and Evidence

First of all, let us make casual observations on the relationship between deficits and private saving. From the empirical point of view, the experience in Japan from 1965 to 1990 and in the United States in the 1980s provides an interesting laboratory for the equivalence proposition.

Japan's deficits rose from almost zero in the mid 1960s to 5.5 percent of GNP in 1980, then gradually declined to less than 2 percent in 1989. As the deficits increased from the mid 1970s to 1980, there was no distinct movement (above and beyond the trend) in private saving. This casts some doubts on the equivalence proposition.

In the United States, the deficit/GNP ratio increased from about 2.6 percent in 1981 to 6.3 percent in 1983. Although the ratio declined toward the end of the 1980s, it was still above 3 percent in 1988. During the first half of the 1980s, as government deficits rose and stayed at high percentages, private saving went down and the real interest rate reached a high level. If equivalence is to hold, private saving should increase as consumers see the necessity of future taxes. This suggests that Ricardian equivalence was probably not holding in this case.

When deficits rise with a tax reduction, consumption is unchanged under Ricardian equivalence; in the Keynesian framework, consumption increases. A popular approach to distinguishing these implications is to estimate an aggregate consumption function (consumption as a function of income) with a deficit term included.[9] (Of course, the researcher must control for other factors, such as private wealth, the interest rate, and the level of government spending.) If a positive coefficient on deficits is obtained (not obtained, respectively), Ricardian equivalence is judged to be rejected (accepted). Many studies, using the US data, have investigated the relationship between deficits and consumption and that between deficits and real interest rates. Measurement problems prevent us from drawing definitive conclusions from these studies. Often, contradictory results have been obtained. Feldstein (1982) found evidence that contradicts the Ricardian equivalence proposition; Kormendi (1983) found evidence favorable to the proposition. In summary, according to Bernheim (1987, p. 291), "[a] succession of studies have established the existence of a robust short-run relationship between deficits and aggregate consumption. While there are many potential explanations for this pattern, it is at least consistent with the traditional Keynesian view."

A strategy used by Homma et al. (1987) is to estimate a consumption function with a tax variable and a government-expenditure variable. Suppose that consumption is a function of permanent income, which is defined as current wealth plus future income minus future tax liabilities. Future tax payments are inferred from past tax collections and government expenditures. If consumption is influenced by government expenditures but not by taxes, it is judged to be consistent with the equivalence proposition. From 1965 to 1975 Japan's deficits were almost zero, so that it is difficult to use deficits directly as an explanatory variable. Homma et al. estimated such a consumption function in quarterly data from 1965 to 1983 and obtained results that are consistent with the equivalence proposition. However, they also tried other empirical methodologies using annual data and obtained results not consistent with the equivalence proposition. Hence, the final conclusion of their study is much more cautious about the validity of Ricardian equivalence in the case of Japan.

SUMMARY

The corporate income tax is heavier in Japan than in the United States. Inheritance taxes have a higher share in the national government's tax revenues in Japan than the estate tax has in the United States, while customs duties have a higher share in the United States. On the spending side, the defense budget is only about 7 percent of the general account in Japan; the United States spends more than a quarter of its federal budget on defense. A large share of

Japan's general-account budget is used for grants to local government. The general budget of Japan is supplemented by a capital-investment account called the Fiscal Investments and Loans Program, which receives funds from postal savings and annuity accounts and which makes loans to various public investment projects. In 1983 the government deficit/GNP ratio was higher in Japan than in the United States. Japan has just gone through a cycle of the rise and fall of government-deficit bonds. The deficit/GNP ratio soared in the latter half of the 1970s because of a Keynesian-type policy that misjudged the growth potential of the Japanese economy; it was contained only by means of a freeze on spending (growth) and an increase in taxes produced by bracket creep.

APPENDIX: GUIDE TO DATA

A convenient source in English for statistics on national taxes in Japan is *An Outline of Japanese Taxes*, published every year by the Tax Bureau of the Ministry of Finance.

Major components of government expenditures and FILP are reported in any economic statistics annual, such as the Bank of Japan's *Economic Statistics Annual*.

More detailed statistics related to public finance are available only in Japanese. The sources include Ministry of Finance, Tax Bureau (ed.), *Zaisei Tokei* [Tax Bureau Statistics Annual] and Ministry of Finance, Internal Revenue Agency [Kokuzei Cho], *Kokuzei Cho Tokei Nenpo* [Internal Revenue Annual Statistics]. Various issues of *Zaisei Kinyu Tokei Geppo* [Fiscal Monetary Statistics Monthly] carry detailed analysis and statistics on Tax Revenues, Expenditures, and FILP (usually one topic in each issue, with a twelve-month cycle.)

NOTES

1. Major European countries have introduced value-added taxes (VATs) at the national level. West Germany and France did this on January 1, 1968, and Britain on January 1, 1973. Thus, the share of "indirect tax" reaches 40–60 percent in these countries. Japan's shift from a "commodity" tax on selected items to a kind of valued-added tax (called the *consumption tax*) indicates that the Japanese tax structure is in a sense moving away from the US system and toward the European system.

2. In the United States, the marginal rate drops to 28 percent for taxable income above $177,720 for a joint return. This peculiar rate schedule was put into effect so that the *average* rate would be 28 percent for any amount of income. In 1991 the schedule was revised so that the marginal rate will be 31 percent, with a phaseout of deductions for higher-income earners. The highest marginal tax rate was 75 percent as recently as 1983 in Japan. In the US it was 70 percent on "unearned" income as late as 1980.

3. For an international comparison see page 60 of Ishi 1989.

4. Exact estimates are difficult, because part of the income-tax reduction in the package could have been regarded as a technical correction for bracket creep due to a real income increase.

5. In effect, the greater of half of the decedent's property, regardless of size, and 80 million yen ($533,333) may be bequeathed to a spouse tax-free. In the case of gifts, a gift of (own) residential housing valued up to 20 million yen ($133,333) may be transferred to a spouse of 20 years or more. Beyond this amount—theoretically, even between spouses—gifts are taxable. In theory, transfer taxes should apply to a family's wealth once per generation. A transfer of wealth from a grandparent to a grandchild would be taxed twice in a normal succession of bequest. Hence, there is a penalty for skipping generations in transfers in both countries. In Japan, if an asset is bequeathed to a grandchild there is a surcharge of 20 percent over the normal tax liability. No such penalty exists in the gift taxation. In the United States, a flat rate of tax equal to the highest rate of the estate tax (55 percent) after a $1 million exemption per taxpayer would be imposed on a generation-skipping bequest or gift. In both countries, if the grandchild's parent has predeceased the grandparent the generation-skipping tax does not apply.

6. Since adopted children were counted as statutory heirs, Japanese millionaires sometimes adopted children with the understanding that the adopted children would not inherit property. Eventually the law was changed to limit the number of adopted children to two (when there are no biological children).

7. Short-term government securities [seifu tanki shōken] with 60-day maturities have always existed in order to fill the seasonal gap. They are designed not to be carried over the fiscal-year deadline (March 31). In this chapter these short-term securities are not considered, because of their temporary nature.

8. Advocates of equivalence can rebut each of these points for different specifications of the economic model; however, we are not directly interested in these questions here. For a survey, see Bernheim 1987.

9. Another approach is to use an Euler equation derived from intertemporal utility maximizations. See Bernheim 1987.

BIBLIOGRAPHY

Asako, K., T. Ito, and K. Sakamoto. 1991. "The rise and fall of the deficit in Japan." *Journal of the Japanese and International Economies* 5, no. 4 (forthcoming).

Barro, R. 1974. "Are government bonds net wealth?" *Journal of Political Economy* 81: 1095–1117.

Barthold, T., and T. Ito. 1991. "Bequest taxes and accumulation of household wealth: US-Japan comparison." In *Political Economy of Tax Reforms*, ed. T. Ito and A. O. Krueger. University of Chicago Press.

Bernheim, B. D. 1987. "Ricardian equivalence: An evaluation of theory and evidence." In *NBER Macreconomics Annual 1987*, ed. S. Fischer. MIT Press.

Bernheim, B. D., A. Schleifer, and L. Summers. 1985. "The strategic bequest motive." *Journal of Political Economy* 93: 1045–1076.

Feldstein, M. 1982. "Government deficits and aggregate demand." *Journal of Monetary Economics* 9: 1–20.

Homma, M., ed. 1990. *Zemināru Gendai Zaisei Nyūmon* [Seminar: Introduction to Modern Fiscal Policy]. Nihon Keizai Shinbunsha.

Homma, M., and M. Atoda, eds. 1989. *Zaisei Kaikaku no Jissho Bunseki* [Empirical Analysis of Tax Reform]. Toyo Keizai Shinpo.

Homma, M., Y. Mutoh, T. Ihori, A. Abe, M. Kandori, and M. Atoda. 1987. "Kōsai no Churitsusei Meidai: Riron to sono Jisshōbunseki [The equivalence proposition of debts: Theory and Evidence]." *Keizai Bunseki* [Economic Analysis], Economic Planning Agency, February.

Ishi, H. 1989. *The Japanese Tax System*. Clarendon.

Kormendi, R. C. 1983. "Government debt, government spending, and private sector behavior." *American Economic Review* 73: 994–1010.

Noguchi, Y. 1987. "Public finance." In *The Political Economy of Japan, vol. 1: The Domestic Transformation*, ed. K. Yamamura and Y. Yasuba. Stanford University Press.

Sakakibara, E. 1990. *Shihon Shuqi wo Koeta Nihon* [Japan Beyond Capitalism]. Toyo Keizai Shinpo.

Chapter 7

INDUSTRIAL STRUCTURE AND POLICY

INDUSTRIAL STRUCTURE

The Japanese industrial structure has been a topic of endless discussions in the American popular and financial press. An obvious reason for its fascination is that the peculiar industrial structure is suspected to be the source of Japan's manufacturing prowess.

Three obvious differences exist between the United States and Japan in the manner in which industries are formed and operated:

• Many Japanese firms belong to *enterprise groups* (called *Zaibatsu* before World War II and *Keiretsu* in the postwar era). Group affiliation interlocks stock shares among industrial enterprises, banks, and other financial institutions. This arrangement also involves preferential loans from the financial institutions in a group. The core of an enterprise group is usually a bank. Unlike American banks, Japanese banks are allowed to own equity in other corporations. The shares of group-member firms owned by banks form an important link in the interlocking structure of enterprise groups. In addition to interlocking shares, banks provide group-affiliated firms with loans, and sometimes with board members. Some firms also plan joint ventures within the group. Some critics argue that exclusive trading within a group presents a barrier that keeps non-group-affiliated firms from entering the market.

• In Japan, "large" corporations differ in organization and operations from "small" and "medium-size" corporations. In a large corporation, many workers stay in the same corporation until their retirement, climbing a seniority promotion ladder. Large corporations rarely hire employees in mid-career. Small manufacturing enterprises typically supply parts to large corporations. They hire tempo-

---

The Two Kinds of Keiretsu

Keiretsu, literally translated as "series" or "group," is used in two different contexts.

First, it signifies a financial grouping that effects horizontal integration—a set of firms in different industries—through cross-holding of stocks and lending from a main bank. The largest six groups of this kind are a focus of study in the present chapter. But other banks develop their own Keiretsu groups; in this sense, *Keiretsu group* is interchangeable with *enterprise group.*

Second, *Keiretsu* is used in the sense of a vertical network for product distribution, with manufacturers looking to Keiretsu subcontractors for parts and selling their products to Keiretsu wholesalers and Keiretsu retailers. Large manufacturing companies, such as Toyota, Hitachi, and Matsushita, have a number of Keiretsu parts suppliers and Keiretsu wholesalers and retail stores. These parts suppliers and sales companies are tied to the manufacturer by long-term business relationships, and often by cross-holding of shares. An implication of the Keiretsu distribution system will be discussed in chapter 13.

---

rary and seasonal workers at relatively low wages. Many small firms in the service sector, including retail shops, are operated by families. The division of enterprises into "large" and "small and medium-size" ones, often called the *dual structure,* has been studied intensively for clues to its origin and its implications. The popular American characterizations of Japan's industrial organization and labor markets apply only to large corporations.

• The relationship between business and government in Japan looks very different from that in the United States. The conventional wisdom emphasizes a cooperative relationship between the government and big business: Government and business jointly choose "target" ("sunrise") industries; they then protect these industries with high tariffs and import quotas and nurture them with preferential loans and other resources. After a target industry reaches maturity, government and business begin a drive to increase exports. MITI (the Ministry of International Trade and Industry) also arranges depression cartels for industries experiencing temporary declines in demand, and coordinates the orderly exit of firms from structurally declining ("sunset") industries.

From Zaibatsu to Keiretsu: The Postwar Transformation

The three major policies imposed by the occupation forces were directed as creating a competitive environment for the postwar Japanese economy. The measures included dissolving the Zaibatsu, breaking up large (monopoly) companies, and establishing an anti-monopoly law.

In prewar Japan there were four large Zaibatsu groups (Mitsubishi, Mitsui, Sumitomo, and Yasuda), involved in such key industries as steel, international trading, and banking. These Big Four controlled about one-fourth of the paid-in corporate capital at the end of the war. The occupation force identified them as monopolies that had aided the government in executing the war, and targeted them for extinction. Implemented in November 1945, the Zaibatsu Dissolution was a plan to sell to the public the shares of stock that the holding companies owned (167 million of the 443 million shares of domestic firms in Japan at the time). In addition, the Dissolution purged 2210 officers from 632 Zaibatsu corporations and some 2500 high-ranking officers and large stockholders from other large companies for their wartime activities. (See Nakamura 1981, p. 24, and Patrick and Rosovsky 1975, p. 465.)

In December 1947 the allied powers enacted the Elimination of Excessive Concentration of Economic Power Law, the goal of which was to break up large companies. Originally the allies targeted 325 large companies. In 1948, however, the policy was changed from one of weakening the Japanese economy to one of helping Japan to become a strong ally. Only eighteen companies were broken up (for example, Nippon Steel became Yawata Steel and Fuji Steel; Mitsui Mining became Mitsui Coal Mining and Mitsui Metal Mining; Mitsubishi Heavy Industries became three regional firms; Oji Paper became Tomakomai Paper, Jujo Paper, and Honshu Paper; and Dainippon Beer became Nippon, Kirin, and Asahi).

In order to ensure a competitive market, the Allied force created the Anti-Monopoly Law of April 1947. This law, which mirrored the anti-trust laws of the United States, prohibits holding companies, a monopoly in any market, cartels, and other collusive activities. This law was amended in 1949, 1953, and 1977 in response to new international competition.

It is widely accepted that these policies, along with land reform and political changes, created a competitive environment and made the distribution of wealth more equitable, thus contributing to Japan's rapid postwar growth. Precise econometric evaluation of the Zaibatsu Dissolution and the elimination of excessive concentration would be very difficult, however.

Enterprise Groups: The Current Status

A modern enterprise (Keiretsu) group is a collection of firms in various industries which hold shares in one another, borrow from the financial institutions in the group, and behave strategically as a group. Each group contains a strong bank, which can provide consulting resources as well as money. Banks are allowed to own equities, so a bank can act both as a lender and as a shareholder, although the ratio of equity holdings to lending is small. There is a limit on the portion of the total number of shares issued by one company that a bank may acquire. Prior to 1977, that limit was 10 percent. The Anti-Monopoly Law Reform of 1977 specified that all financial institutions were to reduce their share holdings to below 5 percent by December 1987.

There are six large enterprise groups: Mitsui, Mitsubishi, Sumitomo, Fuyo, Sanwa, and Ikkan. The first three are former Zaibatsu and are known for strong and close relationships among the member firms. Several companies from former Zaibatsu groups (Yasuda, Asano, Nissan, and Nesu) joined with several new companies to establish the Fuyo group after the war, with the Fuji Bank serving as a strong leader. The Sanwa and Ikkan groups were also formed around strong banks after the war. The Fuyo, Sanwa, and Ikkan groups are sometimes called the "bank-led groups," as opposed to the three close-knit ex-Zaibatsu groups.

Participation in a group's "Presidents' Club" defines the "core" membership of the group. For example, the Mitsubishi group's "Friday Club," started in the mid 1950s, had 29 companies as core members in 1987. The Sumitomo group was the first to recast itself in a new form of enterprise group after the breakup of the Zaibatsu in 1946. Its presidents' club started meeting in April 1951. Mitsui's presidents' club was not started until 1961, although another form of gathering, the "Monday Club," goes back to February 1950. The importance of a presidents' club as a strategic decision-making unit depends on the character of the group.

Table 7.1
Economic sizes of six enterprise groups.

	Number of member firms		Average inter-locking shares (%)	Average intra-group loans (%)	Total employees (w/B&I)	Total assets[b] (w/B&I)	Sales[b] (w/o B&I)
	Total	w/o B&I[a]					
FY 1984							
Mitsui	24	20	17.71	19.68	245,205	46,717	27,824
Mitsubishi	28	24	24.91	23.35	241,533	60,997	28,616
Sumitomo	21	17	24.87	27.15	154,964	54,472	19,587
Fuyo	29	25	15.72	17.21	336,954	59,388	28,315
Sanwa	42	35	16.56	19.57	400,191	63,106	29,334
Ikkan	47	42	13.67	12.01	496,403	66,336	45,860
FY 1987							
Mitsui	24	20	17.10	21.94	238,447	59,525	27,405
Mitsubishi	29	25	27.80	20.17	241,846	85,524	24,088
Sumitomo	20	16	24.22	24.53	153,202	79,197	20,011
Fuyo	29	25	15.61	18.20	322,798	77,929	26,861
Sanwa	44	41	16.47	18.51	377,622	88,148	31,080
Ikkan	47	42	12.49	11.18	466,250	86,345	48,653

a. "w/B&I" ("w/o B&I"): with (without) banks and insurance companies. It is important to consider lending from these financial institutions to other companies in the group.
b. Billion yen.

The strength of ties and loyalties among firms in a group is often measured by the ratio of shares owned by other group firms to total shares issued (the *interlocking shares ratio*) and by the ratio of loans received from banks and insurance companies within the group to total loans received (the *intragroup loan ratio*). Table 7.1 gives these ratios along with the total number of employees, the total assets, and the sales of each group.

The three ex-Zaibatsu groups, known for their close relationships, have high ratios of mutual share holdings and intragroup loans. The Mitsubishi and Sumitomo groups in particular are known for their group orientation. Mitsubishi has the highest ratio of interlocking shares—about a quarter of the total shares of an average Mitsubishi firm are owned by other Mitsubishi firms. The Sumitomo group has the highest intragroup loan ratio and is a close second in the interlocking-shares ranking. The Mitsui group is the weakest in its group orientation among the three ex-Zaibatsu groups. The small value of the Mitsui Bank's deposits may explain the relatively weak interlocking in the Mitsui group. In April 1990, however, the Mitsui Bank merged with the Taiyo-Kobe Bank, aiming to create a stronger, bigger bank. The merged bank became the largest bank in the world, surpassing the Daiichi-Kangyo Bank in total deposits. This may change the role of the bank in the Mitsui group, but it will be at least several years before the Mitsui-Taiyo-Kobe-Bank will be able to put its newly acquired power to use.

The fraction of each company owned by another company in the Mitsubishi group is shown in matrix form in table 7.2. For example, the table shows that in 1987 Tokyo Marine and Fire owned 4.53 percent of the Mitsubishi Bank, and the Mitsubishi Bank owned 4.90 percent of Tokyo Marine and Fire. Financial companies, such as city banks, trust banks, and insurance companies, are big owners of other corporations in the respective groups. (By law, a city bank may not hold more than 5 percent of a company's stock shares.)

Table 7.3 shows how much Mitsubishi-group companies borrow from their group's financial institutions. Many of the manufacturing firms in this group did anywhere from a quarter to a half of their total borrowing from the group's financial institutions. From this table it is easy to conclude that share interlocking and intragroup loans are highly correlated. These ratios serve as a proxy for a firm's degree of group orientation.

The three bank-led groups are less group-oriented. The interlocking-share and intragroup-loan ratios for these groups are considerably lower than those of the Mitsubishi and Sumitomo groups. In addition, some companies maintain double or even triple memberships. Hitachi belongs to all three bank-led groups—Fuyo, Sanwa, and Ikkan. Three companies—Kobe Steel, Nihon Tsu-un (Transportation), and Nissho-Iwai (Trading)—belonged to both the Sanwa and Ikkan groups in 1984. (See Patrick and Rosovsky 1975, p. 498.)

Each group represents a cross-section of the Japanese economy, as tables 7.4 and 7.5 illustrate. In principle, each group tries to maintain one and only one company in any type of business. (This is known as the "one set principle.") The group wants to span all business fields (presumably to enjoy economies of scope as an enterprise

Table 7.2
Share interlocking ratios (percentage of ownee's total shares) in Mitsubishi group.

1984

Ownee[a]	Owner[a] 1	2	3	4	5	6	7	8	Group total[b]
1	—	0	6.13	4.69	2.19	1.51	3.46	1.08	24.69
2	3.09	—	6.11	2.03	3.55	1.79	3.04	1.93	30.28
3	(Mutual company, stocks not publicly offered)								
4	5.00	2.39	4.71	—	2.33	0.39	1.90	0.96	21.98
5	5.56	4.20	5.58	6.48	—	1.61	3.83	0.93	33.84
6	3.17	2.10	5.00	1.50	1.22	—	1.93	0.65	16.23
7	4.77	2.72	3.90	2.73	2.15	1.17	—	0.91	20.43
8	4.61	4.03	4.63	4.05	0.95	0.84	1.38	—	24.52
Average	4.04	2.67	5.35	3.16	1.87	0.74	1.88	0.86	24.91

1987

Ownee	Owner 1	2	3	4	5	6	7	8	Group total[b]
1	—	1.93	5.92	4.53	1.80	1.50	3.16	1.08	24.69
2	3.12	—	5.43	1.97	3.14	1.75	3.02	1.87	28.98
3	(Mutual company, stocks not publicly offered)								
4	4.90	3.99	4.55	—	2.36	0.41	1.89	0.94	23.31
5	4.77	4.81	5.47	5.95	—	1.45	3.19	0.85	31.75
6	3.18	5.57	4.05	1.21	0.98	—	1.56	0.52	17.65
7	3.94	6.17	3.25	2.27	1.73	0.97	—	0.76	20.76
8	4.21	7.09	4.22	3.53	0.67	0.66	1.20	—	25.06
Average	3.74	5.02	4.99	2.90	1.96	0.68	2.76	0.85	27.80

a. Key to numbering of firms: (1) Mitsubishi Bank, (2) Mitsubishi Trust, (3) Meiji Life, (4) Tokyo M&F, (5) Mitsubishi Trade, (6) Mitsubishi Electric, (7) Mitsubishi Heavy Industries, (8) Mitsubishi Real Estate.
b. Includes other companies in the group.
Source: Toyo Keizai, *Kigyo Keiretsu Soran*, 1986 and 1989.

Table 7.3
Intra-group loans in Mitsubishi group, 1987.

	Share interlocking ratio (total)	Loan ratio from		
		M. Bank	M. Trust	Total[a]
M. Trading House	31.75	6.46	4.40	13.13
Kirin Beer	18.77	35.79	2.80	41.56
M. Rayon	25.52	19.78	8.34	30.56
M. Paper	33.65	21.54	12.12	39.66
M. Kasei	22.75	14.61	8.40	26.54
M. Gas & Chemical	26.55	16.08	12.95	30.66
M. Yuka	34.36	17.80	9.50	29.83
M. Jushi	59.93	19.53	16.94	38.61
M. Oil	45.63	23.65	6.12	30.38
Asahi Glass	28.60	5.52	0.18	7.12
M. Mining & Cement	35.02	19.13	19.14	47.20
M. Seiko (Steel)	35.92	16.66	13.63	43.48
M. Metal	21.37	15.91	9.63	28.46
M. Densen Kogyo	52.10	15.30	16.05	32.63
M. Kakoki	35.77	14.63	13.55	33.34
M. Electric	17.65	18.66	13.03	36.67
M. Heavy Industry	20.76	12.92	6.73	21.18
Nikon	27.73	21.22	11.00	38.79
M. Real Estate	25.06	18.21	16.25	44.06
Nihon Yusen	25.70	6.79	2.78	11.81
M. Storage	41.08	22.56	10.24	36.25
Group average	27.80	10.69	6.63	20.17

a. Includes loans from M. Bank, M. Trust Bank, Meiji Life, Tokyo Marine and Fire, and Nihon Trust Bank. The Nihon Trust Bank is not a member of the Mitsubishi President's club.
Source: Toyo Keizai, *Kigyo Keiretsu Soran*, 1989, p. 30–31.

Table 7.4

	Mitsui	Mitsubishi	Sumitomo
Banking	Mi. Bank	Mb. Bank	S. Bank
Trust banking	Mi. Trust	Mb. Trust	S. Trust
Life Insurance	Mi. Life	Meiji Life	S. Life
Marine & Fire	Taisho Marine & Fire	Tokyo Marine & Fire	S. Marine & Fire
Trading	Mi. Bussan	Mb. Shoji	S. Shoji
Mining	Mi. Kozan		S. Ringyo
Forestry	Hokkaido Mining Ship.		S. Coal Mining
Construction	Mi. Construction	Mb. Construction	S. Construction
	Sanki Kogyo		
Food & Drink	Nihon Mills	Kirin Beer	
Textiles	Tohre	Mb. Rayon	
Paper	Ohji paper	Mitsubishi Paper	
Chemicals	Mi. Toatsu	Mb. Kasei	S. Chemical
	Mi. Petrochemical	Mb. Gas chemical	S. Bakelite
		Mb. Yuka; Mb. Jushi	
		Mb. Monsanto	
Oil		Mb. Oil	
Glass, cement	Onoda cement	Asahi Glass	Nihon Ita Glass
		Mb. Kogyo C.	S. Cement
Steel	Nihon Seikojo	Mb. Seiko	S. Kinzoku
Nonferrous	Mi. Kinzoku	Mb. Kinzoku	S. Kinzoku Kozan
metals		Mb. Aluminum	S. Kei Kinzoku
		Mb. Densen Kogyo	S. Denki Kogyo
Machinery		Mb. Kakoki	S. Jukikai Kogyo
Electronics	Toshiba	Mb. Elect.	Nihon Elec Corp.
Vehicles	Mi. Shipbuil	Mb. Heavy Industry	
	Toyota	Mb. Automobile	
Optics		Nikon	
Real estate	Mi. Real Est.	Mb. Jisho	S. Real Est.
Transport. &	Osaka Shosen	Nihon Yusen	S. Storage
communic.	Mi. Storage	Mb. Storage	
Dept. stores	Mitsukoshi		

Table 7.5

	Fuyo	Sanwa	Ikkan
Banking	Fuji Bank	Sanwa Bank	Daiichi Kangyo Bank
Trust banking	Yasuda Trust	Toyo Trust	
Life Insurance	Yasuda Life	Nihon Life	Asahi Life; Fukoku Life
Marine & Fire	Yasuda Marine & Fire		Nissan M&F; Taisei M&F
Trading	Marubeni	Nichimen	C. Itoh
		Nissho Iwai	Kanematsu Gosho
Construction	Taisei Const.	Ohbayashi; Toyo Constr.	Shimizu Constr.
		Sekisui House; Zenitakakumi	
Food & Drink	Nissin Mills	Itoh Ham; Suntory	
	Sapporo Beer		
	Nichi Rei		
Textiles	Nisshinbo; Toho Rayon	Yunichika; Teijin	Asahi Kasei Kogyo
Paper	Sanyo Kokusaku pulp		Honshu Seishi
Chemicals	Showa Denko	Tokuyama Soda; Sekisui chem	Denki Kagaku Kogyo
	Kureha Kagaku	Ube Kosan; Kansai Paint	Kyowa hakkou; Lion
	Nihon Yushi	Hitachi Kasei	Nihon Zeon; Sankyo
		Tanabe Pharm. Fujisawa Pharm.	Asahi Denka; Shiseido
Oil	Toa Nenryo	Cosmo oil	Showa-shell
Rubber	Nihon Cement	Toyo Rubber	Yokohama Rubber
Glass, cement	Nihon Cement	Osaka cement	Chichibu cement

Category			
Steel	NKK	Kobe Seiko; Nissin Seiko	Kawasaki Steel
		Nakayama Seikosho	Kobe Seiko
		Hitachi Kinzoku	Nihon Heavy Ind.
		Hitachi Densen	
Nonferreous metals			Nihon Kei Kinzoku
			Furukawa Mining; Furukawa Ele
Machinery	Kubota Tekko	NTN Toyo Bearing	Niigata Tekkousho
	Nihon Seiko		Iseki Noki; Kashihara
Electronics	Hitachi	Hitachi	Hitachi
	Oki Electric	Iwashaki Tsushinki	Fuji Electronics
	Yokokawa Denki	Sharp	Fujitsu;
		Kyosera	Yasukawa Electronics
		Nitto Denki Kogyo	Nihon Columbia
Vehicles	Nissan	Daihatsu	Isuzu
		Hitachi Ship Bldg	Ishikawajima harima
		Shin Meiwa Kogyo	Kawasaki Heavy Ind.
Optics	Canon	HOYA	Asahi Kagaku
Transport. & Communic.	Tobu Railway	Hankyu Rail	Kawasaki Kisen
	Keihin Kyuko	Nihon Tsu-un	Nihon Tsu-un
	Showa Ship.	Yamashita shinnihon Ship.	Shibusawa Soko
Dept. Stores		Takashimaya	Seibu Dept. store
Finance & Leasing		Orient Lease	Nihon Kangyo Kakumaru Scrties
			Orient Finance
Entertainment			Korakuen Stadium

Table 7.6
Weights of the Big Six in the Japanese economy (percentages).

	Employ-ees	Assets	Capital	Sales	Profit	
					Gross	Net
1975	5.11	15.76	14.74	14.94	8.29	18.55
1980	4.91	15.34	15.09	15.59	12.08	12.84
1985	4.51	14.24	14.29	16.01	14.22	17.16
1987	4.14	12.96	15.00	14.35	11.70	11.88

Note: Companies which belong to more than one group are netted out, so that they are not double-counted.

Source: Toyo Keizai, *Kigyo Keiretsu Soran*, various issues.

group), and it tries not to have two companies in the same type of business (in order to avoid competition between two companies in the same group). There are several exceptions to this principle, however. Some groups lack businesses in some key fields, and there are sometimes many companies in a group involved in the same type of business. Moreover, when a technological advance creates a new field, such as the petrochemical industry in the 1960s, two companies in the same group may develop similar products and cause a major conflict that threatens the unity of the group. For example, Mitsui Petrochemical and Mitsui Chemical fought for market shares in the petrochemical market.

Table 7.6 shows how much weight the Big Six have in the Japanese economy. Combined, the Big Six account for about 5 percent of the labor force and about 16 percent of sales and profits. Thus, a typical worker in the Big Six is roughly three times as productive as a non-Big Six worker. Companies of the Big Six hold about a quarter of the outstanding shares of the 1820 firms listed on the Tokyo and Osaka stock exchanges (table 7.7). Moreover, 38.1 percent of the money lent to these companies come from the financial institutions of the Big Six. In addition, of the 8431 board members who come from outside the respective firms among the listed corporations, as many as 45 percent are sent by Big Six group corporations (mostly by their financial institutions). Therefore, the six corporate groups combined have a significant weight among the big businesses.

Table 7.7
Influence of the Big Six on listed companies (percentages).

	Mitsui	Mitsu-bishi	Sumi-tomo	Fuyo	Sanwa	Ikkan	Total[d]
Stock owership[a]	3.27	5.03	4.11	3.70	5.50	3.41	24.2
Loan share[b]	5.96	7.17	6.75	6.03	7.30	4.44	37.7
Board of directors' share[c]	6.69	7.08	6.58	9.38	8.97	12.44	45.5

a. Stock shares owned by group companies/Total issues.
b. Outstanding loans lent by group financial companies/Total outstanding loans.
c. Number of directors sent from group companies/Total "outside" board members.
d. This is not the sum of the six groups, because holdings of companies that belong to more than one group are netted out.
Source: Toyo Keizai, *Keiretsu Kigyo Soran*, 1989.

Nonbank (Independent) Groups

The other enterprise (Keiretsu) groups are much smaller in scale than the Big Six. Some of them are "vertical" groupings rather than horizontal (across-industry) groupings—that is, a large manufacturer forms a group with its supplies and distributors, and maintains a long-term relationship. For example, Sony is independent of the Big Six enterprise groups. The Sony group has 87 subsidiaries [*Kogaisha*] and affiliated companies [*Kanren gaisha*]. This group of subsidiaries and affiliated companies is mostly vertical, and Sony owns a large portion of the shares of these affiliates. Shin Nippon Steel has 150 subsidiaries and affiliated companies.

A large corporation that associates with an enterprise group may also be the core of its own independent group. For example, Sumitomo Shoji, a general trading company in the Sumitomo group, has its own independent group of subsidiaries and affiliates. Nisho-iwai, another general trading company and a member of both the Sanwa and Ikkan groups, also has its own independent group. Toyota, a Mitsui group member, is the core of an independent group of parts suppliers and subcontractors which are Toyota subsidiaries and affiliates.

Each of the Big Six has a bank and a trading company as its core and a presidents' club that plays an important role. There is significant bank borrowing among group-member companies, and many board members of group firms are former bank employees. An independent group is under less influence from a bank; for example,

Toyota has little debt with any bank and manages a large portfolio of liquid assets by itself.

The Role of the General Trading Companies

A general trading company [*Sogo Shosha*] is a uniquely Japanese kind of company that specializes in exporting and importing. The top nine general trading companies handle 47 percent of Japan's exports, 65 percent of imports, and 18 percent of domestic wholesale sales. The top nine combined had total sales of 84 trillion yen ($420 billion) in 1983. Half of their sales are exports and imports, but the share of third-country trades increased from 5 percent of total sales in 1970 to 16 percent in 1983 owing to a rise in direct exporting and importing by large Japanese corporations.

General trading companies trade a wide range of commodities—everything from instant ramen (cup noodles) to missiles, as a well-known expression has it. When they serve as intermediaries for foreign trade, they often provide the credits and short-term loans associated with the export-import business.

General trading companies have worldwide networks of branches and stations through which they gather information relevant to the export-import trade. Each of the ex-Zaibatsu enterprise groups includes a large general trading company: Mitsui Bussan, Mitsubishi Shoji, and Sumitomo Shoji. In the Zaibatsu days the general trading company played the central role in the group, and this legacy remains.

A Comparison of the Zaibatsu and the Postwar Enterprise Group

The postwar enterprise group is similar to the Zaibatsu in that a group consists of firms of different industries. Each group is made up of a set of companies in different major industries. A typical mix includes commercial banking, trust banking, insurance, mining, petrochemicals, steel, trading, heavy industry, optical, electric, gas, and chemicals.

Unlike a prewar Zaibatsu, a postwar enterprise group has no holding company that dictates the actions of each member of the group. The companies in postwar enterprise groups are independent decision-making units which cooperate with other firms in their group. Sometimes competing interests do emerge within a group and cause conflicts.

A Historical Reflection on Interlocking Shares

One might wonder why Japanese firms interlock their shares. The reasons for this practice have been changing over the years, according to Itoh, Misumi, and Ichimura (1990), whose opinions will be summarized here.

At the time of the dissolution of the Zaibatsu, banks were allowed to hold shares of other companies. As a result, enterprise groups with banks at their cores emerged to replace the Zaibatsu. More prevalent cross-shareholding among non-ex-Zaibatsu companies as well as among ex-Zaibatsu companies did not start until the 1960s, however. When joining the Organization for Economic Cooperation and Development, Japan was asked to open its capital markets to the rest of the world. Driven by a fear of capital inflows, many Japanese companies tried to defend against takeovers. One such move was an amendment to Article 280 of the Commerce Law. The new provision allowed the board of a company to increase its capital by assigning new shares to other firms. Essentially, two companies issue additional shares and assign them directly to each other—that is, they dilute the present stock of shares without obtaining formal approval from the current stockholders. Since more shares exist, and they are in the hands of group-member firms who are "friendly" and "stable" and won't sell them to "outsiders," this action makes it much more difficult for foreign companies to acquire enough shares to gain control over the Japanese firms that do this. The ex-Zaibatsu companies significantly increased their cross-holding ratios from the mid 1960s to the 1970s, as table 7.8 shows. In this sense, the original reason for major cross-holding of shares was to defend against forced takeovers from abroad.

Table 7.8
Cross-holding ratios, 1962–1974.

	Mitsubishi	Mitsui	Sumitomo	Fuyo	Daiichi K.	Sanwa
1962.9	17.30	8.80	20.13	10.49	10.14	7.58
1966.9	16.81	10.52	18.43	11.17	10.85	9.07
1970.9	20.71	14.14	21.83	15.26	17.19	11.18
1974.9	26.57	17.37	24.71	19.10	16.90	13.01

Source: Itoh, Misumi, and Ichimura 1990.

By the time the Japanese capital market became open to foreign companies, there was no threat of takeover activity from foreign companies. In the meantime, Japanese companies became more financially secure. Many observers believe that even if there had been no cross-holding there would not have existed much of a threat of foreign takeovers by the mid 1970s. Cross-holding continued to be the norm through the 1970s and the 1980s, however. One reason for this inertia is that cross-holding acts as a potential disciplining device in a cooperative long-term relationship, either between a parts maker and a big auto company or between a bank and a manufacturer. The holding of shares facilitates close monitoring, and in the event of financial distress the big auto company (or the bank) may send executives to the parts supplier (or the manufacturer).

Recently another round of increases in cross-holding has become evident. More active capital markets in Japan have prompted more merger and acquisition (M&A) activity. T. Boone Pickens obtained his holdings of shares in Koito (a parts supplier in the Toyota Keiretsu) and caused a conflict over his unsuccessful request for representation on Koito's board. Shuwa, a real estate company, bought a large block of shares in Inageya and Chujitsuya, large retail store chains. It seems that the original motivation for cross-holding—to defend against hostile M&A activity—seems to have reappeared in the Japanese capital market.

Economic Consequences of Interlocking Shares

Because interlocking shares are rarely transacted, takeovers are more difficult to execute in Japan than in the United States. Affiliated firms hold a large percentage of any firm's equity and keep it off the market. A group would not allow one of its members to be snapped up and taken away from the group. Hence, it would be nearly impossible to make a successful takeover bid for one of the Keiretsu group's firms. This aspect enables managers in Japan to concentrate on long-term investment strategies rather than on tactics to prevent takeover bids.

With large blocks of stock permanently kept off the market, stock prices may behave differently in Japan. Those firms which hold blocks of shares for interlocking purposes are supposed to prevent not only takeovers but also "excessive" fluctuations in stock prices. By holding a large block of shares, a stable price level (that is, a level that varies between some upper bound and some lower bound) can be maintained, just as a central bank with large foreign reserves can peg the exchange rate. Many argue that since speculators know that market pressures will be absorbed without changing stock prices, fewer speculative attacks will take place. The validity of this claim, however, rests on how well the price level is chosen.

Another consequence of interlocking shareholding is that equity assets of large firms (which hold equities of other companies) may be undervalued. Stocks are usually valued on the balance sheet at their purchase values rather than their market values. Since much of the stock held by group companies was acquired a long time ago, the stock values on the asset side are likely to be undervalued. Shares acquired at the time a stock was first issued may still be valued at their face value, which is 50 yen/share for virtually all stocks. Since information on which stocks are held at which value may not be easily available to outsiders, calculating the net worth of a company may be tricky.

Disentangling a firm's market value from the effects of cross-holding may also be difficult. Suppose that firm A holds half of firm B's outstanding shares, while firm B holds half of firm A's outstanding shares. (Recall table 7.2.) Then the cross-holding situation is equivalent to the situation in which each firm buys back (and retires from the market) half of its own shares. Thus, the stock price per market-available share should rise. Therefore, it is difficult to calculate a virtual stock price free from the effects of cross-holding.

Such complex group relationships would not exist without good economic reasons. We will now explore the advantages that group affiliation can create for the member firms. Note that the Keiretsu studied in this chapter are "financial" Keiretsu (horizontal relationships) rather than "distribution" Keiretsu (vertical relationships). Therefore, the role of stable suppliers and buyers should be de-emphasized here. It is possible, on the other hand, that Mitsubishi Industries would use Mitubishi Shoji for exporting and importing its products; or that Toyota affiliates can count on Toyota as a long-term customer, and Toyota can count on those suppliers. In the insurance field, since automobile-insurance and life-insurance premium rates are regulated, all such firms offer virtually the same product; thus, it requires only a little subtle pressure (or group orientation) to convince corporate and individual customers in group firms to choose to purchase from their group's affiliated insurance companies. The same kind of argument applies to bank deposits, the rates on which are regulated.

One might conjecture that an enterprise group plays the role of a joint profit maximizer—it allocates profits by bilateral (reciprocal) trading contracts and preferential treatment (such as reciprocated lower prices or interest rates for group affiliates). A group might take advantage of "externalities" within it—for example, by sharing technological information, or by coordinating a project requiring the services of a railroad company, a bank, and a construction firm. That is, an enterprise group might "internalize" externalities in the project. An enterprise group might also more easily shift capital and workers from a depressed industry to a booming industry within it. In addition, an interlocked group might provide its members with product diversification and hence with mutual implicit insurance against a downturn in the company. However, the data do not support most of these conjectures. Caves and Uekusa (1976, pp. 72–83) tested whether group affiliation increased profitability and efficiency, allowing for structural differences. Using data from 243 large manufacturing firms over the period 1961–1970, they found that group affiliation, as measured by the "proportion of a firm's equity shares held by its Zaibatsu or principal bank group affiliates," has a negative coefficient in an equation that tries to explain gross profit as a linear combination of total assets. That is, there is no evidence that group membership raises a firm's rate of profit; in fact, it seems to lower it.

Another important finding of Caves and Uekusa is that group firms tend to make significantly higher interest payments than nongroup firms, even though although their financial structures are insignificantly different. From this result, Caves and Uekusa conclude that it is the group banks who enjoy the fruits of maximizing the sum of group firms' profits.

Nakatani (1984) investigated other aspects of the performance of group firms and found that group-affiliated firms, in comparison with nongroup firms, earn lower profits, grow at lower rates, have less variability in performance, pay higher wages, have higher debt/equity ratios, and have lower ratios of dividend payments to capital. These findings are consistent with the hypothesis that their managers are risk-averse and subscribe to an implicit system of mutual insurance in which group firms help one another in times of serious business hardship. Since sensitive information can be available within a close-knit group, moral hazard and adverse selection can be avoided. The implicit mutual insurance is essentially an arrangement to share risks and profits. Help is available in the form of loans and in the form of transfers of management teams and workers. These findings conflict with the view that group-affiliated firms take advantage of externalities within their group to make higher profits.

Hoshi et al. (1991) compared the investment behavior of companies that are affiliated with enterprise groups and those that are not. They found that investment by affiliated companies is not constrained by their cash-flow positions (presumably because of reliable and timely help from the group's main bank), whereas investment by independent companies is subject to cash-flow restrictions. This finding is consistent with a theoretical model of imperfect information in an imperfect capital market. If evaluating investment projects is costly and time-consuming, not all profitable investment proposals considered by an independent firm are funded instantaneously. A group bank serves as a screening agent for the investment projects of the group firms and stands ready to lend funds whenever they are needed.

Another work by Hoshi et al. (1990) is an example of the increasing application of *agency theory* to the Keiretsu relationship. According to this application, the bank in an enterprise group monitors the performance of a company's management. According to the popular view, the bank—since it is both a lender and a stockholder—monitors the management group to see whether it devotes its best efforts to achieving the company's long-term objectives. The bank will tolerate low earnings and poor dividends if they are due to costs associated with a long-term project. This more patient attitude results in more efficient production and higher profits in the long run. In contrast, managers in the United States have to worry about earnings and profits every quarter, striving to satisfy impatient stockholders (including institutional investors) without attracting hostile corporate raiders.

"Dual Structure" and Subcontracting

The term "dual structure" [Niju Kozo] pertains to the existence of two qualitatively different sectors in Japanese industry. In this chapter, it is used in the sense that a group of small firms and a group of large firms have qualitatively different characteristics.[1] In Japan many economic statistics—including commercial sales, earnings, employment, and wages—are often categorized by firm size. In the United States, the size of a firm is not necessarily relevant to its economic performance.

Whether Japan's many small firms are as efficient as the large firms is a matter of controversy. Many small companies are "affiliated" with larger companies and work as subcontractors [shitauke] in a vertical "Keiretsu." For example, Toyota purchases thousands of auto parts from subcontractors, many of which are small firms with fewer than 100 workers. The traditional view is that small companies hire low-skill temporary and seasonal workers, pay them low wages, and offer meager benefits. Thus, the work force is divided into two groups: workers with lifetime employment and high wages at large companies, and workers with temporary employment and low wages at small companies. When an economic downturn comes, the large companies order less from their subcontractors, who then fire some of their temporary workers. According to this view, small subcontractors are a "buffer" for a large company's work force.

Some contend, however, that the quality of workers in small companies is very high. A large company, say Toyota, checks the quality of the parts which are delivered to its auto plant. Toyota engineers then work with small suppliers to improve the quality of their parts. Thus, the long-term relationship between Toyota and its subcontractors is more cooperative than dominant.

INDUSTRIAL POLICY

Industrial policy can be defined as intervention by a government in order to change the market's allocations of resources, most often in favor of manufacturing industries.[2] In Japan, protecting infant industries from foreign competition and using various policy measures to drive exports have been regarded as the essential elements of industrial policy. The Ministry of International Trade and Industry (MITI) plays the major role in executing industrial policies. The term meaning industrial policy, Sangyo Seisaku, was not coined until about 1970, but the Japanese government has implemented policies of the sort that it describes since the end of the Second World

War. For example, right after the war the government targeted the coal and steel industries for special assistance.

From a microeconomic point of view, intervention by the government is justified in a case of "market failure."[3] Some of the factors associated with market failure are scale economies, positive and negative externalities, potential monopolies, "infant industries," needs for basic research and development, and problems with respect to uncertainties such as adverse selection and moral hazards. Examples of theoretically justified policies include construction of infrastructure (which takes advantage of positive externalities), pollution control (which eliminates negative externalities), regulation of the electric-power industry (which tames a natural monopoly), protection of infant industries, and the creation of product standards.

Although market failures can theoretically be corrected by government intervention, it is questionable whether a "correct" policy is implementable in the real world. It is difficult to compare the overall benefits of many policies against their overall costs. For example, it is difficult to measure the benefits that accrue to all the users of a proposed bridge, although it is relatively easy to calculate the cost of building the bridge. It is sometimes difficult to spot an infant industry with a potential for growth. Even if an infant industry is spotted, the government may make a mistake regarding the kind of policies it should then attempt; for example, how many firms should be encouraged to enter an infant industry may be difficult to determine, and any arbitrary choice is likely to be wrong. Maintaining government, implementing regulations, and monitoring the activities of industries cannot be done without cost.

The stated objectives of Japanese industrial policy have been to reduce imports, to foster higher growth in key industries, and to change the industrial structure. Although the government has varied its industrial policies throughout the postwar period, it has consistently undertaken policies in four major categories:

Creating infrastructure for all industries. The government has helped fund the construction of road systems, industrial ports, industrial water supplies, and electric-power plants.

Allocating resources among industries. The government has given subsidies and import protection to certain targeted industries. Infant industries are protected by import restrictions until domestic manufacturers are able to compete with foreign ones. The import restrictions were lifted only after domestic manufacturers became strong and competitive. For example, the restrictions on buses and trucks were lifted in 1961, those on color TVs in 1964, those on passenger automobiles in 1965, those on color film in 1971, those on cash registers in 1973, those on large-memory integrated circuits in 1974, and those on computers in 1975. It would be interesting to know whether the Japanese manufacturers that now dominate the markets for these items could have achieved their dominance without import protection during their infancies.

Industrial restructuring among individual industries. The government has helped individual industries "reorganize" their structure [Sangyo saihensei], cartelize during structural depressions, cartelize for "rationalization" (automation and labor-saving technology), coordinate cuts in operation or capacity, and coordinate plant investment and production. The basic philosophy of Japanese policy in this category is to prevent "excess competition."

Dealing with the problems of small and medium-size firms. Various measures have been taken to protect and help small and medium-size firms, which usually suffer from structural changes described in the preceding item and which are seen as a buffer against the exacerbation of business cycles.

The first two of the above categories concern resource allocations over all industries; the last two concern problems within individual industries.

MITI creates and implements most of the specific policies, but other policies set forth by other ministries can theoretically be included under the heading of Japanese industrial policy. These include agricultural policies administered by the Ministry of Agriculture, Forestry, and Fisheries; regulations on communication industries administered by the Ministry of Post and Communication; regulations on railroads, trucking, and airlines administered by the Ministry of Transportation; and regulations on financial industries administered by the Ministry of Finance. In the following, we will concentrate mainly on the policies adopted by MITI.

There were four stages in the development of the actual industrial policies just described[4]:

• In the late 1940s and the 1950s, the Japanese economy was recovering from the devastation of the war and suffered from shortages of productive capacity and of the foreign reserves needed to import raw materials and consumer goods. There were also general shortages of goods. Since exports and imports were heavily regulated, the economy was isolated from the rest of the world. It was not until 1949 that the uniform exchange rate of $1 = 360 yen was established. The government preferentially allocated raw materials and financial help to key industries. Under the Preferential Production Plan [Keisha Seisan Hoshiki] of 1946–1948, the steel industry received more coal and the coal industry received more steel. Preferential loans, price controls combined with subsidies, and allocations of restricted imported materials supplemented the plan. At this stage, Japanese industrial policy resembled socialist economic planning. Some evaluate this stage as a successful preparation for heavy and chemical industrialization down the road. The government dropped the emphasis on the coal industry in the 1950s, however, and high-priced coal would remain a problem. In the 1950s, "rationalization" [Gōrika] plans became the center of policy.[5] The main tools at this stage were special tax provisions and the use of the Fiscal Investments and Loans Program for the purchase of labor-saving machines and modern plants. In particular, the government adopted accelerated depreciation and tariff exemptions for imported machines in targeted industries. Policies at this point were conducted within the framework of a market economy with tax incentives. The policies can be interpreted as a plan to share the large risk associated with building costly modern machines and plants. The industries targeted for rationalization included steel, coal, shipbuilding, electric power, synthetic fibers, chemical fertilizer, and, in the late 1950s, petrochemicals, machine tools and parts, and electronics. The steel industry benefited from the rationalization plans and became an important export industry. (A large factor in its success was the switch from domestic inputs to imported coal, iron ore, and oil.) The coal industry became unable to survive without subsidies. Some industries, such as automobiles and heavy electric machinery, were protected from foreign competition, but the protection was understood to be temporary. In general, industrial policies succeeded for industries with scale economies, such as steel, and failed for industries without scale economies, such as coal.

• In the 1960s, Japan was gradually integrated into the international economic system. As one of the conditions for membership in international organizations such as the General Agreement on

Tariffs and Trade, the International Monetary Fund, and the Organization for Economic Cooperation and Development,[6] Japan was required to liberalize (i.e., deregulate), or to show a schedule for liberalizing, its import quotas, tariffs, and capital controls. The objective of industrial policy, therefore, shifted to strengthening the industrial structure within the time frame for trade and capital (foreign investment) liberalization. This often meant that MITI organized (or attempted to organize) the mergers of big companies into even bigger ones (as in the Nippon Steel merger), the coordination of fixed capital investment in order to avoid overcapacities, the specialization and coordination of small and medium-size companies, and the establishment of a comprehensive energy policy. Apparently MITI thought that, left alone, many Japanese industries could not survive foreign competition.

• In the 1970s the government greatly transformed its industrial policies, attempting not only to make domestic industries strong enough to withstand international competition but also to pursue objectives other than growth. The government's new objectives included achieving pollution control,[7] or industrial development harmonious with environmental needs, and stricter application of anti-trust policies. Industries with an international competitive edge started to complain about too much government intervention. Anti-monopoly rulings also limited the government's power to conduct intra-industry industrial policies, such as the arrangement of depression cartels. Japanese industrial policy began to move toward the use of the market mechanism and deregulation.

• In the late 1970s and the 1980s, industrial policy brought Japan into conflict with other countries. The rapid expansion of Japanese exports started to stir protests. Japan became haunted by its own success. The first glimmer of a trade conflict had appeared way back in 1971, when the United States and Japan negotiated a textile agreement. In the 1980s, trade conflicts became more frequent and more intense. (Some of the trade conflicts of the 1980s are discussed in chapter 12.) MITI's industrial policy came to include measures to prevent trade conflicts and to control the damage from those that occurred.

How Effective Has Japan's Industrial Policy Been?

Japan's rapid economic growth, supported by high productivity growth in many industries, may be seen as evidence of successful industrial policy. The key industries targeted by MITI—shipbuilding, steel, and computers, to name a few—grew as planned. Cooperative (or coordinated) research between the government and major companies reduced the duplication of investment. Tariff and nontariff import barriers against foreign products, though temporary, ensured a domestic market for producers.

There are those who are critical of Japanese industrial policy, however, and they have three lines of argument. First, many "industries" became successful (that is, grew and began to export) without government help: sewing machines, cameras, bicycles, motorcycles, pianos, and radios during the 1950s and 1960s, and color TVs, tape recorders, magnetic tapes, audio components, watches, pocket calculators, machine tools, textile machines, ceramics, and robotics from the late 1960s to the present. Second, industrial policy was not always implemented as MITI envisioned. Indeed, one failure of MITI's industrial policy turns out to have created a successful industry. MITI tried to "cartelize" the automobile industry in the 1950s and the early 1960s, on the notion that only one or two auto companies were needed for a tiny country like Japan. The automobile industry fought off MITI's pressure, and today we find numerous Japanese automakers not only surviving but prospering throughout the world. Third, actual (attempted) policy cannot always be justified by theory. In other words, the stated reasons for industrial policies are often not consistent with any theoretical justifications. For example, "planned shipbuilding" was implemented right after the war in order to help save foreign reserves. It is not clear that this policy could still be justified at the end of the 1960s. The Oil Industry Law, intended to restrict competition in the industry, was enacted in 1962, when the oil industry did not seem to be suffering from any market failure.

Those who praise Japanese industrial policy usually point to the excellent overall performance of the Japanese economy. They also think that the policy of targeting and nurturing certain industries was successful: Japan's steel and shipbuilding industries became the world's largest after policies to promote them were enacted. Japan's industrial-policy efforts have been "forward-looking"—that is, they have targeted high-growth industries and have taken advantage of scale economies. When protection has been utilized, it was for infant industries, such as semiconductors, which became successful later.

The Case of the Automobile Industry

The automobile industry is frequently cited as an example of a failure of attempted industrial policy. In 1955 MITI developed a plan to set standard specifications for domestic passenger cars, set a price, have a design and performance contest among automakers, and award a license to produce cars to one company. The idea was to exploit economies of scale. Fierce opposition from the automakers stopped the plan.

In 1961 MITI advocated another auto plan, called the Specialization and Grouping Plan, under which automobiles would be classified in three groups: mass production, sport and luxury, and mini cars. Automakers would then limit the number of companies and specifications in each group. This plan, too, was scrapped after protests from the industry. History shows that the plan was ill-conceived, and would have had a terrible effect on the economy. Fortunately it did not materialize, since MITI lacked the legal authority to control the industry.[8]

The Debate in the United States over Industrial Policy

The United States has reacted to Japan's success with fear and envy. Many American businessmen and civic leaders hail Japan's success and envy the cooperation between government and business. It is a good idea, they argue, for government and industry to work in harmony and to cooperate on research, aiding in the painless passing of declining industries and nurturing up-and-coming ones, and it is a good idea for the government to retrain the workers in declining industries to give them currently demanded skills. They think that the United States is misdirecting its resources when it tries to help declining industries (as it has done by bailing out Chrysler and subsidizing Amtrak), and that the government should direct funds to rising industries instead.

Of course, these beliefs are not universal. Many conservatives counter that what MITI does is cartelize economic activity, suppres-

---

The Japanese and American Bureaucratic Systems

In Japan the bureaucratic system is relatively independent of the executive heading the cabinet, so that policy decisions are less politically motivated and more economically oriented. Furthermore, career bureaucrats are expected to stay in the same ministry (with rotations) until their retirement around the age of 55; this ensures continuity and stability in strategic decision making. These two aspects together make Japanese bureaucrats better able to form and implement strategic planning than their American counterparts. Japanese bureaucrats often draft legislation related to industrial policy, as well as implement regulatory details.

There are only three political appointees in the Japanese Finance Ministry: the Minister and the two "parliamentary vice-ministers" [seimu jikan], one of whom traditionally comes from each of the two houses. In contrast, most of the top positions of the US Department of Treasury are occupied by political appointees. In 1986, there were 13 presidential appointees (confirmed by the Senate) and 13 noncareer appointees (approved by the Office of Management and Budget).

A Japanese bureaucrat may well stay in a ministry from his early twenties to his early fifties, joining the private sector only after retirement, whereas in the United States changes of jobs between bureaucracies and the private sector are rather common. The difference between the two systems is illustrated nicely by the colloquialisms used in the two countries: in Japan, retiring bureaucrats moving into the private sector are said to "descend from heaven" [amakudari]; in the United States, individuals moving in either direction are said to be passing through a "revolving door."

---

sing the positive characteristics of free, competitive markets. They argue that government regulation is inherently inefficient. One regulation invites another, and bureaucracies produce copious amounts of red tape. They further argue that declines in certain American industries are due not to Japanese industrial policies but to bad managerial decisions. For example, the US automobile and steel industries allowed wages to climb faster than in other industries and also made unwise investment decisions. Finally, they point out that it is quite difficult to spot sunset and sunrise industries, and that there is no reason to believe that the government is more adept at this than the marketplace.

The industrial-policy debate casts a shadow over US-Japan trade relations. Some American officials regard industrial policies as subsidies to industries that export to the United States, and that such subsidies constitute unfair competition and put Americans out of work. Many of the arguments the Japanese offer in rebuttal fall along one of the following lines of reasoning: (i) All countries have industrial policy in one form or another. The Chrysler bailout is a form of industrial policy; NASA and agricultural price supports are other examples. Therefore, what Japan is doing falls within the bounds of international standards, such as the OECD-approved Positive Adjustment Policy. In this regard, France may be a worse offender than Japan.[9] In fact, the share of government funding in research and development was smaller in Japan than in the United States throughout the 1980s. (ii) Tariffs are, on average, lower in Japan than in any other OECD country. Hence, infant-industry protection is (currently, anyway) not in place. All in all, industrial policy is far from collusion, coercion, and intervention; rather, it is vision and cooperation without commitment. Put differently, industrial policy complements the free market by creating a competitive market process. It is not intended to stifle the free market.

The gap between supporters and critics of industrial policy is still large, and it exists both in academia and in politics. Japanese scholars have been rather critical of industrial policy; however, recent developments in the study of monopolistic competition, scale economies, and economies of scope have induced some scholars to revise their neoclassical views, and the study of infant-industry protection and strategic trade has been revived.

ANTI-MONOPOLY LAW AND DEPRESSION CARTELS

The "democratization policies" of the American occupational force included the breakup of large Japanese companies and the establishment of a strict anti-monopoly law. Later anti-monopoly laws and their interpretations were considerably relaxed, but originally all cartels were prohibited. In the 1953 amendment to the anti-monopoly law (enacted in 1954), cartels for depressed industries and for modernization purposes became formally allowed. In addition, the MITI minister could "advise" the shutdown of a plant or the shortening of its hours of operation. Japanese anti-monopoly law operated with considerable laxity until the 1977 amendment that (for example) limited the bank's shareholding of a company to 5 percent of the company's equity.[10] Even after the 1977 amendment, Japanese anti-monopoly policy was considered less restrictive than its American counterpart. In the Structural Impediments Initiative talks of 1989–1990, the United States demanded that Japan strengthen its anti-monopoly policy.

The legal provisions of Japanese anti-monopoly policy should be differentiated from their actual implementation. First, in Japan cartels may be formed in specified situations under legal provisions that would not exist in US anti-monopoly law. Second, even when the legal provisions are the same, their interpretation and implementations sometimes differ between the United States and Japan. In the rest of this section, the legal provisions that allow cartels in Japan will be explained.

In Japan, if a particular industry is designated as being in a temporary depression,[11] then under Article 24-3 of the Anti-Monopoly Law a cartel may be formed in order to keep the supply low and the price high. After such a cartel is formed, production and investment schedules are coordinated by MITI. In this sense, Japanese industrial policy is based more on direct intervention and control than US policy is. Most depression cartels last less than a year.

A depression cartel is formed so that companies in a depressed industry can share the losses (nearly) equally and a costly bankruptcy or massive layoffs by one company can be avoided. In the case of Japanese coal mining, the cartel offered not only temporary relief but also a means of orderly, gradual exit for all companies in the industry. Japanese industrial policies work for sunset industries as well as for sunrise industries.

Policies that are lenient toward the forming of cartels can be criticized on several grounds (usually by free-market advocates in the United States). For one thing, they tend to protect a chronically inefficient firm in an industry as well as a structually sound but temporarily troubled company. Furthermore, they give any firm an incentive to overinvest during boom periods, because the firm knows that when difficult times come it will be allowed to form a depression cartel (and the production cut will usually be proportional to the production capacity of the firm's factories).

APPENDIX: SOURCES OF DATA

For cross-holding of shares: Toyo Keizai Shinposha, *Interlocking Enterprise Annual* [*Kigyo Keiretsu Soran*], every year; Toyo Keizai

Shinposha, *Enterprise Group in Japan* [*Nihon no Kigyo Group*], every year.

The *Interlocking Enterprise Annual* lists the top 20 shareholders of companies listed on the Tokyo stock exchanges. It also lists the amounts borrowed from major banks (including trust and long-term credit) as well as from city banks. Board members' past affiliations are listed. This book also presents a matrix of interlocking shares among the big six enterprise groups.

Enterprise Group in Japan lists about 1650 parent firms and their affiliates and subsidiaries, totaling 22,000 firms. Firms not listed in the stock exchanges are listed here. Surveys were conducted to find information on stock shares, types of businesses, addresses, sales, number of employees, and so on. Consolidated figures are summarized in the second part.

NOTES

1. The term has additional uses in other contexts. For example, in regard to the prewar labor market it means that city workers commanded high wages while workers in the agricultural sector earned only subsistence wages. In regard to the postwar economy, it means that workers in large companies enjoy higher wages and bonuses, shorter work hours, and more job security than workers in small firms.

2. Recently, a group of prominent Japanese economists have completed and published studies of industrial policy: Komiya, Okuno, and Suzumura (1984) and Itoh, Kiyono, Okuno, and Suzumura (1988). Eads and Yamamura (1987) summarize positive and negative views on industrial policy. I will frequently refer to these works, explicitly and implicitly, in this section. For a political-economy approach, Johnson 1982 is a classic.

3. An equilibrium (demand = supply) of a perfectly competitive market achieves an efficient allocation of resources if there are no scale economies, there are no monopolies, there are no public goods or externalities, there exists perfect and complete information, and there is a complete set of contingent commodities (for example, insurance) with which economic agents can hedge risk. See Itoh et al. 1988 for more along this line.

4. This classification is based on Tsuruta 1982 and on chapters 1–3 of Komiya et al. 1984.

5. In Japan "rationalization" means a cost-cutting effort, with a strong connotation of automation (labor-saving technology) and relocation or layoff of workers. Hence, in the 1960s many labor unions fought for "anti-rationalization."

6. Japan became a member of the OECD in 1964 and an Article 8 member of the IMF in April 1964.

7. Between 1971 and 1973 a series of court cases known as the "big four pollution cases"—all of which were decided against industry—raised Japan's environmental consciousness and shifted Japanese public opinion away from the pursuit of economic growth at any social cost.

8. For further references see Yakushiji 1984, especially pp. 281–283; Tsuruta 1982, pp. 168–174; and Komiya et al. 1984, chapter 11.

9. See pp. 435–448 of Eads and Yamamura 1987 for descriptions of European industrial policy and "lessons for Japan."

10. Other measures include strengthening the power of the Fair Trade Commission to restore competition by, for example, ordering the division of a company in a highly concentrated industry where domestic sales exceed 50 billion yen, where the share of the largest company is over 50 percent or that of the two largest is 75 percent, where new entry is deterred, and where profits have been unusually high for 3–5 years. See pp. 481–486 of Uekusa 1987.

11. For example, the coal mining, aluminum, and shipbuilding industries received cartel designations at times during the 1970s and the 1980s. For details see pp. 490–499 of Uekusa 1987.

BIBLIOGRAPHY

Caves, R., and M. Uekusa. 1976. *Industrial Organization in Japan*. Brookings Institution.

Eads, G. C., and K. Yamamura. 1987. "The future of industrial policy." In *The Political Economy of Japan*, volume 1, ed. K. Yamamura and Y. Yasuba. Stanford University Press.

Hoshi, T., A. Kashyap, and D. Scharfstein. 1990. "Bank monitoring and investment: Evidence from the changing structure of Japanese corporate banking relationships." In *Asymmetric Information, Corporate Finance, and Investment*, ed. R. G. Hubbard. University of Chicago Press.

Hoshi, T., A. Kashyap, and D. Scharfstein. 1991. "Corporate structure, liquidity, and investment: Evidence from Japanese industrial groups." *Quarterly Journal of Economics* 106, February: 33–60.

Itoh, M., K. Kiyono, M. Okuno, and K. Suzumura. 1988. *Economic Analysis of Industrial Policy*. University of Tokyo Press. (In Japanese.)

Itoh, K., T. Misumi, and T. Ichimura. 1990. "Spiral shift of logics of interlocking shareholdings in Japan." Hitotsubashi University *Business Review* 37, no. 3: 15–36. (In Japanese.)

Johnson, C. 1982. *MITI and the Japanese Miracle: The Growth of Industrial Policy, 1925–1975*. Stanford University Press.

Komiya, R., M. Okuno, and K. Suzumura. 1984. *Nihon no Sangyo Seisaku*. University of Tokyo Press. English edition: *The Industrial Policy of Japan* (Academic Press, 1988).

Nakamura, T. 1981. *The Postwar Japanese Economy*. University of Tokyo Press.

Nakatani, I. 1984. "The economic role of financial corporate grouping." In *The Economic Analysis of the Japanese Firm*, ed. M. Aoki. North-Holland.

Patrick, H., and H. Rosovsky. 1975. *Asia's New Giant*. Brookings Institution.

Tsuruta, M. 1982. *Sengo Nihon no Sangyo Seisaku* [Industrial Policies in Postwar Japan]. Nihon Keisai Shinbun.

Uekusa, M. 1987. "Industrial Organization: The 1970s to the Present." In *The Political Economy of Japan*, volume 1, ed. K. Yamamura and Y. Yasuba. Stanford University Press.

Yakushiji, T. 1984. "The government in a spiral dilemma: Dynamic policy interventions vis-à-vis auto firms." In *The Economic Analysis of the Japanese Firm*, ed. M. Aoki. North-Holland.

Chapter 8

THE LABOR MARKET

The Japanese labor market is known for several distinct features, including lifetime employment, seniority wages, and enterprise unions (all said to be unique to Japan). When these features were first pointed out by non-Japanese scholars, they were explained in terms of "cultural" factors. For example, "paternalistic" firms and "loyal" workers were compared to feudal lords and their samurai subordinates. It became clear, however, that such "cultural" explanations do not stand up under close examination. For example, many "unique" features of the Japanese labor market are really postwar phenomena which evolved after much of the traditional Japanese culture had been destroyed or deemphasized.

The economic explanations of these unique features follow two strands. One strand recognizes that unique features do exist and claims that they are rational, optimal responses to institutional arrangements in Japan. For example, lifetime employment, which is an extreme form of an implicit long-term contract, is argued to be a rational institution whose purpose is to enable workers and firms to share risks and profit. Moreover, human-capital investment can be rewarded efficiently only if some kind of long-term contract is arranged. Economists pursuing the other strand argue "against the popular stereotype" (Shimada 1980), typically claiming that the lifetime-employment and seniority-wage systems are nonexistent or much exaggerated.

BASIC STATISTICS

As table 8.1 shows, the male participation rate is slightly higher in Japan than in the United States, while the female participation rate

Table 8.1

	Number employed (1)	Number unemployed (2)	Unemployment rate[a]	Participation Rate[b]
Japan, 1988				
Male	36,020,000	910,000	2.5%	77.1%
Female	24,080,000	640,000	2.6%	48.9%
Total	60,110,000	1,550,000	2.5%	62.6%
US, 1988				
Male	64,820,000	3,655,000	5.3%	76.6%
Female	51,858,000	3,046,000	5.5%	56.6%

a. Calculated as follows: $(2)/[(1) + (2)]$.
b. Calculated as follows: $[(1) + (2)]$/Population, where "Population" consists of persons over age 15 in Japan and persons over 16 in US.
Sources: Toyo Keizai Statistical Annual for Japan; Monthly Labor Review, August 1989.

is much higher in the United States. The latter fact is a reflection of differences in the social acceptance of female workers. The unemployment rate is much lower in Japan than in the United States, owing to institutional aspects (such as lifetime employment) that reduce the rate of voluntary and involuntary job turnover.

Table 8.2 summarizes employment by industry. Japan still has higher primary-sector employment than the United States or Germany. This may be due to Japan's strong protection of its agricultural industry. On the other hand, employment in the service (tertiary) sector commands a larger fraction of the labor force in Japan than in Germany. Table 8.3 shows that Japanese employees work, on average, much longer hours than their American and German counterparts.

CONVENTIONAL WISDOM

Conventional wisdom identifies the following as unique characteristics of the Japanese labor market:

Lifetime employment [*Shushin Koyo*]. It is commonly known that Japanese workers are under "lifetime employment" commitments. That is, firms agree not to lay off or fire workers, and workers pledge an almost unlimited degree of loyalty to their

Table 8.2
Employment in major industrial sectors, 1986 (thousands of workers, percentage of labor force).

	Primary[a]	Secondary[b]	Tertiary[c]	Total
Japan	4,950	19,860	33,720	58,530
	(8.5%)	(33.9%)	(57.6%)	
US	3,163	29,130	77,304	22,813
	(2.9%)	(26.6%)	(70.5%)	
Germany (FRG)	1,344	10,554	13,896	25,794
	(5.2%)	(40.9%)	(53.9%)	

a. Agriculture, forestry, fishing.
b. Manufacturing, construction.
c. Services (wholesale, retail), financial.
Source: Bank of Japan, Comparative Economic and Financial Statistics.

Table 8.3
Other indicators (1986).

	Hours worked per week (average manufacturing production workers)	Number of workers	Days lost in labor disputes
Japan	43.7	75	163,000
US	38.4	119	4,417,000
Germany (FRG)	35.6	155	33,000

firms. Workers neither quit nor refuse any job assignment. Thus, a firm-worker relationship lasts for the occupational lifetime of the worker. This relationship is all implicit and understood, without a written contract. This is a somewhat exaggerated view of the Japanese labor market, although it does apply to the majority of male workers in large firms (that is, roughly 30 percent of all total workers).

Seniority-based wages and promotion [Nenko Joretsu]. Promotions and wage increases in Japanese firms depend on length of service to the company rather than on individual merit. It is very unusual for middle-management job openings in large companies to be filled with persons from other firms.

Enterprise unions (as opposed to trade unions). Japanese unions are typically organized within each firm across different job specifications—in particular, across blue-collar or white-collar workers. It is sometimes argued that enterprise unions are more cooperative with management than are trade unions.

Semi-annual bonuses. Regular employees (including both blue-collar and white-collar workers, from rookies to executives) of almost all Japanese firms receive bonuses twice a year. These bonuses amount to 15–30 percent of annual income.

The annual, synchronized "spring offensive" [Shunto] for contract negotiations. In the United States, many labor contracts extend beyond the current year. Two- and three-year contracts are not uncommon in the manufacturing sector. Negotiations of different companies take place throughout the year; there is no particular "season" in which labor negotiations are bunched together. In Japan, almost all labor negotiations are done in the spring (i.e., March through May), and the contract length is almost always one year.

The dual structure [Niju-Kozo]. There are large discrepancies between large and small companies in terms of wage levels, steepness of wage profiles, and fringe benefits. And, in a sense, only regular employees of large companies enjoy lifetime employment.

Treatment of blue-collar workers. Blue-collar workers are treated more like white-collar workers in Japan. It has been noted that in Japan blue-collar workers are paid "salaries" rather than hourly "wages."[1] The gap in salaries between blue-collar and white-collar workers is small in Japanese firms, and they belong to the same union and eat in the same cafeteria. And Japanese blue-collar workers receive extensive on-the-job training in a variety of skills.

Longer work hours. The average working hours of Japanese employees are longer than those of Americans. In many firms, employees work half the day on Saturday. On weekdays, many Japanese office workers remain at the office late into the evening.

The low and inflexible unemployment rate. The Japanese unemployment rate was between 1 and 2 percent during the 1960s and the 1970s; it increased to between 2 and 3 percent in the 1980s. In the United States, the unemployment rate typically fluctuated between

5 and 10 percent over business cycles in the 1970s and 1980s. The Japanese unemployment rate is much less sensitive to macroeconomic fluctuations than its US counterpart.

Severance payments. In Japan, nearly every worker receives a severance payment [taishoku kin], amounting to two or three years' pay, upon retirement (typically between the ages of 55 and 60). Workers who switch jobs before retirement receive severance payments which have been capitalized up to that point. On the other hand, corporate pensions are still rare in Japan. There is a special deduction in individual income tax for one-time severance payments. In the United States, large severance payments are usually limited to top executives. Average workers usually participate in corporate pension plans and receive annuities, rather than one-time payments, after retiring.

Table 8.4 summarizes this conventional wisdom on the differences between the Japanese and US labor markets. We will examine

Table 8.4
Conventional wisdom.

Japan	United States
Lifetime employment	Frequent job changes
Seniority wages	One job, one wage
Job rotation and multi-functional workers	Promotion in line and single-function workers
On-the-job and in-house training; firm-specific human capital	Human capital transferable across firms
Bonus system widespread	Bonuses only for executives
Enterprise unions	Labor unions across firms
Annual, synchronized contracts [Shunto]	Multi-year staggered contracts
Stable employment (low unemployment rate)	Frequent layoffs (high and volatile unemployment rate)
Flexible compensation	Inflexible compensation
Large severance payments at retirement for all. Corporate pensions rare.	No severance payments other than for top exectives. Corporate pensions common.

Source: Adapted from "Editors' Introduction" to a conference issue of the *Journal of the Japanese and International Economics*, vol. 3, no. 4, December 1989.

the conventional wisdom, and the critiques of it, in the rest of this chapter.

LIFETIME EMPLOYMENT AND SENIORITY WAGES

Lifetime employment and the seniority system are the two features most often cited in the literature as unique aspects of the Japanese labor market. It is important to recognize that these two features are closely connected and should be considered together.

There is now a consensus among researchers that lifetime employment and the seniority wage system are *not* legacies of feudal Japan. Many managerial employees of large companies have enjoyed significant job security since the Meiji era. It was not until the end of World War II that many manual workers obtained implicit promises of job security. Seniority wages were probably created around the time of World War I to prevent skilled workers from quitting their jobs too often in booming industries.[2]

Rotation, Mobility, and Promotion

Since the average job stay of a worker is long, a company can safely train workers at its own expense. Both blue-collar and white-collar workers in typical Japanese firms are trained more extensively than those in typical US firms, and they rotate through different jobs requiring various skills early in their careers.

It is sometimes said that in Japan a generalist is valued more than a specialist. Since the value of an employee is measured by how many different sections of the company he has trained in and how well he understands the connection between these positions, his worth is "company-specific."[3] When the need for a specific skill arises (as happened when the market for financial futures and options trading was created), chosen employees are sent, with all expenses paid, to business schools and companies in the United States to learn the necessary skills and to receive on-the-job training. A Japanese firm rarely, unless pressed by urgent needs, hires ready-made specialists into regular positions in the middle of the promotion ladder.

In-house training at different kinds of jobs, in-house seminars on specialized topics, and all-expenses-paid study at American business schools constitute a broad investment in human capital, made while the worker continues to work for the same Japanese company. In the United States, if a similar human-capital investment is made, the worker may (and often does) decide to change jobs. Employee "loyalty"—the worker's implicit commitment not to quit—is what makes Japanese firms willing to pay for training costs. In order to have workers who possess many different skills, a Japanese company has them invest in various skills early in their careers at the company's expense. These human-capital investments pay off later in the workers' careers.

A steep age-earning profile, seniority-based promotions and wages, and the large lump-sum retirement payments serve as incentives for workers to work hard and to stay with one firm—they expect rewards later.

There exists a fast track of promotion in every company, and the assignment of able workers to posts in this track is intended to keep them loyal and motivated. Comparable monetary compensation usually does not come until later in one's career, however. Even promotions are "deferred." These deferred payments and promotions definitely serve to keep workers in the company. The low mobility of workers under the lifetime-employment system, however, could pose serious problems when large reallocations of workers are necessary—for example, when an industry declines, as in the case of shipbuilding.

The firm would not be able to maintain its lifetime-employment policy without having discretionary power to reassign workers to any job division, or to an affiliated company. Indeed, voiding layoffs during recessions is possible only with flexible job assignment, made possible by broad human investment in the early stages of workers' careers, and by the existence of enterprise unions.

For example, when sales of automobiles declined in the mid 1980s, Nissan sent its workers from idle production lines to dealers, in order to help promote sales. And when the Japanese steel industry began to decline in the mid 1980s, Japan Steel [Shin Nihon Seitetsu], the nation's biggest steel mill, began diversifying by creating biotechnology divisions.

A Japanese firm goes a long way to protect jobs for its workers. When earnings and profits decline sharply, a firm may adjust its bonuses, which amount to about a quarter of the annual compensation of the average worker. Bonus adjustments are another device to help firms weather temporary shocks without having to lay off workers.

In summary, lifetime employment, flexible job assignment, and the nenko wage system should be regarded as a package. With long-term commitments from workers, firms can safely invest in training their workers. Training includes rotating them through different kinds of jobs. Employees do not quit when they become highly trained and valuable. To enforce this long-term commitment, firms use deferred payments and a steep age-earning profile. The worker receives job security. In return, the worker agrees to accept deferred payments (that is, to stick with the firm) and to accept the possibility of assignment to any kind of job. Even if the firm suffers a little, it must hold up its end of the deal: It will not lay off workers. Instead, the firm may shift workers from a redundant division to a growing division, or from a subsidiary (or an affiliated firm) in a sagging sector to one in a booming sector.

The Revisionist View

The revisionist view, developed by Koike (1977, 1981, 1983, 1984) and Shimada (1980, 1981), is that lifetime employment, nenko wages, and enterprise unions are not in fact unique to Japan. Koike, in his various writings, emphasizes that the "uniqueness" is an illusion and that the only difference in the Japanese labor system is that blue-collar workers acquire some universal white-collar traits, such as an upward-sloping age-earning profile and longer service to the same company.

Koike argues, for example, that the upward wage profile is common to white-collar workers in Japan and in European Community countries if one compares wage data using similar statistical sources. What is different about Japan is that the age-earning profile of Japanese blue-collar workers also looks similar to the profile of white-collar workers. Koike calls this the "white-collarization of blue-collar workers." Moreover, the blue-collar wage profile reflects acquired skills, he argues. Koike's observation that blue-collar workers are trained to have different job skills seems to be important.

As for lifetime employment, Koike admits that there are more workers with short job tenure (1–2 years in the same company) in the EC countries and in the United States. This, by the way, is consistent with the higher frequency of job turnover and unemployment among American workers in their teens and twenties. Hence, everybody seems to agree that Japanese workers somehow spend less time on job-searching and job-switching before finding a long-term match. On the other hand, Koike argues that there are also many long-tenure workers in the EC countries and the United States. In fact, the ratio of workers who have served 15 years or longer in a single firm is higher in the United States than in Japan. Moreover, the importance of seniority in layoff decisions in the United States strongly favors workers with longer service. (Layoffs commonly fall on those with the shortest length of service.) Nevertheless, layoffs are not very common in Japan anyway, and the arrangements of the US seniority system say nothing about the presence or absence of lifetime employment in Japan.

Shimada (1980) also argues that extreme stereotypes of the Japanese labor market are false, but he would not deny that the Japanese labor market has certain characteristics that do seem unique. He argues that lifetime employment is a mirage, because (i) there is a mandatory retirement age, (ii) employment does fluctuate, and (iii) employees do separate from their firms. He also argues that "it is not correct to say that such nenko wages are unrelated to productivity." Shimada seems to take the position that length of service, age, and education enhance productivity—that is, he applies human-capital theory to the Japanese system.

Both Koike and Shimada correctly point out that the extreme version of the lifetime-employment system is a mirage, because there is an implicit or explicit mandatory retirement age (traditionally 55) even for employees of large firms and government officials. Although the retirement age is increasing, the most privileged workers as well as regular workers in large firms still have to leave at some age between 55 and 60 (Shimada 1980, p. 8). Many large firms and the government, however, arrange jobs for their employees after "retirement." Affiliates and subsidiaries hire many of these "retired" workers. There are no solid data on this, but casual observation suggests that many high-ranking government officials take jobs with government agencies and private corporations (after one year if the private enterprise is under the jurisdiction of the government post that the person held before retirement), as an "old boy" network matches demand and supply. Large corporations are also known to make conscious efforts to help their workers find a "second life" after age 55, but it would be very difficult to quantify these commitments.

Retirement at an age between 55 and 60 in Japan serves to counterbalance seniority wages and lifetime employment somewhat. By discharging most of these workers from the original firm, it is easy to reshuffle them and place them in suitable positions, given that everybody is supposed to resign. Mandatory "retirement" seems to be another tool for screening workers for different executive jobs. In order to satisfy the implicit contract between worker and firm mentioned above, it does not matter whether workers are allowed to stay in the parent firm or are sent to its subsidiaries and affiliates.

Economic Analysis

In response to the revisionist critique, let us consider how lifetime employment and the nenko wage system can be confirmed or rejected by econometric analysis. (The analysis in this section is heavily dependent on Hashimoto and Raisian 1985.) If workers stay in the same companies longer in Japan and do not change firms until they retire, then we expect the average length of service to the same company to be longer among Japanese workers than among American workers. This should be true for all age groups. Therefore, the test of lifetime employment can be reduced to a test of length of service to the same company.

It would be more difficult to confirm the nenko wage system. A first thought would be to plot average wages against length-of-service (tenure) brackets. If the slope of the plot is steeper for Japan, then it is supporting evidence for the hypothesis that wages depend on length of service. This method would not be conclusive evidence in favor of the nenko wage, however, because other factors, such as education and experience (including that in other companies), must be controlled for. These methods of testing for the existence of lifetime employment and the nenko wage system are well known. Detailed labor-market data are available for Japan and the United States (and sometimes for the EC), but only for selected years.

Another way of confirming these phenomena would be to go directly to representative and comparable firms in Japan and in the United States and ask for personal histories of top and middle managers, and for the salary structure of each company. If lifetime employment and nenko wage promotion are more prevalent in Japan,

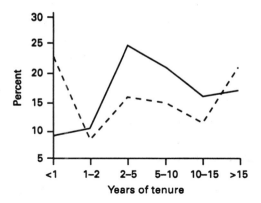

Figure 8.1
Years of tenure, 1960s. Solid line: Japan, 1962. Broken line: United States, 1966.

one should find that top executives there have spent all of their corporate lives in the same company. Casual observations support this view. Of course, some US firms, such as 3M (Minnesota Mining and Manufacturing), are known to encourage continued service among workers and to create reward systems for longer service. It would therefore be difficult to quantify the average length of service from micro company data.

Hashimoto and Raisian (1985) have presented the most conclusive evidence on the issue of lifetime employment and seniority-based wages to date. Figures 8.1 and 8.2, adopted from their paper, show the percentages of male workers with various lengths of tenure in the 1960s and in the late 1970s, respectively. Figure 8.1 (originally presented by Koike) compares the proportion of male workers with various years of service to the same employer for Japan in 1962 and the US in 1966. Contrary to the apparent lifetime-employment characteristics, it was the US in 1966 that had the greater percentage of workers in the 15-years-or-more category. Koike and others have used this to challenge the conventional wisdom concerning lifetime employment in Japan. Figure 8.2 shows that in the late 1970s it was indeed Japan that had the higher proportion of workers in the longer-tenure categories. In fact, the figure shows clearly that Japanese workers hold longer tenure on average. Hashimoto and Raisian attribute the findings evident in figure 8.2 to the fact that not many workers had reached the maximum length of

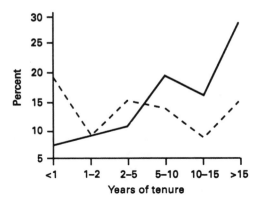

Figure 8.2
Years of tenure, late 1970s. Solid line: Japan, 1979. Broken line: United States, 1978.

service by 1962 (when Koike's study was conducted), because of the disruption caused by the war. In fact, in 1979, average workers were found to stay longer with the same employer in Japan than in the United States.

The next test is to examine the length of tenure in each specific age bracket. The length of tenure should be longer for every age group if lifetime employment does exist. Table 8.5 clearly shows that in each age bracket Japan has a higher proportion of workers with job tenures of 10–20 years and 20+ years. This is strong evidence for lifetime employment in Japan.

Similar tables were constructed for Japan in 1962 and 1977 and for the United States in 1963 and 1978. From these tables, the probability of a worker's staying in his current firm for the next 15 years in the two countries can be calculated. The results are shown in table 8.6. Compare the data on the typical male worker at age 25–34 with job tenure of 5 years or more in 1962. The probability that he was in the same firm after 15 years (i.e., in 1977) was 73.0 percent in Japan and 47.3 percent in the US. Table 8.7 shows how many jobs a typical worker in each age bracket has held in his working life. American workers change jobs roughly twice as often as their Japanese counterparts.

Of course, most job changes occur when workers are young and are looking for a good job before settling down. By age 25, 40 percent of workers' total lifetime job changes have occurred in both coun-

Table 8.5
Job tenure of male workers in Japan (1977) and the United States (1978).

Age	30–34			35–39			40–49			50–54		
Tenure	0–9	10–20	20+	0–9	10–20	20+	0–9	10–20	20+	0–9	10–20	20+
Japan	40.0	59.7	0.3	25.2	65.4	9.4	18.6	50.5	30.9	16.4	46.1	37.5
US	76.4	23.5	0.1	62.9	35.6	1.5	48.3	36.1	15.6	34.1	36.3	29.6

Source: Hashimoto and Raisian 1985.

Table 8.6
Probabilities of retention from 1962 to 1977.

Age in 1962 Experience (years)	teens[a] 0–5	20–24		25–34		35–39	
		0–5	5+	0–5	5+	0–5	5+
Japan	36.4	45.1	65.3	42.7	73.0	37.7	75.9
US	5.6	13.0	30.0	22.2	47.3	24.4	54.5

a. Includes ages 15–19 in Japan and 14–19 in US.
Source: Hashimoto and Raisian 1985.

Table 8.7
Numbers of (cumulative) new jobs held by males of various ages.

Age	16–19	20–24	25–29	30–34	35–39	40–54	55–64	65–69
Japan (1977)	0.72	2.06	2.71	3.11	3.46	4.21	4.91	—
US (1978)	2.00	4.40	6.15	7.40	8.30	10.25	10.95	11.15

Source: Hashimoto and Raisian 1985.

tries: 2.06 out of 4.91 in Japan and 4.40 out of 11.15 in the United States. (See figure 8.3.)

It is a common criticism that lifetime employment may be found only in large firms. In order to check this aspect, Hashimoto and Raisian compared length-of-service statistics for small and large firms. The results (table 8.8) show that job tenure is longer in Japanese firms of each size. This again confirms the importance of lifetime employment for all sizes of firms in the economy.

Evidence on Seniority-Based Wages

Controlling for various economic factors, such as schooling, Hashimoto and Raisian estimate the effects of experience and job tenure on worker earnings. They assume that workers accumulate two major kinds of human capital: general skills (experience), accumulated through all previous work experience, and firm-specific skills, accumulated through tenure at a particular firm. The percentages of growth (over initial pay) in earnings attributable to cumulative experience and to tenure at the firm are shown in table 8.9. This table

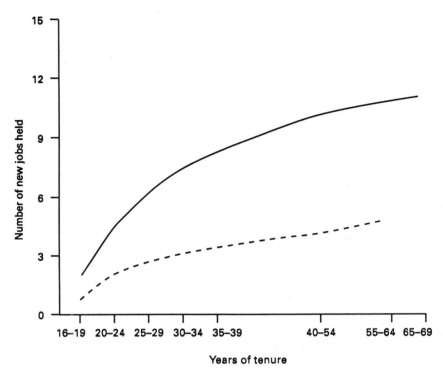

Figure 8.3
Number of new jobs held by male workers in various age brackets. Broken line: Japan, 1977. Solid line: United States, 1978.

Table 8.8
Job tenure (years) of the median male employee, by firm size.

	Firm size[a]			
	Tiny	Small	Medium	Large
Japan	8.0	8.0	8.1	12.0
US	2	3	5	7

a. Firm sizes are defined as follows: in Japan, "tiny" = 1–9, "small" = 10–99, "medium" = 100–999, and "large" = 1000+; in the US, "tiny" = 1–25, "small" = 26–99, "medium" = 100–900, and "large" = 1000+.
Source: Hashimoto and Raisian 1985.

Table 8.9
Earnings profiles: number of years to peak, percentage of growth attributable to experience, and percentage of growth attributable to tenure.

	Firm size		
	Small	Medium	Large
Japan			
Years to peak	24	33	27
Experience	235.6%	267.4%	242.8%
Firm Tenure	150.4%	141.0%	205.2%
United States			
Years to peak	25	30	30
Experience	140.0%	98.6%	109.7%
Firm Tenure	57.9%	28.9%	52.6%

Source: Hashimoto and Raisian 1985.

clearly shows that the earning-tenure profile is steeper in Japan for every size of firm, thus implying that the slope of the wage profile is higher for Japanese employees in each class of firms. When other effects are controlled for, wages are found to be more strongly affected by length of service in Japan than in the United States.

Summary

• Both Japanese and American workers, especially white-collar workers, enjoy prolonged relationships with their firms. In both countries the age-earning profiles are upward-sloping. But Japanese workers tend to change jobs less often, to stay in a company longer, and to have a steeper wage profile. The sharpest difference seems to be that it is not uncommon for a Japanese worker to settle down in the first company for which he or she worked.

• Long service is a necessary but not sufficient condition for promotion in a large company. Workers must start their careers on the bottom rung of the ladder upon graduation from college. Among white-collar workers, it is very rare to see recruitment at the middle or top management level from outside the company (unless it is from affiliated companies in the same enterprise group).[4] Wages seem to be less differentiated among cohorts during their first 5–10 years of work, but incentives for better work do not diminish under

---

Life in a Large Company

The preference to work for a large company is very strong among Japanese college graduates for several reasons. The first reason is job security, even after "retirement." Second, if one finds the atmosphere in a large company too competitive, and promotions too slow, one can easily change jobs in mid-career from a large company to a small one; it is almost impossible, on the other hand, to move in the opposite direction. Third, wages and bonuses tend to be higher in large companies. Fourth, fringe benefits are usually better in large companies. These fringe benefits often include rent-subsidized company housing in choice locations (rent subsidies are not taxable), allowances for commuting (not taxable), allowances for dependents (taxable), the availability of company deposit plans which yield interest rates higher than those banks offer, and company home loans (mortgages). Finally, a certain prestige comes with working for a large company, since all those benefits are well known to the public.

---

the lifetime-employment system. There is always a threat of being labeled as incompetent; this would not affect a worker's salary immediately, but the "incompetent" would be assigned to a post with little responsibility and would be relegated at age 55 to a relatively low-paying "retirement job." Therefore, deferred payment provides a strong incentive for workers to supply good effort under the lifetime-employment system. In fact, being labeled incompetent often bears a greater penalty in Japan than in the US, since there is no chance for a middle manager to make a comeback or to be hired in a comparable position at another company.

• There are fewer distinctions between white-collar and blue-collar workers, and between specialists and generalists, in Japanese firms. Even blue-collar workers are rotated through jobs requiring various skills.

• Many Japanese firms require "retirement" at some point between ages 55 and 60. If a worker has implicit lifetime employment, however, he can expect significant support from the firm in finding another job after he "retires." This institution leads to many nominal job changes for workers in this age bracket. The statistics, however, suggest that many true job changes to occur at that age. A survey of 60-year-old employees would show that the average length of service is greater in the United States than in Japan. Lifetime employment does not mean employment at the same job, or in the same company. Workers give up the choice of job type and location under this system. Therefore, the lifetime commitment can be made only by large firms (especially by those in enterprise groups) which are diversified and which have many subsidiaries and affiliates.

ENTERPRISE UNIONS

Many Japanese firms have unions which cover both white-collar and blue-collar workers. National organizations are often based on industry type (for example, the metal industry) rather than on specific job skills.[5]

In terms of decision-making authority, Japanese unions are much like American unions. The local units at the firm level, like "locals" in the United States, have strong decision-making powers. In the United States, the Ford and Chrysler units of the United Auto Workers can negotiate different contracts. In Japan, even if a team of local units meets with a team of management negotiators, the final decisions can vary across firms. For example, when private railway workers' unions negotiate together against management, the details of their settlements can vary, reflecting the respective firms' performances. In fact, Japanese and American unions are at one extreme, which gives most power to the locals, while the European and Scandinavian unions are at the other extreme. In some European countries, strong central unions negotiate national contracts that bind the local unions.

Both Japan and the United States have experienced sharp, across-the-board declines in union density (i.e., rate of union membership among workers). Between 1975 and 1986, union density declined from 29 percent to 18 percent in the United States and from 34 percent to 28 percent in Japan.

Only recently could the relationship between labor unions and management in Japan be called harmonious. In the 1940s and the 1950s there were frequent strikes and lockouts in major industries. The incidence of labor disputes was high, and violent tactics were often used. Moreover, the labor movement was strongly influenced by leftist ideology. Some of the labor disputes were framed in terms of the "class struggle," and went beyond questions of wage increases and of improved working conditions.[6]

Table 8.10
Percentages of workers formally belonging to unions.

	United States		Japan	
	1973/75	1986	1975	1986
Manufacturing	37	24	40	35
Construction	38	22	18	19
Transp/Communic/Util	50	35	66	56
Service	7	6	26	19
Mining	35	18	41	43
Trade	11	7	11	11
Finance/Insu/RealEst	4	3	20	18
Government	24	36	67	69
All together	29	18	34	28

Source: Freeman and Rebick 1989.

Freeman and Rebick (1989) analyze possible reasons behind the recent decline in union density in Japan and the United States. Table 8.10 shows the changes in union density by sector. Union density has declined across all sectors in both countries. Although the expansion of the service sector, which has the lowest organization rate, has contributed to the overall decline, it accounts for only a modest proportion of it. The uniform decline across sectors deserves a deeper explanation. After examining other evidence, Freeman and Rebick identify the failure of unions to organize locals in new establishments as an important factor in their decline. That failure is, in turn, due to the lower worker interest in and the stiffer management opposition to unionism that followed the oil shocks.

The Japanese labor movement went through a great transformation in 1987–1989. Up to this time, there were four major national union organizations. For more than 35 years, the Sōhyō (which was comparable to the AFL-CIO) dominated the labor movement in Japan, counting a third of organized workers as its members. The Dōmei had 17 percent, the Churitsu Roren had 13 percent, the Shinsan betsu had 1 percent, and other, smaller units had the rest. The Sohyo's member unions had spread throughout the private and public sectors. The leftist faction of the Sohyo was very much supportive of the Communist Party, while the right-center majority supported the Socialist Party. The other three national organizations were primarily anti-Communist. In 1987, unions in the private sector merged across old boundaries among the national organizations into the Rengo (literally, coalition). In November 1989, the Rengo was expanded to include public-sector employees. The new regime consists of the Zenro-ren (a small faction which is strongly supportive of the Communist party) and the Rengo (which represents the rest of the organized workers, who are in principle opposed to the Communists and to the Liberal Democrats).

The Rengo successfully sent members to the House of Counselors as a result of the election of 1989. The current Rengo has 8 million members—that is, two-thirds of organized workers. The Zenro-ren claims to have about 1.5 million members. It remains to be seen how these new national organizations will function, whether the Rengo can reverse the decline in union density, and whether the Rengo will become a major political force in Japan.

DO THE JAPANESE WORK TOO MUCH?

There are many stories about how long and hard Japanese employees work. Typical regular workers (under lifetime commitments) in large firms and in the government work until 10 or 11 P.M. Since everybody works overtime, the overtime pay allocated to a particular division of a firm is usually divided equally.

Workers do not take all the paid holidays they are entitled to. On average, they use only half of their paid vacation—mainly for family occasions, such as weddings and funerals. In 1987, on average (over all industries), each worker had 15.1 paid vacation days, of which only 7.6 were used. The larger firms (those with 1000 or more employees) give 17 paid vacation days, the smaller firms (with 30–99 workers) only 13. And since female workers (in support staff) tend to use up all their paid vacation days, the numbers above overestimate the number of vacation days taken by male lifetime employees.

Many Japanese work until noon on at least some Saturdays. Only 7.3 percent of the 6000 firms surveyed in September 1987 said that they give all Saturdays off, but the larger firms are more generous. Among firms with 1000 or more workers, 37 percent give every Saturday off; among firms with 30–99 workers, only 5 percent of them do so. Hence, about 30 percent of workers have every Saturday off, about 20 percent work every Saturday, and the rest have only

Table 8.11
Average working hours in manufacturing.

	1976	1980	1981	1982	1983	1984	1985	1986	1987	1988	1989
Japan	42.6	43.5	43.2	43.0	43.3	43.8	43.6	42.9	43.2	43.7	42.9
US	37.6	37.3	37.4	36.6	37.5	38.5	38.0	38.1	38.5	38.4	38.5
Germany (FRG)	37.0	37.5	37.1	36.5	36.1	37.0	36.5	36.2	35.9	35.6	40.9

Source: Bank of Japan, International Comparative Statistics, 1990.

certain Saturdays off. Bank and government workers have had five-day work weeks only since 1989.

As table 8.11 shows, Japanese employees work about 10 percent more hours than their American counterparts, and this gap in working hours has not shown any tendency to shrink.

Japanese workers and their families have started to voice—though not too aggressively—demands for shorter work weeks and longer paid vacations. The government's response has been to advocate shorter work hours and more vacation days. In February 1989, with the government's guidance and cooperation, financial markets and institutions began closing every Saturday. Before then, all banks and securities houses were open Saturday mornings. The stock and bond markets were also open, so customers could make deposits, withdraw funds, or place trading orders. It is ironic that just when banks in Japan began closing on Saturdays—on the pretext of promoting shorter work hours, but also inconveniencing some customers—many US banks were beginning to open on Saturday mornings, responding competitively to consumers' needs. Japanese banks did not consider the option of creating several shifts to cover Saturday while guaranteeing five-day work weeks to all workers, so that both customers' and workers' needs would be met.

Japan has four holidays around the end of April and the beginning of May. Traditionally, April 29 was the Showa Emperor's birthday; May 3 was Constitution Day and May 5 Children's Day. After the demise of the Showa Emperor in January 1989, a new law was enacted to keep April 29 a national holiday and, in addition, to make May 4 a new holiday. With the Saturdays and Sundays around those holidays, it is quite possible to have six days off in a span of ten days.

The Japanese Labor Shortage
The young in Japan are said to avoid occupations with three Ks—Kitanai, Kiken, and Kitsui, which roughly translate as dirty, dangerous, and demanding. Construction companies and other enterprises requiring blue-collar workers to work long hours experienced a severe shortage of workers in the second half of the 1980s. Some of those openings have been filled by foreign workers—many of them working illegally—and many companies are now considering adopting shorter work hours, mainly to attract young workers.

The week that falls during this time is called the "golden week." Many large manufacturing companies give a week or even ten days off around this time to avoid frequent startups and shutdowns of their assembly lines. About 56 percent of manufacturing firms, and 34 percent of all industries, take the golden week off and shut down their operations.

THE FEMALE LABOR FORCE

The traditional view of a typical Japanese woman is that she works until she gets married, then "retires" to homemaking for the rest of her life. This view is not accurate now. It was not quite accurate decades ago either, but for different reasons. The participation rate of women in the labor force was relatively high in the 1960s, peaking at about 55 percent in 1960. After declining through the 1960s and the 1970s, it began to increase again in the 1980s. In 1990, the participation rate was just under 50 percent (table 8.12). This fact is not widely recognized, and it may seem surprising that the participation rate was much higher 30 years ago. The key to this puzzle is that the nature of work done by women has changed drastically.

In the 1960s, many women were at work in agriculture and in family businesses. The number of workers in these jobs has been declining steadily since the 1960s. At the same time, the number of female employees in non-agricultural, non-family businesses has gradually increased. The increase in female employees did not make up for the decline in female family-business and agricultural workers during the 1960s and 1970s, but during the 1980s the number of female employees increased by a third. In 1990, one-third of women over age 15 were employed (Table 8.12). Since women tend not to work during their child-bearing and child-raising years, it is safe to say that more than half of the women without small children are working now. Many women now resume working in their late thirties or their forties.

BONUSES AND THE SHARE ECONOMY

The labor market is, of course, quite important for the entire economy. Maintaining low unemployment is always one of the top policy priorities. In order to keep unemployment low, wages and/or hours should be flexible in responding to productivity shocks and

Table 8.12
Employment-related data on Japanese women aged 15 and older (millions).

	Work-age population (1)	Employed total (2)	Employees (3)	Unemployed (4)	Unemploy-ment rate (4)/[(2) + (4)]	Participation rate [(2) + (4)]/(1)	Employee ratio (3)/(1)
1960	33.81	18.07		0.31	1.7	54.4	
1965	37.67	18.78		0.25	1.3	50.5	
1970	41.01	20.03		0.21	1.0	49.4	
1975	43.56	19.53		0.34	1.7	45.6	
1978	44.87	20.83	12.80	0.43	2.0	47.4	28.5
1979	45.36	21.17	13.10	0.43	2.0	47.6	28.9
1980	45.91	21.42	13.54	0.43	2.0	47.6	29.5
1981	46.34	21.62	13.91	0.47	2.1	47.7	30.0
1982	46.87	22.00	14.08	0.52	2.3	48.0	30.0
1983	47.67	22.63	14.75	0.61	2.6	49.0	30.9
1984	48.04	22.82	15.08	0.65	2.8	48.9	31.4
1985	48.63	23.04	15.39	0.63	2.7	48.7	31.6
1986	49.25	23.27	15.74	0.67	2.8	48.6	31.9
1987	49.95	23.60	16.04	0.69	2.8	48.6	32.1
1988	50.59	24.08	16.60	0.64	2.6	48.9	32.8
1989	51.20	24.74	17.38	0.59	2.3	49.5	33.9

Source: Labor Force Survey, various issues.

product-demand shocks. Put differently, paying too much will result not only in higher unemployment but also in higher inflation. How labor contracts are negotiated has profound macroeconomic implications. In this section we will examine bonuses (a particular form of compensation) and labor-contract negotiations from the viewpoint of how they contribute to Japan's macroeconomic performance.

The paying of bonuses to almost all full-time workers is one of the distinctive features of the Japanese labor market. The amount is not trivial. On average, about one-third of annual compensation is paid in the form of bonuses. Bonus income as a fraction of total income tends to be greater for workers in big firms and for workers with longer tenure in a firm.

Several interesting questions immediately arise with respect to the bonus system. Why is a part of annual compensation paid in a lump-sum fashion? Is the bonus a disguised wage, or a device to make labor compensation more flexible? If bonuses are flexible, how do they respond to various shocks? Is the bonus system good for macroeconomic performance? We will attempt to answer these questions in this section.

Many workers in Japan receive bonuses twice a year—the first one in June or July and the second one, which is usually larger than the first, in December. Whereas in the United States bonuses are limited to top executives, in Japan blue-collar and white-collar workers, and rookies as well as top executives, receive bonuses. The two annual bonus payments add up to, on average, the equivalent of 3–5 months' regular pay.

In order to examine how the annual compensation is divided into three types of earnings, let us take the "representative" worker with the following characteristics (in 1987). He is 38 years old, with 11 years of experience. In a typical month, he works 180 hours (roughly 44 hours a week) as regular hours and an additional 14 hours in overtime. He receives 248,500 yen monthly, inclusive of overtime pay. His summer and winter bonuses add up to 839,900 yen, which is equivalent to 3.4 months' wages. The time series of the bonus/wage ratio for all workers reveals an interesting trend. The ratio increased throughout the 1950s and the 1960s, and then peaked around 1973–74. The ratio has been gradually declining since then.

Table 8.13 shows how the bonus/wage ratio varies among workers in different industries, and across firms of different sizes. As a work-

Table 8.13
Wage bonuses and bonus/wage ratio.

Age bracket	Firm size	Average age	Tenure (years)	Monthly earnings	Bonus	Bonus/ monthly earnings
All Industries						
all	all	37.9	10.7	248,500	839,900	3.4
young[c]	all	22.6	2.8	161,900	427,700	2.6
old[d]	all	47.4	16.6	305,800	1,143,600	3.7
all	small[a]	39.6	8.8	215,300	509,900	2.4
young	small	22.6	2.5	153,400	299,800	2.0
old	small	47.4	12.3	243,300	612,400	2.5
all	large[b]	36.8	13.6	297,300	1,272,700	4.3
young	large	22.7	3.1	171,400	556,200	3.2
old	large	47.3	22.3	395,000	1,885,600	4.8
Manufacturing Industries Only						
all	all	38.4	11.8	241,400	810,800	3.4
young	all	22.5	3.2	162,500	452,500	2.8
old	all	47.4	17.2	289,000	1,073,000	3.7
all	small	41.5	9.5	204,800	461,600	2.3
young	small	22.5	2.7	153,600	289,800	1.9
old	small	47.4	12.2	224,200	541,100	2.4
all	large	36.6	14.8	292,200	1,220,200	4.2
young	large	22.6	3.5	172,700	564,800	3.3
old	large	47.3	23.6	380,900	1,777,200	4.7
Financial/Insurance Industry Only						
all	all	36.4	10.6	298,700	1,490,700	5.0

Bonus/Wage Ratio (summary)

	All industries			Manufacturing only		
	all	small	large	all	small	large
all	3.4	2.4	4.3	3.4	2.3	4.2
young	2.6	2.0	3.2	2.8	1.9	3.3
old	3.7	2.5	4.8	3.7	2.4	4.7

a. 10–99 employees.
b. 1000+ employees.
c. ages 20–24.
d. ages 45–69.
Source: Toyo Keizai Economic Statistics Annual, 1989.

er stays in the same firm and earns seniority, bonuses as a fraction of monthly earnings increase. Take, for example, the "all industries" panel in table 8.13, and compare young and old workers of all firm sizes in the "monthly earnings" column. The typical old worker is earning a little less than twice as much as the young worker, but close to three times as much in bonuses.

It is also evident from table 8.13 that workers in large firms enjoy larger bonuses. Workers in their early twenties in a small firm receive bonuses equivalent to 2 months' wages. Workers in their late forties, at the height of their productivity, in a large firm receive the equivalent of 5 months' wages—about 30 percent of their annual pay—in bonuses.

The manufacturing sector seems to be just average in terms of its bonus/wage ratio. The typical worker in the manufacturing sector has a longer tenure than workers in other sectors of the economy. That is, a worker tends to stay longer in the same manufacturing firm, large or small, than in other sectors.

Workers in the financial sector, which includes banks, securities firms, and insurance companies, receive above-average bonuses. This reflects the fact that the Japanese financial sector in the second half of 1980s enjoyed higher earnings and profits, and has given some of them back to workers via bonuses.

There are at least three strands of thought regarding the function of bonuses in the Japanese labor market: cultural and historical explanations, disguised-wage explanations, and profit-sharing explanations.

One view is that bonuses are a cultural legacy of feudal institutions—a paternalistic show of good will by the lord (company) toward the samurai (workers). According to this hypothesis, the amount of the bonus is determined mainly by the discretion of the employer, who paternalistically hands out additional payments when it is possible. Although this has a certain appeal to those who want to explain one unique Japanese institution with another, it is unlikely to explain today's bonus system. It is well known that bonuses were introduced during the 1930s to reward skilled workers in certain industries, and that they spread to all types of workers in all industries only in the 1950s.[7] Statistics show that the weight of bonuses in annual compensation increased throughout the 1950s and the 1960s. It is hard to imagine that cultural traditions became stronger and stronger in those decades.

Another view is that bonuses are merely disguised wages. Those who subscribe to this view emphasize that the approximate size of a bonus is negotiated in Shunto (the annual spring contract renegotiation), and that bonuses are therefore just as sensitive as wages to past economic performance. Bonuses are also fully expected at the time of receipt by both employers and workers. For government officials, the "bonus scale" is as rigid as the wage scale. One could argue further that even merit pay is distributed as bonuses. Since the nenko (seniority) wage system determines the level of wages according to the worker's length of service in the company, the bonus takes the place of what would be a merit raise in the United States. In short, the "disguised wage" hypothesis maintains that whereas American workers receive direct wage adjustments reflecting changes in a company's earnings and profits, Japanese workers are rewarded for the company's earnings and profits in the form of bonuses. This view does not explain why the Japanese labor market had to invent a special institution in order to give fair compensation to its workers, however. In addition, even if bonuses compensate for unexpected profits or special individual merit in a manner equivalent to annual adjustments in wages, they do permit considerable additional year-to-year flexibility. When profits return to normal after a surprisingly profitable year, bonuses can be adjusted downward without major conflict; wages generally cannot. Bonus adjustments can be temporary, in that they can easily be adjusted downward without difficult negotiations or stigma, whereas a wage decrease might prompt a strong protest. As for the merit-increase function, casual observation suggests that compensation variation within the same seniority class is not as large as one might expect until a worker reaches a very high position in the company.

The third argument is that bonuses perform the role of profit sharing (Weitzman 1985), with the amount of the bonus linked to how much profit the firm is able to earn in a year. Theoretically, by sharing some profits, a firm gives its workers an incentive to work harder, and does not have to lay workers off when profits are down.

Weitzman (1985) argued that the bonus system in Japan is the closest thing to the institution he had in mind when he proposed the "share economy" (Weitzman 1984). In order to support the argument, he examined the correlation between bonuses and profits at various aggregation levels. Weitzman (1986) showed that aggregate bonuses in an economy are correlated with aggregate profits. His analysis shows for all industries in postwar Japan that when profits increase by 10 percent, the rate of increase in the level of bonuses accelerates by 1.4 percent.

In a more careful study on the extent of the response of bonuses to corporate profits and value added, by sector, Freeman and Weitzman (1987) found that bonuses are much more sensitive to profits than are wages, both in the aggregate and in each industrial sector. Thus, some unexpected profits are distributed as bonuses to workers— that is, firms engage in profit sharing. They concluded that this profit-sharing system is at least partly responsible for Japan's ability to combine superb Japanese macroeconomic performance and low unemployment.

Critics of the Freeman-Weitzman study point out that many bonuses are rather predictable, and many are even negotiated beforehand in Shunto. Hence, any large, unexpected movements in bonuses are results of extraordinary changes in firms' earnings and profits. The degree to which bonuses could act as flexible compensation may be questioned, although the existence of such an effect (detected as statistically significant coefficients in regressions) is undeniable. Thus, a further study will be needed.

Macroeconomic Implications of Bonuses

According to the "share economy" interpretation, the reason that the bonus system contributes to good macroeconomic performance is clear-cut: The existence of bonuses increases the flexibility of labor compensation. Bonuses are much easier to increase or decrease on short notice, and a decreased bonus carries less of a stigma than a decrease in wages. The flexibility in labor costs may prevent firms from having to lay off workers when positive shocks to profits last only a short period. Therefore, the flexibility in compensation due to bonuses is responsible for Japan's employment stability and low unemployment.[8]

Weitzman (1984) emphasizes that a profit-sharing contract will increase employment and output. The logic goes as follows: Suppose that a profit-maximizing firm, with production function $F(L)$ and product price p, is deciding how many workers to hire. Under a fixed-wage contract, the number of workers is determined by the point at which the marginal product is equal to the wage: $p\,F'(L) = w$. Suppose now that workers are paid a base wage, z, that is less than the wage w, plus a share in gross profit, $s(p\,F(L) - zL)$, so that the total payment is equal to the amount under the wage contract:

$$wL = s(p\,F(L) - zL) + zL.$$

The present worker is indifferent to the new institution. But under the profit-sharing contract, management has the incentive to hire more workers, since additional profits are larger than the base wage:

$$wL = p\,F'(L)L > zL.$$

The share of profits paid to existing workers may be adjusted so that total compensation will not change, while the additional workers may be paid the same as older workers. Put differently, the firm will pay out some of its profits, so the firm is more interested in average profit than in total profit. This has the effect of increasing the employment level (or at least its demand side, causing the "excess-demand condition").

Another aspect of bonuses is that, since compensation is linked to the performance of the company, workers as a collective unit have the incentive not to shirk. (Of course, there is a free-rider problem if individual contributions cannot be monitored and rewarded accordingly.) Since a substantial part of compensation is tied to the company's profit, workers are willing to put in overtime if necessary and to put more effort into their work. In other words, the bonus system as a profit-sharing device will help promote a cooperative relationship between the firm and its workers.

There is yet another dimension to the role of bonuses in macroeconomic performance. A large portion of bonuses are, at least temporarily, steered into saving instead of consumption. The permanent-income hypothesis of consumption predicts that transitory income will be spent on consumption to a lesser extent than permanent income. As bonuses have increased relative to annual compensation, the saving rate seems indeed to have increased. This argument was examined carefully by Ishikawa and Ueda (1984).

Summary and Remaining Questions

It has been suggested that bonuses serve to demonstrate the employer's good will and maintain the cultural heritage, to provide extra flexibility in the wage-adjustment process (particularly regarding merit raises), and to permit collective corporate performance to affect compensation adjustment (profit sharing). Most likely, bonuses play all three roles, and more rigorous studies will be needed in order determine the relative performance of these factors and which role is most important. It is widely believed that the bonus system increases the flexibility of labor compensation, leading to greater stability of employment. To the extent that bonuses are correlated with profits, the bonus system can be regarded as a profit-sharing institution.

THE SPRING OFFENSIVE [SHUNTO]

Most major labor contract negotiations in Japan are concentrated in the spring, roughly from March to May. All contracts are renegotiated annually, whereas in the United States major multi-year contracts are negotiated throughout the year.

Every year around February, Japanese labor unions issue their demands for the forthcoming contract negotiations. The central issue is usually the amount of the annual wage raises.[9] Powerful unions, such as the railway workers and the federation of steel workers, lead the labor side in the negotiations. The management side also coordinates in a federation, called Nikkeiren, which deals with labor relations. Negotiations are carried out both nationally (for a specific industry) and at the local (firm) level. At the federation level, common, market-wide issues, such as average wage increases and number of paid vacation days, are discussed; at the individual-firm level, detailed allocation mechanisms and other firm-specific issues are discussed. Some firms settle the negotiations easily by giving exactly what is demanded by the unions, and some enter prolonged negotiations, but most firms and unions settle their negotiations by the end of May.

Macroeconomic Implications

Annual, synchronized contract negotiation makes wage adjustment more flexible in Japan than in other countries. Taylor (1980) and Fischer (1977) point out that when wage-contract negotiations are staggered, a union's demands depend on what other unions have negotiated in the recent past and on the union's expectations of what other unions will do in the coming months. Thus, rapid adjustments may be impeded by the lack of synchronization, since each union is reluctant to take a wage cut both because future cuts in other union's wages cannot be guaranteed and because past concessions granted in recently negotiated contracts cannot be rescinded. Put differently, there is a coordination failure among the various unions. Japan, with Shunto, escapes these problems.

A wage increase may be called "non-inflationary" if it is equal to the increase in workers' productivity. At the time of wage negotiations, however, the productivity increase over the contract horizon is not exactly known. Suppose for the moment that, at the time of wage negotiations, a union and management attempt to equate the wage increase with the expected productivity increase. The wage contract could become inflationary if the actual productivity increase falls short of expectations. Then the wage contract is judged to have been a "mistake." The fact that in the United States many contracts extend over more than one year means that, once a mistake is made, it lingers for more than a year; in Japan a mistake often is corrected after one year. (The econometric aspect of this is examined in Grossman and Haraf 1989.)

Staggered contracts add yet another layer to the problem. Suppose that a union attempts to obtain a wage increase which is the (expected) average of the wage increases obtained by other unions negotiating before and after it. Taylor (1980) showed that in a staggered-contract world the economic effects of one union's "mistake" would persist well beyond the contract period. The reason behind this is that the unions who negotiate subsequent to the mistake-making union would try not to be left behind in the wage increase. Put differently: If inflation is going to be caused by one union's mistake, other unions must also make mistakes to keep their standards of living intact. This process continues after the expiration of the contract for perhaps two years, because by the time the union that made the original mistake comes around to renegotiate the contract, all the other unions that negotiated over the contract length of this union will have copied the mistake, so that the new contract will also reflect it. One needs "collective action" or some credible policy intervention to undo mistakes in this staggered-contract environment.

Under the synchronized contract system, unions can make a "mistake" together and correct it together. Since all unions negotiate at the same time, expectations of what other unions will do can be resolved at the same time. Therefore, the problem that Taylor pointed out does not occur.

Shunto and the First Oil Crisis

The episode of inflation around the time of the first oil crisis, which was touched upon in chapter 5, is an interesting example of how synchronized wage contracts fail and succeed. Loose monetary policy was already creating inflationary pressure in 1973. When oil prices increased in October, inflation took off. Mistaking this "supply" shock (the oil-price increase) for a nominal shock (monetary inflation), labor demanded a large increase in wages in the Shunto of 1974. As a result, wages increased by 26 percent, the consumer price index increased by 23 percent, and the combination of all these caused a severe recession, with −1.4 percent growth, in 1974. Since the oil-price increase acted as an adverse technological shock (more exports were required to finance the higher import bill, so fewer goods were available for domestic consumption), the increase in nominal wages negotiated in response to the inflation was a "mistake." The mistaken increase only increased inflation further. Realizing what had happened, firms and unions held wages down considerably in 1975. This quick correction can be credited to flexible union leaders and to synchronized contract negotiation.

This story is confirmed in table 8.14. Learning from the mistakes they had made in the first oil crisis, management and unions held wage increases down during the second one. As a result, inflation was only moderate, and real growth was not adversely affected, during the second oil crisis.

WHY IS THE JAPANESE UNEMPLOYMENT RATE SO LOW AND INFLEXIBLE?

It is easy to observe that Japan's unemployment rate is low and stable in comparison with that of the United States. From 1979 to 1988, the US unemployment rate soared from 5.8 percent (in 1979) to 9.7 percent (in 1982) and then declined to 5.5 percent (in 1988). During the same period in Japan, the unemployment rate stayed in a narrow range, between 2.0 (in 1980) and 2.8 percent (in 1986–87). During the 1960s and the 1970s Japan's unemployment rate was even lower—between 1 and 2 percent.

Table 8.14
Wage and productivity increases in Japanese manufacturing industries.

	Growth of real GNP	Inflation in CPI	Nominal wage increase	Labor productivity increase
1971	4.3%	6.5%	13.4%	4.4%
1972	8.5	4.8	15.6	11.1
1973	7.9	11.7	24.2	17.5
1974	−1.4	23.3	26.0	−0.5
1975	2.7	11.6	11.8	−3.9
1976	4.8	9.5	12.1	12.2
1977	5.3	8.1	9.4	5.2
1978	5.2	4.3	6.9	8.7
1979	5.3	3.7	6.1	10.7
1980	4.3	7.8	7.4	6.3
1981	3.7	4.8	6.2	2.3
1982	3.1	2.8	3.8	1.1

Data source: Toyo Keizai, Statistical Annual, 1979 and 1989.

There are several reasons for this difference. First, the definition of the unemployment rate differs between the two countries. (See the appendix to this chapter.) The composition of the labor force and the behavior of particular groups, such as women and young people, are also different in the United States and Japan. It has also been suggested that in Japan flexible wage adjustment through the bonus system and synchronized annual labor contracts eliminate a significant portion of temporary layoffs.

The purpose of this section is twofold. First, we examine whether these and other commonly cited factors explain the differences in unemployment between the United States and Japan. Second, we examine the apparent secular increase in the average unemployment rate over the business cycle as observed in the two countries.

Any consideration of the differences between the US and Japanese unemployment rates should take into account both the levels and the volatility. In the autumn of 1986, for example, Japanese unemployment was 2.9 percent while US unemployment was 7.0 percent. But aside from such differences in level, there is the fact that in the United States the unemployment rate increases sharply during recessions, whereas in Japan the rate hardly responds to macroeconomic conditions. At the bottom of the business cycle in the 1981–82 recession, the US unemployment rate hovered near 10 percent; the Japanese unemployment rate had hardly deviated from its trend level and was at 2.4 percent.

The following are suspected to be factors in the differences between the Japanese and US unemployment rates.

Statistical Problems

Since American and Japanese unemployment statistics are defined differently, the statistical definitions of the unemployment rate must be reconciled before cross-country comparisons can be made. Taira (1983) argued that if unemployment were defined in Japan as it is in the United States it would be significantly higher, but Sorrentino (1984) showed convincingly that the definitions are not very different.

The Youth Factor

In any country, unemployment is usually highest among the young. Thus, the more young people participate in the labor market, the higher the aggregate unemployment rate tends to be. The US-Japan difference in youth unemployment is even more dramatic than that in aggregate unemployment. The US has a higher rate of participation by young people in the labor market (about 54 percent) than Japan (about 17 percent), as well as a higher rate of youth unemployment (23 percent in 1982, declining to 17 percent in 1987) than Japan (5.8 percent in 1982, increasing to 8 percent in 1987). This difference is partly explained by the fact that the American definition of "youth" includes persons between the ages of 16 and 19 whereas the Japanese definition also includes 15-year-olds. About 20–30 percent of the observed difference in aggregate unemployment in the years 1975–1982 was due to the higher participation rate of young Americans.

The importance of youth unemployment remains controversial. (See Ellwood 1982.) Since young people are usually single and can obtain some support from their parents, high youth unemployment does not induce the same amount of social disruption as high unemployment among married males 30–40 years old. If youth unemployment is not a serious problem, then the published data exaggerate the real macroeconomic difference between the United States and Japan. On the other hand, it can be argued that the more frequently someone is unemployed during his youth, the more unemployment-prone he will be later in life, because he will have accumulated less on-the-job experience. On this view, the difference in youth behavior signals big differences in the labor force for all age groups.

Why do young Japanese participate less in the labor market? Schooling in Japan up to college entrance exams is very rigorous, and success has a high payoff. It is much more profitable in the long run to invest in education as a teenager than to invest in on-the-job training, given the Japanese employment and promotion system. And it is quite common for Japanese parents to offer full financial support to their children in college, not to mention high school. Therefore, students have less acute financial needs. Summer vacation is shorter in Japan, so there is no custom of college students' taking summer jobs in the private sector. High school students are normally prohibited by school codes from taking summer jobs. Instead of working, they are encouraged to attend cram (preparation) schools. Furthermore, a popular part-time job for college students is tutoring high school or elementary school students. Since this is a part of the underground economy, it does not show up in employment statistics.

The inclusion of 15-year-olds in the "youth" category should lower the participation rate in Japan. On the other hand, the fact that about 55 percent of 18-year-old Americans go to college, versus only 30 percent of Japanese 18-year-olds, should work to increase the participation rate in Japan.

Agriculture and Family Businesses as a Factor

In the United States, a family member who works more than 15 hours on a family farm or in a family business is counted as employed; in Japan, it is only one hour. Even so, there is virtually no unemployment in these sectors.

Since it is easy to absorb surplus labor in the agricultural sector, the larger the agricultural sector, the lower the unemployment rate. Since Japan has a greater portion of its population employed in the agricultural sector than the United States, this may be a large source of differences in the aggregate unemployment rate.[10] If so, the gap in the aggregate unemployment rate is merely reflecting differences in economic structure.

If the United States had an agricultural sector—where there is virtually no unemployment—as large as Japan's, the US unemployment rate would have been lower. The magnitude of this effect, however, is estimated as only half a percentage point.

Temporary Layoffs

Japanese firms' commitment to lifetime employment includes avoiding temporary layoffs. Suppose that American firms behaved in the Japanese manner, not laying off workers even when experiencing a downturn. There is a category in US statistics called "temporary layoffs." A hypothetical US unemployment rate can be calculated by regarding these temporarily laid-off workers as "employed." Naturally, this adjustment is most significant when the US economy is in recession, as it was in 1981–82. These adjustments are summarized in table 8.15.

Other Factors

After all these adjustments, half of the unemployment gap between the United States and Japan still remains unexplained. What other factors have been neglected?

• Since the aggregate female participation rate was higher in Japan until 1980, and the gap between the two countries is still very small, that does not seem to be a factor. A closer examination reveals, however, that the participation of women as *employees* (rather than self-employed or family workers) is much higher in the United States.

• It may take less time for a worker to find a lifetime employer in Japan, where careful screening is done by employers.

• Although temporary layoffs are accounted for in the above analysis, they may still be a source of differences. Some Japanese firms make every effort to help surplus workers find alternative jobs in affiliates and subsidiaries, and keep them on the payroll until they have found work elsewhere.

Table 8.15
Unemployment rates. (See note 10.)

	1975	1976	1977	1978	1979	1980	1981	1982
(1) US (pub)	8.46	7.70	7.06	6.07	5.85	7.14	7.61	9.69
(2) Japan (pub)	1.88	2.01	2.04	2.24	2.09	2.02	2.21	2.36
(3) US (hypo)	5.07	5.01	4.70	4.04	3.82	4.49	5.01	6.29
difference								
(4) = (1) − (2)	6.58	5.69	5.02	3.83	3.76	5.12	5.40	7.33
(5) = (1) − (3)	3.9	2.69	2.36	2.03	2.03	2.65	2.60	3.40
(6) = (5)/(4)	51.5	47.3	47.0	53.0	54.0	51.8	48.2	46.4

(4): published difference
(5): accounted difference
(6): ratio of accounted gap to various adjustments

Marginal contribution of each factor[a]

	1975	1976	1977	1978	1979	1980	1981	1982
(7) Layoff	6.67	6.60	6.20	5.38	5.04	5.72	6.30	7.74
(1) − (7)	1.79	1.10	0.86	0.69	0.81	1.14	1.31	1.95
(7)/(4)	27	19	17	18	22	28	24	27
(8) Agriculture	7.81	7.12	6.54	5.63	5.45	6.70	7.18	9.16
(1) − (8)	0.85	0.58	0.52	0.44	0.40	0.44	0.43	0.53
(8)/(4)	13	10	10	11	11	9	8	7
(9) Youth	7.07	6.41	5.86	4.97	4.81	6.04	6.49	8.45
(1) − (9)	1.39	1.29	1.20	1.10	1.04	1.10	1.12	1.24
(9)/(4)	21	23	24	29	28	21	21	17

a. Hypothetical US rates after adjusting for the respective factor.

- In view of the bonus system and the Shunto negotiations, one might say that Japan is a flexible-pay country, whereas the United States is an inflexible-wage country. Flexible pay enables Japanese firms to afford to offer stable employment.

SUMMARY

The Japanese labor market has several distinct features that differentiate it from its American counterpart, although the two labor markets may not be as different as they seem as first sight. Most notably, many Japanese workers are hired directly out of school for "lifetime employment." This is most prevalent among large firms and among male "regular" workers. Only a few workers (certainly many fewer than in the United States) quit during the early stages of their careers. Japanese firms rarely lay off or fire workers. The age-earning profile is rather steep, so there is little incentive for workers to move after several years. "Lifetime employment" and the steep age-earning profile traditionally extend until age 55. Recently it has become common to stay in a "lifetime" job until age 60, but sometimes without much increase in wages after age 55.

In Japan, the relationship between management and workers is harmonious, and work practices are relatively cooperative—not necessarily owing to "cultural" reasons. There are economic explanations. Most obviously, the implicit long-term contract accounts for much of the observed bonding between firms and workers. Long-term contracts emerge as a result of risk-sharing, and in order for these contracts to be enforceable the wage profile must be upward-sloping. Although the commitment to lifetime employment limits a company's ability to adjust the size of its labor force as market conditions change, flexible bonuses and annual wage negotiations make the total compensation for labor more flexible in Japan than in the United States.

Since the steep wage profile and the commitment to lifetime employment provide strong incentives for workers to remain with a firm, a Japanese firm can invest heavily in its human capital. In-house education ranges from on-the-job training in various jobs to all-expenses-paid study trips to US business schools. In return for its human-capital investment, a firm may shift workers from one division to another, and sometimes to affiliates and subsidiaries, according to its strategy and to shifts in demand. Workers, in order to keep their end of the lifetime-commitment bargain, must accept any job assignments.

Any piecemeal effort to implant Japanese practices in the American system, either by an American firm or by a Japanese firm, would be difficult if not impossible. It will be interesting to see whether Japanese firms are able to successfully implement "Japanese management" practices when they invest directly in the United States. Since Japanese firms are now becoming involved in American automobile ventures, we will soon have evidence on this point.

The bonus system and the annual, synchronized wage negotiations have contributed to employment stability in Japan. These
mechanisms enable the compensation of workers to respond to
changes in the economic environment.

APPENDIX A: CONCEPTS AND THEORIES OF UNEMPLOYMENT

General Definitions

In Japan the *potential workers* in the labor market are considered to
be those persons in the population aged 15–64. (The age range is
16–64 in the United States.) Statistics are collected every month by
means of surveys. An *unemployed person* is one who does not have
a job, but does want one. The following equations summarize the
relationships among the basic concepts:

Population = Labor force + Nonparticipation,

Labor force = Employed + Unemployed,

Employed = Self-employed + Family-employed + Employees,

$$\text{Unemployment rate in Japan or US} = \frac{\text{Unemployed}}{\text{Labor force}},$$

$$\text{Unemployment rate in UK or Germany} = \frac{\text{Unemployed}}{\text{Employees} + \text{Unemployed}}.$$

It is important to keep in mind that if a person without a job says
that he is "not looking for one" when answering a survey, then he is
classified as "not in the labor force." The person is "unemployed"
only if he says that he did not work during the survey week and was
actively "looking for a job."

There are subtle issues, such as how to treat those who have jobs
but are on paid vacation, those who are promised a job but have not
started one yet, those who help family businesses on and off but are
not paid explicitly, and those who are ill and not in a condition to
work or even to go job hunting. These borderline cases are sometimes treated differently in the United States than in Japan. Correcting these statistical differences hardly changes the overall statistics,
however.

How workers move between employed and unemployed status is informative. A worker who enters the job market for the first time may become employed with or without experiencing unemployment. After being employed, a worker may lose his job and become unemployed. A job loss could be voluntary or involuntary.

Most of those who are self-employed and family-employed are in the agricultural and small-business sectors. Therefore, the stage of economic development would affect the composition of workers by industries. More workers in manufacturing industries usually makes the unemployment rate sensitive to economic fluctuations. It is sometimes important, depending on one's research purposes, to break down the employed and the unemployed by age, gender, and race.

The unemployment rate, though very popular as an overall indicator, may not be a good summary statistic of labor-market conditions. Two examples illustrate this point. First, a worker who holds an undesirable job and wants to change jobs will not be recorded as "unemployed from better job," and a worker who has settled for a part-time job or for a family business is classified as "employed." During the transition from an agriculture-dominant society to an industrial economy, economic (industrial sector) fluctuations may be absorbed by such "disguised unemployment" (also called "under-employment") without showing up in the unemployment statistics. Second, there are some "marginal" workers who move between employment and nonparticipation. These workers are known to "drop out" of the labor force when unemployed, and thus are not counted in the unemployment "statistics." Women—particularly married women as second wage-earners—tend to behave in this way. The decision of a married women to participate in the labor market depends on her youngest child's age, her husbands' employment status and income, and the overall condition of the labor market (including the unemployment rate and the wage rate). The participation decisions of married women are known to be more sensitive to labor-market conditions than those of male heads of households. In some cases, it is difficult to draw the line between being unemployed and being out of the labor force. Some speculate that in Japan jobless women tend to *say* that they did not look for a job (and thus to be classified as nonparticipating) even if they looked for one but could not find one (classified as unemployed).

Theories of the Labor Market

The Spot Market

Labor demand functions can be derived from a firm's profit-maximization decision. Market conditions and (labor-saving) technological progress affect the demand for labor. If a firm takes its output price and the wage as given, then labor demand is determined by the point at which the marginal value product (price times the marginal productivity of labor) is equal to the nominal wage. Labor supply is the result of the following household decision: Given the price and wage levels and the total endowment of "time," the household decides how much time should be devoted to work (to earn money to pay for consumption) and how much time should be allocated to "leisure." The neoclassical analysis of the labor market emphasizes that the employment and wage levels are determined by the intersection of demand and supply, just as for any other commodity in a competitive market.

If the wage is not perfectly flexible, it is possible that unemployment (excess labor supply) will be caused by a lack of aggregate demand. When aggregate demand takes a downturn, the demand for labor (inputs) decreases for any given wage rate. If the wage rate is not adjusted quickly enough to reduce the labor supply and prevent demand from falling sharply, the labor market will be in excess supply—unemployment will rise. Many economists believe that this happens during the downturns of business cycles, although they disagree on why wages are inflexible. Unemployment due to these business downturns is a big problem for society and a challenge to macroeconomics and economic policy.

Search Theory and Frictional Unemployment

Job hunting takes considerable effort and time. It may be a reasonable assumption that it is more efficient to look for a job when one is not working. In that case, a worker might quit a job and then search for a new one when he contemplates a job change.

The best search strategy in a wide range of situations is the *reservation strategy*, according to which the worker has a minimum wage level that is acceptable and continues to look for a job until he finds one with a wage at or above this level. (It is sometimes optimal for a searcher to revise his reservation level during the search process.)

Those who quit their job in order to search for another would be classified as "unemployed," but this is a temporary status and part of a normally functioning economy. Even in the "full-employment" economy, one finds a certain number of persons unemployed; this is due to the statistical definition. Unemployment of this nature is called "frictional unemployment." In certain models in which inflation is assumed to be caused by the difference between aggregate supply and aggregate demand, the frictional level of unemployment is referred to as the "natural rate of unemployment." The idea is the same. There is a level of unemployment that is natural and normal for an economy.

From the macroeconomic point of view, those who are voluntarily unemployed while job hunting are not a concern for those who make economic policy. The problem is that we do not know *a priori* how much unemployment is frictional and how much unemployment is due to a lack of aggregate demand.

Unions, Labor-Contract Theory, and Human-Capital Theory

The labor market is usually treated very differently from other markets in Keynesian macroeconomic models. Wages are often assumed to be fixed, or at least to be inflexible. In fact, wage statistics show that the nominal wage is sluggish. There is good reason for this. Union negotiations usually fix the wage rate for a certain period. Some US unions negotiate three-year contracts, and others one- or two-year contracts. In Japan, virtually all labor contracts extend one year. Longer contracts necessarily imply sluggish nominal wage behavior over the contract periods. Moreover, unions might bring a "monopolistic" element into the labor market. Those who emphasize unions as a bargaining unit assume that unions attempt to maximize labor's share of firm revenues, or to maximize the welfare of current union members (insiders). This prevents the labor *market* from being competitive; in particular, it prevents it from adjusting the wage rate according to market excess demand and supply.

Implicit (or long-term) labor-contract theory emphasizes the long-term relationship often observed between workers and firms. Suppose that an economy is exposed to productivity shocks—for example, suppose that the marginal product of labor (labor demand) fluctuates at random. If the wage level is determined in the neoclassical fashion, the wage will fluctuate as the demand for labor fluctuates, given a constant level of labor supply.

Suppose that workers are risk-averse and firms are risk-neutral—that is, workers prefer to have to a fixed income (wage) rather than be exposed to the risk of wage fluctuations, and firms are willing to insure the risk. An optimal arrangement in this environment is that the firms and the workers agree (implicitly or explicitly) to a fixed wage before true productivity becomes known. Then, if productivity is below the mean, the firm takes a loss; if productivity is above the mean, the firm makes an extra profit. The profit and the loss balance on average. In a sense, a fixed wage is the result of income insurance: the worker pays a premium during good times (when the excess of productivity over the wage yields excess profits for the firm) and receives coverage during bad times (when the excess of the wage over productivity yields a loss for the firm).

This arrangement may not be feasible, however, if workers can quit the firm and move to another at any time without incurring a substantial cost. This can be understood by means of the following thought experiment: In good times (periods of high productivity), there is a gap between marginal productivity and the contract (fixed) wage. Any firm has an incentive to offer a worker in another firm a wage slightly higher than the contract wage, and the worker will accept it unless the originally contracted firm matches the offer. Therefore, firm A's attempt to steal workers from firm B will increase the wage at firm B to the marginal productivity level, and vice versa. The wage during good times must be at the (high) marginal productivity level. But if this is the case, then the excess profit disappears. Since the premium (excess profit) is not paid, the coverage will not be given. Thus, the insurance scheme or implicit contract will break down if it is played as a one-shot game.

If the implicit contract is to be repeated, however, the insurance scheme becomes viable. Suppose that the same contract is repeated many times. Take, for example, the two-period case. In the second period, the wage must be bid up when productivity is high, because of the competition just described. But in the first period, workers could accept wages below the marginal product of their labor in order to be insured in the future. In other words, the premium is paid in the first period for coverage in possible bad times in the future. Thus, long-term labor contracts as insurance would take the form of "front-end loading."

Under this scheme, implicit contract theory would predict, on average, an upward-sloping wage profile and downward rigidity in wages. (See Holmstrom 1981 for details.) In fact, any kind of "deferred payments" (including a steeper wage profile, severance and retirement payments, and accumulations in nonportable pension funds) could be used to enforce implicit contracts between workers and firms.

Another way to ensure that workers stay with their firms is to provide firm-specific skills—skills that are useful and productive only in the company in which they were acquired.

In the case of an upward-sloping wage profile, neoclassical theories would explain that human capital, with accumulation of firm-specific and general skills, increases with the length of service. Implicit contract theory would explain that even if productivity does not increase with the tenure of workers at the firm, the wage could increase because of "front-end loading."

It can also be shown that wages are less flexible than productivity. During the downturns of business cycles, productivity declines while real wages do not decrease substantially. This observation is quite consistent with what implicit contract theory would predict.

In an economy in which implicit labor contracts, human capital, or the influence of unions is important, the static neoclassical theory of wage determination fails to be a valid framework for understanding the labor market.

APPENDIX B: GUIDE TO JAPANESE LABOR STATISTICS

Standard labor statistics for the United States are found in *Monthly Labor Review* and *Employment and Earnings*. The following Japanese publications are comparable:

Labor Force Survey [Rōdōryoku Chōsa]. This survey reports statistics on employment and unemployment, with many subcategorical breakdowns based on sectors and firm sizes. Workers are surveyed to determine their employment status during the week ending on the last day of each month. A handy annual report is published in the spring of each year by the Statistics Bureau's Management and Coordination Agency. A special survey is conducted once a year to gather more detailed information about workers' employment status.

Monthly Labor Survey [Maitsuki Kinrō Tokei Chōsa]. This survey is a standard source for wage statistics. Among other statistics, wages (regular and overtime), bonuses, and working hours (regular and overtime) are reported. Also reported are the number of persons employed—in particular, the number of "regular workers"—and the changes in this number due to accession (new hires and reentrants) and severance (voluntary and involuntary quits). Statistics are tabulated by firm size and industrial sector. In contrast to the Rōdōryoku Chōsa, employers are surveyed. (Note that the meaning of the average level of wages for establishments may change when the composition of workers within establishments changes. This caution applies to time-series interpretations as well as cross-section comparisons.)

When more detailed information about the structure of wages is required, the following publication should be consulted:

Basic Survey on Wage Structure [Chingin Kōzō Kihon Tōkei Chōsa]. This annual survey, taken in June, shows the detailed structure of wages. It breaks down wages according to educational attainment, duration of service, and occupational career for many different job types. The survey covers all private establishments with more than five regular employees and all public establishments with more than ten. Both surveys are published by the Statistical Bureau's Management and Coordination Agency.

Every five years (on October 1), a large-scale Employment Status Survey [Shūgyō kōzō kihon chōsa] is conducted. About 930,000 persons are surveyed on whether their "usual" work status consists of being employed or unemployed. For those who are employed, the following questions are asked: occupation, working days in a year, whether the person desires additional work or a job switch, annual income, and current and previous job tenure. Those who do not hold a usual job are asked whether they wish to work and why. Part-time work by household members is surveyed, too. The definition of being employed or unemployed in this survey is different from that in the Rōdōryoku Chōsa, however. In that survey, whether a person engaged in actual (paid) work during the survey week is the test for employment (this is consistent with the US definition); in this survey, whether a person engaged in work which is considered "usual" to this person is the test for being employed.

For statistics concerning labor unions, the *Basic Survey on Trade Unions* should be consulted. Among other statistics, union membership in various industries is reported in this publication.

Assorted labor statistics are reported in the *Yearbook of Labor Statistics*, published annually since 1948 by the Policy Planning and Research Department of the Minister's Secretariat of the Ministry of Labor. In this book, original sources, definitions, and explanations of technical terms are given in Japanese and in English.

NOTES

1. The Japanese-English expression "salary-man" refers to a regular employee, white-collar or blue-collar, who receives a monthly paycheck. The category does not include temporary workers, part-time workers, the self-employed, or small-business owners.

There are other categories for female workers. Female workers on the fast (elite) track, although their number is increasing steadily, are still rare; female executives already at the top of the ladder in large corporations and civil service are almost nonexistent. Hence, the gender problem of female "salary-men" has not become an issue. Female executives are in the category of (professional) career women, which covers both employees and the self-employed. Female support-staff workers in large corporations are expected to quit upon marriage or upon the arrival of the first child. They are called "OLs" (office ladies).

2. The quit rate in the 1930s among skilled Japanese textile workers, the majority of factory workers then, was as high as for any group of workers in the United States in the 1980s. It is easy to understand that the promise of lifetime employment and seniority-based wages would work to retain skilled workers. Only after the Second World War did the present practice of lifetime employment and the nenko wage system spread to other sectors, including blue- and white-collar workers. See Galenson and Odaka 1976 (especially p. 614) and Taira 1970 (p. 156) for more historical details.

3. Thus, the bidding away of middle managers does not occur in Japan. It is also true that bringing in a manager from outside would be detrimental to the morale of the workers, since it takes away a possible future promotion. The fact that in-house, company-specific training is valued more is one of the reasons that the demand for business schools in Japan seems to be very low.

4. In other words, there are necessarily dropouts, because of the pyramid structure of the promotion ladder, but there is no outside hiring at the middle and top levels. There is a fierce struggle in large companies to survive this competition.

5. For some special job specifications, there do exist national organizations. For example, Japan Airlines must deal with a flight attendants' union, a pilots' union, and a ground workers' union separately. But this is rather an exception.

6. On the relationship between labor and political parties, see Shirai 1983.

7. Note that for some white-collar workers, bonuses might have been introduced earlier. Also, some end-of-year tips [kokorozuke] were handed down to workers and servants. However, they were quite different from the institutionalized bonuses that were introduced after the Second World War.

8. See Sachs 1979 and Gordon 1982.

9. Wage increases are usually divided into an automatic nenko-wage (seniority) increase and the "base-up" (the across-the-age increase). For an individual, some of the wage increase is automatic by age. The "base-up" is more of a true wage increase.

10. Odaka (1980) suggests that some workers released from the industrial sector after the first oil crisis were absorbed by the agricultural sector. To calculate a hypothetical unemployment rate, define the following notation:

P16 = US youth population = 16,205,000,

JPART16 = Japanese participation rate = 0.176,

JUNE16 = Japanese unemployment rate = 0.058,

U16 = US actual unemployment rate (16–19 yr),

E16 = US actual employment rate (16–19 yr),

U20 = US actual unemployment rate (20+ yr),

E20 = US actual employment rate (20+ yr).

Then

U16H (US hypothetical youth unemployment) =
P16 × JPART16 × JUNE16,

E16H (US hypothetical youth employment) =
P16 × JPART16 × (1 − JUNE16)

and

$$\text{US actual unemployment rate} = \frac{U16 + U20}{U16 + U20 + E16 + E20}$$

$$= 9.7\% \text{ (in 1982)},$$

$$\text{US hypothetical unemployment rate} = \frac{[U16H + U20]}{[U16H + U20 + E16H + U20]}$$

$$= 8.45\% \text{ (in 1982)}.$$

Source: author's calculations. Data source: See table 8.14.

Because of rounding errors and second-order effects, the sums of the differences due to layoffs, agriculture, and youth do not add up to the total accounted differences.

BIBLIOGRAPHY

Ellwood, D. 1982. "Teenage unemployment: Permanent scars or temporary blemishes?" In *The Youth Employment Problem: Its Nature, Causes, and Consequences*, ed. R. B. Freeman and D. A. Wise. University of Chicago Press.

Fischer, S. 1977. "Long-term contracts, rational expectations, and the optimal money supply rule." *Journal of Political Economy* 85: 191–205.

Freeman, R. B., and M. E. Rebick. 1989. "Crumbling pillar? Declining union density in Japan." *Journal of the Japanese and International Economies* 3: 578–605.

Freeman, R. B., and M. L. Weitzman. 1987. "Bonuses and employment in Japan." *Journal of the Japanese and International Economies* 1: 168–194.

Galenson, Walter, and Konosuke Odaka, "The Japanese Labor Market." In *Asia's New Giant*, ed. H. Patrick and H. Rosovsky.

Gordon, R. J. 1982. "Why US wage and employment behaviour differs from that in Britain and Japan." *Economic Journal* 92, March: 13–44.

Grossman, H. I., and W. S. Haraf. 1989. "Shunto, rational expectations, and output growth in Japan." *Empirical Economics* 14, no. 3: 193–213.

Hashimoto, M., and J. Raisian. 1985. "Employment tenure and earnings profiles in Japan and the United States." *American Economic Review* 75: 721–735.

Holmstrom, B. 1983. "Equilibrium long-term labor contracts." *Quarterly Journal of Economics* 98, supplement: 23–54.

Ishikawa, T., and K. Ueda. 1984. "The bonus payment system and Japanese personal savings." In *The Economic Analysis of the Japanese Firm*, ed. M. Aoki. North-Holland.

Koike, K. 1977. *Shokuba no Rodo Kumian to Sanka* [*Unions and Participation*]. Tokyo Keizai Shinposha.

Koike, K. 1981. *Nihon No Jukuren* [*Skilled Labor in Japan*]. Yohikaku.

Koike, K. 1983. "Internal labor markets: Workers in large firms." In *Contemporary Industrial Relations in Japan*, ed. T. Shirai. University of Wisconsin Press.

Koike, K. 1984. "Skill formation systems in the US and Japan." In *The Economic Analysis of the Japanese Firm*, ed. M. Aoki. North-Holland.

Odaka, K. 1980. "Employment sharing in Japan." In *Unemployment in Western Countries*, ed. E. Malinvaud and J.-P. Fitoussi. Macmillan.

Sachs, J. 1979. "Wages, profits and macroeconomic adjustment: A Comparative Study." *Brookings Papers on Economic Activity* 2: 279–332.

Shimada, H. 1980. *The Japanese Employment System*. Japan Institute of Labor.

Shimada, H., A. Seike, T. Furugori, Y. Sakai, and Y. Hosokawa. 1981. *Rodo Shijo Kiko no Kenkyu [Research on the Labor Market Mechanism]*. Institute of Economic Research, Economic Planning Agency, Tokyo.

Shirai, T., ed. 1983. *Contemporary Industrial Relations in Japan*. University of Wisconsin Press.

Sorrentino, C. 1984. "Japan's low unemployment: An in-depth analysis." *Monthly Labor Review*, March: 18–27.

Taira, K. 1983. "Japan's low unemployment: Economic miracle or statistical artifact?" *Monthly Labor Review*, July: 3–10.

Taira, Koji. 1970. *Economic Development and the Labor Market in Japan*. New York: Columbia University Press.

Taylor, J. B. 1980. "Aggregate dynamics and staggered contracts." *Journal of Political Economy* 88: 1–23.

Weitzman, M. L. 1984. *The Share Economy*. Harvard University Press.

Weitzman, M. L. 1985. "The simple macroeconomics of profit sharing." *American Economic Review* 75: 937–953.

Weitzman, M. L. 1986. "Macroeconomic implications of profit sharing." In *Macroeconomics Annual 1986*, ed. S. Fischer. MIT Press.

Chapter 9

SAVING AND THE COST OF CAPITAL

Japan has a high rate of personal saving—much higher than the rate in the United States. Many hypotheses have been put forth to explain this.[1] In this chapter we will investigate the reasons for, and the implications of, Japan's high rates of saving and investment.

The comparative investigation of saving is important in many respects. Although private saving is mainly the result of household decisions, it has two important macroeconomic implications. In order to explain these macroeconomic implications, it is convenient to recall the *saving-investment identity* (discussed in detail in appendix B at the end of this chapter):

Saving – Investment = Government budget deficit + Trade surplus.

Although this identity does not imply any causal relationship, the following observations are immediately apparent:

• High saving generally reduces the capital cost of investment, since more saving tends to make funds available to financial intermediaries at a lower interest rate.[2] Saving *ex post* equals investment, if the government's budget and the international trade account are balanced. Therefore, high saving is likely to be accompanied by high investment, especially when capital controls are in place. High investment, in turn, makes it possible to adopt the most advanced technology for production, embodied in capital goods such as machines. This line of reasoning suggest that high saving can be the source of rapid growth.

• High saving might imply a tendency to run trade surpluses rather than deficits. In fact, the recent decrease in investment in Japan caused the saving-investment gap to widen. The gap is absorbed by outflows of capital. Since large capital movements were supposed to be the cause of the overvalued-dollar problem, one might be led to criticize Japan's high saving rate as a cause of the US-Japan trade imbalance.[3] The causal chain from too much saving to trade imbalances, however, seems to be rather remote and seems to be based on various assumptions. It is true, by the accounting identity mentioned above, that the gap between national saving and investment is equal to the current-account surplus. It is not clear whether saving and investment "cause" the current-account surplus. The identity does not teach us about causal directions.

DEFINITIONS AND JAPANESE DATA

Any discussion of saving must begin by specifying *whose* saving is to be considered. An economy can be divided into three major sectors: individuals (households), corporations, and the government. Individuals and corporations may be aggregated into the "private" sector. There are different definitions of the saving rate according to these divisions.

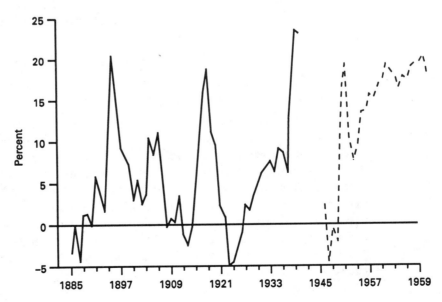

Figure 9.1
Personal saving rate, 1885–1971.

The most frequently used saving rate is the *personal saving rate*, which is the portion saved out of personal disposable income. Figure 9.1 shows the long-term personal saving rate for Japan. Before the Second World War, there were three surges in the personal saving rate: one corresponding to the time of the Sino-Japanese War (1894–95), one to the First World War (1914–1919), and one to the war with China in the late 1930s.

Second, there is the *private saving rate*. In addition to household saving, corporate saving (undistributed profits) is counted here. The private saving rate is the ratio of private saving to net national product. Figure 9.2 shows the private saving rate since 1885 in Japan. The movements in private saving closely resemble those in personal saving.[4]

The third definition of the saving rate is the *national saving rate*, which includes the government's role in saving. It is difficult to determine whether some government activities constitute consumption or saving and investment. (Should the construction of a battleship be considered consumption, or investment?) In practice, however, most government activities, including the purchasing of

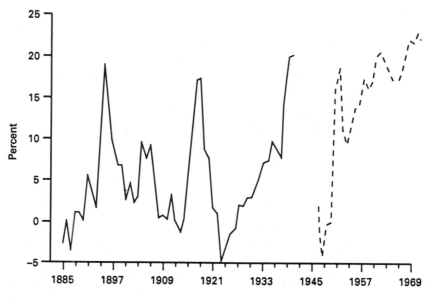

Figure 9.2
Private saving rate, 1885–1971.

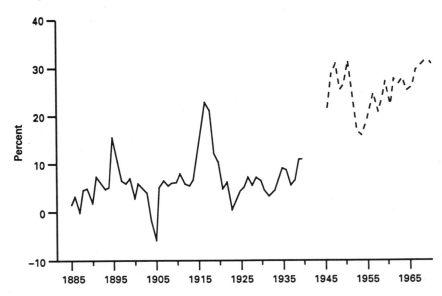

Figure 9.3
National saving rate, 1885–1971.

weapons, are considered government consumption. Therefore, with
the behavior of other sectors held constant, if the government is
running a deficit the national saving rate will go down; if the government is running a surplus the national saving rate will go up.
Figure 9.3 depicts the long-term behavior of Japan's national saving
rate. The three prewar humps in the personal (and also the private)
saving rate disappear when we examine the national saving rate,
since the government was incurring budget deficits during major
wars. In the case of Japan's national saving rate, it is very clear that
the prewar saving rate was much lower than the postwar one.

US-JAPAN COMPARISON

Figure 9.4 compares the personal saving rates of Japan and the
United States after the Second World War, and table 9.1 compares
the personal and national saving rates for selected years for the
two countries. In 1984 the personal saving rate, the ratio of personal
saving to personal disposable income, was about 16 percent in
Japan and 6 percent in the US.[5]

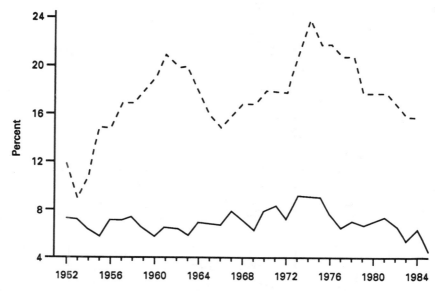

Figure 9.4
Personal saving rates of Japan (broken line) and United States (solid line).

Table 9.1
Personal and national saving rates.

1965	1970	1971	1972	1973	1974	1975	1980	1984
Japan								
(1) 0.16	0.18	0.18	0.18	0.21	0.24	0.22	0.18	0.16
(3) 0.21	0.31	0.28	0.28	0.30	0.27	0.22	0.21	0.18
United States								
(1) 0.07	0.08	0.08	0.07	0.09	0.09	0.09	0.06	0.06
(3) 0.10	0.07	0.07	0.07	0.10	0.07	0.04	0.05	0.05

(1) = Personal saving rate = Personal saving/Personal disposable income.
(3) = (net) National saving rate = (Personal + corporate +gov't savings)/
Net National Product. US disposable income is adjusted for interest paid by
consumers to corporations.

Source: Hayashi 1986.

There are several reasons why we might be interested in looking at different measures of savings, however. Although personal saving rates are very different between the two countries, if the national saving rates (including the savings of corporations and the government) are similar then the effects of saving on macroeconomic performance should not be very different. In fact, if one believes in the Ricardian equivalence principle (recall chapter 6), it is not meaningful to look at personal saving rates, since increases and decreases in personal saving may be due to consumers' undoing what government and corporations do.[6] The second reason for investigating different saving rates is to make inferences and judgments regarding different hypotheses of saving behavior. Different hypotheses can be tested with respect to saving rates other than or in addition to the personal saving rate. For example, the life-cycle theory of consumption predicts certain patterns of saving and asset accumulation for different age brackets. When the government introduces pay-as-you-go social security, as Japan did in 1973, the personal saving rate should drop, especially among individuals who are near retirement age. The effect on the national saving rate should be less prominent in this case, since the government's consumption will increase. Suppose that corporate saving is merely deferred dividends. Then even if corporate saving (retained profits) is increased, *private* saving will not be affected, although *personal* saving will be reduced.

DATA FROM A CROSS-SECTIONAL SURVEY

In its annual Family Saving Survey [Chochiku Dōkō Chōsa], the Statistics Bureau of Japan's Management and Coordination Agency asks an elaborate array of questions regarding, among other things, the levels and changes in the balances of housing, land, financial assets, and debt, the composition of financial assets, and details on annual income.[7] In this survey, saving is defined as the sum of the increase in financial assets, net of debt, and the net increase in land and housing. The latter is the difference between spending on construction, repairs, improvement, and sales, which captures depreciation and capital appreciation at the point of spending and sale. Stocks and bonds are valued at par [gakumen]. Annual income includes all types of compensation, including semi-annual bonuses but excluding severance (retirement) pay [taishoku kin], sales of

Table 9.2
Saving rate by age of head of household, 1988.

	Age bracket										
	Ave.	−24	25–29	30–34	35–39	40–44	45–49	50–54	55–59	60–64	65–
All	21.1	10.7	9.9	21.3	18.2	25.9	19.0	17.6	22.8	31.8	18.5
Employees	20.3	11.0	7.1	18.2	19.1	24.1	17.4	16.2	27.4	30.3	23.0

Source: Family Saving Survey, 1988.

Table 9.3
Saving rates, 1988.

Head of household	Major cities	Medium cities	Small towns	Villages	Region									
					Hokkaido	Tohoku	Kanto	Hokuriku	Tokai	Kinki	Chugoku	Shikoku	Kyushu	Okinawa
All	20.7	22.2	21.8	18.8	19.1	12.1	19.9	27.1	24.5	25.0	19.8	12.1	21.9	36.4
Employee	22.7	19.6	22.4	15.0	17.2	9.3	19.0	26.3	27.3	21.3	17.9	16.0	20.5	54.2

Source: Family Saving Survey, 1988.

housing and land, and inheritance. The saving rate is calculated at the ratio of saving to annual income.

As table 9.2 shows, the average saving rate in 1988 was 21.1 percent for all types of households and 20.3 percent for employees' households. The saving rate fluctuates around 20 percent between the ages of 30 and 65. Those in their late forties and early fifties save less, presumably because of the educational expenses of their children. Saving continues after age 65, although the saving *rate* declines.

Table 9.3 shows that the saving rate is uniform over households living in cities of different sizes and in towns, although there seem to be a few discrepancies among the regions of Japan. The Hokuriku, Kyushu, and Okinawa regions register relatively high saving rates, while the Tohoku and Shikoku regions register relatively low saving rates. The exceptionally high saving rate in Okinawa is due to the heavy investment in land during this particular year. No obvious economic or cultural factors explain the regional discrepancies with regard to rates of saving.

STYLIZED FACTS

We now have the following stylized facts about the time-series characteristics of the Japanese saving rate:

• The personal saving rate rose throughout the 1960s and up to 1973–74.

• The private saving rate peaked in 1970, whereas the personal saving rate peaked in 1974.

• The adjusted national saving rate decreased significantly in the late 1970s and in the 1980s. It is now very close to the US level.

• The saving rates, especially the national saving rate, were not high during the prewar period.

• Household savings cannot be reliably predicted on the basis of the household's geographic region or the size of its home town.

• The saving rate is consistently high across age brackets. Even households headed by an individual 65 or older have positive saving rates. (See Dekle 1990 and Hayashi, Ando, and Ferris 1988.)

Any theory attempting to explain the "high Japanese saving rate" should be consistent with these observations.

WHY IS THE JAPANESE SAVING RATE SO HIGH?

Technical and Real Differences

The Family Saving Survey has one notable technical deficiency: one-time severance pay [taishoku kin] is not included.[8] A lump-sum payment upon retirement from one's principal job is still more prevalent than an annuity-style pension in Japan. The amount is equivalent to four to ten times the recipient's annual salary. Saving (net changes in financial and real assets) would not differentiate between money saved out of regular salaries and bonuses and money saved out of severance pay. Hence, those in the 55–60 age bracket would report an apparently high saving rate.

The above-mentioned problem does not affect the aggregate saving rate in time-series studies in which national-account data are used. Hayashi (1986) notes three differences between the Japanese and American definitions of personal saving rates. First, in the US, the interest paid by consumers to businesses is included in personal disposable income. (This would make the published US saving rate lower than the common definition, but the difference is very small.) Second, depreciation in Japan is valued at "historical cost" rather than at "replacement cost." Thus, personal disposable income, which is valued net of depreciation, is overstated, as is the personal saving rate, since as Y (personal disposable income) increases, $(Y - C)/Y$ increases with C (personal consumption) held constant. Hayashi estimated the difference between the historical-cost adjustment and the replacement-cost depreciation adjustment. The downward adjustment to personal income due to this correction reduces the personal saving rate by about 2 percentage points at the most. The greatest adjustment is for 1973–74, when inflation reached its peak. Third, in the Japanese data, spending on durable goods is classified as consumption (or, put differently, these goods undergo instant 100 percent depreciation). The correct measure, according to theory, would classify durable expenditures as saving, which would depreciate (as services from durables are received as consumption) at a certain rate. This adjustment would adjust the saving rate upward, though not significantly. Therefore, Hayashi concludes that there are significant differences in the personal saving rates of the United States and Japan—about 10 percentage points—even after technical adjustments are made.

Table 9.4
Technical adjustments to saving rates, as estimated by Hayashi (1986).

	1965	1970	1971	1972	1973	1974	1975	1980	1984
Japan[a]									
Personal saving/NNP[b]	0.12	0.13	0.13	0.13	0.16	0.19	0.18	0.15	0.14
Private saving/NNP	0.15	0.23	0.20	0.21	0.20	0.16	0.14	0.14	0.12
National saving/NNP	0.17	0.25	0.21	0.21	0.20	0.16	0.11	0.09	0.08
United States[a]									
Personal saving/NNP	0.05	0.06	0.06	0.05	0.07	0.07	0.07	0.05	0.05
Private saving/NNP	0.10	0.08	0.09	0.08	0.09	0.08	0.09	0.06	0.08
National saving/NNP	0.10	0.07	0.07	0.07	0.10	0.07	0.04	0.05	0.05

a. Both countries' rates are calculated using the US Bureau of Economic Analysis accounting method, which classifies all types of government expenditures as consumption.
b. Net national product.

Hayashi goes on to adjust corporate and government saving rates in the two countries to make them comparable. In particular, he makes adjustments for government expenditures on tangible assets and durables. Hayashi applied the above-mentioned depreciation scheme to the private sector, using the US Bureau of Economic Analysis practice of classifying government expenditures as consumption. Since the largest fraction of government expenditures in Japan goes to investment, this accounting practice depresses Japanese government saving.

Table 9.4 shows the estimated saving rates in the two countries that Hayashi obtained using the common concepts. The table makes the following points:

• There is a considerable difference between the two countries in the rate of personal saving.

• In Japan, the private saving rate behaves differently from the personal saving rate. In particular (as mentioned above), the personal saving rate peaked in 1974, whereas the private saving rate peaked in 1970.

• If we classify government expenditures as consumption, the national saving rates in the two countries shows a much smaller difference than other measures and published data.

Cultural Explanations

One might think that saving is a cultural phenomenon, and that the Japanese, like all good students of Confucianism, are "thrifty." The most persuasive evidence against this cultural explanation is found in a comparison of Japanese saving rates during the prewar and postwar periods. It is safe to assume that Confucianism is less important in postwar Japan than it was in prewar Japan. Thus, if culture is a key factor, the prewar saving rate should have been higher. However, as figures 9.1–9.3 and table 9.5 indicate, the personal, private, and national saving rates were all higher during the postwar period.

Cross-sectional evidence casts further doubt on the cultural explanation. It is reasonable to assume that those living in rural towns and villages preserve the traditional culture better than those living in cities. But saving rates seem to be uniform across cities and towns

Table 9.5
Average saving rates for Japan before and after World War II.

	Personal	National
1885–1940	5.5%	6.2%
1946–1971	13.5%	22.0%

of different sizes. The regional discrepancies in saving rates cannot be correlated with any cultural discrepancies.

Japan's Underdeveloped Social Security System

One possible explanation for the high saving rate argues that because Japan provides less in the way of government pensions, the Japanese must save for retirement more than their American counterparts. Yet although Japan's social security system has expanded rapidly since 1973, Kurosaka and Hamada (1984) found no significant (negative) relation between the ratio of social security benefits to national income and the (personal) saving rate. And Hayashi (1986, table 13) found no significant change in the saving rate of "retired old couples" in Japan after 1973. Moreover, in the prewar period, when virtually no social security was available, the saving rate was lower.

The Bonus System

Ishikawa and Ueda (1984) argue that the bonus system contributes to Japan's higher saving rate, noting that the ratio of bonuses to regular compensation is closely correlated with the personal saving rate. They point out, in particular, that the bonus ratio and the personal saving rate both peaked in 1974, and then they slowly started to decline together. Moreover, economies without an extensive bonus system, such as the United States and prewar Japan, show considerably lower saving rates. Ishikawa and Ueda concluded that the bonus system was a factor in the high saving rate but that the effect was small. Without the bonus system, they estimated, the saving rate would have been reduced by 3 percentage points from the actual average of 20 percent for 1958–1978. Moreover, uncertainty about a lifetime income a large portion of which is paid in the form of bonuses might make precautionary saving higher.

One piece of evidence that conflicts with the bonus hypothesis is the movement of the private saving rate, if a bonus can be thought of as a mere transfer of corporate saving into personal saving. (This is another way of saying that bonuses are a form of profit sharing.) Bonuses would explain the high rate of personal saving but not the high rate of *private* saving. Moreover, some aspects of the behavior of private saving, such as the peak of 1970, cannot be explained by the bonus hypothesis.

Tax Incentives

There were widespread provisions for the tax exemption of interest income in Japan. Interest income from the following assets was tax exempt until April 1, 1988 (with the specified limits on the amount of principal)[9]:

"maru-yu" (deposits in banks, and securities and mutual funds) (3 million yen)

"special maru-yu" (government and municipal bonds, new issues and secondary, up to 5 years after issue) (3 million yen)

"zaikei" (housing and pension savings; earmarked savings applied to employees aged 54 or younger, for the purpose of housing purchase or retirement endowment funds) (5 million yen)

postal savings (3 million yen)

postal "zaikei" (earmarked savings for housing purchases (0.5 million yen).

By fully using each of these options, a young employee who wants to save for a housing purchase could receive tax-free interest from a principal amount of up to 14.5 million yen ($100,000, at $1 = 145 yen). Even beyond the tax-exempt ceiling, there were financial instruments (discount bonds issued by long-term credit banks and governments) that were taxed at a low rate (16 percent) regardless of the income-tax bracket of the bondholder. About 58 percent of personal savings were in one of the above forms of tax-exempt savings (Bank of Japan 1986, p. 158).

Again, even if people are induced to save at one time, their savings must be spent at another time. Therefore, the channel from tax incentives to higher saving rates must be reached by tilting consumption behavior so that the younger generation is induced to save more. In other words, a higher rate of interest must affect the lifetime consumption pattern. Would the tax incentives cause enough intertemporal substitution of consumption to affect the saving rate? One piece of evidence against this hypothesis is Hayashi's (1986) finding that saving does not seem to be sensitive to changes in the interest rate in Japan. Similar studies in the United States often yield inconclusive findings.

High Housing and Land Prices

The annual Public Opinion Survey on Saving finds that many Japanese are saving for a house. Since land is so much more expensive in Japan than in the United States, becoming a homeowner takes longer in Japan. It is in his thirties that the representative (median) Japanese citizen buys a house, whereas home ownership is expected to come about ten years earlier in the United States. The mere fact that housing and land are more expensive does not theoretically predict the high saving rate in Japan, however. Real estate that is more expensive to purchase will generate more revenue when sold. Again, the lifetime saving rate and the aggregate saving rate should not change if borrowing and lending can be carried out freely in order to smooth out this lumpy transaction.

The question is whether and how the saving pattern over a person's lifetime changes as a result of housing purchases. Housing purchases require that a certain portion of the sale price be paid up front, in the form of a down payment. If the younger generation is liquidity-constrained, then saving toward down payments will distort the consumption pattern further. In other words, the very young, who should be dissaving, will have to save for a down payment. Saving is difficult for the average young Japanese worker, whose age-earning profile is steeper than that of his US counterpart. Furthermore, in Japan the down-payment ratio (the fraction of the sale price to be paid up front) is usually higher than in the United States, and the mortgage horizon is usually 20 years rather than 30 years as in the United States. Another related factor that might affect housing decisions is the availability of mortgages and the tax deductibility of interest payments. In Japan the deductible amount of interest payments is minimal; in the US mortgage interest payments are fully deductible for those who itemize.

Hayashi, Ito, and Slemrod (1988) investigated the impact of these down-payment constraints on the aggregate saving rate with a simulation model in which the parameters were chosen to reproduce the timing of Japanese and US housing purchases and saving rates. They concluded that the theoretical prediction is correct in direction, but that down-payment constraints themselves do not contribute much to the gap between the saving rates of Japan and the United States. They also evaluated in a simulation model the impacts of changes in the tax laws regarding the tax exemption of interest income and the tax deductibility of interest payments. The model predicts that if the US were to adopt the system that was used in Japan prior to April 1, 1988, the US saving rate would rise by only 1.5 percentage points.

The Permanent-Income Hypothesis and Unexpected Income Growth

More theoretical explanations require explicit specification of the determinants of consumption and savings. Suppose that consumption is determined to be a constant fraction of permanent income, and that the common perception of permanent income lags behind movements in actual personal disposable income. Then, if permanent income increases, saving rates will increase in the time it takes for people to realize that permanent income has gone up. It follows that, since people continued to underestimate economic growth during the 1950s and the 1960s, they would have continued to save more than otherwise. This hypothesis is difficult to prove or disprove because of the lack of data on expectations, but since the forecasts in the Japanese government's economic plans always underestimated actual economic performance during the 1950s and the 1960s it might be reasonable to argue that there did occur a series of pleasant economic surprises. Moreover, as rapid economic growth came to an abrupt halt in 1973–74, the saving rate started to decline. Even after the second oil crisis, however, the *level* of the Japanese saving rate remained higher than that of any other developed nation. Clearly, surprises alone cannot explain Japan's high saving rate.

The Life-Cycle Hypothesis and High Income Growth

The life-cycle hypothesis (LCH) is the most widely accepted hypothesis of saving in macroeconomic theory. On this theory, individuals are assumed to save and dissave to smooth out their consumption streams. In particular, people save when they are young primarily because they must finance their retirements. Suppose that there are no gifts or bequests, so that lifetime income equals lifetime expenditures. When the population or the income of subsequent generations grows, it is still possible to have a positive aggregate saving rate in such an economy. Mechanically speaking, aggregate savings occur whenever society's net savers save more than society's dissavers. In this context, aggregate savings will occur if the young and middle-aged generation (made up of the society's net savers) is larger in population size and/or in income than the old and retired generation (the net dissavers). (See appendix C to this chapter.) Since Japan has a small proportion of aged people and rapid growth in personal income, the gross prediction of the LCH seems to be borne out.

Applied strictly, the LCH would predict that saving rates for people in the same age bracket should be similar in Japan and the United States, but that the overall saving rates could differ because of differences in the income growth rates over generations and/or in demographic composition between the two countries. This theoretical prediction is not supported by the data, however. First, saving rates in all generations (age brackets) in Japan are higher than for their US counterparts. Second, the biggest puzzle is that Japanese over the age of 60 do not seem to "dissave" but, rather, continue to save a significant fraction of their income.

This last problem may be due in part to a bias in data collection. Since age brackets for the Family Saving Survey are defined for household heads and there is a tendency for retired couples in Japan to live with sons and daughters, the sample of households headed by persons of age 60 and older is biased toward the very wealthy, who can afford to be independent or who dominate their sons and daughters in terms of income and remain the highest earners in the merged household. This point is well known among researchers. Hayashi inferred the behavior of retired couples in various ways in order to get around the problem; he concluded, even after correcting for the bias, that Japanese retired couples seem to be saving too much. (See, for example, Hayashi 1986, p. 191, table 10. See Dekle 1990 for evidence from a different data set.)

The Bequest Motive

The Japanese tend to have extended and close-knit family relationships. The positive saving rate among elderly Japanese implies that elderly couples intentionally or accidentally leave bequests for their descendants. Is this an aspect of "culture"? Do societies with benevolent parents and strong dynastic ties save at high rates?

There is an economic explanation why bequests may occur in high-saving-rate countries. First, since the timing of death is not known, it is difficult to dissave as the life-cycle hypothesis would prescribe. The elderly would be afraid of spending their life savings before their death. Hence, their consumption patterns would be conservative, unless they could obtain perfect annuities. Thus, accidental or imperfectly anticipated death will increase aggregate saving.

More important, suppose that bequests serve as a way of repaying debts accumulated during the last days of life for the elderly. Explicitly or implicitly, the elderly contract with their children who are to take care of them (financially and psychologically) in exchange for fixed-amount bequests to be made upon death. Since the timing of death is uncertain, the extended family serves as an annuity for the elderly. The rarity of annuities from corporate pensions and the prevalence of one-time lump-sum severance make the extended family more important in Japan than in the United States, cultural factors aside.

Put differently, bequests are used to ensure that somebody will look after the elderly. Although it may be morally controversial that bequests are used for this "strategic" purpose (see Bernheim et al. 1985), the theoretical predictions conform with the stylized facts.

Once the bequest motive is introduced, the bequest tax structure which favors real estate (recall chapter 6) will tilt the portfolios held by elderly Japanese toward real assets. If land prices increase substantially, the survey suggests, the elderly accumulate real assets. The bequest-motive explanation of the high saving rate (whether it is strategic or accidental) is still at a preliminary stage, and there is little econometric evidence to help quantify the importance of these considerations.

THE COST OF CAPITAL AND INVESTMENT

Conventional wisdom holds that the typical Japanese firm has an edge over its American counterpart because the Japanese firm has access to "cheap money." Interest rates have been held down by regulation in Japan, and a bank with which a Japanese firm has a long-term relationship (if not a stock cross-holding relationship) may provide funds at a low interest rate. The debt/equity ratios of Japanese firms have been markedly higher than those of their US counterparts until recently. More recently, high stock prices have made it possible for large Japanese firms to raise funds in the equities market easily and cheaply. The low cost of capital was the primary engine that gave Japanese firms a competitive advantage in world markets.

Does this conventional wisdom hold up under rigorous examination? Ando and Auerbach (1988a, 1988b, 1990) investigated this subject thoroughly, comparing the cost of capital for average US and Japanese firms using micro data (the Compustat tapes for the United States and the Nikkei Financial Data tapes for Japan). Ando and Auerbach estimated the before-tax cost of capital faced by firms. Borrowing costs were estimated by dividing interest payments by the outstanding debt and then adjusting for inflation. There are two ways to measure the required (before-tax) return to equities, the returns to existing capital, or the cost of raising funds in the equities market. The first measure corrects for three understatements in the inflationary environment: the depreciation amount, the cost of inventories when "first in, first out" accounting is used for inventories, and real capital gains from net liabilities (because a real burden of net nominal liabilities goes down as inflation). The second measure calculates the return from the viewpoint of the investors in the market. This measure calculates the holding-period yield (dividends plus capital gain) to the shareholders in a company plus the taxes paid by the company. The latter measure includes capital gains, but it is relatively volatile and not very informative in the short run.

Table 9.6 shows the returns to capital in the United States and Japan. It demonstrates that, if the accounting-earnings measure is

Table 9.6
Alternative measures of returns to capital.

| | United States | | Japan | | | |
	Adjusted accounting earnings (1)	Market return (2)	Adjusted accounting earnings (3)	Market return (4)	(3) plus cross-holding correction (5)	(3) plus cross-holding and land correction
1985	12.1%	25.3	7.03	10.32	8.47	33.50
1986	9.3	19.2	5.60	27.44	6.77	23.21
1987	10.3	9.4	4.36	5.04	5.00	19.37
1988	12.7	14.0	4.37	31.40	5.45	15.98
Average, 1967–88	11.9%	9.8%	7.02%	8.20%		

Source: Ando and Auerbach 1990.

used, there exists a gap of about 5 percentage points between Japan and the United States. Using the market-return measure, the gap between the two countries is much smaller.

The cross-holding of stocks is widespread in Japan. Although dividends earned from holding other stocks are reported in earnings, capital gains from holding other stocks are not reported in the accounting earnings. Because of the low dividend ratio in Japan (see chapter 14), this may cause significant underestimation of returns to capital. In order to correct this, Ando and Auerbach attempted to estimate the impact of cross-holding on the returns-to-capital measure. The earnings/price ratio (the reciprocal of the PER) was adjusted in the same manner in which the PER is adjusted in chapter 14 of the present volume, but this adjustment was done at the aggregate level. With this correction, the return to capital in Japan increases by about one percentage point. This is shown in column 5 of table 9.6. This still leaves a significant gap between the United States and Japan in terms of returns to capital.

The last correction is to adjust capital gains made on land that the company holds. Land prices have increased much faster than the general price level in the long run. These unrealized capital gains do not appear in financial statements unless the assets are sold. Ando and Auerbach attempted to estimate the unrealized gains on land holdings by using aggregate data on land held by the nonfinancial corporate sector, but this correction causes somewhat puzzling jumps in the Japanese return to capital, as is evident in the last column of table 9.6. Japan suddenly becomes a country with a high cost of capital when capital gains on land are adjusted. A possible resolution is to consider that capital gains on land cannot be utilized when factories and headquarters are built on it. Hence, capital gains on land could not be counted as earnings on the same level with dividends.

Ando and Auerbach also found that the differences between the accounting-measure costs of capital are more prominent for broad-based samples (Ando and Auerbach 1988b) than for selected samples of large companies (Ando and Auerbach 1988a), and that the following potential explanations for the gap between the costs of capital in the two countries are not very important: the difference in corporate tax burdens, the greater access of Japanese corporations to tax-deductible borrowed funds, and the differences in accounting practices for dealing with nonconsolidated subsidiaries.

Ando and Auerbach (1990) conclude that the apparent differences in the cost of capital between the United States and Japan may reflect imperfect integration of the capital markets and differences in investors' individual tax treatment in the two countries. The fact that the cost of capital for large firms is similar in the two countries supports the above speculation, because large firms presumably have easier access to international capital markets. Small firms must rely on domestic markets, however, and then the high saving rate in Japan helps finance them with relatively low-cost capital.

APPENDIX A: GUIDE TO DATA ON CONSUMPTION AND SAVING

Family Income and Expenditure Survey (FIES) [Kakei Chōsa]

This survey aims at providing comprehensive data on incomes and expenditures for all the non-agricultural households of two or more members and other related information. The FIES covers all the consumer households in Japan *except for those engaged in agriculture, forestry, or fishing, and one-person households.* About 8000 households are randomly selected for the survey out of about 26 million qualified households.

Disposable income and consumption expenditures are measured monthly. Consumption expenditures are categorized into different purposes and different items. Consumption is measured by volume, price, and expenditures. Statistics are tabulated by household characteristics (such as income and the age and occupation of household heads) and by geographic areas (such as "all samples," "all cities," and "large cities").

Sampling coverage was revised in 1962. "All cities" before 1962 corresponds to "cities with population of 50,000 and over" after 1963. In 1981 the categorization of consumption items was revised. New categorizations are backdated in annual series to 1962 and in monthly series to 1970. For those consumption-expenditure categories that have small samples, such as automobiles and other consumer durables, care should be taken when performing econometric analysis.

The annual report becomes available around June every year. A monthly report is also available two to three months after the survey month.

Family Saving Survey [Chochiku Dōkō Chōsa]

Financial saving, liabilities of households, and their changes from the preceding year are surveyed. The survey tabulates the details of saving and liabilities with respect to various household characteristics, such as age bracket, income, number of household members, and geographic area. Stocks are evaluated at market value, and life-insurance saving at the accumulated value of premium payments.

The survey samples about 6300 households which have been sampled recently in the FIES. Half of the sample households are carried over from the year before. Since the sample households are a sub-sample of the FIES, single-member households and households in the businesses of agriculture, forestry, and fishing are excluded from sampling. For example, elderly households with a widow(er) only are excluded from this survey. This would bias the average financial holdings of elderly households upward.

The annual report is published in March and becomes available publicly around May every year.

National Survey of Family Income and Expenditure [Zenkoku Shōhi Jittai Chōsa]

This is the most comprehensive survey of consumer behavior. It differs from the above-mentioned two surveys in its sampling of single-member households and agriculture, forestry, and fishery households as well as other types of households, and in its large sample. Households are categorized by age and occupation of household head and by type of household (a couple only, a couple and a child, a parent and a child, etc.). The types of stores in which particular consumer items are purchased are tabulated. With respect to consumer durables, the survey asks the time of purchase of the good and whether it was bought as a replacement or as an addition.

The cost of comprehensiveness is that the survey is conducted infrequently and for only three months. The survey has been carried out every five years since 1959. Households are surveyed for their income, expenditures, and asset holdings in September, October, and November of the survey year. (Single households are surveyed only in November.) Seasonal effects due to the sampling months should be noted. About 4000 single-member households and 50,000 other households are sampled.

Comprehensive Survey of Living Conditions of the People on Health and Welfare [Kokumin Seikatsu Kiso Chōsa]

This survey, begun in 1986, integrates four different surveys which had been conducted separately. One big survey, covering about 240,000 households, is scheduled to be conducted every three years. Small-scale surveys are conducted during the other two years. The big survey asks questions in three categories: household composition, health conditions, and income and saving. (The last category is asked of only 40,000 households.) Questions in the household-composition category include the age of the household head, the ages and genders of other household members, and the types of pensions subscribed to or benefited from. Questions on health conditions include how sick a household member is, how often family members go to the hospital, and how long the members have been hospitalized. Income and saving (financial assets and housing conditions) questions are cross-tabulated along different household types, such as households with an elderly member (65 or older).

APPENDIX B: THE SAVING-INVESTMENT IDENTITY

In introductory macroeconomics, we learn that saving equals (*ex post*) investment. This is true only in a closed economy with a balanced government budget. At the intermediate level, we learn the following income identity. With the usual notation of Y = aggregate income, C = consumption, I = investment, G = government expenditures, X = exports, M = imports, S = Saving, and T = Taxes, observe first the aggregate-income identity and the definition of consumption:

$$Y = C + I + G + X - M,$$

$$C = Y - T - S.$$

With these two equations, we can rewrite saving as

$$S = Y - C - T$$

$$= I + G + X - M - T.$$

Hence,

$$S - I = (G - T) + (X - M). \tag{A1}$$

In words, the accounting identity reduces to

Saving − Investment = Gov't deficit + Trade surplus.

Another accounting relationship shows that the current-acount surplus equals the capital outflow (less the foreign-reserve increase and bank headquarter-branch accounting, derived in chapter 6). Simply put,

Trade surplus = Capital outflow.

This equation gives us an insight into the macroeconomic implications of saving. In a simple context without foreign trade or government deficits, an increase in saving results in an increase in investment—that is, an increase in the capital stock (minus the replacement of depreciation of the current stock). The increase in the capital stock implies a higher rate of productivity growth for the economy. This reasoning is often used to promote the stimulation of saving as an economic policy target. (For example, see Summers 1985.)

Equation A1 can be interpreted in a different way: government deficits must be financed by a surplus of saving over investment and/or trade deficits.

In sum, other things being equal:

• A high saving rate is likely to sustain a high level of investment, which results in faster economic growth.

• A high saving rate will finance government deficits without causing a high real interest rate or borrowing from abroad. The increase in government deficits will leave a larger government debt to future generations.

• A high rate of saving will produce foreign lending (capital outflow). This will, in the long run, establish the country as a world lender.

In Japan the saving rate has been consistently high. During the 1950s and the 1960s, the first implication, higher investment, was realized. After the oil crisis of 1973–74, investment plummeted and government deficits grew very rapidly. In the 1980s, with government deficits reduced and investment still lagging behind the pace of the 1960s, capital outflow soared. This last episode will be analyzed in detail in the next chapter. Japan showed, at different times, how the three macroeconomic implications of high saving operate in reality.

Table 9.7

Generation		Time			
		$t-1$	t	$t+1$	$t+2$
$t-1$	Income	$(1+g)^{-1}Y$	0		
	Consumption	$(1+g)^{-1}C_1$	$(1+g)^{-1}C_2$		
t	Income		Y	0	
	Consumption		C_1	C_2	
$t+1$	Income			$(1+g)Y$	0
	Consumption			$(1+g)C_1$	$(1+g)C_2$

APPENDIX C: THE LIFE-CYCLE HYPOTHESIS OF SAVING

Suppose that each generation goes through two periods: "youth" and "old age." A person works when young and retires completely when old. Hence, a person born in period t is assumed to earn labor income Y in period t and no labor income in period $t+1$. Suppose that the lifetime utility function of this individual is $u(C_1) + bu(C_2)$, where b is the discount (time preference) rate. Suppose that the discount rate equals the interest-rate factor $1/(1+r)$. Then the optimal consumption pattern can be shown to be that consumption when young is equal to consumption when old:

$$C_1 = C_2. \tag{1}$$

Income less consumption becomes an asset for the young. Interest is earned on it and is paid out in the next period, when the individual becomes old. The sum of principal and interest is consumed during the "old age" period.

Suppose that labor income of a new generation is higher than that of the parental generation, owing to exogenous technological progress, at a growth rate denoted by g. (Alternatively, population growth could be assumed with no growth in labor income. Algebraically the results are identical.) Table 9.7 illustrates how generations overlap. By equation 1, the optimal consumption pattern becomes $C_1 = C_2 = (1+r)Y/(2+r)$. Note that, for each generation, no bequest is assumed (that is, there is no unused saving over a person's lifetime). The crux of this model is that even though lifetime saving equals zero for each generation, there is positive aggregate saving when the economy is growing.

Let us look at aggregate income and consumption during period $t + 1$. The total labor income earned by the generation born at time $t + 1$ is $(1 + g)Y$, and the interest income earned by the preceding generation is $rY/(2 + r)$. Hence, aggregate income is

$$Y_{t+1} = (1 + g)Y + rY/(2 + r).$$

Aggregate consumption is

$$C_{t+1} = C_2 + (1 + g)C_1 = (2 + g)(1 + r)Y/(2 + r).$$

The average saving rate, s, is as follows:

$$s = 1 - (C/Y) = g/(2 + r).$$

It is easy to show that s is an increasing function of g. That is, if the economy grows faster, the aggregate saving rate increases. The point of this theory is that in a growing economy there are more savers (when individuals are weighted by economic size—in this case, income) than dissavers. This is true even though everyone spends all his or her lifetime income. This idea won the Nobel Prize for Franco Modigliani.

NOTES

1. There have been many studies and surveys on this important issue. Two that should be consulted are Horioka 1990 and Hayashi 1986.

2. One might object to this statement on the grounds that exports and imports will arbitrage away any international differentials in returns to investment if the transaction costs of international capital movements are low. (See chapter 11.) In fact, Feldstein and Horioka (1980) posed it as a puzzle that high-saving countries tend to invest more. See the section on the cost of capital later in this chapter, and also Krugman 1989, on why high saving tends to result in high investment even in the era of internationally integrated capital markets.

3. Secretary of State George Shultz reportedly criticized "too much" saving by the Japanese in a speech at Princeton University in the spring of 1985. See also Horioka 1989.

4. The identical personal and private savings for 1885–1905 are due to problems with the data.

5. One might question, as was the case with the unemployment rate, whether the two counties' definitions of the saving rate are comparable. This problem will be discussed below.

6. The Ricardian neutrality proposition states that, given the level of government expenditures, it is equivalent to finance the expenditures by

issuing bonds (deficit financing) or by imposing taxes. The reason is that the private sector saves in the case of deficit financing in order to pay for the future increase in taxes necessary to pay for the debt. This neutrality holds only when several key assumptions are satisfied. Empirical evidence concerning Ricardian neutrality is mixed.

7. See the explanation of the Kakei Chōsa in appendix A. The 1985 survey was conducted between December 20, 1985, and January 15, 1986.

8. Indeed, severance pay is explicitly excluded from annual income in the survey questionnaire. See "1988 Family Saving Survey," p. 328. I thank Professor Kazuo Sato for pointing out this anomaly.

9. The government bonds and savings securities issued because of the Russo-Japanese War were the first to offer tax-exempt interest. The Tax Exemption System for Small Saving [Maru-yu] was established in 1963. Interest from postal savings has been tax-exempt since 1920. The new law passed in 1987 phased out the Maru-yu account starting April 1, 1988. Interest income is now taxed at a flat rate of 20 percent, regardless of other income. The accounts of the elderly (65 and older), the handicapped, and single-parent households are still tax-exempt.

BIBLIOGRAPHY

Ando, A., and A. Auerbach. 1988a. "The corporate cost of capital in Japan and the US: A comparison." In *Government Policy towards Industry in the United States and Japan*, ed. J. Shoven. Cambridge University Press.

Ando, A., and A. Auerbach. 1988b. "The cost of capital in the United States and Japan: A comparison." *Journal of the Japanese and International Economies* 2, no. 2: 134–158.

Ando, A., and A. Auerbach. 1990. "The cost of capital in Japan: Recent evidence and further results." *Journal of the Japanese and International Economies* 4, no. 4: 323–350.

Bernheim, B. D., A. Shleifer, and L. H. Summers. 1985. "The strategic bequest motive." *Journal of Political Economy* 93, no. 6: 1045–1076.

Dekle, R. 1990. "Do the Japanese elderly reduce their total wealth? A new look with different data." *Journal of the Japanese and International Economies* 4, no. 3: 309–317.

Feldstein, M., and C. Horioka. 1980. "Domestic saving and international capital flows." *Economic Journal* 90: 314–329.

Hayashi, F. 1986. "Why in Japan's saving rate so apparently high?" In *NBER Macroeconomics Annual 1986*, ed. S. Fischer. MIT Press.

Hayashi, F., A. Ando, and R. Ferris. 1988. "Life cycle and bequest savings: A study of Japanese and US households based on data from the 1984 NSFIE and the 1983 Survey of Consumer Finances." *Journal of the Japanese and International Economies* 2, no. 4: 417–449.

Hayashi, F., T. Ito, and J. Slemrod. 1988. "Housing finance imperfections, taxation, and private saving: A comparative simulation analysis of the United States and Japan." *Journal of the Japanese and International Economies* 2, no. 3: 215–238.

Horioka, C. Y. 1989. Saving, IS Balance, and US-Japan Trade and Investment Friction. Discussion paper 208, Institute of Social and Economic Research, Osaka University.

Horioka, C. Y. 1990. "Why is Japan's household saving rate so high? A literature survey." *Journal of the Japanese and International Economies* 4, no. 1: 49–92.

Ishikawa, T., and K. Ueda. 1984. "The bonus payment system and Japanese personal savings." In *The Economic Analysis of the Japanese Firm*, ed. M. Aoki. North-Holland.

Krugman, P. 1989. *Exchange-Rate Instability*. MIT Press.

Kurosaka, Y., and K. Hamada. 1984. *Makuro-Keizai Gaku to Nihon Keizai* Nihon Hyōron Sha.

Summers, L. H. 1985. Issues in National Savings Policy. Working paper 1710, National Bureau of Economic Research.

Chapter 10

INTERNATIONAL TRADE

During the 1950s and the 1960s, international trade, along with domestic investment, was an engine for the high growth of the Japanese economy. As a resource-poor nation, Japan must import raw materials and oil. In addition, Japan clearly does not have a comparative advantage in agricultural and lumber products. In order to pay for its consumption of oil and agricultural products, Japan manufactured various products from raw materials and exported them. By adding value, Japan could earn enough foreign currency to pay for the imported materials used to produce both export goods and goods for domestic consumption. An important part of Japan's industrial policy in the 1950s and the 1960s was the assignment of foreign currencies earned from exports to industries that were expected to earn more foreign currency (relative to their use of foreign currencies in inputs). The country thrived, and it moved toward an industrial structure that would produce "high-value-added" products—goods with high earning power in terms of foreign currencies. Japan's main export products changed from textiles and radios in the 1950s to tape recorders, televisions, ships, and steel in the 1960s. During the 1970s, automobiles and steel became Japan's prime exports. Automobiles continued to be Japan's most important export commodity during the 1980s.

The foreign-exchange rate was fixed at 360 yen per dollar from 1949 to 1971. This rate overvalued the yen during the 1950s, in that it would have caused trade deficits if no foreign-exchange controls to limit imports had been in place. By the late 1960s, the yen was undervalued at the prevailing rate. Even at the peaks of its business cycles, Japan managed to accumulate trade surpluses. When exchange rates began to float in 1971, many thought that every nation's trade would automatically come into balance. Two decades under the floating-rate regime have made it clear that this is not the case. Changes in the trade balance lag significantly behind changes in the exchange rate.

Japan has often been criticized for its export success by its trading partners. Rapid rises in Japanese exports often led to allegations of dumping, an unfair trade practice. More recently, Japan has been accused of keeping its markets closed to foreign goods. Many now believe that during the first half of the 1980s the dollar was overvalued from the level that would balance the trade account of the United States. As Japan benefited from exporting more automobiles and consumer electronics to the United States, economists argued in favor of using fiscal and monetary policies to correct the imbalance. When exchange-rate adjustment finally happened in 1985, an adjustment in the trade balance was expected to follow after a year or so. In fact, the major turnaround in the current-account imbalances of Japan and the United States did not occur until 1987–88. The unusually slow adjustment stimulated more research on the responses of exports, imports, and domestic prices to changes in the exchange rate. In the presence of exchange-rate fluctuations, economists found, firms are unwilling to change their export prices or their domestic prices. Researchers tried to explain this behavior through models involving sunk costs, imperfect competition with differentiated products, and dynamic optimization of firms. They found that firms often differentiate prices according to the destination of the commodity (that is, they price to market) and change profit margins in response to exchange-rate fluctuations in order to keep retail prices constant. These behaviors prevent exchange-rate changes from "passing through" to retail prices. These phenomena cannot be analyzed in a traditional, classical model of international trade in which perfect competition is assumed.

In more recent discussions of trade conflicts, "intra-industry" trade has played a significant role. When commodities are differentiated by brand names and designs, as are automobiles and consumer electronics, it is natural to import and export (different makes of) the same commodities. (This is just the opposite of what the classical comparative-advantage argument would predict.) Intra-industry trade is considered to be the natural outcome in advanced countries. At least in terms of a crude index of intra-industry trade, Japan appears to be an outlier among the advanced industrialized countries. This has been used by critics of Japan's policies as evidence of a closed domestic market.

TRADE STRUCTURE

Comparative Advantage

The classical theory of international trade usually starts with a lecture on the concept of comparative advantage, according to which a country's trade structure is determined by its resource endowments and its technology. Japan is a resource-poor country not endowed with significant quantities of oil or other raw materials. On the other hand, Japan's labor productivity in automobiles and other manufactured industrial goods relative to that in agricultural and chemical products is higher than that of the United States. That is, Japan has a comparative advantage in manufactured goods, and the United States has a comparative advantage in agricultural and chemical products. Classical trade theory predicts that competition in world markets will force Japan to specialize in manufacturing and the United States to specialize in agricultural and chemical industries. In fact, this is the case, as we will see in the rest of this section. Japan imports resources and exports manufactured goods (Leamer 1984; Saxonhouse 1983, 1986) whereas the United States and the countries of Western Europe export and import the same types of products. The extent to which Japan exercises its comparative advantage is rather extreme.

The Balance of Payments

A country's international trade is recorded in its balance-of-payments statistics.[1] Exports and imports constitute the merchandise trade balance; transportation, travel, and investment incomes, among other things, constitute the service trade balance; and unilateral transfers include economic assistance and pension payments. The sum of these three balances, called the *current-account balance*, is the most representative statistic by which to judge a country's position in international trade.

Japan has recorded surpluses in the trade balance and deficits in the service balance. During the 1970s and the 1980s, Japan's current-account balance tended to be in surplus except for the years

Table 10.1
Japan's balance of payments, 1980–1989 ($ billion).

	Merchandise imports (1)	Trade imports (2)	Balance (3) = (1 – 2)	Service balance (4)	Travel balance	Investment income	Transfers (5)	Current account (3 + 4 + 5)
1980	126.7	124.6	2.1	-11.3	-3.9	0.9	-1.5	-10.7
1981	149.5	129.6	20.0	-13.6	-3.9	0.8	-1.6	4.8
1982	137.7	119.6	18.1	-9.8	-3.4	1.7	-1.4	6.9
1983	145.5	114.0	31.5	-9.1	-3.6	3.1	-1.6	20.8
1984	168.3	124.0	44.3	-7.7	-3.6	4.2	-1.5	35.0
1985	174.0	118.0	56.0	-5.2	-3.7	6.8	-1.7	49.2
1986	205.6	112.8	85.8	-4.9	-5.8	9.5	-2.1	85.8
1987	224.6	128.2	96.4	-5.7	-8.7	16.7	-3.7	87.0
1988	259.8	164.8	95.0	-11.3	-15.8	21.0	-4.1	79.6
1989	269.6	192.7	76.9	-15.5	-19.3	23.4	-4.2	57.2

(4) Service balance includes transportation, travel, investment, and royalty incomes.
(5) Transfers includes pensions, remittance, and economic assistance.
Source: Ministry of Finance, *Zaisei Kin-yu Tokei Geppo*, June 1985 and August 1990.

The Transportation Account and the Travel Account
Receipts on the transportation account of Japan include payments made by foreigners for Japan Airlines' services; payments on the account include Japanese payments for United Airlines' services. The travel account basically measures how much the Japanese spend while they are traveling abroad. This is estimated by counting dollars and traveler's checks purchased before travel, international credit-card usage, and yen used abroad by Japanese tourists. The last component is estimated by counting the yen returned to Japan from abroad in cash. In July 1988 the method of counting yen returned from abroad was modified to include more types of accounts in the definition of returned yen.

Perhaps half of the jump from $5.7 billion to $11.3 billion in the travel account (see table 10.1) is due to this change in the statistical definition. The government did not resist the change in the definition at all, because the Japanese government was trying very hard to find ways to reduce exports (receipts) and increase imports (payments) in order to avoid trade conflicts with the United States.

of the two oil-price crises, 1973–1975 and 1979–1980. Table 10.1 breaks down the current account of Japan.

As can be seen from the table, the trade balance is the major component of the current account. Japan's service balance has always been in deficit. In particular, the transportation balances and travel balances have exceeded the modest surpluses in investment income. Toward the end of the 1980s, the magnitudes of both investment-income surpluses and travel-account deficits rose sharply. The investment-income surpluses rose because Japan has accumulated a large amount of foreign assets that yield interest and dividends; the travel-account deficits rose partly because more Japanese are traveling abroad and spending more and partly because the definition of the travel account was changed in 1988.

Figure 10.1 shows, for Japan and the United States, the ratio of the current account to the GNP, with the current account scaled to the size of the economy, for the period 1973–1989. Figure 10.2 plots the yen/dollar exchange rate for the same period.

Observe that the current accounts of the two countries generally move in opposite directions. It is often the case that Japan's current-account deficits occur in years in which the United States' current account is in surplus, and vice versa. This is indicative of the close

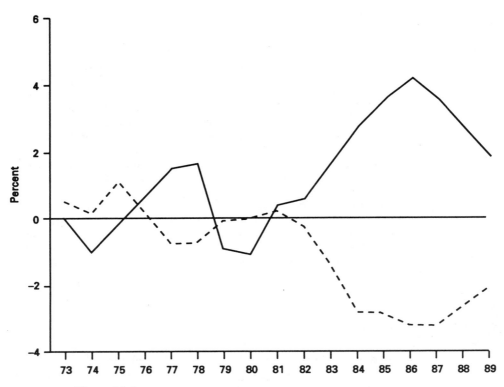

Figure 10.1
Ratios of current account to GNP for Japan (solid line) and United States (broken line).

interdependence of the two economies. As we will see shortly, the US market is the number-one destination for Japanese exports, and Japan tops the source list of US imports. As figure 10.1 shows, Japan's current-account balance was near zero in 1973 and slightly negative in 1979, and the US current account was also almost balanced in both years. Although this is a crude measure, we may define the "equilibrium" yen/dollar exchange rate as the reference point for the yen/dollar rate at which the current accounts of the two countries are close to being in balance. Specifically, let us take the average of the yen/dollar rate for the first three quarters of 1973 and of 1979, define the equilibrium yen/dollar rates for 1973:II and 1979:II, and then interpolate and extrapolate the rates at the constant appreciation rate implied by the two reference points. The

Figure 10.2
Yen-dollar exchange rate, 1973–1990. Broken line represents equilibrium rate.

broken line in figure 10.2 shows the long-run "equilibrium" exchange rate constructed in this way. Although this definition of the equilibrium rate is only a first approximation, it nonetheless gives a lot of insight into the relationship between the exchange rate and the current-account balances of the two countries.

It is obvious that dollar appreciation (situations in which the solid line in figure 10.2 moves above the broken line) is associated with Japanese current-account surpluses and US current-account deficits, after a time lag. This is true for an entire period, the most dramatic case being the first half of the 1980s. The imbalance of current account/GNP ratios grew dramatically from 1981 to 1985 as the dollar continued to hover at a level higher than the equilibrium rate. This corresponds to the dramatic appreciation of the dollar. Moreover, the turning point in the exchange-rate trend usually precedes the turning point in the trend of the current account/GNP ratio by a year or two.

Trade by Commodity

Japan has traditionally been an importer of oil, foodstuffs, iron ore, coal, and other raw materials, and an exporter of manufactured goods such as consumer electronics, steel, ships, and automobiles. Table 10.2 shows the composition of recent imports and exports. Note that Japan earns one-fourth of its export revenues from automobiles, and more than 90 percent from machinery, transportation equipment, and industrial products (versus about 60 percent for the United States).

The most notable development on the Japanese import side in the second half of the 1980s is that the share of fuels in imports declined sharply. In 1980 half of Japan's imports were "fuel" (mostly crude oil); in 1985 the figure was 43 percent; in 1987 it was down to 27 percent. Several factors were responsible for the decline. First, oil prices in terms of dollars plummeted in 1986. Second, the yen appreciated sharply, so that the dollar price of the same volume of fuel imports was reduced. Third, fuel consumption (volume) per unit of GNP was declining, thanks to energy-saving measures. Fourth, the appreciation of the yen accelerated imports of manufactured goods. The share of machinery, transportation equipment, and other industrial goods in imports increased across the board. Foodstuff imports also rose steadily during the 1980s.

Japan still imports foodstuffs, raw materials, and fuels, and then produces industrial, manufactured commodities (most notably automobiles) for export. In the second half of the 1980s, however, there were signs that this may change, with manufactured exports and imports expanding and the relative share of fuel imports declining.

Trade by Destination

Table 10.3 shows the trading structures of Japan and the United States by trading partner. For Japan the United States is the most important trading partner, both in exports and in imports. Over a third of Japan's exports go to the United States—more than double the share of Japan's exports going to all the European Community

Table 10.2
Exports and imports, by commodity.

Exports: percentage composition

	Food stuffs	Raw materials	Fuels	Chemicals	Machinery and transportation				Other industrial			
					Total	General	Electrical	Automobile	Total	Textile	Steel, iron	Optical[a]
Japan												
1980	1.2	1.2	0.4	5.1	58.6	(15.7)[b]	(16.3)	(22.7)	32.4	(4.0)	(11.9)	(5.0)
1985	0.7	0.8	0.3	4.3	67.9	(25.5)	(20.6)	(24.4)	24.9	(2.8)	(7.7)	(4.8)
1987	0.7	0.7	0.4	5.0	70.6	(22.0)	(20.6)	(25.7)	21.7	(2.4)	(5.5)	(5.1)
United States												
1980	14.2	12.1	3.8	10.5	38.9	(19.3)	(5.6)	(6.8)	18.3	(1.7)	(1.5)	(3.7)
1985	10.7	8.9	4.9	10.4	46.0	(21.1)	(8.0)	(9.5)	14.5	(1.2)	(0.6)	(4.2)
1987	9.3	8.8	3.2	10.5	45.2	(19.8)	(8.8)	(8.9)	15.3	(1.2)	(0.5)	(4.1)

Imports: percentage composition

	Food stuffs	Raw materials	Fuels	Chemicals	Machinery and transportation				Other industrial			
					Total	General	Electrical	Automobile	Total	Textile	Steel	Optical[a]
Japan												
1980	10.5	17.7	50.1	4.2	6.0	(2.9)	(1.5)	(0.5)	10.8	(1.2)	(0.6)	(1.2)
1985	12.2	14.5	43.8	6.2	8.3	(3.9)	(2.4)	(0.6)	13.5	(1.6)	(1.2)	(1.7)
1987	15.3	15.5	27.1	7.8	11.4	(4.8)	(3.4)	(1.8)	21.6	(2.2)	(1.7)	(2.1)
United States												
1980	8.0	4.8	32.9	3.6	25.5	(7.2)	(6.1)	(11.0)	23.6	(1.0)	(3.3)	(1.8)
1985	6.8	3.4	15.5	4.2	39.5	(11.3)	(10.4)	(16.5)	28.2	(1.4)	(3.1)	(2.2)
1987	6.3	3.1	11.1	4.0	43.3	(13.3)	(11.0)	(17.9)	29.7	(1.5)	(2.3)	(2.5)

a. Optical apparatus and precision instruments.
b. Parentheses indicate shares of particular commodities included in "Machinery and transportation" or "Other industrial."
Original source: OECD, Statistics of Foreign Trade.
Source: Bank of Japan, *Comparative Economic and Financial Statistics*, 1990.

Table 10.3
International trade, by destination (percentage shares).

	Exports from Japan to							
	US	UK	FRG[a]	France	EC[b]	IC[c]	Oil-D[d]	non-oil-D
1980	24.5	2.9	4.4	1.6	14.0	45.3	14.2	32.4
1985	37.6	2.7	4.0	1.2	11.9	57.6	7.7	29.4
1988	34.1	4.0	6.0	1.9	17.8	60.4	4.4	29.9
	Imports to Japan from							
	US	UK	FRG	France	EC	IC	Oil-D	non-oil-D
1980	16.8	1.1	1.8	0.9	5.4	31.7	42.7	22.1
1985	19.4	1.1	2.3	1.0	6.9	37.7	30.7	27.1
1988	22.5	1.9	4.5	1.7	14.0	47.5	15.1	30.3
	Exports from US to							
	Japan	Canada	UK	FRG	France	EC	IC	Oil-D	non-oil-D
1980	9.4	17.9	5.8	5.0	3.4	26.7	56.8	7.7	31.7
1985	10.7	25.0	5.3	4.2	2.9	23.0	60.9	5.6	29.8
1988	11.7	22.2	5.7	4.4	3.1	23.5	62.2	4.2	30.8
	Imports to US from							
	Japan	Canada	UK	FRG	France	EC	IC	Oil-D	non-oil-D
1980	13.4	17.2	4.5	5.0	2.1	16.2	50.3	22.8	23.6
1985	20.3	20.0	4.6	5.8	2.6	19.9	64.6	5.9	24.8
1988	20.6	18.5	4.3	5.9	2.7	19.3	62.6	4.9	31.4

a. Federal Republic of Germany.
b. European Community.
c. Industrialized countries.
d. Oil-producing developing nations. Original source: IMF, Direction of Trade.
Source: Bank of Japan, *Comparative Economic and Financial Statistics*, 1990.

countries combined. A little less than a quarter of Japan's imports come from the United States; this is more than Japan imports from all the EC countries combined, and also more than from all the oil-producing nations combined. Immediately after the second oil shock, the oil-producing nations combined had a higher import share, but this share declined after 1985 for the reasons explained above. Thus, Japan and the United States have become more and more interdependent.

EXCHANGE-RATE ADJUSTMENT AND THE J-CURVE EFFECT

The argument behind the *J-curve effect* can be formalized as follows. Japan's trade balance in yen is the value of its exports minus the value of its imports. The value of exports is the real export volume times its price in yen; the value of imports is the real import volume times its price, where the import price is the product of the foreign price times the yen/dollar exchange rate:

Trade balance (yen) = Export price (yen) × Export volume

$$-(\text{yen}/\$) \times \text{Foreign price}(\$) \times \text{Import volume}.$$

The export volume is a function of foreign income, Y^*, and the relative price of exported goods in the destination country, which is the export price in yen, p, divided by the product of the yen/\$ exchange rate, e, and the foreign price, p^*:

Export volume = $EX(Y^*, p/ep^*)$, with partial derivatives, $EX_1 > 0$, $EX_2 < 0$;

Import volume = $IM(Y, p^*/ep)$, with partial derivatives, $IM_1 > 0$, $EX_2 < 0$.

Suppose that at the initial position the trade balance is zero and then the yen depreciates (higher yen/\$). Suppose for the moment that domestic prices, p, and foreign prices, p^*, stay constant. Then the export volume should rise and the import volume should decline, because Japanese goods become cheaper relative to foreign products. This should have a positive effect on the trade balance. But these volume changes may take time if, for example, export and import contracts are written several months in advance. Until the volumes EX and IM change, the trade balance goes negative, because the yen/$ exchange rate, which is now greater, multiplies the same import volume.

Now suppose that the yen were to depreciate, making Japanese goods cheaper abroad so that the Japanese would sell more, and making foreign goods more expensive in Japan. This should reduce Japan's trade deficits eventually. It was observed in the 1970s that this process takes a considerable amount of time, because the movements in exports and imports lag behind price changes for various reasons. When trade volumes do not respond to exchange-rate changes, the trade balance moves in the "wrong" direction: yen depreciation makes Japan's trade deficits rise in the short run. The phenomenon in which the trade balance moves to deficits and then rises to surpluses is called the *J-curve effect*. As figure 10.2 shows, casual observation supports the existence of the J-curve effect. For a more rigorous investigation of this effect, we should consider the domestic prices and the incomes of Japan and its trading partners.[2]

NEW TRADE THEORY AND TRADE POLICY

Increasing Returns and International Trade

In the second half of the 1970s, and in the 1980s, a new breed of international trade model appeared. The classical theory, which dominated the research at the time, typically assumed that perfect competition ruled all markets, and that returns to scale with the typical technology were constant. Economists analyzed policy distortions, such as tariffs, quotas, taxes, and subsidies, but they assumed that the firm's behavior in the typical model was very simplistic. The new models introduced aspects of industrial organization, such as increasing returns, imperfect competition, and oligopolistic behavior, into existing international models. Dynamic (intertemporal) maximization under uncertainty became the norm. (See Helpman and Krugman 1985.)

The new models can help explain the possibilities of using trade policy as an aggressive tool for economic development. A model with increasing returns typically yields the implication that the company that first moves to expand will enjoy a large market share for a long time. Hence, subsidies given to firms in order to nurture sunrise industries would be justified by future returns. The new models can also be used to justify some strategic trade policies, such as temporarily shielding a domestic market from foreign competition while domestic firms grow and enjoy scale economies. (This is known as *infant-industry protection*.) This theoretical advance is quite important in providing theoretical underpinning to Japanese trade policy.

The typical evaluation of Japanese trade policy is that the country protected its infant industries well. During the 1950s and the 1960s, Japan put up high tariff and nontariff barriers protecting industries such as automobiles and ships, in order to give domestic manufacturers a chance to sell and expand in domestic markets. By producing for the domestic market, the manufacturers could expand and exploit scale economies without competition from abroad. As domestic manufactures caught up technologically, and as workers' skills improved, Japanese firms become competitive in the world market (that is, typically, the US market). Only then were import restrictions lifted. This process of infant-industry protection was successfully repeated for many commodities. (Of course, for some Japanese industries that later became successful in world markets, including the consumer-electronics industry, such protection was almost nonexistent.)

Pricing to Market and Pass-Through

Suppose that a camera can be manufactured in Japan at a cost of 30,000 yen. With a markup of 100 percent at the manufacturer level, the wholesale price is 60,000 yen. This camera is also exported to the United States. Depending on how the manufacturer prices the exported camera, we can consider several cases. Suppose the exchange rate changes from 200 yen/$ to 100 yen/$. The typical Japanese manufacturer uses imported components and raw materials for inputs. Yen-denominated costs go down because of the appreciation of the yen. The capital and labor costs in Japan do not change. As a result, the full costs go down somewhat. Now the question is how the export price will change. If the profit margin remains constant, let us see how the retail price in the United States will change. See table 10.4. Note that the change in the exchange rate is fully reflected in the change in the retail price in the destination market. This is *full pass-through*. Since the firm charges the same wholesale price in the domestic market and in the export market,

Table 10.4
Full pass-through; no pricing to market.

	Before		After	
Exchange rate	200 yen/$		100 yen/$	
Full production cost	30,000 yen		20,000 yen	
Maker's profit margin	for domestic 30,000 yen	for export 30,000 yen	for domestic 20,000 yen	for export 20,000 yen
Domestic wholesale price	60,000 yen		40,000 yen	
Export price		$300		$400
Distribution margin	30,000 yen	$150	20,000 yen	$200
Retail price	90,000 yen	$450	60,000 yen	$600

Table 10.5
Partial pass-through; pricing to market.

	Before		After	
Exchange rate	200 yen/$		100 yen/$	
Full production cost	30,000 yen		20,000 yen	
Maker's profit margin	for domestic 30,000 yen	for export 30,000 yen	for domestic 20,000 yen	for export 10,000 yen
Domestic wholesale price	60,000 yen		40,000 yen	
Export price		$300		$300
Distribution margin	30,000 yen	$150	20,000 yen	$150
Retail price	90,000 yen	$450	60,000 yen	$450

there is no "pricing to market."[3] At the going rate of exchange, there is no difference in the domestic and foreign prices.

In the example of table 10.4, the US retail price soars from $450 to $600 owing to the exchange-rate change. This is not acceptable for purposes of maintaining a share of the US market. Then the Japanese firm may lower its profit margin in order to keep the US retail price constant. If it lowers only the profit margin for exports, this is an example of pricing to market. See table 10.5.

Note in table 10.5 that the change in the exchange rate resulted in no change in the retail price in the export destination market. This is *zero pass-through* for export pricing. Since the firm charges different wholesale prices for the domestic market and for the export market, this constitutes pricing to market. In the second example, one may think of a more drastic variant: If the profit margin for the domestic wholesale price is raised to 200 percent, then the domestic retail price after the yen appreciation will become 90,000 yen. The benefit of yen appreciation is pocketed by the manufacturer and is not passed on to consumers. This is the case of zero pass-through for the domestic market. (Although pass-through and pricing to market are illustrated together here, one is neither necessary nor sufficient for the other.)

The yen/dollar exchange rate dropped dramatically from 260 in February 1985 to 120 in December 1987. That is, the value of the yen in terms of the dollar more than doubled in less than three years. The most rapid appreciation occurred between September 1985 and August 1986, when the rate went from 240 to 150 yen/dollar. The trade balance did not respond for two to three years, however. This lag was longer than a traditional J-curve argument would predict. In connection with lags of this kind, the behavior of multinational firms in response to exchange-rate changes became a topic of intensive investigation during the 1980s. This is another application of the new trade theory.

Multinational firms are able to shift production from one country to another, within various economic and political limits. When the dollar appreciated, US-based multinational firms moved their production abroad. For example, Ford began producing its Fiesta in Europe. Yen appreciation is also one of the reasons why Japanese automakers built factories in the United States.

The costs a multinational firm incurs in building a factory and in setting up a network of distributors and dealers are sunk costs (Krugman 1989). This explains why trade balances become unresponsive to swings in the exchange rate. Consider the example of a US firm that built a factory outside the US during the first half of the 1980s, when the dollar was relatively overvalued. In the second half of the 1980s, the dollar depreciated rapidly. However, the firm may not move its production facility back to the United States, even if the exchange rate moves in the opposite direction. The firm may think that the exchange-rate changes are temporary, and may try to adjust its profit margin to absorb the exchange-rate fluctuations. This is a rational behavior. Even in the long run, the firm may not pull out from overseas production, since the sunk cost of building the factory is not recoverable even if the firm closes down the factory. This explains why exports from the United States, which declined as a result of the dollar appreciation of the first half of the 1980s, did not rise immediately during the rapid dollar depreciation of 1985–1987. Many Japanese firms built distribution networks and incurred other fixed costs in order to increase their exports to the United States in the first half of the 1980s. Even after the yen started to appreciate in 1985, Japanese firms tried to hold onto their market shares, which were built up thanks to sunk costs. In the short run, many Japanese firms decreased their profit margins to absorb the yen appreciation, so that dollar-denominated prices would not change. In the initial stages of the yen appreciation, these firms may have thought that the exchange-rate changes were temporary, and may have tried to hold onto their market shares by preventing price fluctuations. (Of course, they adjusted their expectations after several months as the yen did not return to its old level.) In the long run, many Japanese firms, most notably automakers, decided to build factories in the United States. There is an additional aspect to these pricing and production behaviors: When exchange-rate fluctuations are large (volatility is high), firms tend to delay decisions on foreign operations (Dixit 1989a, b). Owing to the pricing and production decisions of multinational firms described above, exchange-rate changes do not pass through to domestic prices. If full pass-through takes some time, adjustment of the trade account in response to exchange-rate changes takes a long time.

The above stories may work without considering the possibility that a firm employs the "pricing to market" strategy. First, suppose that producers make differentiated products. For example, Honda automobiles are differentiated from Fords in design, in expectations of reliability, and in other characteristics, although they become substitutes when prices are sufficiently different. Second, there are enough barriers so that customers in one market cannot easily obtain a commodity from the other market. That is, Honda of Japan could make different models for Japan and the United States, and a customer in one country would not be able to obtain a model made for the other market.

If the domestic and foreign markets have different kinds of customers, in particular with respect to price elasticities, then different pricing (that is, different markup ratios over the same full cost) in the different markets will yield higher profits than a constant mark-up would. Hence, firms will charge different prices in different markets for manufactuered goods differentiated by brand names, designs, and expected quality, though not for generic goods such as wheat and steel.

Economists trying to demonstrate pass-through effects and pricing to market must overcome several difficult problems. One might think that it is appropriate merely to regress export prices or retail prices of imported goods on the exchange rate, but this will yield incorrect results for several reasons. First, technological changes constantly lower costs. If a particular industry in Japan happens to implement a technological change that lowers marginal costs in the same year in which the exchange rate appreciates, the export price may be lowered, but not necessarily as a result of pricing to market. Second, for a country like Japan that imports many raw materials, the appreciation of currency lowers input prices, which also lowers costs.[4] The change in the export price, which appears to respond to exchange-rate appreciation, is in fact a combination of lowered costs and lowered profit margins. Of the two, we are interested in only the latter, which comes from the pass-through effect. Marston (1990, 1991) measured the pricing behaviors of American and Japanese exporting firms in the mid 1980s. In order to control for changes in cost conditions, he compared the ratio of domestic wholesale prices to the export prices that the firms charged. He conducted the study for different industrial sectors in both countries and concluded that the export prices of the Japanese firms changed more in response to exchange-rate changes than the export prices charged by the American firms. That is, pricing to market was more prominent among the Japanese firms.

INTRA-INDUSTRY TRADE

As explained above, the structure of Japanese trade seems to be perfectly reasonable from the perspective of the theory of comparative advantage. But Japan's trading partners have complained that Japan has not imported enough and has thus run up large surpluses—and citing comparative-advantage theory does not necessarily help a great deal in maintaining political relationships. Moreover, some economists have developed a simple measure and an accompanying argument to highlight the "peculiar" structure of Japan's trade. They point out, first, that the comparative-advantage argument ignores how "gross" exports and "gross" imports are determined, predicting only "net" exports. Of course, Japan should record net trade surpluses in manufactured goods and trade deficits in fuel. But what is "wrong" with Japan is that its "gross" imports of manufactured goods are too low for its economic size. Germany, another country with large trade surpluses in the 1980s, does import significant quantities of manufactured goods. The reason why manufactured goods should be both exported from and imported into the same country is that those products, which include automobiles and consumer electronics, are differentiated by brand name and design. (Recall the new trade theory once again.) If the tastes of people in different countries were distributed similarly, so that one-third of the Japanese public preferred to own a (Toyota) Lexus, another third a BMW, and the remaining third a Lincoln Continental, and these fractions were similar for the Americans and for the Germans, we would expect to see *intra-industry trade*—that is, each of the three countries would engage in both importing and exporting automobiles.

A simple measure of intraindustry trade has been developed: Take the sum of exports and imports for the ith industry, $EX_i + IM_i$, and then subtract the absolute value of the difference of the two, $|EX_i - IM_i|$. If this industry is exclusively an export or an import industry, then the subtraction yields zero. If exports and imports are equal in size, then $EX_i + IM_i$ is the difference. If we sum this measure over different industries and then normalize by the total size of trade, we obtain the following measure of intra-industry trade:

$$m = \sum_{i=1}^{n} [(EX_i + IM_i) - |EX_i - IM_i|] \bigg/ \sum_{i=1}^{n} (EX_i + IM_i).$$

Index m takes a value between 0 and 1. A higher m indicates a higher degree of intra-industry trade. Table 10.6 shows Lawrence's (1987) estimates of such a measure. Japan, along with Australia, is an outlier in this table. Moreover, Lawrence notes that the number of Japanese manufacturing industries that had unduly low imports in 1983 increased to nine out of twenty from only three in 1970.

Can we take this as conclusive evidence that the Japanese markets are closed to foreign goods? Does the number indicate that

Table 10.6
Intra-industry trade index.

	21 sectors	94 sectors
Australia	0.41	0.22
Belgium	0.87	0.79
Canada	0.67	0.68
Finland	0.58	0.49
France	0.88	0.82
Germany	0.69	0.66
Italy	0.71	0.61
Japan	0.30	0.25
Netherlands	0.77	0.78
Norway	0.62	0.51
Sweden	0.66	0.68
UK	0.82	0.78
US	0.67	0.60
Korea	—	0.48
Switzerland	—	0.61

Source: Lawrence 1987.

Japan's trade policies, including tariff and nontariff measures, are intended to keep foreign goods out of Japanese markets? There are several factors that should be considered before we draw this kind of conclusion. First, if people in different nations have different tastes, a low intra-industry index does not imply that policy is at fault. For example, if Japanese consumers like Toyota's designs over those of BMW and Ford, even for any reasonable price differentials, then it is natural to see mostly Toyotas on Japanese streets. Neither economic theory nor policy can fault (or change) consumers' tastes.[5] Second, distance from other markets (which is part of the endowment of a nation), and transportation costs, may be crucial in determining how much intra-industry trade occurs. Both Japan and Australia have low intra-industry trade in table 10.6, and both countries lack large neighboring countries with advanced industrial products.[6] Saxonhouse (1989) attempted to synthesize the comparative-advantage model of international trade and the model of intra-industry trade driven by differential products. He estimated equations for gross imports and gross exports of 61 trade sectors in 41 countries for 1979, using factor endowments of capital, education, labor, petroleum, coal, and arable land as explanatory variables. According to his results, the actual patterns of Japan's gross imports can be closely forecast by using the estimated coefficients on endowments for all countries excluding Japan. Hence, he concludes that Japan's distinctive intra-industry patterns can be explained by its national endowments.[7]

There seems to be a consensus that Japan's intra-industry pattern is an outlier among industrial nations. Whether this is due to Japan's policies or to factor endowments and consumers' tastes is a focus of debate. This topic is important in the current policy debate between Japan and the United States, and it will be discussed further in chapter 12.

SUMMARY

Japan's distinctive trade structure is a clear example of classical comparative-advantage theory. Japan imports oil from the Middle East and exports manufactured goods (most notably automobiles) to other industrial nations (most notably the United States). Few manufactured goods are imported into Japan, although this pattern seems to be changing. The trade relationship between Japan and the United States has strengthened in recent years.

In the second half of the 1980s, a large exchange-rate adjustment occurred. Current-account adjustment was slow to follow the exchange-rate adjustment. One of the reasons behind the slow adjustment, in addition to the usual J-curve effect, was a less-than-full pass-through: The exchange-rate changes did not pass through to domestic retail prices, because firms decided to hold onto market shares built up with sunk costs. This effect was often associated with a pricing-to-market strategy in which firms priced manufactured goods differently in domestic and foreign markets. Japanese firms appear to display pricing-to-market behavior.

One of the distictive features of the Japanese trading structure is that manufactured imports are low. Comparative-advantage theory predicts that Japan should have low "net" manufactured imports. But critics assert that Japan's "gross" imports are too low, which implies the existence of nontariff barriers. Japan is allegedly found to engage in too little intra-industry trade. The debate as to whether this is due to Japan's various policies of keeping out foreign products, to Japanese consumers' tastes, or to factor endowments continues.

NOTES

1. The Balance of Payments Monthly is prepared by the Bank of Japan and published by the Ministry of Finance every month. The balance-of-payments statistics are included in major statistical monthlies and year-books. Detailed tables are available in a special annual issue of *Zaisei Kinyu Tokei Geppo*, usually published in August. The balance of payments is published in terms of both yen and dollars.

2. In recent years, the Economic Planning Agency's White Papers have included a section on the J-curve, including its estimation.

3. The pricing-to-market strategy is defined as a firm's charging different prices to different markets for the same or a very similar make of the same commodity. It can be understood as a variant of price discrimination by monopolists in terms of brands and design. (See any intermediate microeconomics textbook.) The literature on pricing to market and pass-through includes Froot and Klemperer 1989, Hooper and Mann 1989, Krugman 1987, Mann 1986 and 1991, and Marston 1990 and 1991.

4. Ohno (1989) has corrected for the effects of cost reductions due to imports, using an input-output table with sectoral price data.

5. Lawrence acknowledges the possibility of taste differences as the cause of a low intra-industry index. If so, there is little that policy can do. Was the rapid increase in manufactured imports (for example, BMW and Mercedes automobiles) in the second half of the 1980s also due to changes in consumers' tastes, or did it reflect various policy measure aimed at lowering nontariff barriers on the part of Japan?

6. A proponent of intra-industry trade might note that in the age of the Boeing 747-F (the freight model) the economic distance of transpacific trade is not so much farther than that of transatlantic trade. An opponent would assert that the various ways to cross land borders among EC countries are much more important than the existence of the Boeing 747-F. It would be interesting to net out all trades in North America, all trades in the EC, and all trades in the Asian countries and then calculate an index of intra-industry trade for Asia, North America, and the EC.

7. See also the discussions of the Saxonhouse paper by Tyson (1989) and Bowen (1989).

BIBLIOGRAPHY

Bowen, H. P. 1989. "Comment: Saxonhouse paper." In *Trade Policies for International Competitiveness*, ed. R. C. Feenstra. University of Chicago Press.

Dixit, A. 1989a. "Entry and exit decisions of a firm under uncertainty." *Journal of Political Economy* 97: 620–638.

Dixit, A. 1989b. "Hysteresis, import pricing, and pass-through." *Quarterly Journal of Economics* 104, May: 205– 228.

Froot, K. A., and P. D. Klemperer. 1989. "Exchange rate pass-through when market share matters." *American Economic Review* 79, no. 4: 637–654.

Helpman, E., and P. Krugman. 1985. *Market Structure and Foreign Trade: Increasing Returns, Imperfect Competition, and the International Economy*. MIT Press.

Hooper, P., and C. L. Mann. 1989. "Exchange rate pass-through in the 1980s: The case of US imports of manufactures." *Brookings Papers on Economic Activity* 1: 297– 337.

Krugman, P. 1987. "Pricing to market when the exchange rate changes." In *Real-Financial Linkages among Open Economies*, ed. S. W. Arndt and J. D. Richardson. MIT Press.

Lawrence, R. Z. 1987. "Does Japan import too little? Closed minds or markets?" *Brookings Papers on Economic Activity* 2: 517–554.

Leamer, E. E. 1984. *Sources of International Comparative Advantage*. MIT Press.

Mann, C. L. 1986. "Prices, profit margins, and exchange rates." *Federal Reserve Bulletin* 72, no. 6: 366–379.

Mann, C. L. 1991. "The effects of exchange rate trends and volatility on export prices: Industry examples from Japan, Germany, and the United States." *Weltwirtschaftliches Archiv* 127: 588–618.

Marston, R. C. 1990. "Pricing to market in Japanese manufacturing." *Journal of International Economics* 29, no. 3/4: 217–236.

Marston, R. C. 1991. "Price behavior in Japanese and US manufacturing." In *The US and Japan: Trade and Investment*, ed. P. Krugman. University of Chicago Press.

Ohno, K. 1989. "Export pricing behavior of manufacturing: A US-Japan comparison." *International Monetary Fund Staff Papers* 36, no. 3: 550–579.

Saxonhouse, G. R. 1983. "The micro- and macroeconomics of foreign sales to Japan." In *Trade Policy for the 1980s*, ed. W. R. Cline. MIT Press.

Saxonhouse, G. R. 1986. "What's wrong with Japanese trade structure?" *Pacific Economic Papers*, no. 137: 1–36.

Saxonhouse, G. R. 1989. "Differentiated products, economies of scale, and access to the Japanese market." In *Trade Policies for International Competitiveness*, ed. R. C. Feenstra. University of Chicago Press.

Tyson, L. D. 1989. "Comment: Saxonhouse paper." In *Trade Policies for International Competitiveness*, ed. R. C. Feenstra. University of Chicago Press.

Chapter 11

INTERNATIONAL FINANCE

FROM THE BRETTON WOODS SYSTEM TO THE FLOATING-RATE REGIME[1]

After the Second World War, a new exchange-rate regime (to become known as the Bretton Woods system) was established. Under the system, the values of major countries' currencies were tied to the US dollar, and the dollar was convertible to gold. The convertibility of the dollar was credible in the 1940s and the 1950s because the United States held a substantial quantity of gold to back externally held dollars. The International Monetary Fund (IMF) was created to monitor and enforce the exchange-rate regime. The value of the yen was fixed at the rate of 360 yen per dollar in 1949, although it took three more years for Japan to join the IMF. The rate of 360 was maintained until the summer of 1971.

In Japan, strict capital controls were maintained under the fixed-exchange-rate regime. Borrowing from and lending to foreign countries by private parties were severely limited. All dollars earned from exports had to be exchanged into yen, so that dollars were centrally held by the Bank of Japan; and imports had to be approved by the respective ministries, where the necessary dollars were allocated. In this environment, the trade surpluses or deficits were mirrored almost one for one in the increases of decreases in foreign reserves. With limited foreign reserves and capital controls, the fixed-rate regime meant that the health of the domestic economy was sometimes sacrificed in order to maintain the fixed exchange rate. The rule was simple: When foreign reserves were depleted because of trade deficits, imports were cut even if this meant slowing down the entire domestic economy. When all countries abided by this rule and the exchange rate was gradually adjusted to reflect some "fundamental" changes, such as differences in productivity growth rates, the fixed-exchange-rate system worked best. The Bretton Woods system showed signs of disintegration toward the late 1960s, however, because the exchange-rate adjustments needed to correct for the differences in productivity growth proved to be politically difficult. Another problem was that the United States sustained trade deficits, so externally held dollars gradually increased. By the end of the 1960s, some currencies (notably the Japanese yen and the German mark) were undervalued while the US dollar was overvalued. Moreover, the amount of dollars held outside the United States far outweighed the gold reserves of the United States.

In August 1971, President Nixon announced that the convertibility of the dollar was suspended, and that an import surcharge of 10 percent would be imposed. The exchange-rate market was thrown into chaos. Foreign-exchange markets were temporarily closed while policy makers groped for appropriate levels for exchange rates. By the end of August, major currencies, including the yen, started to float. After four months of searching for new "equilibrium" rates, the Smithsonian Agreement was struck in December 1971. The major industrialized countries agreed to new exchange rates with wider bands of fluctuation. The central rate for the yen was 308 per dollar, a 16.9 percent revaluation from the Bretton Woods rate of 360. From December 1971 to February 1973, efforts were made to ensure that exchange rates stayed within the bounds of the Smithsonian Agreement.

By the end of 1972 it was clear that the Smithsonian rates were not working. The yen was consistently near the ceiling allowed under the agreement. Yet both Japanese trade surpluses and US deficits grew larger in 1972. In February 1973 the United States unilaterally devalued the dollar, and within a month Japan and major European countries decided that the Smithsonian rates were not sustainable. A true floating-exchange-rate regime had begun.

Since 1973, the yen has been floating—that is, the rate has been determined continuously in the market, although the monetary authorities have occasionally intervened in the market. Even official intervention is part of overall supply and demand in the market.

The major European countries formed the European Monetary System (EMS) in March 1979. They created the European Currency Unit (ECU), whose value is defined as a weighted average of the member countries' currencies. As of October 1990, the membership of the EMS includes Germany, France, Britain, Italy, the Netherlands, Belgium, Luxembourg, Denmark, Ireland, Spain, Greece, and Portugal. The first ten countries form the Exchange Rate Mechanism (ERM); the exchange rates of their currencies are virtually fixed (plus or minus 2.25 percent, with the exceptions of Britain and Spain with 6 percent). Britain, a member of the EMS since its formation, did not join the ERM until 1990. The German mark was the representative currency of the ERM for the 1980s. In the 1980s, dollars, yen, German marks, and British pounds were free to fluctuate in relative value in the marketplace. Many smaller countries pegged their rates to one of the four (now only three, since Britain joined the ERM) major currencies, or to a basket of those currencies.

Figure 11.1 is a plot of the yen/dollar exchange rate from 1972 to 1989. Since the vertical axis measures the value of the dollar in terms of the yen, the yen is said to appreciate (or, equivalently, the dollar is said to depreciate) when the curve goes down; the yen depreciates (or the dollar appreciates) when the curve goes up.

Major yen appreciation (dollar depreciation) occurred in 1978 and in 1985–86; major yen depreciation occurred in 1973–74, 1979–80, and 1981–1985. Two of the three major episodes of yen depreciation, 1973–74 and 1979–80, were due to the two oil crises. Since Japan produces less than 1 percent of the crude oil it consumes, it cannot substitute for oil in the short run. Oil-price increases mean that Japan has to export more goods in order to buy the same amount of oil. For Japan, an oil-price increase acts just like an adverse productivity shock, so the yen has to depreciate. The causes and consequences of the dollar's strength in 1981–1985 will be analyzed below.

The dollar depreciation (yen appreciation) of 1978 was prompted by deterioration in the US trade balance. The dollar depreciated until President Carter announced measures to "defend the dollar" on November 1, 1978. The other episode of sharp yen appreciation (1985–86) will be carefully analyzed below.

The floating-exchange-rate system has survived for more than fifteen years without a major problem. Two major oil crises have caused exchange-rate changes, but they agree with theoretical predictions. However, strong criticisms of floating rates surfaced in the mid 1980s, and they have led to a search for an alternative system.

Figure 11.1
Yen-dollar exchange rate, 1972–1989.

JAPANESE CAPITAL CONTROLS

The Japanese financial markets were practically closed off from the rest of the world before 1974. Importers could not freely obtain foreign currencies; they had to apply for and obtain currency allocations from the government. Those who would travel abroad were subject to restrictions on how much foreign exchange they could obtain. Moreover, the Japanese were not allowed to obtain foreign securities or real estate, and foreigners were not allowed to purchase most Japanese securities or equities. These kinds of restrictions on international movement of financial capital are called *capital controls*. Under a flexible-exchange-rate system, however, there are several reasons why both the private sector and the monetary authority want liberalization (deregulation) of financial markets.

First, exporters, importers, and investors in foreign assets may
want to *hedge* and *speculate* against exchange-rate fluctuations. For
example, suppose that Japanese exporters who hold export contracts
due in three months make a contract now to buy yen (sell dollars) on
the data of the export sales, so that their income in terms of yen will
not be affected by possible exchange-rate fluctuations. In order to
carry out this transaction of foreign exchange in the future, the exporters must be matched with someone—most likely, importers—
who would like to carry out the reverse transaction. Matching these
customers would be rather difficult without an established market.
Once the market is created, speculators who bet on movements in
exchange rates by taking positions will have to be invited in order to
"deepen" the market. Hedging and speculating require investments
in comparable instruments, and restrictions on the purchase or sale
of financial instruments (that is, capital controls) become an obsta-
cle to smooth foreign trade and investment.

Second, under a flexible-exchange-rate regime the Bank of Japan
need not purchase the foreign currencies brought back to Japan as a
result of current-account surpluses. Thus, those companies in the
private sector that accumulate foreign exchange will want to diver-
sify their portfolios into different kinds of assets in foreign de-
nominations. For this reason, pressures to deregulate the holding of
foreign assets were mounting in the mid 1970s.

Capital controls were relaxed in several steps during the 1970s.
The history of deregulation coincides with the roller-coaster path
of the yen/dollar exchange rate. The Japanese monetary authority
clearly had the objective of exchange-rate stabilization, so the restrictions on outflow (inflow) were lifted when the monetary authority desired to prevent rapid yen appreciation (depreciation). There
was a short spell of capital-control tightening between 1977 and
1979. For example, the margin reserve requirement for "free" yen
accounts held by nonresidents was increased to 50 percent in
November 1977 and to 100 percent in March 1978, then reduced to
50 percent in January 1979 and 0 percent in February 1979. Nonresidents were prohibited from purchasing any Japanese securities with
maturities less than five years and one month from March 1978 to
February 1979. This is one of a few cases in which controls were
tightened only to be deregulated shortly thereafter.

Tables 11.1–11.3 summarize the chronology of the major steps
toward integrating the Japanese financial market into world mar-

Table 11.1
Chronology of capital-control deregulations and their motives, 1971–1973.

1971

August 15: Convertibility (to gold) of the dollar suspended.

August 28–December 19: Yen under floating-rate regime.

December 19: Smithsonian rate (308 yen ±2.5%) established.

1972

(Yen appreciation pressure prompted policies of encouraging capital out-flows and discouraging inflows.)

February: Resumption of controls on receipt of advances of export proceeds (amounts above $10,000 required approval).

March: Japanese banks permitted to purchase foreign securities. Foreign investors prohibited from acquiring fiscal bills (FBs).

June: Imposition of a 25% marginal reserve requirement on nonresident free yen accounts. Tightening of controls on receipt of advances of export proceeds (approval required for all transactions above $5,000).

July: Increase in marginal reserve requirement on nonresident free yen accounts. Japanese residents allowed to purchase foreign real estate.

October: Foreign investors' purchases of Japanese securities limited to amount sold by other foreign investors.

1973

February: Yen became "cleanly" floating.

(October: Oil crisis caused yen depreciation, which prompted policy actions to encourage capital inflows.)

November: Relaxation of controls on the receipt of advances of export proceeds from $5,000 to $10,000 as the approval threshold. Abolition of limits (to the amount sold by other foreigners) on the acquisition of Japanese equities by foreigners.

December: Abolition of limits (to amounts sold by other foreigners) on acquisition of Japanese bonds by foreigners.

Adapted from Fukao 1990, with modifications.

Table 11.2
Chronology of capital-control deregulations and their motives, 1974–1978.

1974

(Further yen depreciation prompted policy actions to restrict capital outflow as well as to encourage inflow.)

January: Relaxation of controls on receipt of advances of export proceeds from $10,000 to $100,000 as the approval threshold. Prohibition of resident purchases of short-term foreign currency securities.
Approval required for opening of new foreign currency deposits.

July: Relaxation of controls on the receipt of advances of export proceeds from $100,000 to $500,000 as the approval threshold.

August: Liberalization of acquisition of FBs by foreign investors.

1975

June: "Voluntary restraints" on purchase of foreign securities lifted for all institutions except banks.

1977

(Yen appreciation prompted policy actions to encourage outflows.)

March: Abolition of "voluntary restraints" on purchase of foreign securities by banks.

June: Abolition of controls on acquisition of short-term foreign securities by residents (hitherto *de facto* prohibited). Acquisition of equities and bonds by nonresidents shifted to automatic approval.

November: *De facto* prohibition of nonresident acquisition of FBs, through cessation of public subscription for FBs. Introduction of 50% marginal reserve requirement on nonresident free yen accounts.

1978

(Further yen appreciation prompted more restriction of inflows.)

March: Introduction of controls on acquisition of yen-denominated bonds by foreign investors. (Acquisition of general bonds of less than five years and one month remaining maturity prohibited.) Marginal reserve requirement of 100% reintroduced for nonresident free yen accounts.

Adapted from Fukao 1990, with modifications.

Table 11.3
Chronology of capital-control deregulations and their motives, 1979–1986.

1979

(Rapid yen depreciation prompted to encourage inflows.)

February: Abolition of controls on acquisition of Japanese bonds by foreign investors. Abolition of marginal reserve requirements on nonresident free yen liabilities.

May: Nonresidents permitted to engage in Gensaki market. Abolition of controls on receipt of advances of export proceeds. Permission to introduce short-term impact loans (untied foreign currency borrowings by Japanese companies).

1980

March: Repeal of interest-rate ceilings on free yen accounts held by foreign governments.

December: The new Foreign Exchange and Foreign Trade Control Law enacted. (All capital transactions allowed unless explicitly prohibited)

Complete liberalizations of the foreign currency deposits of residents at foreign exchange banks in Japan; of impact loans; of the acquisition of foreign securities by residents when made through designated securities dealers (except for transactions deemed direct investment which are subject to notification); of the acquisition of domestic securities by nonresidents when made through designated securites dealers (except for transactions deemed direct investment which are subject to notification); of foreign real estate investments by residents. Shift from nonresident free yen accounts to nonresident yen accounts, since the total removal of convertibility restrictions on resident yen accounts eliminated the need to distinguish between "free" and "nonfree" yen.

1984

April: Abolition of the "Real demand principle" in the forward market.

June: Abolition of spot position controls (yen conversion quotas) on foreign-exchange banks. (This gave banks total freedom to borrow in foreign currencies and invest the funds locally in yen.)

July: Liberalization of the acquisition of domestic real estate by nonresidents.

1986

December: Establishment of the Japan Offshore Market (JOM). Offshore transactions between banks and non-residents (deposits, borrowings, and loans) were separated from domestic transactions, so that such transactions were exempted from reserve requirements, interest rate controls, deposit insurance, and withholding tax.

Adapted from Fukao 1990, with modifications.

kets. The enactment of the new Foreign Exchange and Foreign Trade Control Law in December 1980 was particularly important. Before the enactment of this law, any capital movement was prohibited unless explicitly allowed; afterward, capital movements in general were allowed unless specifically prohibited. Allowing foreign investors to participate in the securities and Gensaki markets was a big step toward liberalizing capital inflow, and foreign investment in the Japanese stock market increased substantially in the early 1980s.

Japan's domestic institutional structure and domestic regulations can still be impediments for foreign investors, however. For example, foreign investors may legally purchase stocks of a company in order to take control of its management, but in many cases the interlocking shares described in chapter 4 make such a move practically impossible for many companies. Foreign investors could legally purchase Japanese long-term government bonds; however, as was mentioned in chapter 5, a large block of new issues of long-term bonds are negotiated between the Ministry of Finance and a syndicate of Japanese financial institutions. (In 1984 foreign securities firms were invited to join the syndicate, and a portion of the long-term bonds were auctioned. In 1989 this portion was 40 percent.)

In April 1984 the so-called *real demand principle* was abolished. Previously, a Japanese resident who wanted to carry out a forward contract had to show that the there existed a real demand—for example, export or import transactions, or maturing foreign securities.[2]

After these steps of deregulation, there remain practically no capital controls that prevent Japanese or foreign investors from moving their portfolios into and out of Japanese assets.

COVERED INTEREST PARITY

In a world without capital controls, investors try to find the best investment opportunities in the world. In this environment, the choice of country-specific assets will depend on the size of the investment, the horizon for the investment, and the investors' attitudes toward risk. Since many investors in major developed countries such as the United States, Japan, Great Britain, and Germany are looking for opportunities constantly, most if not all arbitrage opportunities are exploited. That is, if one asset has a relatively

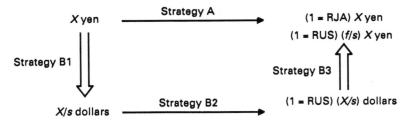

Figure 11.2
Covered interest parity. s: spot yen/dollar exchange rate. f: k-period forward yen/dollar exchange rate. RJA: k- period interest rate on yen-denominated asset. RUS: k-period interest rate on dollar-denominated asset.

attractive yield, many investors want to purchase this asset, so that the yields on the assets with comparable risks must be equalized. One such arbitrage relationship is *covered interest parity.* Investigating covered interest parity between yen-denominated assets and dollar-denominated assets is one way to test econometrically the extent to which the capital market of one country is integrated with the capital markets of the rest of the world.

Suppose a Japanese investor wants to earn returns on an investment of X yen over the next three months. If this investor invests the fund in a yen-denominated asset (say, strategy A), then the fund grows to $(1 + RJA)X$ yen after three months, where RJA is the interest rate on this yen-denominated asset. As an alternative, the investor may invest in a dollar-denominated asset (say, strategy B). In this strategy, the fund of X yen is first converted ino X/s dollars, where s is the spot yen/dollar exchange rate; then that number of dollars is invested in an asset yielding an interest rate of RUS. After three months, the fund grows to $(1 + RUS)X/s$. The investor can make a contract in the forward market to obtain f yen per dollar. All three steps in this strategy are carried out simultaneously. Hence, the fund will grow to $(1 + RUS)Xf/s$ yen in three months. Strategy A and strategy B are illustrated in figure 11.2.

Note that the yen-denominated asset, which yields the interest payment of RJA, and the dollar-denominated asset, which yields the interest payment of RUS, are assumed to be equivalent in default risk. The Eurodollar deposit rate and the Euroyen deposit rate are an excellent pair from this point of view, but they would not make a good test of the capital controls of a country, since both rates are quoted "offshore" (outside the domestic capital market and regulations). The CD (certificate of deposit) rate in the United States and the CD rate in Japan are comparable in our sense. If a (risk-free) US treasury-bill (TB) rate is used as RUS, the comparable (risk-free) TB rate of Japan should be used for RJA; however, the TB market in Japan has not yet fully developed.[3]

Any difference between strategy A and strategy B would make arbitrage profitable without exchange-rate risk. Hence, (1 + RJA) and (1 + RUS)f/s must be equal. This equality is called covered interest parity. Deviations from parity,[4] beyond nominal transaction costs, would signal the existence of capital controls.[5] Hence, a violation of covered interest parity implies that a country's capital market is not integrated into the world capital market. In this sense, covered interest parity is a test of capital controls, or a test of capital-market integration. The parity should hold for any maturity of assets and the corresponding forward exchange—for example, for one week, for one month, and for three months. Forward-market contracts are typically not available for horizons longer than one year. Hence, many studies conduct tests in the one-month horizon, the three-month horizon, or the six-month horizon.

As was described in the preceding section, Japan began dismantling its capital controls in the 1970s and completed the job in December 1980. It is interesting to test the covered-interest-parity relationship in order to consider the effectiveness of these deregulation steps. One problem in implementing the test in Japan is that domestic interest rates were typically controlled (recall chapter 5). The TB rate was not available[6] until the mid 1980s, certificates of deposit were not issued until May 1979, and other bank deposit rates were under strict regulation. As was mentioned in chapter 5, the exception to these controls in the 1970s was the Gensaki (repurchase agreement) rate. In what follows, the 3-month Gensaki rate is used for RJA and the 3-month Eurodollar deposit rate is used for RUS. Other studies have compared the 3-month Eurodollar deposit rate and the US domestic CD rate, and found that differences between them are within the bounds of transactions costs.

Figure 11.3 is a plot of the deviations from covered interest parity from 1972 through 1984. The amplitude of fluctuations declined through the 1970s. Since the new law was implemented, in December 1980, covered interest parity has held without exception.

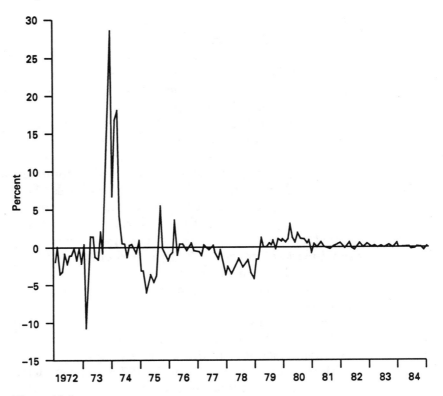

Figure 11.3
Deviations from covered interest parity.

Wild fluctuations in the measure of deviation from 1972 to 1974 signal the existence of capital controls. For example, in December 1973 the deviation was as high as 28.5 percent (in terms of annualized percentage-point differential). In that month, the Gensaki interest rate was 13.85 percent and the Eurodollar rate was 10.13 percent, while the spot exchange rate was 280 yen/dollar and the forward rate was 302 yen/dollar. This is in contrast to the case in February 1973, when the deviation from parity was below −10 percent. These large deviations would have invited large capital inflows and outflows (and would have been arbitraged away) if capital controls had not been present. Put differently, the determination of the Japanese interest rates was quite independent of the forward premium (the difference between the log spot and forward-exchange rates) and the foreign interest rate. This was possible because Japan's capital markets were isolated from the rest of the world. Apparent unexploited gains from arbitrage in the early 1970s were due to strong capital controls, such as restrictions on the acquisition of foreign securities by Japanese residents, restrictions on foreign investors' participation in the Gensaki market, and sales of forward contracts only in the case of "real demand."

Between 1975 and February 1979, deviations from parity were in a direction such that there existed apparent arbitrage gains toward yen-denominated assets. That was particularly true at the beginning of 1975 and in 1978. Capital controls on inflow were binding in that they combined with strong demand for yen to generate rapid appreciation of the yen until the end of October 1978. As was explained above, purchases of Gensaki by nonresidents were not allowed until May 1979, and other restrictions on foreign borrowing by Japanese citizens were lifted in December 1980. It can be seen from figure 11.3 that covered interest parity between Gensaki and dollar-denominated assets held after these changes. (See Ito 1986 for a detailed examination of covered interest parity, explicitly taking into account the bid-ask spread—a major transaction cost.)

In sum, from the evidence on covered interest parity, the Japanese short-term capital market has been integrated into the world capital market since 1980.

In the covered-interest-parity relationship explained above, no exchange-rate risk is involved in arbitraging return differences between the domestic and foreign securities. Supposed that foreign securities are not "covered"—that is, that forward transactions are not contracted when foreign securities are purchased. In other words, the third step of strategy B is carried out not in the forward market, but in the spot market at the time the securities mature. In this case the relationship involves exchange-rate risk. If the currency of the investor appreciates during the investment period, then strategy A *ex post* turns out to be a better strategy; if the currency depreciates during the investment period, then strategy B *ex post* turns out to be a better strategy. Of course, the exchange rate in the future is not known at the time of investment. Suppose that the investor is "risk-neutral."[7] If the investor expects that the future exchange rate (of the domestic currency) will appreciate more than the forward rate, however, the investor will not cover his position; if the investor expects that the future exchange rate will depreciate more than the forward rate, the investor will take the cover. Therefore, in the efficient market, the above-mentioned arbitrage can be freely conducted, with many risk-neutral investors, and the forward rate becomes equal to the investors' expected future exchange rate.

Thus, when investors are risk-neutral and the forward market is efficient, the deviation from uncovered interest parity, defined as

$$\text{UDEV} \equiv (1 + \text{RUS})s^e/s - (1 + \text{RJA}),$$

where s^e is the expected future spot rate, should be zero according to the hypothesis of uncovered interest parity. Since covered interest parity is a sheer arbitrage relationship and does not presume any risk neutrality, it is more likely to hold. By direct verification (see above), the parity has indeed appeared to hold between the yen, the dollar, and the appropriate interest rates of three-month securities since 1980. Note that, given covered interest parity, uncovered interest parity implies that the forward rate equals the expected rate: $f_{t,k} = s^e_{t,k}$.

However, testing hypotheses of this type is usually difficult, since the expectation variable, $s^e_{t,k}$, is not generally observable.[8] One assumption which is commonly adopted or tested is that the expectation of the exchange rate is formed "rationally"—that is, that investors use all historical data and other information in order to form the most accurate possible expectations.

Rational expectation of the future exchange rate implies that $s^e_{t,k} = s_{t+k} + e_{t+k}$, where e_{t+k} is a random variable with zero expected value and without serial correlation. We have the following hypothesis for an unbiased forward rate: If risk-neutral investors form rational expectations in the efficient market, then the relationship $f_{t,k} = s_{t+k} + e_{t+k}$ holds.

This hypothesis, which implies that the forward rate is an unbiased predictor of the future spot exchange rate, can be tested easily. Many papers have investigated this relationship for various foreign-exchange rates over different sample periods. Some papers reject the hypothesis; some do not.[9] The problem with this hypothesis is that, since three controversial assumptions are needed to derive the relationship, it is not clear what is actually tested. When a researcher finds rejection, it is not immediately obvious whether rational expectations are rejected, risk neutrality is rejected, the efficient-market hypothesis is rejected, or all of the above are rejected. In the early literature, however, the test is usually called the "test of uncovered interest parity and risk-neutrality," assuming *a priori* rational expectations and the existence of efficient markets.

A YEN FOR YEN?

Misalignment in the First Half of the 1980s

In 1980, the United States' exports and imports were balanced; incidentally, Japan also had a balanced current account. The average exchange rate for the year was about 227 yen per dollar. If a balanced current account is the criterion for the equilibrium yen/dollar exchange rate, it was somewhere between 220 and 230. (Admittedly, this is a very rough calculation. On the other hand, even a sophisticated model would produce a similar result for 1980.) From the productivity and inflation differentials between the two countries, many economists predicted that the yen would appreciate against the dollar through the first half of the 1980s. Moreover, the interest rate was much higher in the United States, so the forward rate for yen had a premium over the spot rate. Put differently, the forward rate "predicted" the coming yen appreciation. However, just the opposite happened. The yen *depreciated* in 1982, falling from 220 in January to 270 in October. After rebounding and staying in the 230s and 240s from 1983 to mid 1984, the yen depreciated again, from 230 in mid 1984 to 263 in February 1985.

The first half of the 1980s was the period of the "dazzling dollar," which appreciated against all odds. After the fact, many economists explained the overvaluation of the dollar as follows: At the beginning of the 1980s, the Federal Reserve Board adopted a tight monetary policy in order to kill the inflation inherited from the 1970s. The prime rate topped 20 percent in 1980 and remained in the high teens until the summer of 1982. On the fiscal side, tax cuts and an increase in military expenditures caused large fiscal deficits.[10] The federal deficit soared from $64 billion in 1981 to $176 billion two years later. The combination of tight monetary and loose fiscal policy caused the high interest rate, as any reasonable theory would predict. The high interest rate, in turn, created the overvalued dollar by attracting foreign capital.

Many believed that the overvaluation of the dollar (caused mainly by capital flows) was detrimental to the competitiveness of US goods. In fact, the US current account went from a $6 billion surplus in 1981 to a $107 billion deficit in 1984. In this sense, the dollar was "misaligned."

The Reagan administration tended to deny any linkage between fiscal deficits and high interest rates, or between high interest rates and an overvalued dollar. The administration interpreted the strong dollar as the reflection of a strong US economy and the trust of world investors:

Increases in the real value of the dollar were initially associated with the actual and perceived shift to a tighter monetary policy in the United States and the attendant effects of this policy shift on nominal and real interest rates. As the recovery began in late 1982, however, the persistence of high US real interest rates and a strong dollar were most likely due primarily to rapid real growth in the United States relative to that in the rest of the world. The robust expansion, low inflation, and business tax cuts all improved the after-tax real return to new business investment and raised the return on dollar-denominated assets in general, making the United States more attractive to investors worldwide. The increased demand for dollar-denominated assets bid up the real foreign exchange value of the dollar. (Council of Economic Advisors, Economic Report of the President, February 1986, p. 52)

Many economists point out, however, that the fiscal deficits continued to be a major factor even after 1982. A simple calculation shows that the fiscal deficits, combined with declining domestic saving in the private sector, necessarily implied capital imports— that is, current-account deficits.

Another argument that the US administration put forward was that regulations and other structures in Japanese financial markets prevented capital from flowing into Japan. The Japanese regulations, which made the Tokyo market closed to the rest of the world, were responsible for the unattractive, undervalued yen. In order to correct the overvaluation of the dollar, the US administration argued that yen-denominated assets ought to be more attractive. In 1983, following this logic, the Reagan administration called for the creation of a committee to discuss Japanese financial markets, with the intention that deregulation would bolster the demand for yen-denominated assets and cause appreciation of the yen. This line of argument led to a dialogue between the United States and Japan regarding deregulation of the Japanese financial markets, to which we now turn.

The Yen/Dollar Working Group and Deregulation

The so-called yen/dollar working group (officially the Joint Japan-US Ad Hoc Group on Yen/Dollar Exchange Rate, Financial and Capital Market Issues), initially proposed in the summer of 1983, was officially set up during President Reagan's visit to Japan in November. The group, headed by Vice Minister of Finance Tomomitsu Ōba and Under Secretary of the Treasury Beryl W. Sprinkel, met six times between February and May of 1984 and submitted a report to Finance Minister Noboru Takeshita and Treasury Secretary Donald Regan.

The report suggested major steps toward deregulation, including gradual deregulation of deposit interest rates and the introduction of money-market certificates and large time deposits. Restrictions on banks' issues of CDs were relaxed, as well. But the link between deregulation of Japanese capital markets and the prospect of any yen appreciation was weak and unclear. Some of the deregulatory steps were thought to have eased the Japanese market's access to foreign capital; some of the other measures only encouraged the Japanese institutions to invest abroad. For example, abolishing all restrictions on the conversion of foreign-currency funds into yen (June 1984) eased capital inflow into Japan at a time when the funds demanded by investors in Japan exceeded the domestically available funds. Giving foreign securities houses permission to deal in Japanese government bonds made it easier for foreign investors to include the Japanese government bonds in their portfolios, and also gave foreign firms in Japan lucrative business opportunities. Allowing Euroyen bonds to be issued to foreign firms was considered a way to increase the demand for the yen as a medium of exchange or as a part of asset portfolios. The impact of these steps on the demand for yen as a medium of exchange and a portfolio investment, however, was quantitatively rather limited. Moreover, abolishing the "real demand principle" for the forward market (April 1984) brought down transaction costs for Japanese and foreign investors in general and was neutral for the value of yen. (See Frankel 1984 for an excellent survey of the negotiations and economic consequences of the yen-dollar working group.)

Table 11.4
Current accounts in the 1980s.

	Japan		United States	
	CA ($ million)	CA/(Nominal GNP) (percentage)	CA ($ million)	CA/(Nominal GNP) (percentage)
1980	−10,738	−1.01	1,887	0.07
1981	5,118	0.44	6,214	0.20
1982	6,977	0.22	−9,362	−0.30
1983	20,942	1.77	−47,057	−1.38
1984	35,148	2.80	−106,786	−2.83
1985	49,169	3.69	−115,103	−2.86
1986	85,845	4.37	−138,828	−3.27
1987	87,015	3.64	−153,964	−3.40
1988	79,631	2.78	−126,548	−2.60

Source: Bank of Japan, Comparative Economic and Financial Statistics, various years.

Japan's Capital Exports

As the dollar appreciated against the yen, the surpluses in the Japanese current account grew rapidly while the deficits in the US current account mushroomed. Table 11.4 shows that the current-account imbalance grew rapidly from 1983 to 1987. The trend turned around only after the massive changes in exchange rates that followed the Plaza Agreement (explained below).

The Japanese current-account surpluses mean that Japan receives more dollars than it pays out. In a casual sense, the surpluses could be spent either to accumulate foreign reserves or to invest abroad. The latter is called a *capital outflow* (or *capital export*). As table 11.5 shows, Japan's long-term capital outflows grew as its current-account surpluses grew in the 1980s. In more recent years, however, the long-term capital outflows have become 50 percent larger than the current-account surpluses. The difference is financed by borrowing short-term capital. Japanese investors are acting like banks, in that they are willing to incur short-term liabilities in order to have long-term assets.

Table 11.5
Japan's international balance of payments ($ million).

	Current account	Capital accounts		Change in foreign reserve
		Long-term (1)	Short-term (2)	
1973	−136	−9,750	2,407	−6,119
1974	−4,693	−3,881	1,778	1,272
1975	−682	−272	−1,138	−703
1976	3,680	−984	111	3,789
1977	10,918	−3,184	−648	6,244
1978	16,534	−12,389	1,538	10,171
1979	−8,754	−12,976	2,735	−12,692
1980	−10,746	2,324	3,141	4,905
1981	4,770	−9,672	2,265	3,171
1982	6,850	−14,969	−1,579	−5,141
1983	20,799	−17,700	23	1,234
1984	35,003	−49,651	−4,295	1,817
1985	49,169	−64,542	−936	197
1986	85,845	−131,461	−1,609	15,729
1987	87,015	−136,532	23,865	39,240
1988	79,631	−130,930	19,521	16,183
1989	57,157	−89,246	20,811	−12,767

Put differently, Japanese investors wanted to purchase foreign assets (denominated in dollars and other currencies) as a part of their long-run diversification strategy, but they were afraid of the possibility that the yen might appreciate further. Therefore, borrowing short-term dollars to finance their long-term investments was a solution. In fact, the increased volatility in the yen/dollar rate since September 1985 has made Japanese investors hedge their dollar-denominated assets.

Table 11.6 shows the components of long-term capital outflows. First, the long-term capital accounts are divided into Japanese capital and foreign capital. Then, each capital account has different types of capital: bonds, equities (stocks), and direct investment. Most of the increase in Japanese capital outflows from 1982 to 1986 took the form of bond investment, particularly in US treasury bonds. In the

Table 11.6
Japan's long-term capital account.

Japanese capital

	Direct investment	Export credit/loan	Securities		Other	Total (3)
			Stock	Bonds[a]		
1979	2,898	6,814	575	5,290	717	16,294
1980	2,385	3,270	−213	3,966	1,409	10,817
1981	4,894	7,814	240	8,537	1,324	22,809
1982	4,540	11,141	151	9,592	1,994	27,418
1983	3,612	11,014	661	15,381	1,809	32,459
1984	5,965	16,859	51	30,744	3,156	56,774
1985	6,452	13,244	995	58,778	2,346	81,815
1986	14,480	11,117	7,048	94,929	4,521	132,095
1987	19,519	16,725	16,874	70,883	8,829	132,830
1988	34,210	22,150	2,993	83,956	6,574	149,883
1989	44,130	26,497	17,887	95,291	8,313	192,118

Foreign capital

	Direct investment	Export credit/loan	Securities		Other	Total (4)	Total net[b] (3)−(4)
			Stock	Bonds[a]			
1979	239	−202	329	3,953	−1,001	3,318	12,976
1980	278	−247	6,546	6,567	−3	13,141	−2,324
1981	189	−201	5,916	7,304	−71	13,137	9,672
1982	439	−196	2,549	9,311	337	12,449	14,969
1983	416	−29	6,126	8,633	224	14,759	17,700
1984	−10	−74	−3,610	10,804	14	7,124	49,651
1985	642	−46	−673	17,414	−64	17,273	64,542
1986	226	−74	−15,758	16,303	−63	634	131,461
1987	1,165	−120	−42,835	36,754	1,334	−3,702	136,571
1988	−485	−100	6,810	13,488	−760	18,953	130,930
1989	−1,054	17,804	6,998	78,146	978	102,872	89,246

a. Including foreign bonds.
b. This value is the negative of long-term capital flow (column (1) of table 11.5).

mid 1980s, Japanese investors bought 30–50 percent of new treasury bond issues. But from 1986 to 1987, investment in equities (stocks) increased more than any other component, and in 1988 it was direct investment that increased most. This shows that Japanese investors started diversifying by purchasing different types of foreign assets.

It is quite remarkable that foreign capital was withdrawn from the Japanese market in the mid 1980s. In particular, there was a spectacular selloff of Japanese equities in 1987. In the same year, Japanese investors were big buyers in the New York stock market. In part, this asymmetric investment behavior reflects exchange-rate movements and volatility; in part, it reflects opposing opinions about the strength of the Tokyo stock market. Foreign investors were afraid that stock prices, measured in terms of their price-earning ratios (PER), were too high in the Tokyo market, while Japanese investors were quite confident in the Tokyo stock market.

In sum, a yen for yen never materialized during the 1980s. Instead, Japan's capital exports, largely the counterpart of current-account surpluses, became prominent. A rapid rise in Japan's capital exports became a source of friction. The 1989 purchases of Columbia Pictures by Sony and of Rockefeller Center by Mitsubishi Real Estate became highly publicized and controversial in the United States. Some critics argued that the "fire sale" of US assets is detrimental to US national interests. On the other hand, when signs of hesitation appeared in Japan's capital exports, the US stock and bond markets became jittery. The capital markets of the United States and Japan are now closely interdependent, and any policy should take this fact into account.

EXCHANGE-RATE DYNAMICS AND NEWS

From the experience of the floating-exchange-rate regime, the following stylized facts about exchange-rate dynamics have emerged[11]:

• Exchange-rate changes in the short run (say, up to one month) cannot be predicted. In other words, the exchange rate is, in the short run, a random walk.

• The volatility of the exchange rate changes over time. When it moves, it moves a lot; at other times it stays within a narrow band. Put differently, periods of turmoil alternate with periods of tranquility. This is evident in figure 11.1. The large changes usually occur in "steps," with a bumpy slope, and a sharp rise is sometimes followed by a sharp decline.

- Covered interest parity holds in the absence of capital controls.

- Uncovered interest parity may not hold. Even if one finds a period over which it indeed holds, the deviation of the forward rate from the realized spot rate is large in magnitude. In that sense, the forward rate is a poor predictor of the future spot rate.

In light of the stylized facts summarized above, a majority of researchers now believe that foreign exchange may be regarded as a portfolio asset of institutional investors, and that foreign-exchange rates may be treated as asset prices. This view is based on the fact that there are many large investors and speculators who manage funds constantly in the foreign-exchange markets as well as in the securities markets. Large money-center banks, securities houses, insurance companies, and pension funds manage a portion of their assets internationally. For all practical purposes, they bet on changes in exchange rates as well as on the interest-rate differentials between different countries. This portfolio behavior causes capital flows and, in turn, exchange-rate changes.

If all pieces of information are taken into account at every second in determining the exchange rate, then exchange-rate movements cannot be predicted (at least in the short run). Thus, the first stylized fact is implied. It is a characteristic of an asset market that prices move instantly when relevant information becomes common knowledge in the market. Put differently, the asset price, or the exchange rate in this case, is determined with all available information taken into account. Any price movement reflects the arrival of new information.

In the long run, exchange rates are determined by "fundamentals," such as the money supplies, GNPs, and productivities of different countries. Short-run movements, however, are dominated by the arrival of new information regarding the fundamentals. Hence, the exchange rate moves not when the money supply actually changes but at the exact moment when the market comes to expect that the money supply will move in the near future. Such a belief may be formed, for example, when the GNP announcement for the last quarter was disappointing (the central bank may then increase the money supply in order to prevent a recession), or when the inflation rate last month was announced to be much higher than the then-believed rate (the central bank may then tighten the market in order to prevent inflation).

The market is called efficient if information spreads among the participants quickly and if prices move to reflect information immediately after the arrival of the information. (There are at least three versions regarding types of information.) Many consider the exchange-rate market to be an efficient market. There are two ways to investigate the relationship between exchange-rate changes and the arrival of news. First, by examining the behavior of the exchange rate around the time of the announcement of important economic news, such as money-supply or price-level announcements, we may infer the sensitivity of the exchange rate to new information. Second, by picking out the days on which the magnitude of the exchange-rate movement was large we may infer the arrival of news behind such a large change. In the former method, specific economic news which theory suggests is relevant to the exchange rate will be selected first. The researcher must know *a priori* the determinants of exchange rates. In the latter method, determinants are inferred from analysis instead of being assumed.

The foreign-exchange market is open virtually 24 hours a day from Money to Friday somewhere in the world, and the Bahrain market is open on Sunday. As news relevant to foreign exchange hits the world, the exchange rate moves in a market that happens to

---

Time Differences

Japanese Standard Time, observed in all of Japan, is 9 hours ahead of Greenwich Mean Time (GMT). In the United States, Eastern Standard Time is 5 hours behind GMT. Therefore, when it is 7 P.M. in New York in the winter (or 8 P.M. in the summer), it is 9 A.M. on the next day in Tokyo; 9 A.M. in New York in the winter is 11 P.M. on the same day in Tokyo. (Japan does not observe daylight saving time now, although it did from 1948 to 1952.)

Thus, the Tokyo financial markets (the foreign-exchange and stock markets, for example) are closed when the New York financial markets are open, and vice versa. For this reason, which of the two markets will be the first to respond to a given political or economic event depends on the timing. One reason financial institutions open foreign offices and branches is to be ready to move swiftly in the market whenever news breaks anywhere in the world.

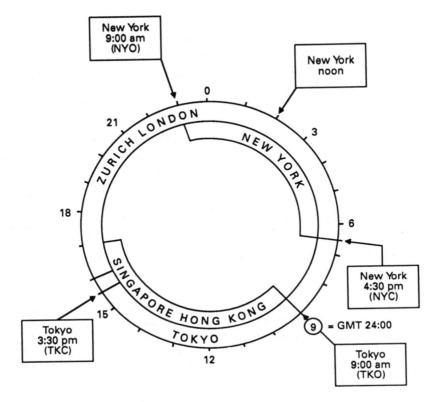

Figure 11.4
Hours of major markets relative to Tokyo time, depicted on 24-hour clock.
(When daylight saving time is in effect in New York, the hours of the New
York market should be shifted counterclockwise by one hour.)

be open. It is usually the case, however, that relevant economic and
political news of a certain country is revealed during the market
hours of that country. Hence, time differences make it possible to
identify the origin of news. Figure 11.4 illustrates how the trading
hours of various markets overlap.[12]

In any 24 hours on a weekday, there are only $2\frac{1}{2}$ hours ($3\frac{1}{2}$ when
the US is on daylight saving time) between the closing of the New
York market and the opening of the Tokyo market in which there
are no major currency markets open in the world. Why is this important? According to the efficient-market hypothesis, all responses
to the arrival of information take place instantaneously. When the
time interval is short, it may better isolate the change of the ex-

change rate due to the information. For example, if a large jump in the exchange rate was observed in the Tokyo market one day, but not in the New York market, then it is reasonable to infer that some important new information about Japan's economy or policy was revealed in the Tokyo market.

The association of news with changes in the exchange rate is illustrated in figure 11.5. For the month of March 1985, the arrivals of news are pointed to in the time horizon which plots the exchange-rate changes in Tokyo and New York. Note that on the time horizon changes in the exchange rate in the two markets do not overlap. As the efficient-market hypothesis indicates, the opening exchange rate of the Tokyo market is approximately the previous day's closing rate of the New York market, which closed 2–3 hours earlier, rather than the previous day's closing rate of the Tokyo market.

Another way to illustrate how news is associated with large exchange-rate changes is to pick particular days and market hours when large jumps occurred. Table 11.7 describes the large jumps that occurred from 1980 to March of 1985. Most of these jumps are explained by news. However, there are some exceptions. These exceptions, if they are too numerous, pose a serious challenge to the efficient-market hypothesis (at least to the strongest version of the hypothesis). The notion that the exchange and stock markets are "too volatile" is based on the observation that some changes are caused by sheer speculation.

Various models of exchange-rate determination identify as the most important regularly announced economic variables the money supply, the price level, and industrial production. For example, two scenarios are possible when last month's money supply is revealed to be greater than expected. In one scenario, in which the central bank is believed to follow a monetarist policy, the market participants expect that the central bank will tighten the money market (that is, raise the real interest rate) in the near future, in order to offset the effect of a greater-than-expected money supply. In the other scenario, in which the central bank is not following a monetarist prescription, the market interprets the greater-than-expected money supply as a sign of future inflation. Inflationary fears will raise the nominal interest rate, given the level of the real interest rate. Both scenarios predict a higher nominal interest rate in reaction to the announcement of a greater-than-expected level of the money supply. This has been confirmed by studies (Roley and Walsh

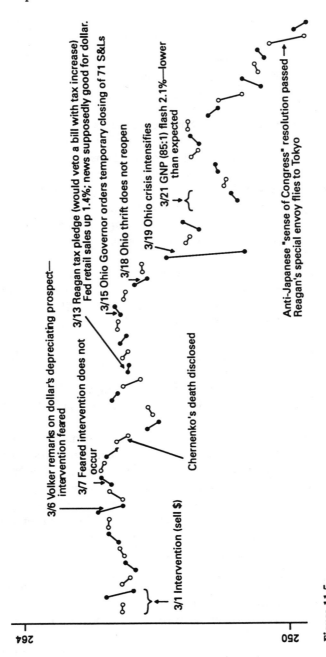

Figure 11.5
Association of news events and yen/dollar rate, March 1985. o———o: opening and closing of New York market. ★———★: opening and closing of Tokyo market.

Table 11.7
Large[a] exchange-rate changes, April 1980–March 1985.

	Market	Change (Yen/$)	Explanations given in newspaper
1980			
4/1	Tokyo	+3.6	Feeling of too-strong yen compared with European currencies.
4/9	Europe	−4.6	Sharp decline in dollar due to the anticipation of peak of US interest rate.
4/10	New York	−3.8	Anticipation of interest-rate peak in US; Bundesbank rumored to tighten monetary policy.
4/11	Tokyo	+3.5	(no explanation)
4/16	New York	−3.8	Chase Manhattan lowers prime rate.
4/23	New York	−3.9	Chase Manhattan lowers prime rate again.
5/6	Tokyo	−3.2	Decline in interest rates in US.
5/12	Europe	−3.7	(no explanation)
5/16	Europe	+4.0	Vote of no confidence in Ohira cabinet passed in Diet.
5/28	Tokyo	+3.1	Eurodollar interest rate bottoms; US trade deficit shrinks.
12/30	Europe	−3.3	Prime rate declines in US.
1981			
3/2	New York	−3.05	Reagan's "tight budget" address.
3/2	Pacific	+3.35	(profit-taking?)
8/4	Tokyo	−4.3	Reaction to strengthening of dollar in recent days due to expectations of continued high US interest rates; intervention by the Bank of Japan.
8/4	Europe	+3.2	(profit-taking?)
8/7	New York	−3.2	(no explanation)
8/17	New York	−3.15	Unexpected increase in US money supply; uncertainty about future of US interest rate.
12/11	Pacific	+3.3	Bank of Japan lowers official discount rate.

a. I.e., more than 3 yen in one market session.

Table 11.7
(continued)

	Market	Change (Yen/$)	Explanations given in newspaper
1982			
7/16	New York	−3.2	US interest rates declined further; M1 announcement lower than expected.
8/18	New York	+3.25	Reaction (profit-taking) to yen appreciation in the Tokyo market (+2.7) and Europe market (+2.6). (?) Increased likelihood of Mexican default.
8/27	Europe	+4.9	Cross-arbitrage with strengthening mark.
10/7	New York	−4.4	Federal Reserve announces relaxation of monetary policy. The monetary regime changes.
11/16	Europe	−4.25	The OPEC countries invest in yen.
1983			
1/11	New York	+4.0	The "Chicago speculators" sell yen.
1/24	Tokyo	+3.0	Expectations about further easing of US monetary policy not materializing. (?)
1983			
1/26	Tokyo	−3.0	OPEC meeting produced no result.
2/8	New York	+3.05	(no explanation)
2/22	New York	+3.3	Nigeria decreases its oil price more than expected. (?)
1984			
3/2	New York	−4.5	(no explanation)
1985			
2/18	Europe	+5.15	(no explanation)
3/19	New York	−4.55	Ohio banking crisis
3/19	Pacific	+3.30	(profit-taking?)

1985; Urich and Wachtel 1981). Although the two possible scenarios yield the same answer for the domestic money market, they have different implications for the exchange rate. If the real interest rate rises, then capital inflows will cause appreciation of the currency; if inflation becomes likely, the currency will depreciate.

Engel and Frankel (1984) examined the effect of money-supply announcements on exchange-rate changes, measured as the difference between the closing rate on the announcement day in New York and the closing rate on the previous day in New York. They showed that the dollar tended to appreciate when the money supply in the United States was announced to have been higher than expected. This is consistent with the observation that the market considered US monetary policy from 1979 to 1982 to be close to what a monetarist would prescribe.

Ito and Roley (1987) showed that the sensitivity of the yen/dollar rate to money announcements in the United States disappeared after 1984, and that Japanese money announcements never had any effect on the yen/dollar exchange rate. In their study, responses to money announcements were measured in the respective markets; that is, changes (from noon to closing) in the New York market were tested against US money announcements, and changes in the Tokyo market (from opening to closing) against Japanese money announcements. The latter evidence would be puzzling if the Bank of Japan followed monetarism, as some monetarists believe. This evidence supports the view, explained in chapter 5, that the Bank of Japan did not follow a monetarist policy.

NEWS ANALYSIS: ONE YEAR AFTER THE PLAZA AGREEMENT

On Sunday, September 22, 1985, ministers of the Group of Five (G5)—the United States, Japan, Germany, the United Kingdom, and France—gathered at the Plaza Hotel in New York to devise a plan to push down the value of the US dollar. The announcement by the G5 ministers that they regarded the dollar as overvalued and that they would take measures to correct the overvaluation created strong selling pressure on the dollar as soon as the market opened on September 23. The closing rate in New York on September 23 was about 8 yen/dollar lower than the closing rate on the preceding Friday. This was the beginning of the end of the dollar's overvaluation. The yen appreciated from 240 yen/dollar just before the G5 meeting

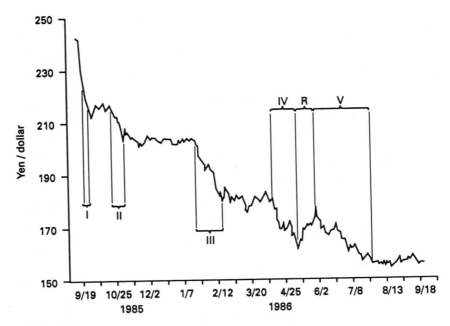

Figure 11.6
The yen/dollar rate at TKC (closing time of Tokyo market) in the period after the Plaza Agreement.

to 150 yen/dollar nine months later. This 60 percent change in the value of the yen in nine months was the largest in magnitude in the yen's history. The experience of these nine months deserves close scrutiny.[13]

Figure 11.6 shows how the yen's appreciation progressed over the nine months. It clearly shows that the appreciation occurred in several waves. In one wave there was an appreciation of 10 yen/dollar or more in as short a period as one week, although a wave sometimes lasted one month. Between waves, the yen stayed relatively stable.

During the week that followed the G5 announcement, the yen appreciated more than 15 yen/dollar. This was the first wave. The second wave occurred in late October, when an appreciation of another 10 yen/dollar occurred in two weeks. In the third wave, from late January to mid-February, there was an appreciation of more than 20 yen/dollar. The last wave—which was slow, taking the months of June and July—carried the yen to 150 per dollar.

Taking advantage of time differences, we can decompose the daily change in exchange rates (over 24 hours) into the change in the Tokyo market (TK_t = Tokyo closing − New York closing of the preceding day), the change in the European market (EU_t = New York opening − Tokyo closing), and the change in the New York market (NY_t = New York closing − New York opening). With the notion introduced in figure 11.4, the decomposed, nonoverlapping changes are defined as follows[14]:

$$TK_t \equiv TKC_t - NYC_{t-1},$$

$$EU_t \equiv NYO_t - TKC_t,$$

$$NY_t \equiv NYC_t - NYO_t.$$

Then, for a specified period (a week or a month), we can calculate the sum of changes in each market. For example, the accumulated change in the Tokyo market from the first day to the tenth day is $TK_1 + TK_2 + \cdots + TK_{10}$. Table 11.8 summarizes the accumulated changes in the three markets for subperiods (waves) of the year following the Plaza Agreement.

The weekend of the Plaza Agreement is very illustrative of how the exchange rate responds to "news." The Group of Five meeting at the Plaza Hotel was arranged hastily. By the closing time of the New York market on Friday, September 20, it was known that the meeting had been called; however, the market did not anticipate that the meeting would produce any significant policy changes. The yen/dollar rate stood at 239 at the closing of the New York market on that Friday, little changed from the day before. When the first major market opened after the announcement—New Zealand's Wellington market—on Monday, September 23, the yen instantly appreciated by 5 yen/dollar to 234. (The Tokyo market was closed because of a bank holiday on that Monday.) The London market closed at 232 yen/dollar, and yen appreciation continued in the New York market. By the time the New York market closed that day, the yen had appreciated to 230/dollar. The yen/dollar rate did not change in the Tokyo market on the following Tuesday although the Bank of Japan reportedly sold 1.3 billion dollars, which amounted to one-third of the total trading volume of the Tokyo market that day. Many investors bought the dollars the Bank of Japan was selling, mistakenly thinking that the dollar would rebound soon. Hence, this evidence suggests that the dollar essentially depreciated on the basis of the

Table 11.8
Decomposition of yen/dollar changes.

Dates	Total change[a]	Accumulated yen changes in market		
		Tokyo[b]	Europe	New York
9/20–9/23	−7.75	(Tokyo closed)		−7.75
9/23–9/30	−14.95	−0.85	−1.425	−12.675
10/1–10/24	0.12	4.225	−1.525	−2.005
10/25–11/7	−10.745	−7.70	−1.80	0.055
11/8–12/17	−3.675	−0.12	−0.305	−4.30
12/18–1/23	−0.30	−0.41	−0.78	−0.825
1/24–2/19	−21.10	−7.775	−6.84	−7.415
2/20–4/15	−2.40	0.64	−4.125	1.21
4/16–5/12	−17.45	−6.91	−1.385	−6.095
5/13–6/2	11.70	5.50	2.92	5.90
6/3–7/31	−21.25	−6.78	−5.665	−7.155
8/1–9/26	0.985	2.135	−5.85	3.28

a. Total change is defined as the change from the NY closing of the last day of the preceding regime to the last day of the current regime with two exceptions: The first row is the change from the NY closing on September 20, Friday, to the NY opening of September 23, Monday. Note that the Tokyo market was closed on September 23, due to a banking holiday. The total change in the second row is defined as the change from the opening of the NY market on September 23 to the NY close of September 30.

b. The daily change in the Tokyo market is defined as the yen/dollar change from the NY close of the preceding business day to the Tokyo close of the day. The daily change in the European market is defined as the yen/dollar change from the Tokyo close to the NY opening of the day. The daily change in NY market is defined as the yen/dollar change from the NY opening to the NY close of the day. The accumulated changes within specified dates are the sum of the daily changes in the respective dates. Because of country-specific banking holidays, the four market changes do not add up to the total change of the dates.

announcement that policy makers had decided to coordinate in driving down the dollar.

The First Wave: One Week After the Plaza Agreement

The statistics on the first wave in table 11.6 show that 85 percent (12.675/14.95) of the yen's appreciation in the week after the Plaza Agreement took place in the New York market. This indicates that US policy changes were the largest factor in changing market participants' expectations. Two other pieces of evidence are relevant to the question of what caused the sharp yen appreciation (dollar depreciation). First, if we examine the movements of other currencies, we find that the correlation of the changes in the yen/dollar rate with those of the pound/dollar or the mark/dollar rate in the New York market was quite high during the week after the Plaza Agreement. This suggests that the dollar was the major source of exchange-rate disturbances, and that the rest of the currencies moved together against the dollar. Second, interest-rate differentials were not a factor, because the interest-rate differential between Japan and the United States stayed about the same during the week.

This evidence is consistent with the view that one of the most important results of the G5 meeting was the change in US policy from benign neglect to international coordination. During the Regan-Sprinkel regime, the Treasury Department took the position that the dollar was strong because of the strong US economy. They denied that there existed a link between US fiscal deficits and high interest rates, or a link between high US interest rates and the strong dollar. Under the Baker regime, which started in the spring of 1985, the need for greater international coordination was recognized. This was reflected in the Plaza Agreement. It was a surprise (news) to the market that the Federal Reserve intervened in cooperation with other central banks, although the amount of its intervention was less than that of the Bank of Japan in the week after the Plaza Agreement. The New York market must have become convinced day by day of the change in US policy.

The Second Wave: The Bank of Japan's Role in October 1985

The exchange rate hovered around 215 yen/dollar for the first three weeks of October. However, the Japanese authorities—probably in consultation with foreign authorities—judged that the yen had not appreciated enough and feared that the dollar might creep back up to its previous level. Accordingly, the Bank of Japan decided to step up its action. The Bank of Japan announced a major policy change on Thursday, October 24: Governor Sumita, in a regular press conference, announced that the Bank would adopt a policy of high short-term interest rates. The presumption was that narrowing the interest-rate gap between the United States and Japan would create another round of yen appreciation.

On October 25, the Tokyo market opend at 216.55. As the short-term interest rate soared in morning trading, the yen appreciated sharply. The Tokyo closing rate that day was 214.90. Yen appreciation continued for two weeks as more and more market participants became convinced of the sincerity of the new monetary policy. The interest-rate differential narrowed significantly, owing to the sharp increase in the yen interest rate. It is quite natural that the narrowed interest-rate differential worked in favor of investment into Japan, thus causing the yen to appreciate.

During this wave, as table 11.6 shows, most of the yen appreciation occurred in the Tokyo market, in sharp contrast to the first wave. This suggests that new information became available in the Tokyo market. As the short-term interest rate rose in Tokyo, the yen appreciated in the Tokyo market. Other evidence includes a low correlation between movements in the yen and in European currencies, suggesting that this wave involved yen appreciation instead of dollar depreciation. In sum, the second wave of yen appreciation after the Plaza Agreement was due to the Bank of Japan's monetary policy alone, and news was appropriately revealed and acted upon in the Tokyo market.

After the second wave of yen appreciation, the rate stayed just above 200 yen/dollar for more than $2\frac{1}{2}$ months. There are pieces of evidence that indicate that the Japanese monetary authorities, in concert with other monetary authorities, made an attempt to stabilize the yen at around this level. First, people who were involved in the Plaza Agreement confessed later that a target of 200 yen/dollar was mentioned at the Plaza meeting.[15] Second, during the New Year's holiday (the Tokyo market closes from January 1 to January 3 each year) in 1986, the yen appreciated quietly in the New York market. On January 2, the yen closed at 198.55 in the New York market. Then news came from Japan: Governor Sumita of the Bank of Japan had said in a New Year's press interview that the yen should be kept at around 200. As soon as the content of this interview was reported in the New York market on January 3, the yen went back above the 200 level.

Third, the events of January 24, the beginning of the third wave, lend further support to the view that the Japanese authorities tried to maintain a target for the yen/dollar exchange rate. Finance Minister Takeshita was in Washington, on his way home from the London G5 meeting of January 18 and 19. At a press conference, he reportedly said that he would allow the yen to go below the 200 level. The Tokyo market was informed of Takeshita's remark by a wire service at around 3 P.M., 30 minutes before the closing of the market. The yen jumped from 201 to 198 in a matter of 20 minutes; then profit taking brought it back to 199.50 by the 3:30 P.M. closing. Finance Minister Takeshita came home that evening, long after the Tokyo market had closed, and gave another news conference in Tokyo. He said: "If the exchange rate moves to the 190s as a natural result of the market movement, it should not be artificially brought back [to more than 200]. Though it varies depending on the sector, the 190s would be acceptable by industry."[16] This news conference in Tokyo was reported in the European and New York markets, which were still open. The yen appreciated to 198 in London and then to 196.60 in New York.

The Third Wave: The Oil-Price Effect

The yen appreciated by 21 yen/dollar within four weeks of the Takeshita announcement. A long-expected discount-rate cut by the Bank of Japan, which took effect on January 30 (having been announced a day earlier), did not stop the strong appreciation. In fact, the major cause of the yen appreciation in this wave was a rapid decline in the price of oil. A minor role was played by the decline in the United States' long-term interest rate, which reflected a change in US fiscal policy. The spot price of a barrel of crude oil (North Sea Brent in London) declined from $26 in the beginning of January to $19 dollars in one month, and then to $13 in the beginning of March. An oil-price decline usually causes the yen and the mark to appreciate, since Japan and Germany are oil-importing countries.

Table 11.6 reveals that yen appreciation during this period took place almost equally in the three markets (Tokyo, Europe, and New

York). What is interesting is that the contribution of the European market in this wave is very large compared to that during the other periods. Recall that the first wave of appreciation was attributed to the US policy shift in favor of international coordination, and the second wave to Japanese monetary policy. What was new about the third wave was that the yen appreciated in the European market as well. This gives us information about the force behind the third yen-appreciation wave. The movement of oil prices occurred mainly during the European market hours. The yen moved as soon as oil-price news became available. The rather low correlation between movements in the pound and in the yen during the third wave of yen appreciation is further evidence for this view.

The Fourth Wave

As the third wave brought the yen/dollar rate into the 180s, Japanese policy makers and business leaders became resistant to further yen appreciation. Many in Japan began to think that the yen had appreciated enough. They had hoped that the yen at 180 would soon correct the trade imbalance between Japan and the United States. Many business leaders in export industries complained about a sudden loss of price competitiveness of their products. In fact, real GNP growth for the first quarter of 1986 was negative. The sudden yen appreciation caused exports to decline, and uncertainty about further yen appreciation made the business outlook pessimistic (which, in turn, depressed investment). This recessionary movement was then dubbed a "yen-appreciation recession" [Endaka Fukyō], only to be forgotten shortly. It became obvious by the summer that Japan had managed to adjust to the new environment of the strong yen.

The fourth wave started when the second internationally coordinated discount-rate cut became a certainty. From April 16 to May 12, the yen appreciated by more than 17 yen/dollar, breaking its all-time high on April 21 in Tokyo. The monetary authorities in Japan did not want to cause further appreciation of the yen. Short-term interest rates went down quickly, and yen-selling interventions continued.

As table 11.6 indicates, most of the appreciation took place in Tokyo and New York. This gives a clue, in that the most important news about the fourth wave was US monetary policy. In fact, it was well known that the coordinated discount-rate cut was led by the

US central bank, so that the US authorities were most enthusiastic about the interest-rate decline. Since the correlation between the yen and the pound is relatively high, oil was not the factor. In fact, oil was relatively stable (in the range of $11–$13 per barrel) during the fourth wave.

The Fifth Wave

A long and gradual yen appreciation took place during the early part of the summer of 1986. There was appreciation of about 20 yen/dollar from June 3 to July 31. Since this appreciation was much more gradual than that during the other waves, it may be inappropriate to discuss it in the same manner as the others.

The yen appreciated uniformly in the three markets. The largest effect was in the European market, again suggesting that the effect was due to oil-price declines, as was the case in third wave.

During the fifth wave, the spot price of a barrel of oil indeed declined from $13 to $9 per barrel. The yen reached a level of 154 yen/dollar on August 1, and then stayed very close to this level until March 1987.

THE TARGET ZONE

Criticisms of the Floating-Exchange-Rate Regime

Before the floating-exchange-rate regime began, many economists thought that floating rates would restore the independence of domestic policies, since exchange rates would automatically equilibrate the trade balance. As the fundamental factors that determine the exchange rate moved, the exchange rate was supposed to adjust to a new equilibrium. The developments of the late 1970s and the early 1980s showed that this view was mistaken. Even in the 1970s, exchange-rate movements were found to be too volatile, containing sharp rises and falls without corresponding changes in underlying factors. These movements were often regarded as indicative of the formation and popping of speculative bubbles.

A more serious challenge to the floating exchange rate came in the first half of the 1980s. Because of the combination of tight monetary policy and loose fiscal policy in the United States, the dollar appreciated significantly from 1981 to the beginning of 1985.

Although numerical estimates vary, many believe that the exchange rate deviated from the long-run equilibrium level for more than two years. As a result of dollar overvaluation, the trade balance of the United States worsened sharply.

Hence, many realized by the mid 1980s that a floating-exchange-rate system neither automatically maintains a trade-account balance nor prevents short-term volatility. But in the modern world of capital-market integration it is impossible to go back to the fixed-exchange-rate system. Under these circumstances, a proposal was made under which the governments of the G7 countries (G5 plus Canada and Italy) would agree on central exchange rates and bounds around them, and then make a commitment to keep exchange rates within the bounds.

The Target-Zone Experiment

Judging from newspaper reports, many think that the period of quiet target-zone policy started with a joint press release of the Miyazawa-Baker agreement of October 31, 1986. In this agreement, the yen/dollar exchange rate at the time (160) was considered to be near the level that is consistent with fundamentals. In the press conference, however, Finance Minister Miyazawa denied the existence of a target zone.

The range set by the Baker-Miyazawa agreement is believed to have been 155–170, or approximately ±8 yen (5 percent) of the rate of the time (that is, 161.5 at the close of the Tokyo market on October 31). The timing of the establishment of the target zone was ideal. By October, expectations in Japan had adjusted to the reality that an appreciated yen, say in the range 155–170, was here to stay. It happened that the yen suddenly depreciated from 155 to 160 within three days in late October.[17] The Japanese authority must have calculated that it was acceptable, if the United States agreed, to keep the exchange rate around the "current level." The US authority, fearing that the yen might depreciate further, agreed to put a ceiling on how much the yen should appreciate in return for a promise that the Japanese government did not want the yen to depreciate further. Thus, we may conjecture that Japan insisted on an appreciation limit of 155, slightly above the record high back in August, wishing to push the yen back to 170, while the United States insisted on not reversing the trend of the yen's appreciation.[18]

The first test came in early January 1987, when the yen appreciated from the high 150s to the low 150s very quickly. Finance Minister Miyazawa flew to Washington to consult with Treasury Secretary Baker, presumably to reaffirm the two-month-old target zone. The Bank of Japan heavily intervened as the rate approached 150. On January 7, 1987, an intervention started for the first time since the target zone became effective. The Bank of Japan, in concert with Germany and France, intervened in support of the dollar at around 158 (*Nihon Keizai Shinbun*, January 8, 1987). It seemed that the Bank of Japan was signaling that 158 was the defense line. The yen appreciated further, however, as Treasury Secretary Baker made a statement on January 8 to the effect that the dollar's depreciation was a logical consequence of developments in the world economy. On January 14, the yen appreciated from 155.5 at the opening to 153.8 at the closing of the Tokyo market, in spite of the intervention by the Bank of Japan.

Thus, in mid January the market received mixed signals. The Japanese government, which made it clear that it did not want further yen appreciation, resorted to strong intervention. It was reported that the Bank of Japan bought about 8 billion dollars during the first two weeks of January 1987 (*Nihon Keizai Shinbun*, January 15, 1987). This rather heavy intervention, triggered at the level of 158, supports the guess that the lower bound was 155.

In February 1987, the United States reportedly proposed to establish a reference range for the exchange rate in preparatory discussions for a G7 meeting. In a meeting held at the Louvre, the Group of Seven (though Italy was absent) reaffirmed its willingness to stabilize the exchange rate around the then-current rate, since it was believed to be consistent with underlying fundamentals, but avoided any mention of specific numbers for the range. The Louvre agreement was interpreted in the market as saying that the target zone was 150–160 (*Nihon Keizai Shinbun*, February 23, 1987). A study based on interviews contends that the Louvre agreement had 153.50 as the yen/dollar central rate, with 2.5 percent and 5 percent as soft and hard bands around the central rate (Funabashi 1988, p. 186).

The next test of the target zone came in late March. On March 23 (a Monday), the yen went under 150 in the New York market. The Federal Reserve intervened, but purchased only several million dollars. The yen appreciation continued on March 24. In the Tokyo market the Bank of Japan intervened, buying 1.7 billion dollars on March 24. The Federal Reserve also intervened from its own account, as opposed to acting as an agent for other central banks, purchasing 0.7–0.8 billion dollars on March 24 (*Nihon Keizai Shinbun*, March 26, 1987). These figures showed that the lower yen-appreciation limit set in the Louvre agreement was indeed 150. During the rest of the week, market forces, which saw that the yen had to appreciate in order to help avert protectionist legislation in the United States, made the yen appreciate further despite massive intervention by central banks. On March 27, the yen closed at 149 in the Tokyo market when the Bank of Japan reportedly bought 2 billion dollars. The yen appreciated to 147 in the New York market on the same day, prompting the Federal Reserve Bank of New York to intervene for five straight days.

The Group of Seven met again on April 8, 1987. Since there was no new content in their subsequent announcement, the yen appreciated from 145.6 (April 8, Thursday, Tokyo closing) to 142.5 (April 13, Monday, Tokyo closing).[19]

At the Group of Seven meeting of April 1987, or sometime around it, the target zone must have been changed to reflect the new reality. When intervention cannot prevent appreciation and when no drastic change in fundamentals (such as the interest rate) is possible, the target zone should be rebased. The new range was probably 140–160.[20] (It could have been 140–155.) When the yen gradually depreciated to 150 in July, there were no signs of intervention in support of the yen. Clearly the ceiling of the range was higher than 150.

On August 14 (a Friday) the United States announced that the trade deficit for the month of June had been $15.7 billion, much larger than expected. It was also revealed that the January–June 1987 trade deficits had been higher than those of 1986. After this news, the yen appreciated from 152.4 (August 14, Friday, Tokyo closing) to 143 (August 21, 1987, Tokyo closing) without much in the way of intervention or other signals from monetary authorities. It was clearly within the target zone.

As the yen approached the lower limit of 140, there were several signals of the existence of a limit. As was mentioned above, the existence of the target zone was revealed (leaked?) on the front page of *Nihon Keizai Shinbun* on August 20. On several occasions (for example, August 19, 26, and 27), the Bank of Japan intervened in support of the dollar (*Nihon Keizai Shinbun*, August 21 and 28) at around 144. The Federal Reserve joined in this intervention on August 27 and September 1, supporting a rate around 141. These facts support the conjecture that there was in fact a target zone with 140 as a lower (appreciation) bound for the yen. Since the yen was stabilized at above 140 for the month of September and most of October, the signals sent by the monetary authorities of the G7 countries—Ministry of Finance, Treasury Department, etc.—seem to have worked this time.

The target zone was abandoned, or at least temporarily shelved, soon after Black Monday (October 19, 1987). In the beginning of October there were many signs that the Bank of Japan and the Federal Reserve wanted to guide the interest rate higher as a precautionary measure against possible inflation. The near crash of the New York stock market, however, prompted the Federal Reserve to pump in liquidity in order to prevent panic. When it became clear that stock prices would not recover promptly, and the lower interest rate would give a lift to the United States' stock market and economy, expectations in the exchange market changed drastically.

The lower limit of 140 was broken on October 28 in the New York market without much resistance from the monetary authority. Over the following two weeks, many reports and interviews came out of the United States suggesting that the Louvre Agreement had been abandoned and that the US would put a higher priority on easing monetary policy. This news convinced the market that the target zone was gone, and the yen appreciated to a level of 133–134. The yen appreciated further, breaking the 130 mark on December 10, after the announcement of a large US trade deficit for the month of October ($17.6 billion). Although the Bank of Japan and the Federal Reserve intervened, selling pressure was too strong. A target zone has been mentioned much less frequently since October 1987. For most of the time since then, exchange-rate movement has been contained within a relatively narrow range (120–140 yen/dollar) anyway. The G7 monetary authorities continue to monitor exchange-rate movement and intervene in the market occasionally, when the exchange rate moves out of the usual range (as when the yen/dollar rate approached 160 in the spring of 1989). It is not clear whether a particular range is considered or a policy action is formed on an *ad hoc* basis when the rate moves too quickly.

A Lesson from the Target-Zone Experiment

The target zone of October 1986 was introduced at a very good time. Both sides could agree that the current level was a good place to stay.

Was the target zone effective? Since two of the virtues of the target-zone proposal are its flexibility and its discretionary nature (the ranges can change in response to changes in economic fundamentals), one cannot judge the success or failure of a target zone by examining the duration of a particular range. Its effectiveness should be measured by the volatility of the exchange rate when it is in effect versus a situation in which there is no such thing. If the existence of a target range makes investors likely to take profits earlier and losses later than usual, this will contribute to relative stability. The market perception of the target zone has a stabilizing effect, as Krugman (1988) demonstrated might be possible in a simple theoretical model. If the market believes that the rate cannot go beyond the ceiling or the floor, Krugman showed, the actual dynamics *within* the range will be more stable with a target zone than without one. According to news reports from the market, this seemed to be the case when the exchange rate was within the target zone. (Let us call this a Krugman effect.)

The problem with the target zone occurs when the range is challenged. If the central banks try to defend an unrealistic rate, this will create strong speculation against the central banks and result in a sudden change in the exchange rate after the defense line is broken. This only creates additional volatility. Therefore, the key to success is determining how wide the range should be, how much resistance should be applied to defend the range, and when the range should be revised.

A one-year-long target zone from late October 1986 with revisions in the range was successful in that the exchange rate was contained within the range without too much distortion of domestic policies and that movements within the range were rather stable (the Krugman effect). The problem was the timing of changes in the range. Although this is hindsight, no-longer-appropriate target zones could have been abandoned easier and earlier.

Should the target zone be announced? Immediately after the Baker-Miyazawa announcement, market participants were guessing what the American and Japanese monetary authorities had agreed upon. They sensed that there was a target range, but they did not know the ceiling and floor numbers. This made the market quite nervous and sensitive to any news, even rumors, about the range.[21] Another example is the experience of January 1987, when the market received conflicting signals from the Japanese and US governments. This confusion made the market too sensitive to officials' statements, thus adding to the volatility of the exchange rate. This sensitivity to statements by government officials arises because the need to guess the range increases the volatility of the exchange rate. In this case, being secretive about the range creates a destabilizing effect.

On the other hand, there are several arguments in favor of a "quiet" target zone. First, if the market happens to believe that the target range is narrower than the actual one, which was the case in November and December of 1986, there is an added bonus to the Krugman effect. Second, being quiet about the target zone would help save face when the range must be adjusted. Theoretically, the authorities could even change the range without being detected at all, but the first argument holds only in exceptional cases and the second argument conflicts with the primary purpose of the target zone. In order to have a positive Krugman effect, the authority must convince the market of the existence of the range. Policy makers cannot gain benefits from their reputation without risking losses in their reputation, at least sometimes. If they were to reserve the right to change the range at any time, changing the target zone would not necessarily damage their reputation. The benefits of a "loud" target zone seem to outweigh those of a quiet target zone.

Summary

Figure 11.7, which illustrates the target zones and the actual exchange-rate movements after October 1986, gives the impression that, although the target zone gave a reference range, the zone was rather "soft." The range has been revised when it has not been defended easily. The existence of the zone was not announced officially. Hence, the experience since 1986 has been an ongoing experiment, and the result of the experiment has not been established.

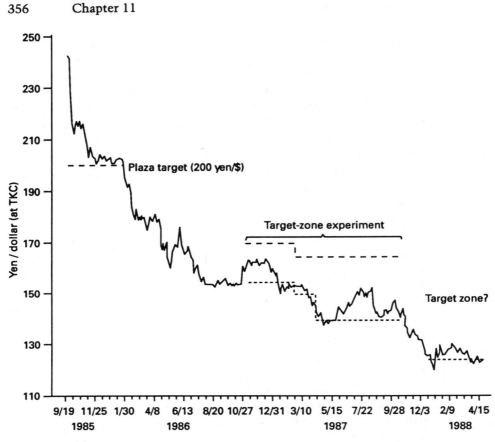

Figure 11.7
Target-zone experiment.

CONCLUDING REMARKS

In the chapter we have considered many topics in international finance, especially exchange-rate dynamics. Since these topics have been developed only recently, some of the materials may seem unorthodox for this kind of book. Exchange-rate movements are an important aspect of any economy, however. In the wake of the large misalignment of the exchange rate in the 1980s, there exists strong interest, both academic and political, in investigating exchange-rate regimes. Many economists now subscribe to the idea of a target zone. When the European Community integrates its members' currencies, the need for coordination between the dollar and the yen is expected to increase. An assessment of exchange-rate management during the second half of the 1980s is important in this respect.

APPENDIX: THE FORWARD MARKET AND THE FUTURES MARKET

There is a distinction between the forward market and the futures market, although both deal with foreign-exchange transactions at future dates.

The forward market consists of contracts (that is, promises) to make foreign-exchange transactions of specified amounts on specified dates. No margins (down payments) are required. Contracts may be arranged case by case between the bank and its customers. Banks are always quoting "ask" (or "offer") and "bid" prices for

Table 11.9
Forward vs. futures markets.

	Forward Market	Futures Market
Margin requirements?	No	Yes
Cash flows before the expiration of the contract?	None	Initial margin must be paid; then as the exchange rate moves, a certain proportion of margin must be maintained.
Who uses this market?	Exporters, importers, speculators	Speculators
Units and dates	Custom made	Standardized
Who holds contracts?	Contracts between banks and customers; plus interbank market between banks	Contracts between the clearing house and its members
Squaring the position possible?	Not really	Yes, by transacting the same amount in the opposite direction
Actual delivery	Hedgers hold contracts until maturities.	Speculators square the position before the expiration of contracts
Options trading?	No	Available
Daily price limit?	No	Yes

foreign currencies, in both spot and forward markets. The bid-ask spread shows the commission of the bank. A major function of the forward market is "hedging." Suppose that a Japanese exporter of automobiles to the United States expects revenues of X dollars in 3 months. The export company may want to determine the revenue in yen. If the company does not want to expose itself to foreign-exchange risk, it can sell the dollars (buy the yen) forward.

In contrast, futures contracts consist of standardized amounts of future transactions to take place on preset dates. Speculation is typically done in the futures market. Almost all contracts are canceled out by equal and opposite transactions, and nobody takes "delivery" on their contracts. For details, see pp. 98–100 of Grabbe 1986.

In Japan, only the forward market has been available. Even in the forward market, until April 1984 there was a regulation that forward contracts without "real demands" were not allowed.

The differences between the two markets are illustrated in table 11.9.

NOTES

1. Monthly series of the yen/dollar, mark/dollar, and other exchange rates are published in almost all statistical yearbooks. Daily series of the exchange rates are available from commercial data services, or from daily newspapers. A convenient book of daily exchange rates, along with various interest rates, from 1973 to 1987, is the 1988 *Money Market Index*, published by Toyo Keizai Shinposha. The data in this book are also available in CD-ROM from the same publisher. Unfortunately, updates have not been published in hard copy.

2. On forward contracts and the forward market, see the appendix to this chapter.

3. Recall the description of the short-term capital market in chapter 5.

4. Deviation from covered interest parity is defined as $DEV \equiv (1 + RUS)f/s - (1 + RJA)$. In the literature of covered interest parity, the parity is often expressed as $\log(f) - \log(s) = RUS - RJA$. This definition and our definition are close enough when one recognizes the approximation $\log(1 + x) \simeq x$, which is good when x is small enough (say, 0.05).

5. Other possible reasons for an observed deviation from parity are political risk, differences in tax treatment of domestic interest income and foreign interest income, domestic regulations, and observation errors. First, if investors suspect that the fund cannot be converted back to the original currency in the future (that is, the forward contract will not be honored) for

some reason (for example, a change in political regime), then the deviation may occur. Second, if domestic interest income is taxed differently from foreign interest income, then arbitrage will not work. As mentioned in the text, some interest rates are regulated. In this case, the arbitrage for that asset does not work either. Hence, it is important to find assets in two countries that are comparable in default risk, tax treatment, and regulation. Finally, in empirical implementation of a test of covered interest parity, as in any other empirical test, observation errors must be carefully avoided. In particular, simultaneous observations of the spot and forward exchange rates and the two interest rates are essential, since rates are moving rather quickly. Ideally, observations must be taken at the same moment. But the domestic rates in Japan and in the United States may not be quoted at the same moment, owing to the time difference. A minimum standard for this test would be to take the rates on the same day (say, within 12 hours).

6. In some data banks or publications, one may find the "TB" rate of Japan during the 1970s. The asset was in fact the fiscal bond, which was issued to smooth out seasonal irregularities of fiscal revenues and expenditures. The fiscal bond was issued by the Ministry of Finance directly to the Bank of Japan at a regulated interest rate. There was no secondary market for investors, although the bond was sometimes sold by the Bank of Japan as a tool for open-market operations. The rate was renamed the "FB" rate in the mid 1980s. Consequently, it is not possible to use the TB rate for Japan for a test of covered interest parity, although the TB rate is the standard rate used to check covered interest parity for other OECD countries.

7. An investor is called *risk-neutral* if he is indifferent between a sure payment of x dollars and an uncertain payment that has an expected return of x dollars. Suppose you are offered a coin-flip bet that pays $10 for heads and nothing for tails. If the coin is fair, risk-neutral investors will value the bet at $5. In this section, as in many models in the literature, all investors are assumed to share a common belief.

8. Survey data on foreign-exchange rates are available. See Domingues 1986, Frankel and Froot 1987a,b, and Ito 1990 for econometric analyses using survey data.

9. For tests of uncovered interest parity, see Boothe and Longworth 1986, Cumby and Obstfeld 1984, Frenkel 1981, Geweke and Feige 1979, Hansen and Hodrick 1980, and Ito 1988.

10. The tax cut was recommended by "supply-siders," who were influential in the early stages of the first Reagan administration, with the argument that an income-tax cut would stimulate labor supply and fixed investment. The increase in supply volume would more than compensate for the decrease in the tax rate.

11. For other stylized facts see Mussa 1979 and Cumby and Obstfeld 1984.

12. One institutional difference in the foreign-exchange markets should be noted. The trading hours of the Tokyo interbank market are strictly reg-

ulated: 9:00 A.M.–noon and 1:30–3:30 P.M. Of course, the customer market is open anytime the bank and a customer want to trade. During the lunch break, the interbank screen goes blank and no interbank trading is possible in Tokyo. Any large customer order made during the lunch hours is relayed to Hong Kong or Singapore (in order for the bank to avoid exchange-rate risk). In the New York or the London market, there is no restriction on the trading hours in the customer or the interbank market. What are shown as the opening and closing rates in the New York market are the rates at the beginning and the end of "active trading" (usually 9:00 A.M. and 4:30 P.M.). If the market stays active, however, the closing quote may come as late as 5:00 P.M.

The Tokyo rates, the last trading rates, are quoted in the *Nihon Keizai Shinbun* daily newspaper, while the New York rates, ask and bid, are provided by the Federal Reserve Bank of New York. The New York rates used in this chapter are the averages of bid and ask rates.

13. The rest of this section is a summary of Ito 1987.

14. Alternatively, TK here can be further decomposed into the "precise" $TK_t = TKC_t - TKO_t$ and the Pacific $PC_t = TKO_t - NYC_{t-1}$. See Ito 1987 and Ito and Roley 1987 for uses of the alternative definition.

15. In an interview for *Toyo Keizai*'s special issue of May 22, 1987, Tomomitsu Ōba confirmed that 200 was the target at the time of the Plaza Agreement. See also Funabashi 1988, p. 18, for a quote naming 200 as the target by Finance Minister Takeshita: "I will not leave office before the yen revalues up to 200."

16. The quote in the text is a literal translation from the *Nihon Keizai Shinbun* of January 25, 1986. This same quote was translated as "the nation's industry could live with the dollar valued at 190 yen" in the *Wall Street Journal* of January 27. Note that the Japanese version states the broadly defined 190s, with the connotation that the target does not go too far below 200, while the English version states 190 as the level. The developments in Europe and New York later the same day were closer to the English version. The point, however, is that the statement signaled a switch in policy.

17. A conspiracy theory contended that the Ministry of Finance leaked information just before the agreement in order to manipulate the base of the exchange rate. See Funabashi 1988, p. 162.

18. Funabashi (1988, p. 163) reports that the Japanese side was aiming at pushing the yen/dollar rate back to 170 at the time.

19. During the week before the G7 meeting, during which the yen appreciated from 149 to 145, the Ministry of Finance and the Ministry of International Trade and Industry were applying pressure, in various forms, on institutional investors and exporters not to sell dollars. I am not sure that these pressures were essential to achieving a target zone.

20. Funabashi (1988, p. 189) reports that Baker suggested rebasing the yen/dollar central rate to the current rate of 146, with 2.5 percent and 5 percent bands around it.

21. For example, on November 6 a rumor swept through the market that an appropriate level was 154–160. This brought the yen from 164 to 161 in an hour (*Nihon Keizai Shinbun*, November 7, 1986).

BIBLIOGRAPHY

Boothe, P., and D. Longworth. 1986. "Foreign exchange market inefficiency tests: Implications of recent findings." *Journal of International Money and Finance* 5: 135–152.

Cumby, R. E., and M. Obstfeld. 1984. "International interest-rate and price-level linkages under flexible exchange rates: A review of recent evidence." In *Exchange Rates: Theory and Practice*, ed. J. F. O. Bilson and R. C. Marston. University of Chicago Press.

Dominguez, K. M. 1986. "Are foreign exchange forecasts rational?" *Economics Letters* 21: 277–281.

Engel, C., and J. Frankel. 1984. "Why interest rates react to money announcements: An explanation from the foreign exchange market." *Journal of Monetary Economics* 13: 31–39.

Frankel, J. A. 1984. *The Yen/Dollar Agreement: Liberalizing Japanese Capital Markets*. Institute for International Economics.

Frankel, J. A., and K. A. Froot. 1987a. "Short-term and long-term expectations of the yen/dollar exchange rate: Evidence from survey data." *Journal of the Japanese and International Economies* 1: 249–274.

Frankel, J. A., and K. A. Froot. 1987b. "Using survey data to test standard propositions regarding exchange rate expectations." *American Economic Review* 77:133–153.

Frenkel, J. A. 1981. "Flexible exchange rates, prices, and the role of 'news': Lessons from the 1970s." *Journal of Political Economy* 89: 665–705.

Fukao, M. 1990. "Liberalization of Japan's foreign exchange controls and structural changes in the balance of payments." *Bank of Japan Journal of Monetary and Economic Studies* 8, no. 2: 1–65.

Funabashi, Y. 1988. *Managing the Dollar: From the Plaza to the Louvre*. Institute for International Economics.

Geweke, J., and E. Feige. 1979. "Some joint tests of the efficiency of markets for forward foreign exchange." *Review of Economics and Statistics* 61: 334–341.

Grabbe, J. O. 1986. *International Financial Markets*. Elsevier.

Hansen, L. P., and R. J. Hodrick. 1980. "Forward exchange rates as optimal predictors of future spot rates: An econometric analysis." *Journal of Political Economy* 88: 829–853.

Krugman, P. 1988. Target Zone and Exchange Rate Dynamics. Working paper 2481, National Bureau of Economic Research.

Ito, T. 1986. "Capital controls and covered interest parity between the yen and the dollar." *Economic Studies Quarterly* 37: 223–241.

Ito, T. 1987. "The intradaily exchange rate dynamics and monetary policies after the Group of Five agreement." *Journal of the Japanese and International Economies* 1: 275–298.

Ito, T. 1988. "Use of (time-domain) vector autoregressions to test uncovered interest parity." *Review of Economics and Statistics* 70: 296–305.

Ito, T. 1990. "Foreign exchange rate expectations: Micro survey data." *American Economic Review* 80: 434–449.

Ito, T., and V. V. Roley. 1987. "News from the US and Japan: Which moves the yen/dollar exchange rate?" *Journal of Monetary Economics* 2: 255–277.

Mussa, M. 1979. "Empirical regularities in the behavior of exchange rates and theories of foreign exchange rates." *Carnegie-Rochester Conference Series on Public Policy* 11, autumn: 9–57.

Roley, V. V., and C. E. Walsh. 1985. "Monetary policy regimes, expected inflation, and the response of interest rates to money announcements." *Quarterly Journal of Economics* 100, supplement: 1011–1039.

Urich, T. J., and P. Wachtel. 1981. "Market responses to the weekly money supply announcements in the 1970s." *Journal of Finance* 36: 1063–1072.

Part III

CONTEMPORARY TOPICS

Chapter 12

US-JAPAN ECONOMIC CONFLICTS

Japan and the United States have had strong trade flows in both directions. Since significant economic interests underlie the trade relationship, conficts over trade have emerged from time to time. The nature of these conflicts changed significantly during the 1980s.

The traditional pattern of conflict was this: A rapid increase in a particular type of Japanese export to the United States (textiles, steel, color TVs, automobiles) set off an alarm. Competing American manufacturers complained to the trade authorities, claiming damages from dumping. Negotiations between the American and Japanese governments followed. The negotiated settlement took the form of price controls (such as unilateral import surcharges imposed by the US and a price-fixing system known as the trigger price system) or quantity controls (such as voluntary export restraints). Japanese firms, especially those in the manufacturing sector, were portrayed in the United States as efficient organizations producing high-quality products—and sometimes the glory of high economic growth and strong exports was extended to the Japanese society in general.

But the nature of the conflicts changed dramatically in the mid 1980s. First, the range of issues broadened to include "structural" problems in Japan. The current debate concerns not only how many vehicles may be exported to the United States, but also whether the ceiling on deposit interest rates in Japan provides low-cost capital for Japanese industries and whether the long-term, group relationships [keiretsu] among distribution channels act as barriers against penetration by foreign products. Second, the tactics of American negotiators shifted toward a "result-oriented" policy with respect to American manufacturers' access to the Japanese market.

Third, high-technology products, which face growing markets in both the United States and Japan, became a focus of conflicts. It is not necessarily the case that US high-technology manufacturers suffer from a surge in imports from Japan. The issue is, again, American market access to Japan.

These changes reflect new developments in economic theory and political reality. This is an unusual mix. In economic theory, the emergence of the "new trade theory" (recall chapter 10) had an enormous impact on policy debates. New trade theory, for example, prescribes infant-industry protection for "sunrise" industries with increasing-returns technology. This can be used as a rationale for targeting the market access of high-technology industries while they are still in a developmental stage. Moreover, "managed trade," which includes various aspects of non-free-trade policy, has been advocated by a number of prominent international economists.

Politically, the Reagan administration (1981–1989) was a staunch supporter of free trade. Thus, it was rather sympathetic to the Japanese claim that the growth in Japanese exports was the result of Japanese producers' offering superior products at reasonable prices. Owing to the particular mix of economic policies (explained in chapter 10), US trade deficits grew rapidly from 1982 to 1987. The Democratic majority in Congress attempted to criticize the trade imbalances as proof of the administration's failure in economic policy. Trade unions in the manufacturing sector were traditionally supporters of the Democratic Party, and many of these unions suffered heavily from Japanese imports. It is also likely that the split government (Republican president, Democratic Congress) contributed to bringing economic issues into the political arena with a more aggressive tone.

In Japan, deregulation to increase economic efficiency is always politically difficult, since it always implies a loss of oligopolistic rents for existing firms. The political situation in Japan, including the Liberal Democratic Party's unchallenged long tenure, prevented regulations from being dismantled when they were no longer necessary. However, demands from the United States were welcomed by those Japanese policy makers and economists who were in favor of deregulation. Such demands were used as strong threats to "persuade" vested interest groups: Infuriating the United States was seen as a possible path to protectionism, and being pressured by the

United States was usually an acceptable and face-saving excuse for constituents.

THE "JAPAN AS NUMBER ONE" SYNDROME

In the late 1970s, the American public developed a strong interest in Japan's economy and society. Until then, most Americans had thought of Japan mainly in terms of high-quality cameras, TVs, and automobiles; their interest usually ended with these particular products. It is fair to say that the Japanese economy in general was not a subject of interest for ordinary citizens. Ezra Vogel's book *Japan as Number One: Lessons for America* appeared in 1979 just when interest in the workings of the Japanese economy was spreading among the American public. Vogel portrayed Japan's economy and society as more efficient and better managed than their US counterparts. His book contributed significantly to updating the perception of Japan among Americans who had not paid close attention to this important trading partner.

The most striking aspect of the Japanese economy is undoubtedly the success of its manufacturing firms. In search of the source of this success, many authors—to name a few, Ouchi (1981), Pascale (1981), and Abegglen and Stalk (1985)—examined Japanese management. Interest shifted toward explaining how Japanese management succeeded in motivating workers to produce high-quality products and in streamlining the production process. Quality circles,[1] just-in-time delivery,[2] and "bottom-up" decision making[3] entered the vocabulary of American business.

Moreover, other features of Japanese labor relations became widely known to those in American businesses and business schools: careful screening in the hiring of workers, lengthy on-the-job training with frequent rotation among different jobs, and flexible job assignment. And there was new attention to the more "democratic" relationship between top or middle management and blue-collar workers in Japan (for example, people in middle management positions share parking lots and cafeterias with blue-collar workers), which supposedly enhances the communication from bottom to top and helps bring out ideas for improvement.

A more serious problem with US industries, according to critics, is that top management is preoccupied with short-run profits, because the stockholders (especially institutional investors) put too much emphasis on quarterly profits. American managers are said to be more interested in producing profits in the short run than in investing for the future. Japanese managers, in contrast, do not have to worry about pressures from stockholders, because a large fraction of a company's outstanding stock is in friendly hands as a result of cross-holding. (Recall chapter 7.) Japanese stockholders are said to be content with low dividend payouts if they are rewarded by capital gains in the long run. Corporate performance is announced only semi-annually in Japan, not quarterly. Cross-holding enables Japanese management to concentrate on long-term planning without worrying about quarter-to-quarter performance or about hostile takeovers.

Increasing success in automobiles and videocassette recorders intensified the positive image of Japanese products in the first half of

---

Smart Bombs, Dumb VCRs

After confidence in American technology increased significantly in the wake of the Gulf War of 1990–91, some Americans started to ask an interesting question. Senator George Mitchell put it this way: "If we can make the best smart bomb, can't we make the best VCR?"

The standard answers to this question are as follows: Commercial success of consumer durables depends on product development rather than on technological breakthroughs. Product development, which emphasizes cost-cutting by mass production and the use of known technology, is quite different from the development of military technology, in which sophistication is often bought at any price and mass production is rarely brought into play.

Other answers to this question bring out interesting aspects of American nervousness about trade conflicts. First, since the Patriot and the Tomahawk do not contain frontier technology anyway, the success of these weapons does not necessarily indicate the superiority of US technology in general. Second, as more nonmilitary technology (such as computer chips) finds use in weaponry, loss of competitiveness in commercial technology may well imperil the national security of the United States in the future. This is the reason behind the new interest in preserving America's lead in supercomputers, computer software, airplane design, airplane engines, biotechnology, and other areas of high technology.

(This "box" is based in part on an article entitled "In US technology, a gap between arms and VCRs," which appeared in the *New York Times* on March 4, 1991.)

the 1980s. Although trade conflicts as a macro phenomenon promoted the image of Japan as an unfair trading partner in the second half of the 1980s, the positive views of Japanese management (at least, in the US manufacturing sector) have not been lost. Serious self-examination of American management continues. (See McCraw 1986 and Dertouzos et al. 1989.)

In the second half of the 1980s, organizational aspects of the Japanese firm became the focus of economic investigation. In contrast to the writings on Japanese management, research on the Japanese firm is oriented more toward microeconomic theory than toward management practice.[4] This line of research emphasizes the fact that the typical Japanese firm has an organizational mode that "horizontally" coordinates communications among different departments—as opposed to hierarchical, specialized control—so that the firm can easily adapt to changes in business and market conditions.

Aoki (1990) emphasizes two long-term relationships as key components in the success of the Japanese firm: lifetime employment (which, with hierarchical promotion, motivates workers to work hard) and long-term bank-firm relationships (which facilitate the monitoring of management). Aoki's contribution is to show that these two long-term relationships are mutually necessary. Since workers' human capital is locked into a company, as they slowly move up the hierarchical ladder, the firm must be robust to changes in the business environment. The continued existence of the firm, though it may change its main business activity from one sector to another, is essential to its workers. The bank-firm relationship gives this kind of insurance. Aoki further argues that corporate decision making is influenced by the interests of financial supporters (namely, banks) and employees, the two major players who have the strongest stakes in the corporation.[5]

AMERICAN FRUSTRATIONS

Conflicts before the Mid 1980s

The first important trade negotiations between Japan and the United States took place in the early 1960s and concerned textiles. Steel was addressed in the late 1960s and the early 1970s. Textile exports have been regulated by the Multi-Fiber Agreement since

October 1974. Steel export prices were placed under a trigger-price system in the late 1970s, and the steel export share has been controlled since October 1984.

A dumping complaint against Japanese TV exports to the United States became an intense issue in the beginning of the 1970s. An anti-dumping surcharge on Japanese TVs was imposed in March 1971; in July 1977 it was replaced by export restraints, which held until June 1980.

Machine tools were the subject of the next conflicts. Their prices were controlled from March 1978 to December 1986, after which the price controls were replaced by quantity controls of the voluntary export restraint (VER) type.[6]

The Automobile VER

In 1980, with the Chrysler Corporation close to bankruptcy, the United States and Japan negotiated a three-year "voluntary" export restraint (VER) limiting Japan's automobile exports to the US to 1.68 million passenger cars for each one-year period from April 1, 1981, to March 31, 1984. The restraint was renewed with a higher ceiling of 1.85 million cars from April 1, 1984, to March 31, 1985, and renewed once again with a 2.3 million ceiling from April 1, 1985, to March 31, 1985, and renewed once again with a 2.3 million ceiling from April 1, 1985, to March 31, 1986. This ceiling has been renewed every year since 1986, although it has not been reached since 1987. In 1990, the number of Japanese automobiles exported to the US was around 1.8 million. MITI has renewed the VER out of a fear that abolishing it would somehow rekindle anti-Japanese feelings in the US Congress.

The VER form of trade restraint was favored for several reasons. The US government can avoid blame by pointing out that it is unilateral Japanese action. Since MITI arranges the quota, the Japanese automakers are exempted from possible anti-trust lawsuits. Moreover, it was presumed beforehand that VERs would not violate the GATT agreements.

In that the VER started as the negotiated result of a US-Japanese trade conflict, it was not a "unilateral" but rather a mutual agreement. However, it later became a truly unilateral action on the part of the Japanese government. On March 2, 1985, President Reagan, citing a study that concluded that the US consumers had suffered as a result of it, announced that the US government would not ask the Japanese government for a continuation of the VER. After some debate, MITI settled on unilateral action with a new ceiling of 2.3 million cars. This action, however, was not well regarded in the US Congress, and it contributed to the passage of the resolution naming Japan as an unfair trading partner.[9]

The VER is essentially a quantity-fixing cartel. The economic consequences of such a cartel are predictable by microeconomic theory, and in fact the automobile VER of 1981, revised and extended through the 1980s, basically produced the predicted results: The quantity-limited Japanese producers increased their profit margins on exported cars, first by loading them with optional accessories and then by gradually shifting from small to mid-size cars. The US automakers took advantage of the limited number of Japanese imports and their relatively high prices. The VER has contributed— though this is difficult to quantify—to the recovery of Chrysler, which was a profitable company by the mid 1980s. Honda, Toyota, Nissan, and Mitsubishi raced to build factories in the United States.[8]

The real big loser under the VER system was the American consumer. To some extent, smaller Japanese automakers that were relative newcomers to exporting, such as Subaru and Daihatsu, suffered because MITI did not assign them high enough quotas.

Partly because of the yen's sharp appreciation and partly because of increasing production by Japanese automakers in the United States, exports of automobiles from Japan to the United States have been declining. It seems that the number of cars exported from Japan to the United States will remain at a less-than-problematic level; however, the quantity of Japanese autos produced in the United States may become an issue.

From the "Resolution of 1985" to Super-301

Throughout the 1980s, tensions between the United States and Japan increased. Anti-Japanese sentiment in the US Congress increased considerably as the trade imbalance between the United States and Japan grew rapidly from 1984 to 1987. Trade conflicts were no longer sectoral issues concerning specific Japanese exports; they were now national issues involving the US-Japan political-economic relationship in general. Market access for American products in Japan became a concern, and Japan's market structure and institutions (such as keiretsu) became debating points. The US strategy changed from one of attempting to limit imports from Japan to one of attempting to make the Japanese market accessible to American products.

The change was symbolized by a resolution passed by the US Senate in March 1985 naming Japan as an unfair trading partner. This was partly a response to frustrations over MITI's decision to increase the ceiling of the automobile export quota (see above) and partly an anticipation of a drive toward an omnibus trade bill.

In September 1986, a semiconductor agreement was signed by the two governments in order to settle a dumping case. The semiconductor agreement had three components: A "fair price" for each of the Japanese semiconductor exporters would be calculated by the US Department of Commerce in order to prevent dumping in the US market, the Japanese would do their best to prevent dumping in third-country markets, such as Hong Kong and Singapore, and the Japanese would help to increase the market shares for American semiconductors in Japan. In return, the US government agreed to drop its dumping case against the Japanese semiconductor makers. There was also a confidential side letter, in which it was stated that the Japanese government "would make efforts to assist the US companies in reaching their goal of a 20 percent market share within five years" (Prestowitz 1988, p. 65).

In April 1987, the United States announced that Japan was found to have been violating the agreement (especially the second and third parts) and decided to impose retaliatory tariffs (up to 300 percent) on various Japanese products, such as laptop computers and large-screen color TVs. The Japanese reaction to this was overwhelmingly negative. Some critics in Japan asserted that the accusations of dumping in Hong Kong were not verifiable, and that the US producers did not devote much time or effort toward winning higher market shares in Japan. The existence of the confidential side letter did not help the American case, either. These two events greatly enhanced, on the one hand, the image of a "bullying" US in Japan, and, on the other hand, the image of an "unfair" Japan in the US. Japan was portrayed as a trading partner that uses any means to increase exports to other countries and that cannot keep an agreement.

Around the time when the semiconductor agreement was violated, several debates over Japanese trading practices took place.

First, the extremely low levels of manufactured-goods imports to Japan became an issue. Drucker (1986) used the provocative term "adversarial trade," suggesting that Japan exports in order to destroy other countries' industries. Among economists, the problem was seen as one of low intra-industry trade. (Recall chapter 10.) Japan's image as in adversarial, unfair trader was ostensibly supported by its large current-account surpluses and low manufactured-goods imports. Economists had no difficulty attributing the trade-account imbalances to the particular mixes of fiscal and monetary policies chosen by the Japanese and US governments.

Second, complaints about limited access to Japanese markets for a broad range of products and commodities were brought up. Negotiations on Japanese restrictions on the importation of several agricultural products, including beef and citrus fruits, took place between 1985 and 1988. It was decided that Japan's import ceilings on beef and oranges would be raised gradually. All quotas on beef and citrus imports were removed and replaced by tariffs in April 1991. Although importing rice into Japan is still banned, the issue was brought up in 1986 and in 1988 by the American Rice Miller Association, only to be rejected by the US Trade Representatives.[7] In 1985 the Market-Oriented Sector-Specific (MOSS) talks, intended to improve American access to Japanese markets, were begun. Four categories—telecommunications, electronics, forest products, and medical equipment and pharmaceuticals—were chosen for discussion (see Prestowitz 1988, pp. 296–299).

In 1986, the construction business became another topic of market-access discussions. Since the Japanese government's procurement programs designated eligible construction companies (all of them domestic), new entry was almost impossible in the case of large construction projects in Japan. After complaints from the United States on this issue, the construction of the New Kansai Airport near Osaka became a test case for market access. An agreement on bidding procedure was struck in November 1987, and the Kansai Airport Corporation proceeded to accept foreign bids on the construction of the terminal building.

Alarmed by the increasing trade imbalances, the Japanese government also took several steps—some more cosmetic than serious—specifically aimed at increasing imports. In 1985, Prime Minister Nakasone suggested that each Japanese citizen purchase $100 worth of imported goods, so that the trade surplus would be cut by $12 billion. (Nakasone himself went out and purchased a tie and a bottle of wine.) The government also handed out fliers in downtown Tokyo encouraging Japanese citizens to buy imports. October was designated "import promotion month." MITI began to feature the motto "Spread friendship worldwide by promoting imports" on its stationery. In addition, "action programs" to increase imports and to absorb Japanese products through greater domestic demand were drawn up. Tariffs on forest products, tobacco, cigarettes, and aluminum were lowered one after another in 1987 and 1988.

Prime Minister Nakasone also formed a commission headed by the former Governor of Bank of Japan, Haruo Maekawa. The task of the Maekawa Commission was to recommend a strategy for the structural adjustment of the Japanese economy to reduce current-account surpluses and to improve the standard of living (quality of life). The Maekawa Commission issued a report (the Maekawa Report) in April 1986, and another report (the so-called new Maekawa Report) by the Economic Council [Keizai Shingikai] was delivered to the prime minister in May 1987.

The Maekawa Report specifiically recommended the following items:

domestic demand stimulation, aiming at improving the quality of life

transformation of industrial structures in order to encourage imports

improving access to the Japanese market by foreign companies

alignment of the exchange rate toward a level consistent with fundamentals

promotion of international policy coordination.

It was well understood from the beginning that the economic structure of Japan would have to be transformed from an export-dependent one to a domestic-demand-oriented one.

Import promotion was a response to US criticisms that the Japanese market is closed to foreigners. In addition to the strict quotas on such commodities as as beef, oranges, and rice, the two countries have discussed the close-knit Japanese distribution system, government procurement procedures, and licensing. Reducing these barriers was supposed to increase imports and hence to narrow the current-account imbalance.

Stimulating "domestic demand," or absorption, was also intended to slow the growth of exports (assuming a constant productive capacity). Promoting housing construction (via deregulation and subsidies) and improving the infrastructure was to shift resources from export-oriented production to domestic-oriented production. Steps to implement these policies should include policies to increase the land supply and, thus, to lower land and housing prices. Lower land prices will enable members of the younger generation to purchase larger houses without requiring greater savings for down payment. Such a shift in relative prices would lower the saving rate of the young generation and thereby lower the aggregate saving rate and decrease the outflow of capital.

THE SUPER-301 CLAUSE AND STRUCTURAL IMPEDIMENTS INITIATIVES

The Omnibus Trade Bill and Super-301

Despite improvements in the areas of imports and overall trade, the political relationship between the United States and Japan soured in 1988. Critics in the United States continued to dwell on Japan's failure to increase imports, and some Japanese became irritated by what they interpreted as US bullying of Japan (Ishihara and Morita 1988). In the summer of 1988, the Omnibus Trade and Competitiveness Act of 1988, the result of efforts put forth by several congressmen over several years, was signed into law by President Reagan. This act contained the "Super-301" clause, which strengthened Section 301 of the Trade Act of 1974. Under the new legislation, the US Trade Representative (USTR) can name countries as unfair trading partners. Barriers to specific commodities listed for these countries must be negotiated over the 18 months following the designation, and if the progress made in the negotiations is determined to be insufficient the US government can impose retaliatory measures. It was clear from talks and press conferences held by various congressmen that Japan was the major target of this legislation.

In May 1989 the USTR designated Japan as an unfair trading partner, along with India and Brazil, under the Super-301 clause. Forest products, satellites, and supercomputers were named as the products subject to barriers. Japan protested that negotiation under threat of sanctions is unacceptable. Progress, however, was made on the procurement and import procedures of the commodities in question. In 1990, after a year of negotiations, it was determined that Japan had made enough progress so that no sanctions would be imposed.

Although the outcome of the 1989 Super-301 designation was less dramatic than had been feared, the episode left a significant mark on the recent history of US-Japan trade conflicts. Those who see Japan as a closed market regard the Super-301 clause as a powerful tool that produces a credible threat in the negotiation process and thus helps open the Japanese market; critics in Japan regard it as an unacceptable measure that could lead to protectionism by mutual retaliation. Since the determination of who is an unfair trading partner is done unilaterally by the USTR, it is regarded by the Japanese (and many European countries) as a violation of multilateral trading frameworks such as the General Agreement on Tariffs and Trade (GATT). Some Japanese view the Super-301 clause as an attempt by the United States to become the sole judge of trading conflicts between the two countries.

Structural Impediments Initiatives

It is notable that talks on the Structural Impediments Initiatives (SII) took place in parallel with the Super-301 developments of 1989. The SII negotiations began in the fall of 1989; their purpose was "to identify and solve structural problems in both countries that stand as impediments to trade and to balance of payments adjustment with the goal of contributing to the reduction of payments imbalances" (*Final Report of Structural Impediments Initiative*). The talks yielded a report, which was submitted to President George Bush and Prime Minister Toshiki Kaifu in May 1990. The report listed six items on the Japanese agenda: saving and investment patterns, land policy, the distribution system, exclusionary business practices, keiretsu relationships, and pricing mechanisms.

The Japanese government, recognizing that Japan lags behind other developed countries in social overhead capital accumulation, promised to increase public expenditures on housing, sewers, public parks, waste-disposal systems, traffic safety, port facilities, airports, and seashore preservation and improvement. Increasing public investment would improve the current-account imbalances between

Japan and the United States by changing the saving-investment balance identity (explained in chapter 9). In order to increase supplies of housing and of residential land, the Japanese government promised to consider revision of the Land Lease Law and the House Lease Law, to increase efficiency in use of idle and underutilized land owned by the national or local governments, and to improve city planning to facilitate the conversion of agricultural land in residential areas. The distribution system was discussed in the SII talks because American exports are kept away from Japanese consumers by Japan's distribution system: overcrowded airports work against speedy customs clearance of imports, and a law restricts increases in the number of large retail stores (which tend to carry imports) for the sake of protecting small, family-run retail stores. Thus, modernizing the distribution system was considered to contribute to increasing Japan's imports. "Exclusionary business practices" and "keiretsu relationships" were targeted to be modified in order to promote more business chances for foreign countries in Japan. The government will encourage Japanese companies to purchase parts and other merchandise from foreign firms, and will aggressively enforce the Anti-Monopoly Act. The Japanese government will also implement policies to lower the prices of goods that could be purchased much more cheaply outside of Japan. These policies include deregulation, enforcement of the Anti-Monopoly Act, promotion of imports, and lowering of utility rates. This is a rather comprehensive list of promises for promoting Japanese consumers' welfare as well as promoting imports. Of these issues, the next two chapters will cover the distribution system and the land problem.

The SII talks were unique in the history of US-Japan negotiations in that Japan also pointed out what Japanese see as problems of the United States—for example, a lack of saving, a lack of worker training, and a deficient educational system. This aspect, however, was not publicized in the United States.

The Revisionist Argument

One version of the so-called revisionist argument goes as follows: Japan has been successful in closing its markets to foreign products, while Japanese products freely increase their shares in US markets.[10] In order to remove impediments in Japan against various US products, the US government has been negotiating with Japan for a long time. The removal of one impediment has led to the discovery of another barrier. As negotiations drag on, Japanese producers catch up with the imported technology and sell enough units to lock in market share (brand loyalty) in Japan. Hence, it is not enough to ask for equal opportunity (a "level playing field"). Instead, the United States should demand a clear quantitative target, such as market shares for foreign producers, and have the Japanese figure out how to achieve that target. Simply put, the Japanese economy works differently; therefore, a strategy deviating from what is recommended by the usual economic theory can be justified.[11] Put differently, the economic structures and political processes in Japan are so much different from those in the West that different rules of negotiation are justified. Neoclassical economic theory does not apply to Japan, some contend. The "different rules" they consider include targeting import quantities or market shares, and they believe that Japan should be responsible, using any means that suit the Japanese political process, for achieving the targets.

Some economists also advocate a similar strategy. Dornbusch (1990) argues that quantity-based managed trade, such as having Japan agree on import targets, with the use of a super-301-type threat, would enhance the US standard of living by balancing the trade account without depreciating the dollar too much. Tyson (1990) argues for subsidizing US high-tech industries to help them keep a competitive edge with respect to their Japanese counterparts, because high-tech industries have increasing-returns technology. However, standard criticisms from supporters of free trade apply to these arguments: Protectionary measures by the US invite similar actions by other countries. Moreover, it is difficult to imagine that Japan would agree to quantity-based targets. The volume edited by Lawrence and Schultze (1990), which contains Dornbusch's and Tyson's papers, offers several opposing views on this issue.

THE USE OF "GAIATSU"

There is a view that the present pattern of trade conflicts, in which the United States makes demands and Japan concedes, can be understood as the result of domestic constraints in both countries. Criticisms of Japan have provided a convenient scapegoat in the US political arena and have served as much-needed "foreign pressure" [gaiatsu] to persuade Japanese vested interest groups to give in to deregulation proposals in Japan. This clever scheme has broken down recently, however, as a result of the changing nature of US demands.

The US government—especially the Reagan administration—may not have been truly serious in criticizing Japan's trade surpluses or the low degrees of Japanese market penetration by US companies, and the Japanese government tolerated the appearance of being pushed around. Economists preached, and the US government may have realized early on, that the real culprit behind the US trade deficit was the US budget deficit and not the Japanese trade surplus. Yet in the 1980s alone the United States demanded export restraints on automobiles, financial-market deregulation, and increases in the import quota for beef, oranges, and pharmaceutical and lumber products, to name but a few demands. It is well recognized among economists, however, that these measures would have had only marginal effects on the US-Japan bilateral trade imbalance. The United States continued to press these issues because various groups in the United States stand to benefit from blaming Japan, and because Congress uses the Japan problem to pressure the White House. Because the Republican administrations since 1980 have supported free trade, the Democratic-controlled Congress has been able to put pressure on them by dramatizing how closed the Japanese markets are and by presenting the case that American manufacturers are hurt by Japan's closed markets. It is not difficult to find unhappy American executives who will testify on the subject of market penetration. Knowing that Congress would take this strategy, the Republican administrations have tried to appear tough on Japan.

The Japanese government recognized that the United States' demands were sometimes not helpful in resolving the trade deficit, but it played along because it saw that these demands might often benefit the majority of Japanese by increasing their productive efficiency and yielding benefits to Japanese consumers. From the Japanese point of view, some of the structural adjustments should have been carried out regardless of their potential effects on the balance of trade. Whether economic measures that enhance the quality of life reduce or increase external surpluses, if the policies improve efficiency adequately they should be regarded as worthwhile. The external balance of trade should not be the sole criterion for judging the desirability of a policy adjustment or the effectiveness of a policy.

These observations explain why the Japanese government appears to welcome foreign pressures when Japan needs a radical change in its economy. Japanese bureaucrats take the US demand as a mandate and work out the technical details of achieving it. Even if structural changes mean that some vested interest groups are hurt, the bureaucrats can point to the United States as a villain. Lobbyists for the vested interest group on the losing side are able to report back to their clients and constituents and explain the lost battle while still saving face: "There was nothing I could do; it was what the Americans wanted."[12]

This scheme was working well until the United State placed trade sanctions on Japan in response to an alleged violation of the semi-conductor agreement and used the Super-301 designation against Japan. Both actions, unlike other US "demands," were intensely disliked by the Japanese. The new types of US demands, such as the result-oriented strategy, were not acceptable to the Japanese.

Many in Japan feel that the differences in economic structure and political process between Japan and the United States do not justify any deviations from traditional multilateral trade negotiations. If the United States' trade deficits are the problem, they are due more to the United States' fiscal deficits than to any Japanese actions. A majority of the Japanese believe that the United States is being unreasonable by dictating unilaterally what it wants to sell. As was argued above, so long as American "demands" contained measures that improved Japan's efficiency (for instance, by dismantling regulations) they were generally welcomed. Once the "demands" turned into simple quotas and preferential treatment for US goods, however, resentment among the Japanese intensified. Of course, it is valid to point out that Japan has no right to single out which demands should be welcomed. The use of "foreign pressure" to avoid serious debate over domestic policy has now backfired.

CONCLUDING REMARKS

It is crucial to understanding the recent US-Japan trade conflict to realize that the problem is macroeconomic and "structural." For example, the conflict is not over whether Japanese firms gained market share in the United States by unfair dumping practices or by superior management. Instead, the heart of the problem is whether the differences in national saving-investment behavior are politically justifiable, and whether the system of political economy that made the Japanese economy grow can survive when its very success has made Japan one of the world's largest economies. Japan's economic strategy will be closely watched and will be quickly criticized if it is determined to treat domestic products preferentially. The world has become more interdependent, and conflicts are bound to arise if common trading rules, such as the GATT, are agreed upon and adhered to by the major trading partners.

NOTES

1. Quality circles are group meetings of workers whose purpose is to exchange ideas for improving the quality of products.

2. Just-in-time delivery is a system of monitoring and delivery in which inventories of parts are kept to a minimum on the assembly line and at the factory. Parts are delivered to manufacturing companies from parts makers a little at a time, with "stock-outs" carefully avoided, and then delivered as needed to assembly lines. The system obviously saves inventory costs and floor space in the factory. It also encourages workers to be more careful when handling parts.

3. The Japanese decision-making system is said to be of the "bottom-up" type, as opposed to the American "top-down" system. In Japan, ideas for product development and strategic planning are often drafted at the middle-management level and sent up to top management. The stylized American way is that the top management draws up important plans and sends them down for implementation.

4. The rest of this section summarizes the excellent survey by Aoki (1990).

5. According to Aoki (1990), Weitzman's idea of a "share economy" (recall chapter 8), which emphasized the sharing of profits by workers, is extended to the sharing of decision making.

6. Although these sectoral issues which became problems in the 1960s and 1970s provide interesting cases for studying international negotiations, we will not go into their details; the main emphasis of this chapter is on the conflicts that developed in the 1980s.

7. After the US president's announcement, the prime minister, MITI, and the Japanese automobile executives debated what to do. The automobile industry insisted on ending the restraints. MITI surveyed the target export number for each automaker and found that the targets collectively reached 2.7 million cars. The prime minister, worried about growing protectionist

sentiment in the US, is reported to have asked that the number be kept down to around 2.05 million.

MITI had two options at this time: (i) Let the restraint expire and have automakers set their targets freely but use implicit "guidance" to avoid an excessive exports. If the number became too high then MITI could invoke a formal restraint. (ii) Extend the restraint with a higher ceiling. As late as March 21, it appeared that the first option was to be used, but finally the second option was chosen, with a new ceiling of 2.3 million cars. MITI seemed to have thought that the automakers would not be able to hold exports down without formal restraint. Moreover, the first option may have invited an antitrust suit from the US Federal Trade Commission. MITI must have thought that this compromise would be welcomed by American protectionist politicians on the ground that the restraint was extended, though with a higher ceiling. (This paragraph is based on articles published in the newspaper *Nihon Keizai Shinbun* on March 21, 27, and 29, 1985.)

The reactions in the US were overwhelmingly negative, however. President Reagan, reportedly "embarrassed" by the decision, said that it would not substitute for Japanese efforts to open up the country to US exports. Worse still, the US Senate passed a Sense of Congress Resolution on March 28 asking the president to take tougher measures—retaliatory if necessary—to correct the unfair trading practices of the Japanese. The resolution, submitted by Senator John Danforth, was originally written to call for the extension of the voluntary export restraint on automobiles. Since the VER was continued but with an unsatisfactory ceiling, the Senate quickly amended the resolution to take a broader perspective.

On April 12, 1985, in the midst of critical reaction from the United States, Prime Minister Nakasone admitted in his answer to a question in the Diet that the decision to increase the number was a "mistake." MITI was surprised and frustrated by the criticism from the prime minister (*Nihon Keizai Shinbun*, April 13). This was a rare instance of MITI failing on the political front, both internationally and domestically.

8. Honda's Ohio plant was the first Japanese automobile factory in the United States. Nissan built a plant in Smyrna, Tennessee. Toyota and General Motors built a plant jointly in Fremont, California; then Toyota built its own plant in Kentucky.

9. The case was transferred to the Uruguay Round of the General Agreement on Tariffs and Trade.

10. As the so-called revisionists and their representative works, Chalmers Johnson (1982), Clyde Prestowitz (1988), James Fallows (1989), and Karel van Wolferen (1989) are frequently mentioned. However, emphasis and logic are slightly different among those four authors. The following argument is probably closest to Prestowitz's argument.

11. A clear case of such result-oriented policy was the report submitted to the US Trade Representatives by the Advisory Committee for Trade Policy and Negotiations in February 1989. Incidentally, result-oriented policy was

actually practiced in the side letter accompanying the semiconductor agreement.

12. The Japanese public had been extremely receptive to "American demands," taking them as things to be accomplished without evaluating their merits in terms of economic efficiency or consumers' welfare. The US demands tended to be seen as a mandate that could not be refused. This "black ship syndrome" (the reference is to Perry) is still dominant in Japan. For example, Japan's deregulation of financial markets was justified in terms of what was demanded by the US and the "current of the time" instead of on its merits to the majority of the Japanese public. Why didn't the government simply say that it was good for economic efficiency? Because the bureaucracy has an easier time blaming the US for dismantling the vested interests than it does persuading the vested interests by means of economic theory.

BIBLIOGRAPHY

Abegglen, J. C., and G. Stalk, Jr. 1985. *Kaisha, the Japanese Corporation.* Basic Books.

Aoki, M. 1990. "Toward an economic model of the Japanese firm." *Journal of Economic Literature* 28, no. 1: 1–27.

Dertouzos, M. L., R. K. Lester, R. M. Solow, and the MIT Commission on Industrial Productivity. 1989. *Made in America: Regaining the Productive Edge.* MIT Press.

Dornbusch, R. 1990. "Policy options for freer trade: The case for bilateralism." In *An American Trade Strategy: Options for the 1990s,* ed. R. Z. Lawrence and C. L. Schultze. Brookings Institution.

Drucker, P. F. 1986. *Frontiers of Management.* Harper & Row.

Fallows, J. 1989. *More Like Us: An American Plan for American Recovery.* Houghton Mifflin.

Ishihara, S., and A. Morita. 1988. *'No' to ieru Nihon* [*The Japan that Can Say No*]. Kōbunsha. (An English edition containing Ishihara's chapters and additional materials was published by Simon & Schuster in 1991.)

Johnson, C. 1982. *MITI and the Japanese Miracle.* Stanford University Press.

Lawrence, R. Z., and C. L. Schultze, eds. 1990. *An American Trade Strategy: Options for the 1990s.* Brookings Institution.

McCraw, T., ed. 1986. *America vs. Japan.* Harvard Business School Press.

Ouchi, W. 1981. *Theory Z.* Addison-Wesley.

Pascale, R. T., and A. G. Athos. 1981. *The Art of Japanese Management.* Warner Books.

Prestowitz, C. V., Jr. 1988. *Trading Places*. Basic Books.

Tyson, L. D. 1990. "Managed trade: Making the best of the second best." In *An American Trade Strategy: Options for the 1990s*, ed. R. Z. Lawrence and C. L. Schultze. Brookings Institution.

Vogel, E. F. 1979. *Japan as Number One: Lessons for America*. Harvard University Press.

Chapter 13

THE DISTRIBUTION SYSTEM

The Japanese distribution system has become the focus of extensive criticism, both abroad and within Japan. The Japanese market is "closed," complain many foreign manufacturers who have tried and failed to export to Japan. Their complaints center around the hostility of the Japanese distribution system to new entrants. Japanese wholesalers and retailers are said to be unwilling to put discounted imported commodities on the shelves, because they are pressured by the distributors of the competing Japanese products (which are still the bread and butter of their business) not to do so. Of the American "success stories" in Japan, some (such as Coca-Cola, Seven-Eleven, and Kentucky Fried Chicken) are franchises; others entered the Japanese market through joint ventures with the Japanese. Somehow the Japanese distribution channels seem to be closed without help from inside.

Criticisms come also from Japanese consumers. Many Japanese products are cheaper in New York than in Tokyo. This phenomenon was most pronounced during the period 1986–1988, when the advertised prices of Japanese-made cameras and VCRs in New York discount stores were much cheaper than the prices in the discount stores of Tokyo. Korean cars, which were successfully marketed in the United States in the mid 1980s, are virtually absent from Japan. Famous European brand-name goods, such as Louis Vuitton, Hermes, Chivas Regal, and Courvoisier, are sold in Japan at extraordinary premia. The "price differential between home and abroad" [Naigai Kakaku Sa] has become an important political problem in Japan. Many suspect that Japanese distributors are marking up imported goods with big margins and pocketing any profits from reduced costs due to yen appreciation (recall the example of "pass-through" in chapter 10).

Several peculiar aspects of the Japanese distribution system are suspected to cost Japanese consumers: Many small, family-run retail stores have survived, thanks to restrictions on the construction and operating hours of large retail stores, such as department and discount stores. The structure of the wholesale system has extra layers which seem unnecessary. The distribution-keiretsu stores carry only one domestic brand of a given product, thus discriminating against other domestic brands as well as against imports. Exclusive agents for many imported goods enjoy monopolistic rents, reducing the volume (and the dollar value) of imports.

Before we proceed with our analysis, it is important to distinguish two issues. The first issue is whether the Japanese distribution system is "efficient" in comparison with the systems of other countries; the second is whether the distribution system acts as a deterrent against new entrants, foreign or domestic. Note that the distribution system could be a nontariff barrier, even if it is "efficient" when measured by the direct and indirect costs of moving commodities from manufacturers' assembly lines to consumers. If what goes into the distribution pipeline is restricted for some reason, the pipeline may be both efficient and discriminatory.

THE CONVENTIONAL WISDOM

The many studies comparing the Japanese distribution system with those of other countries have yielded, in common, these findings:

• Japan has more retailers per capita than other countries. Many of these retailers are small, and many are family businesses.

• In Japan there are more wholesalers involved in distributing a good from the manufacturer to the retailers.

• There exist in Japan wholesalers and retailers who deal exclusively in one manufacturer's brand.

• There are many "unique" (peculiar, nontransparent) trading practices in Japan.

• The Japanese procedure for obtaining permits for large retail stores restricts the construction of such stores.

- There are in Japan many sole-representative importers who claim exclusive rights to import certain brands.
- Long-term relationships are important in Japanese business.

Numerous, Small Establishments

The average Japanese wholesale or retail store is small in terms of number of employees and value of annual sales. The conventional wisdom says that, because they are small, these stores cannot adopt technological advances (such as point-of-sale inventory control by means of bar-code scanning) that would create scale economies, and that this discriminates against imports and new domestic products because financially weak establishments are less likely to risk experimenting with new products.

The characteristic of numerous small establishments is evident from the three parts of table 13.1. First we compare the number of

Table 13.1

	Japan	United States	Germany (FRG)
Workers per wholesale establishment			
1982	9.3	12.6	10.1
1985	9.4	na	9.6
Workers per retail establishment			
1982	3.7	8.1	5.9
1985	3.9	na	5.8
Wholesale establishments per 1000 residents			
1982	3.3	1.5	2.0
1985	3.1	na	1.9
Retail establishments per 1000 residents			
1982	14.5	8.3	6.7
1985	13.5	na	6.6
Square meters of retail floor space			
1982	55.4	na	167.9
1985	58.0	na	na

Source: Maruyama et al. 1989.

Table 13.2
Time series on Japanese wholesale and retail establishments.

	1958	1960	1962	1964	1966	1968
Wholesale						
Establishments	193,000	226,000	223,000	229,000	287,000	240,000
Workers	1,551,000	1,928,000	2,129,000	2,524,000	3,042,000	2,697,000
Workers per est.	8.0	8.5	9.5	11.0	10.6	11.2
Retail						
Establishments	1,245,000	1,288,000	1,272,000	1,305,000	1,375,000	1,432,000
Workers	3,273,000	3,489,000	3,550,000	3,811,000	4,193,000	4,646,000
Workers per est.	2.6	2.7	2.8	2.9	3.0	3.2

Source: MITI Census of Commerce.

workers (both employees and self-employed persons) per establishment. Japanese retail stores are, on average, operated by about four persons. In fact, more than half of the retail stores have only one or two persons running them. The number of persons per establishment is about half of that in the United States and two-thirds of that in (West) Germany. The number of workers per wholesale establishment in Japan is about three-fourths of that in the United States but comparable to that in Germany. Second, the number of establishments per 1000 residents is much higher in Japan than in the United States or Germany. This is true at both the wholesale and the retail level. Retailers and wholesalers are about twice as dense in Japan as in the United States or Germany. Third, the average Japanese retailer has about a third of the floor space of his German counterpart.[1]

Are these Japanese characteristics changing? Table 13.2 shows the time series of the number of workers per establishment for the wholesale and retail sectors. The average number of workers per establishment has declined recently, after peaking in 1972. There is no evidence that the average size of wholesale establishments is increasing at all; however, the number of workers per retail establishment has been increasing steadily. Especially since 1982, the number of establishments has declined, while the number of workers continues to grow. Even at the increased growth pace achieved over the period 1982–1988, however, it would take Japan 20 years to catch up with Germany and 40 years to catch up with the United States in terms of workers per establishment.

1970	1972	1974	1976	1979	1982	1985	1988
256,000	259,000	292,000	340,249	368,608	428,858	413,016	436,502
2,861,000	3,008,000	3,290,000	3,512,973	3,672,638	4,090,919	3,998,437	4,331,601
11.1	11.6	11.2	10.3	10.0	9.5	9.7	9.9
1,471,000	1,496,000	1,548,000	1,614,067	1,673,667	1,721,465	1,628,644	1,619,599
4,926,000	5,141,000	5,303,000	5,579,800	5,960,432	6,369,426	6,328,614	6,850,478
3.3	3.4	3.4	3.5	3.6	3.7	3.9	4.2

The Many Layers within the Wholesale Industry

The Japanese distribution system is said to have many layers, and to be complicated, in that many distributors are involved in the pipeline from the manufacturers' warehouses to the consumers. Sometimes as many as three different wholesalers are involved between manufacturer and retailer. This makes the distribution system inefficient—that is, distribution costs as a percentage of consumer prices are higher than optimal.

The primary wholesaler may be a manufacturer's subsidiary. In that case, it deals with the manufacturer's own brands exclusively. (This is particularly prevalent in the fields of consumer electronics, cosmetics, detergents, and cameras.) In other cases, a primary wholesaler deals with other brands. A secondary wholesaler is typically a regional distributor, and a tertiary wholesaler is a local distributor. At one extreme, a large-scale retailer (say, a chain of large supermarkets) typically obtains goods from a wholesaler, whereas in the United States a similar chain would obtain goods directly from the manufacturers.

As a measure of the number of layers in the wholesale industry, it is popular to use the W/R sales ratio, which compares the sales volumes of the wholesale and retail levels (table 13.3). Japan's high W/R ratio is interpreted as a reflection of the numerous layers in the wholesale industry, with sales of the same commodity being double- or triple-counted as wholesale sales. A high W/R ratio may

Japan

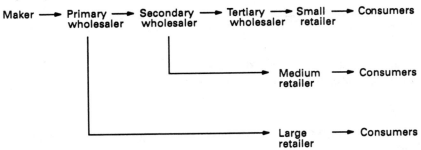

United States

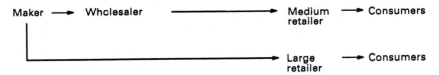

Figure 13.1
Typical merchandise flows.

Table 13.3
Wholesale[a]/retail ratios.

		Japan	United States	West Germany
Sales	1982	3.53	1.09	1.67 (1978)
	1985	3.44	0.97 (1986)	1.80 (1984)
Inventories	1982	1.60	0.82	1.17 (1981)
	1985	1.55	0.85 (1986)	1.17 (1984)
Number of establishments	1982	0.225	0.176	0.290 (1978)
	1985	0.229	na	0.292 (1984)

a. Wholesale-trade data are based on merchant wholesalers.
Source: Maruyama et al. 1989.

Table 13.4
Proportion of wholesale sales by class of customer.

Customer class	Japan (1982)	United States (1982)	West Germany (1986)
Other wholesalers	41.9	24.8	16.2
Retailers and repair shops	24.0	28.0	30.0
Export	7.4	9.8	14.9
Households and individuals	0.6	1.6	2.8
Industrial users		15.0	26.8
Manufacturing and mining	26.1		
Others		20.8	9.2

Source: Maruyama et al. 1989.

be the result of other characteristics, however, such as retail establishments' being especially small. If the value of retail sales per establishment is small because of a small scale of operations, the W/R ratio will be high. Hence, the W/R ratio alone is not conclusive evidence of the multi-layered nature of the Japanese wholesale industry.[2]

We can also measure sales to other wholesalers as a proportion of total sales. As table 13.4 clearly shows, more sales between wholesalers take place in Japan than in other countries—one piece of evidence that Japan has a multi-layered wholesale industry.

Theoretical Explanations

There are two opposite views of how to understand the existence of many small retail stores and the multi-level wholesale system in Japan. The first view is that these characteristics are the efficient results of consumers' preferences and limited space (see Flath 1988, 1989a and Maruyama 1988); the second is that they are largely the results of regulation (see McCraw and O'Brien 1986).

The logic of the first view goes as follows: Numerous, small retail establishments (neighborhood stores) are the rational result of Japanese consumers' diets and buying habits. The Japanese consumer prefers to shop every day in small quantities in neighborhood stores. Fresh fish must be purchased every day. Moreover, consumers' refrigerators are too small to store a weekly inventory of food, and automobiles are inefficient for use in urban areas because of the traffic congestion. Although the stores are small, which seems inefficient, they are usually family-run establishments adjacent to the owner's home, with low overhead costs and rents. All these small retail shops require extra layers in the distribution system, since organizational (monitoring) costs fix the optimal number of retailers (or other wholesalers) per one wholesaler.

The second view is that these characteristics are indications of some distortions in the Japanese distribution system. Even though the roads are congested, public transportation is fully developed and punctual, so consumers are quite mobile. There is no reason to suppose that retailers must be close by. In fact, many Japanese office workers buy food at grocery stores in the basements of department stores near train stations on their way home from work. Sashimi (raw fish) is popular, but it is not an everyday meal. And even with numerous, small retail stores, the ratio of wholesalers to retailers could be lower, since retailers are located close together. In short, according to this view the wholesale/retail ratio should be *lower* in Japan than in other countries,[3] and the stylized facts described above should be the results of regulations.

Keiretsu and "Unique" Trading Practices

Japanese manufacturers develop exclusive distribution systems (distribution *keiretsu*). Panasonic stores, Sony stores, Toshiba stores, and others carry a wide range of electronic products, but all from one brand. This vertical semi-integration makes it difficult for new entrants, including importers, to penetrate the market. A new entrant would need to establish its own network of distributors, an operation involving a large risk that few foreign firms would like to take.

Japan's unique trading practices, including return policies, salespersons on loan, and price-maintenance and rebate systems, make the distribution system seem complicated and inefficient.

The belief that a simple price incentive (discount) for a newly introduced product is insufficient to establish a niche is another stumbling block for price competition. Moreover, discount (manufacturers') coupons delivered with newspapers, which are widespread and popular in daily and especially in Sunday papers in the United States, are banned in Japan by mutual agreement among newspaper publishers, out of fear that they might cause cutthroat competition among large newspapers.

Retail prices are often "maintained" by implicit agreements between manufacturers and the retailers, which operate via wholesalers. Rebates between retailers and wholesalers are just one means of nonlinear pricing. It is alleged that the terms of rebates are often not spelled out beforehand, but left to the discretion of wholesalers and manufacturers.

The conventional wisdom on keiretsu is as follows: Keiretsu stores at the wholesale and retail levels are controlled by the respective manufacturers. In the keiretsu stores, manufacturers control which brands will be carried, how much of a discount from "standard retail prices" (or "retail price wished by the maker," in the literal translation) can be allowed, and how unsold inventories will be dealt with. In this sense, the essential aspect of a keiretsu in the distribution sector is its package of "vertical restraints" (Flath 1989b).

Often wholesalers and retailers deal exclusively with a single manufacturer. (Some argue that many keiretsu stores now deal with more than one brand (*Nihon Keizai Shinbun* 1989, p. 84), but no estimate of the number of such stores is provided.) Returns of unsold merchandise from retail stores to wholesalers are often allowed even if the retail stores bought the merchandise. In order to maintain resale prices, the manufacturer must accept returns of unsold goods; otherwise, retail stores would face too much risk in their earnings in the presence of uncertain demand. In a sense, the "liberal returns policy" [Henpin Sei] and the price-maintenance system can be understood as the results of profit maximization by an oligopolist who produces differentiated products, who has keiretsu power to impose vertical restraints, and whose retailers face an uncertain demand curve (Flath 1989a; Flath and Nariu 1989). According to this view, there is nothing unfair or inefficient about the "liberal returns policy." If there is any problem, it is the institution (or the lack of strict enforcement of fair-trade laws) that allows oligopolistic vertical restraints by manufacturers with differentiated products.

Many department stores and other large retail stores are staffed with "persons on loan" from manufacturers who use them to promote their own goods in retail stores. Although they are on the manufacturers' payrolls, they act as salespersons, promoting and sometimes demonstrating products (particularly new ones) and sometimes gathering information on customers' reactions for later use in product development.[4] In twelve of Japan's department stores, these "persons on loan" outnumber the store's own sales staff. When productivity in the retail sector is examined by size of establishment, those stores with more than 500 employees have extremely high productivities (Maruyama et al. 1989). A significant portion of the high productivity is believed to be due to "persons on loan."

The Large-Scale Retail Store Law [Daiten Ho]

A law that restricts the construction and the operating hours of large retail stores makes it difficult for discount stores, department stores, and supermarkets to take advantage of scale economies. Since these stores carry more imports than smaller-sized retail stores do, this law works against the interests of foreign manufacturers as well as against those of Japanese consumers.

In 1956 the Department Store Law, which requires a permit for every new department store, was enacted in order to curb the growth of department-store chains. Large supermarkets, discount stores, and other large chain stores, which were not covered by the Department Store Law, then became popular. In order to cover these new types of retail stores, the Large Scale Retail Store Law [Daiten Ho], which requires the "reporting" of construction, replaced the Department Store Law in 1974. It was revised in 1979 to its current form.

Restricting the growth of traditional department stores allowed large supermarkets to experience a tremendous jump in sales by adding more stores and merging smaller ones. "Supermarkets" in Japan should be understood as large, nonspecialized discount stores, like American K-Marts, with relatively large grocery sections. Large supermarkets now occupy the top four places in the ranking of large retail stores in Japan.

The Daiten Ho covers two types of stores: stores of 1500 or more square meters (3000 square meters in large cities) and stores of 500–1500 square meters (500–3000 square meters in large cities). The construction plan for a large retail store must be submitted to the governor of the prefecture; then the Shō Chō Kyō (the committee for "adjusting" retail activities) in the community, which is organized under the Chamber of Commerce, "discusses" the plan. For the first type of store, the report from the Dai Ten Shin (the subcommittee on large retail stores) goes to the MITI minister. For the second type of store, the report goes to the prefectural governor. The "adjustment" items include floor space, opening date, store hours, and number of days closed per year. To all appearances, when a plan is submitted, it will be discussed with neighboring shopping malls and stores and will be approved in due time. The letter of the law does not tell the whole story, however. MITI, through "ministry guidance" [gyōsei shidō], controls the interpretation and implementation of the law. In fact, in the early 1980s the implementation was tightened so that it became not uncommon to take more than two years after submission of a plan for final approval. In essence, the law and its implementation can make it prohibitively costly to open a large retail store when the neighboring stores voice opposition.

Table 13.5 shows how the application to build a large retail store is handled. The most time-consuming part of the process is not a part of the law but merely the "practices" and gyōsei shidō of MITI. In particular, the "pre-explanation" is not a part of the legal code or of gyōsei shidō but just a traditional practice. Some local governments do not accept an application for a building permit without an agreement from the Chamber of Commerce, however. The local businesses could simply boycott the "pre-explanation," so that it could take a long time before an application could be filed. (In one case, about seven years passed between the announcement of a plan to open a store and the actual opening.)

Flath (1988) investigated how the number of other types of stores changed as the number of department stores changed in various prefectures. He found that whereas the number of drug stores was not affected by the number of department stores, the numbers of food, liquor, and apparel stores were quite sensitive to the number of department stores. This explains how the Daiten Ho allows some types of small stores to survive.

It should also be noted that the Daiten Ho protects existing department stores from planned department stores. Existing department stores often lobby with small stores in the neighborhood against planned openings of competing department stores. Because of this, the Daiten Ho did not become a dividing line between large

Table 13.5
Implementation of Daiten Ho.

1. Store A plans to build a large-scale retail store.

2. Store A presents a Pre-Explanation [Jizen Setsumei] to the local government, the Chamber of Commerce, and local businesses regarding four conditions: opening day, floor space, closing time, and number of store holidays

3. Local Chamber of Commerce and local stores give "agreement."

4. Store A files an Article 3 Application (application for a building permit) with the Governor.

5. The Governor sends the application to the MITI minister.

6. The MITI minister asks the local Chamber of Commerce whether Store A will affect existing local businesses.
   a. If no, Store A may file an Article 5 Application with the Governor and it will be approved.
   b. If yes, then proceed to 7.

7. Store A and local business must hold a meeting called "Pre-Sho Cho Kyo" [Jizen Sho Cho Kyo]. This takes about 8 months.

8. Store A files an Article 5 application with the Governor.

9. The Governor sends the application to the MITI minister.

10. The formal Sho Cho Kyo (an abbreviation for Shogyo Katsudo Chosei Kyogikai) examines the opening day, the floor space, the closing time, and the number of store holidays. The Sho Cho Kyo consists of local retail stores, local consumers, and scholars.

11. The Chamber of Commerce expresses its opinion.

12. The Large Scale Retail Store Commission [Shingikai] examines the case.

13. The local government expresses its opinion.

14. The MITI minister makes recommendations on conditions for building.

15. The MITI minister gives his approval.

(The process from steps 8 to 15 must occur within 5 months, according to Article 5.)

stores' interests and small stores' interests. This explains the slow
change in the law.

Sole-Representative Importers

Many products are still imported to Japan by exclusive representatives of the manufacturers, although an increasing number of products (including particular brands of Scotch whiskey and American
and European automobiles) have recently been imported more competitively. Sole-representative importers have, in many cases,
charged monopolistic prices with high margins on their brand-name
imports, which shows that Japanese consumers are ready for "conspicuous consumption" and that parallel imports are difficult for
some reason. Parallel imports (that is, imports through independent
wholesalers or third-country markets, without the authorization of
the manufacturer or the representative importer) have been difficult
because repair and other services after purchase are often not provided by the representative importer or the independent stores in
Japan.

Personal and Long-Term Relationships

It is often said that in order to make business deals in Japan it is
essential to establish a long-term relationship, marked by frequent
personal socializing, in addition to a reliable delivery record and a
reputation for consistent quality and after-sale service. Requiring a
long-term relationship for trading between firms puts companies
that produce high-quality products in a favorable light. The other
side of the same coin, however, is a barrier against companies trying
to break into the market.[5]

The emphasis on long-term relationships and the keiretsu distribution system discourage stores from discounting merchandise to
levels significantly below the manufacturers' suggested retail prices.
The most famous episode involved Daie, now the top retail chain in
Japan, and the consumer-electronics giant Matsushita. When Daie
sold Matsushita products at a 20 percent discount in 1965, Matsushita stopped shipping products to Daie. Daie sued Matsushita for
anti-trust violations in 1967. To this day, Matsushita refuses to deal
directly with Daie.

MEASURES OF EFFICIENCY IN THE DISTRIBUTION SECTOR

There have been many studies of productivity and efficiency in the distribution sector. The most popular measure of the productivity and efficiency in this sector has been "sales per employee," as in Ingene 1982. When appropriate data are available, "value added per employee" is also used, as in Beckman 1957.[6]

The Japanese distribution system has been studied in international comparisons by Tajima and Miyashita (1985) and Maruyama et al. (1989); see also Ryutsu Keizai Kenkyusho (1988). Ito and Maruyama (1990) examined gross margin, operating expenses, and operating profits, using data from the Commerce Census of the United States and a similar source for Japan. The Ministry of International Trade and Industry (1988, p. 73) and Nishimura and Tsubouchi (1989) calculated gross margins from the input-output table.

Do the "unique" features of the Japanese distribution system add up to make it an inefficient system, as is often claimed? Several measures have been used in attempts to answer this question.

Sales per Worker, Sales per Establishment, and Value Added

"Sales per worker" or "sales per establishment" has been a popular measure of "performance" and "efficiency." These measures were used by Takeuchi and Bucklin (1977) and cited by Rangan (1989). From the data presented here in table 13.6, Rangan concluded that "the performance of the Japanese counterpart was significantly worse." This conclusion is most likely irrelevant for the Japanese distribution sector of the 1990s, however. The data set is old, and the measure may not really reflect "performance" or "efficiency." Table 13.7 presents more recent data on the same measure. In this table Japan does not look inefficient, except in "retail sales per establishment." The Japanese wholesale sector appears comparable to or better than the wholesale sectors of the other countries.

There are three caveats. First, productivity in the Japanese wholesale sector may be overestimated, because large-scale trading houses [Sogo Shosha] are included in the wholesale sector. Trading houses engage in export-import business and in international trade involving third countries as well as in domestic retail business. Second, as suggested above, productivity in the retail sector may be biased upward because of "persons on loan" in large department

Table 13.6
Productivity measured by retail sales,[a] 1952–1968.

		Japan	United States
Sales per establishment	1952	5.8	96.6 (1948)
	1958	10.6	123.7
	1968	28.0	175.9 (1967)
Sales per worker	1952	2.6	19.0 (1948)
	1958	3.7	22.8
	1968	8.0	28.2 (1967)
Number of establishments per 1000 residents	1952	14.1	11.3 (1948)
	1958	15.7	10.3
	1968	17.8	8.9 (1967)

a. Sales are in thousands of dollars, converted at 360 yen/$, deflated using
the Japanese retail-price index, 1968 base year (Japan).
Source: Rangan 1989, citing Takeuchi and Bucklin 1977.

Table 13.7
Productivity measured by sales.[a]

	Japan	United States	West Germany
Sales per worker, wholesale			
1982	390.5	272.4	173.5 (1979)
1985	448.7	na	299.8
Sales per worker, retail			
1982	62.3	68.5	51.4 (1979)
1985	72.4	na	80.3
Sales per establishment, wholesale			
1982	3614.7	3430.6	1750.8 (1979)
1985	4219.4	na	2870.8
Sales per establishment, retail			
1982	230.3	554.2	302.9 (1979)
1985	281.3	na	465.8

a. Sales are in thousands of dollars, measured at the PPP exchange rate of
the OECD: $1 = 2.54 DM in 1979; $1 = 237 yen in 1982; $1 = 222
yen = 2.48 DM in 1985.
Source: Maruyama et al. 1989.

Table 13.8
Ratio of value added per worker in various sectors (1985).

	Japan	United States	West Germany
Distribution sector / Industry Total	0.76	0.70	0.68
Manufacturing sector / Industry Total	1.19	1.12	0.95
Distribution sector / Manufacturing sector	0.64	0.63	0.71

Source: Maruyama et al. 1989.

stores. Another contamination in the data is the inclusion of eating and drinking establishments, which are not fully a part of the distribution system, in the retail business statistics. Third, the amount of sales is not a good measure of productivity, since it does not reflect any input costs. Compare a retail store that deals in expensive products (say, diamonds) with high input costs (at the wholesale level) and a retail store that deals in less expensive products (say, toys) having low purchase (input) prices. Even if the number of workers, their wage rates, and the net profits are the same, the former store would have a higher level of sales per worker. Moreover, double-counting in the multi-layered wholesale sector may cloud the picture.[7]

Hence, a more accurate measure of productivity is value added. Table 13.8 shows the value added, net of input costs, in the distribution sector relative to that in the manufacturing sector. Using this measure, was find that the value added per worker is as high in Japan as in the United States. According to this measure, there is no evidence that the Japanese distribution sector is less efficient than that of the United States.

Gross Profit Margin

When we regard the efficiency of the distribution system in terms of how much extra a consumer must pay on top of the manufacturer's costs in order to obtain a good, an appropriate measure is the *gross profit margin* (defined as the difference between sales revenues and

Table 13.9
Gross profit margin ratios.

	Japan	United States	Germany (FRG)
Wholesale			
1978	11.9		
1981		na	12.7
1986	11.2	19.4	12.6 (1985)
Retail			
1978	27.0		
1981		na	34.5
1986	27.1	31.0	34.2 (1985)

Source: Maruyama et al. 1989.

merchandise costs, with the latter including merchandise purchase costs plus the change in the value of inventories during the period). Viewed from the other side of the balance sheet, the gross profit margin is equal to the sum of net profits and operating expenses, with the latter including the employee payroll, rents on establishments, and advertising, transportation, and depreciation costs. The gross profit margin divided by the sales volume is called the *gross-profit-margin ratio*.

Contrary to popular belief, the Japanese gross profit margin is quite comparable to, and indeed lower than, that of the United States (table 13.9). Operating expenses and net profits are not particularly high in Japan. Apparently, Japan's small retailers do not suffer from inefficiency.

There are some caveats to this conclusion.[8] First, although the small retail shops do not keep transportation costs and purchase costs down (physical distribution costs are high, and no volume discounts are available from wholesalers), they do operate on low rents with small payrolls. In fact, as was mentioned above, many of the small retail outlets are operated by the owners, who maintain their principal residence in the rear of the building, and many of the shopowners are elderly couples who do not require high net profits or high payrolls.

Second, the "average wholesale" and "average retail" figures for Japan may be misleading, owing to some structural outliers. Large-

Table 13.10
Distribution Margin: Census Approach.

	Japan	United States
Aggregate margin, distribution sales[a]		
1978	15.6	
1986	15.5	25.3
Aggregate margin, retail sales[b]		
1978	63.4	
1985	57.6	49.7

a. Wholesale data are based on merchant wholesalers.
Source: Maruyama et al. 1989.

scale wholesalers or retailers may pull the average up, or some non-distribution-industry subgroup, such as "eating and drinking places," may be distorting the average figures. According to Ito and Maruyama (1990), however, the same pattern is verified for industry-specific data, so the Japanese distribution sector cannot be judged inefficient.

Third, considering retail and wholesale margins separately may be misleading in light of the fact that the wholesale/retail ratios of Japan and other countries are quite different. Even if the gross margin is not larger for Japan, the fact that goods pass through many "layers" may multiply costs. The margin of the distribution system as a whole should be constructed so that it represents the notion of how much a consumer must pay on top of the manufacturer's costs.

The last concern is taken up in table 13.10, which reports the aggregate margins for wholesalers and retailers. These margins are calculated as follows:

$$(MW + MR)/R = (MW/W) \times (W/R) + (MR/R),$$

where MW = gross margin of wholesalers, MR = gross margin of retailers, R = retail sales, and W = wholesale sales. The table also shows that the Japanese aggregate margin is slightly higher than that of the United States. In sum, the gross margin figures do not reveal any inefficiencies in the Japanese distribution system.

Table 13.11
Distribution margins calculated by input-output method.

	Japan		United States, 1977
	1980	1985	
MITI (1988)		29.78	39.44
Official base	33.4	34.4	35.7
Wholesale	9.9	8.2	na
Retail	23.5	26.2	na
Nishimura (1989)	36.8	38.6	35.7

Source: Nishimura and Tsubouchi 1989.

The Distribution Margin: The Input-Output Approach

There is another way to calculate the gross margin in the entire distribution sector (the distribution margin, for short). MITI (1988) calculated the distribution margin from input-output tables, and reported that the US distribution margin is about twice the Japanese one. Nishimura and Tsubouchi (1989) corrected the MITI figures by reclassifying repair services and government-controlled distribution services (for tobacco, rice, and other goods), and found that the distribution margin for Japan is comparable to its US counterpart. The numbers are reported here in table 13.11.[9]

CONCLUDING REMARKS

Although the Japanese distribution system appears to be very different from its American counterpart, its performance as measured by value added, gross margin, operating expenses, and labor costs is quite comparable. Hence, we cannot conclude that the Japanese characteristics are symptoms of inefficiency.

When the findings discussed above are combined with other pieces of evidence, such as that retail prices are generally higher in Japan and that the behavior of Japanese exporters can be viewed as "pricing to market" (see Marston 1989), the following scenario seems plausible: The keiretsu or other structures that make vertical restraints and resale-price maintenance possible may segregate the Japanese market from the rest of the world. Such segregation makes pricing-to-market behavior possible, and Japanese manufacturers seem to be exercising this power. In this sense, the distribution system is guilty of causing price differentials between Japan and other countries.

On the other hand, whatever rents accrue from vertical restraints and pricing-to-market behavior are not shared by the distribution sector, and the distribution sector itself does not incur extra operating expenses which may apparently result from the Japanese characteristics. The Japanese distribution system is as efficient as its US counterpart, once the system receives goods from manufacturers.

NOTES

1. This may be due to high land prices in Japan. (See chapter 14.)

2. Note that the W/R sales ratio can be decomposed into the product of

Sales per wholesale establishment
   Sales per retail establishment

and

Number of wholesale establishments per 1000 residents
   Number of retail establishments per 100 residents

Therefore, if sales per establishment in the retail sector in one country are extremely low, the W/R ratio will be higher, even though the other components are comparable with those of other countries.

3. As David Flath has pointed out, when numbers of stores per thousand households are compared for different prefectures in Japan, Tokyo (the most densely populated prefecture) and Hokkaido (the most sparsely populated) record the lowest ratios. The average number of retail stores (excluding eating and drinking places) per prefecture is 45.5 per 1000 population; Tokyo reports 35.1 and Hokkaido 34.1. The comparable number for the entire US is 23.8.

4. Flath (1989a) applies Telser's (1960) argument of resale-price maintenance to the vertical-restraint behavior (keiretsu) among Japanese firms. But Telser's argument, which emphasizes the merit of "demonstration," can be applied to the "persons on loan" as well.

5. Kyocera, with a short history as a high-tech firm, had trouble finding customers for its semiconductors in Japan until it established a reputation in the US market. When Suntory, traditionally a distiller of whiskey, entered the beer market, which was then controlled by Kirin, Sapporo, and Asahi, it had trouble finding wholesalers and retailers who would provide shelf space for Suntory beer until Asahi gave Sapporo help through Asahi's keiretsu wholesalers and retailers.

6. There are some conceptual difficulties associated with the use of these measures as criteria for efficiency. Bucklin (1978) and Achaval (1984) have also expressed caution.

7. In order to understand why sales per worker would be an incorrect statistic in a multi-layer wholesale system, consider the following example. Suppose that $100 is charged for sales of a product from a single-layer wholesale sector to the retail sector, and that 10 people are working in the (single-layer) wholesale sector. Then $10 of sales per worker would be recorded as the relevant statistic in this single-layer system. Next, suppose that the same product is sold 3 times in the multi-layer wholesale sector (recall figure 13.1): for $50 by 5 people in the first wholesale layer, for $70 by 7 people in the second layer, and for $100 by 10 people in the third layer. Then the volume of sales per capita in each layer is still $10, and it is shown as such in the Japanese statistics. But the "net" (or true) volume of wholesale sales per worker—that is, how many people are needed to pass the goods to the retail level—should be $100/(10 + 7 + 5), a much lower number than $10 per person.

8. Some American economists speculate that the apparent high gross margin among US wholesalers and retailers is a reflection of high incidences of shoplifting, employee theft, and burglary. Unfortunately, we do not have data on damages in the distribution sector from such crimes.

9. For details of the adjustment see Nishimura and Tsuboushi 1989. There are two caveats to remember when comparing the Nishimura-Tsubouchi table and our table. First, the Nishimura-Tsubouchi table includes only consumer goods, whereas our table theoretically includes both consumer and producer goods. Second, the survey on which our table is based is an establishment survey, whereas the input-output-table approach does not double-count trades within the wholesale industry.

BIBLIOGRAPHY

Achaval, D. D., ed. 1984. "Productivity in retailing." *Journal of Retailing* 60, no. 3 (special issue).

Beckman, T. 1957. "The value added concept as a measure of output." *Advanced Management* 22: 6–9.

Bucklin, L. 1978. *Productivity in Marketing*. American Marketing Association.

Flath, D. 1988. Why Are There So Many Retail Stores in Japan? Working paper 17, Center on Japanese Economy and Business, Columbia University.

Flath, D. 1989a. The Economic Rationality of the Japanese Distribution System. Working paper 29, Center on Japanese Economy and Business, Columbia University.

Flath, D. 1989b. "Vertical restraints in Japan." *Japan and the World Economy* 2: 187–203.

Flath, D., and T. Nariu. 1989. "Returns policy in the Japanese marketing system." *Journal of the Japanese and International Economies* 3, March: 49–63.

Ingene, C. A. 1982. "Labor productivity in retailing." *Journal of Marketing* 46: 75–90.

Ito, T., and M. Maruyama. 1990. Is the Japanese Distribution System Really Inefficient? Working paper, National Bureau of Economic Research.

Marston, R. C. 1989. "Price behavior in Japanese and US manufacturing." Presented at NBER conference on "The US and Japan: Trade and Investment."

Maruyama, M. 1988. *Ryūtsū no Keizai Bunseki* [The Economic Analysis of Distribution]. Sobunsha.

Maruyama, M., Y. Togawa, K. Sakai, N. Sakamoto, and M. Arakawa. 1989. "Distribution system and business practices in Japan." Presented at Seventh EPA International Symposium, Economic Research Institute, Economic Planning Agency, Japan.

McCraw, T. K., and P. A. O'Brien. 1986. "Production and distribution: Competition policy and industry structure." In *America Versus Japan: A Comparative Study*, ed. T. K. McCraw. Harvard Business School Press.

Ministry of International Trade and Industry. 1988. *White Paper, 1988*. Ministry of Finance.

Nihon Keizai Shinbunsha. 1989. *Nichibei Masatsu* [US-Japan Conflicts]. Nihon Keizai Shinbunsha.

Nishimura, K. and H. Tsubouchi. 1989. Commerce margins in Japan. Discussion paper 89-J-8, Faculty of Economics, University of Tokyo.

Rangan, V. K. 1989. "Efficiency in the distributive system." Presented at Fourth MITI/RI Conference.

Ryūtsū Keizai Kenkyusho. 1988. *Ryūtsūgyō no Kokusai Hikaku ni Kansuru Chōsa Kenkyū* [Research for the International Comparison of the Distribution Industry].

Tajima, Y., and M. Miyashita. 1985. *Ryūtsū no Kokusai Hikaku* [The International Comparison of Distribution]. Yuhikaku.

Takeuchi, H., and L. P. Bucklin. 1977. "Productivity in retailing: Retail structure and public policy." *Journal of Retailing* 53, no. 1: 35–46.

Telser, L. 1960. "Why should manufacturers want fair trade?" *Journal of Law and Economics* 3: 86–105.

Chapter 14

ASSET PRICES: LAND AND EQUITIES

Asset prices have been a focus of intensive studies for Japanese economists and policy makers since the mid 1980s. Recently, both land and stock (equity) prices have soared to levels that many consider too high. High land prices have raised housing prices so much that many potential buyers in their thirties and forties believe that they are priced out of the market for owner-occupied housing, and high equity prices have scared foreign investors away from the Tokyo stock market.

The real puzzle here is the fact that both land and equities have high "price-earning ratios." In theory, an asset price is determined by the present value of the stream of its future earnings—rents in the case of housing, dividends in the case of stocks.[1] The current levels of land and stock prices in Japan do not seem to be justified on the basis of the present-value calculation (unless prices increase rapidly enough to keep producing capital gains indefinitely). Hence, high price-earning ratios may be the reflection of ever-increasing price levels. Many consider this kind of process as indicating bubbles rather than as being based on fundamentals.

Since investors attempt to arbitrage among different kinds of assets, it is not a coincidence that land and stock prices share common characteristics. On the other hand, the relationship between the two prices could be understood more directly. In a sense, the stock price, which determines the market value of a company, reflects investors' assessments of the company's liquidation value. Land is an important part of a company's assets. Hence, as land prices go up, so do stock prices. Accordingly, high stock prices may result from high land prices.

The acuteness of Japan's high land prices can be seen by comparing the total valuations of the land areas of Japan and the United States in the balance sheets of the nations. At the end of 1984 the national land wealth of Japan was 940 trillion yen, equivalent to $4.6 trillion at 200 yen/dollar; that of the United States was $3 trillion. After the sharp appreciation of the yen in 1985–86 and the sharp increase in Japan's land prices since 1985, the total land value of Japan (1637 trillion yen = $12.6 trillion, at 130 yen/dollar) is considered to be about three times that of the United States. Since the total area of Japan is about 1/25 that of the United States, the average unit cost of land is about 60–75 times as much in Japan as in the United States.

The high cost and low quality of Japanese housing prompts complaints from Japanese citizens. High housing prices are especially worrisome for those who cannot expect to inherit adequate housing from their parents. Episodes of sharply rising housing prices, especially in 1973–74 and 1986–87, have created a sense of widening inequality between those who already have a house and those who do not. Such sentiments may signal difficult political problems to come. Faced with growing interest in the issues of land use, housing, and the "equality of life," the government has proposed efforts to improve conditions in all three areas. In fact, the problem of housing and land has been accorded top priority in many recent government reports and long-term plans.

AN INTERNATIONAL COMPARISON

To better understand the housing situation in Japan, it is helpful to document some key facts from both a time-series perspective and a cross-section perspective. First, we will examine the quantity, quality, and cost of housing in Japan. Second, we will review government policies regarding housing costs.

Is There Enough Housing?

In the 1960s and the 1970s, Japan made large public and private investments in housing. In fact, the number of houses has been increasing so much that the Ministry of Construction has said that the housing problem is one of quality, not quantity. The total number of

Table 14.1
Housing statistics for Japan.

	1958	1963	1968	1973	1978	1983
(A) Houses (thousands)	17,934	21,097	25,591	31,059	35,451	38,607
(B) Households (thousands)	18,647	21,821	25,320	29,651	32,835	35,197
(C) = (A)/(B)	0.96	0.97	1.01	1.05	1.08	1.10

Source: Ministry of Construction Housing Survey.

Table 14.2
Ownership ratios and housing per capita, 1983.

	United States	Japan
(a) Occupied units	84,638,000	34,705,000
(b) Owner-occupied	54,724,000	21,656,000
(c) Rental	29,914,000	13,049,000
(d) Owner ratio, (b)/(a)	64.7%	62.4%
(e) Population	234,799,000	121,049,000
(f) Population 21+	159,444,000	86,039,000
(g) (a)/(e)	36.0%	28.7%
(h) (a)/(f)	53.1%	40.3%

Data sources: (Japan) Ministry of construction (1986); (United States) Statistical Abstract (1989, p. 688).

houses is greater than the total number of households, and the "ownership ratio" in Japan is comparable to that of the United States. (See row C of table 14.1 and row d of table 14.2.) These facts are quoted often by policy makers, who argue that the focus of housing policy should be shifted toward seeking improvements in the quality of housing. (See Ministry of Construction 1986, p. 13; Sawamoto and Minohara 1987; Building Center of Japan 1985.)

These statistics, however, are deceptive. Note that a decision of children to form an independent household, or one by an elderly couple to maintain an independent household, depends on the relative cost of housing. Hence, the fact that the ratio of housing to households is above 1 does not necessarily mean that housing is adequate.

Table 14.3

	United States ($ billion)	Japan (trillion yen)		Japan ($ billion @ 150 yen/$)
Tangible assets (end of 1984)	12,168.4 (100%)	1,696.5 (100%)		11,310.2
Residential structures	3,433.1 (28%)	154.8	(8%)	1,032.2
Land	3,057.9 (25%)	926.1	(55%)	6,174.2
GNP	3,772.2	298.6		1,990.6
Area (million hectares^a)	937.3	37.2		

a. 1 hectare = 10,000 sq. meters = 2.471 acre.

Table 14.4

	1972	1975	1980	1984
Housing investment/GNP (both nominal, in %)				
Japan	7.5	7.6	7.2	5.0
United States	4.5	3.3	3.9	4.1
Housing investment/Total investment (capital formation)				
Japan	22.0	23.4	21.5	17.8
United States	25.1	20.1	21.2	22.8

Japan lags behind other advanced countries in quantity of rental housing as well as in quantity of owner-occupied housing, a fact that is not evident from the "ownership ratio" statistic. A better measure would be the ratio of people owning homes to the population of the cohort. As rows g and h of table 14.2 clearly show, the number of independent housing units per capita is less is Japan than in the United States. The statistics suggest that the shortage of affordable housing discourages the formation of households by younger people and encourages the formation of "merged households" for the elderly. Unmarried Japanese men and women tend to live with parents when they attend school or work in the same town or city, and the elderly in Japan tend to live with their children.

The last argument might be challeged on the grounds that the evidence reflects "culture" rather than "economic backwardness."

Table 14.5

	United States	Japan[a]	West Germany
Rooms/house	5.1	4.7	4.5
Persons/room	0.5	0.7	0.6
Area/new house	134.8	84.4	90.0

a. Source: Ministry of Construction, Nihon no Jukaku Jijo.

Table 14.6

	United States	Japan	Germany (FRG)
Access to flush toilet (in total housing)[a]	97.6	58.2	97.1
Sewerage access (access/total population)[b]	72.0	34.0	91.0
	(Chicago)	(Tokyo)	(Berlin)
Park area per capita (1000 sq. meters)[b]	23.9	2.2	26.1

a. Ministry of Construction, Nihon no Jukaku Jijo.
b. Kokusai Hikaku Tokei.

The ratio of independent households among the elderly, however, appears to rise with household wealth in both time-series and cross-section data. Many surveys also have suggested that the elderly in Japan wish to maintain independent households, though in close proximity to their children.

What Is the Quality of the Housing Stock?

The Japanese house is typically smaller than the American house: fewer rooms per house, more people per room, and less space per house (table 14.5). Moreover, the quality of facilities and amenities is below international standards (table 14.6).

Is Housing Too Expensive for the Young?

Various studies (for example, Hayashi et al. 1988 and Horioka 1988) suggest that housing is much more expensive in Japan than in the

Table 14.7
Ratio of housing prices to annual income.

	1950	1955	1960	1965	1970	1975	1980	1983
All Japan	1.1	2.3	3.2	4.4	5.4	6.2	6.4	6.7
Tokyo only	1.0	1.8	2.8	5.0	5.8	6.6	7.5	7.9

Sources: Horioka 1988; Economic Planning Agency 1985.

United States. The typical price of a new home is roughly 2 to 3 times the annual income of the typical American; it is 5 to 8 times the annual income of the typical Japanese (table 14.7). Hence, a large down payment is required to purchase a house. Hayashi et al. (1988) report that the age by which half of a generational cohort has purchased a house is about 30 in the United States and about 40 in Japan. Because of different practices in the two countries' financial markets, about 35 percent of the house price is paid as a down payment in Japan, versus about 25 percent in the United States. Furthermore, a typical mortgage matures in 20 years in Japan, versus 30 in the United States. In short, housing in Japan is relatively expensive, and so the typical Japanese person purchases a house later life than his American counterpart.

Are There Enough Housing Loans?

In the 1950s and the 1960s, the availability of housing loans was very limited in Japan. Since the end of the first oil crisis, the banking sector has dramatically expanded housing lending to the household sector (table 14.8). Traditionally, housing loans have been provided by the Housing Finance Corporation [Jutaku Kinyū Kōko], a government agency. Interest rates on housing loans have been stable and low (with a cap of 5.5 percent), but eligibility criteria and loan ceilings have been rather strict. Moreover, one condition for a low-interest loan is that the floor space must be below a specified limit, regardless of the location of the housing unit. Even though subsidized loans could be justified from the viewpoint of equity, this floor-space requirement has undoubtedly discouraged the development of larger units.

Table 14.8
Housing loans.

	Banking Sector[a]				Housing Loan Corp.			
	New Loans		Outstanding Loans		New Loans		Outstanding Loans	
	Number (1,000)	Amount (billion yen)	Number (1,000)	Amount (billion yen)	Number (1,000)	Amount (billion yen)	Number (1,000)	Amount (billion yen)
1980	418	2,664.7	3,168	14,509.0				
1985	424	3,590.2	3,575	17,739.5	424	2,765.5	5,569	21,215.6
1987	780	9,404.5	3,776	23,630.7	512	4,326.1	5,831	25,449.8

a. Both bank and trust accounts.

Table 14.9
Rates of inflation and growth, calculated on the basis of changes over five-year periods.

	1955–60	1960–65	1965–70	1970–75	1975–80	1980–85
Land[a]	180.0	174.3	81.6	92.9	20.1	29.3
CPI[b]	10.3	35.1	8.7	72.8	36.7	13.3
Real GNP[c]	54.7	55.0	71.7	24.0	26.9	21.1

a. Source: Zenkoku Shigaichi Tochi Kakaku shisuu, Urban area index, Real Estate Institute.
b. Source: Bank of Japan.
c. Source: Economic Planning Agency.

Summary

Much could be done to improve Japanese housing, both in quantity and in quality. In a sense, the root cause of the housing problem is land prices. As table 14.3 shows, much of Japan's national wealth is held in land rather than in housing structures. This shows either that Japanese houses depreciate quickly, that the Japanese under-invest in housing, or that they cannot afford to invest in housing.

EVIDENCE FROM LAND-PRICE TIME SERIES

In Japan, land prices have been increasing much more quickly than the wholesale price index (WPI) or the consumer price index (CPI) ever since the end of World War II. The Land Legend [Tochi Shinwa] says that land is the best asset in which to invest because its price never goes down. As table 14.9 shows, the average price of urban land has generally outpaced the CPI over five-year intervals, but the relative rate of price increase has changed over time. Figure 14.1 plots the change in real land prices measured by the logarithm of land prices minus the logarithm of the WPI. Table 14.9 and figure 14.1 confirm that land prices rose much faster from the late 1950s to the early 1970s than during the later period. This observation gives us a hint that land-price increases correlate positively with the GNP growth rate.

Figure 14.2 plots the average nationwide land inflation rate against the land inflation rate of the six major metropolitan areas. During the three peak inflation periods (1961–62, 1973, and 1986–87), inflation in large cities was above the nationwide average. Over

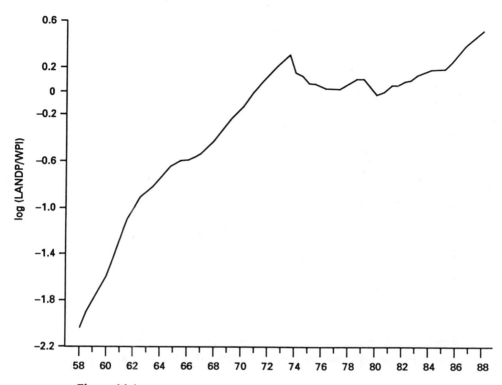

Figure 14.1
Land prices relative to wholesale price index.

the period 1985–1988, land inflation was mostly concentrated in the six largest cities.

Figure 14.3, which plots the rates of inflation in the prices of industrial, residential, and commercial land, shows that inflation in the price of industrial land outpaced inflation of land used for other purposes in 1961–62, that the price of residential land grew fastest in 1973–74, and that prices of commercial land increased most rapidly in 1986–87. The evidence presented in figures 14.3 and 14.4 confirms that the most recent wave of land-price increases was mainly concentrated in the large cities and pertained to commercial uses of land. In this sense, the evidence is consistent with the observation that the most recent episode of land-price inflation was due to Tokyo's having become one of the financial centers of the world. Two years after Tokyo land prices started their sharp in-

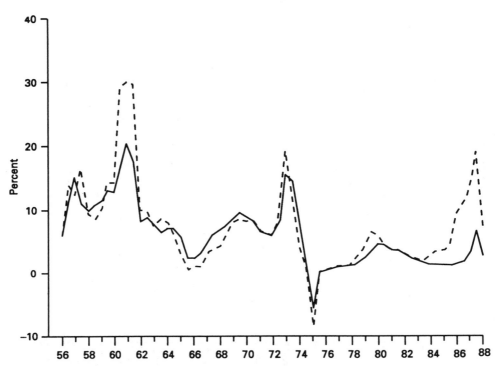

Figure 14.2
Land inflation rates: national average (solid line) and six major metropolitan areas (broken line).

crease, price increases started to spread to other major cities. Although the other cities experienced land-price increases in 1988–1990, the rates of those increases were much lower than the typical Tokyo increase rates of earlier years.

In search of determinants of land prices, figure 14.4 compares the GNP growth rate, the WPI inflation rate, and the land inflation rate. It is not obvious from the graph how these three variables are related. Figure 14.1 offers little indication that the increase in the land price deflated by the WPI (simply "land price" hereafter) was a bubble, except for the possibility that a mini-bubble formed in 1973–74. Price changes differed by use (reflecting different demand changes) and by location (the largest cities and other urban areas). A mini-bubble would be followed by a mini-crash, which could explain the decrease in land price in 1974–75.

Land Prices and Assessments
There are several different "official" land prices: the market price, the monitoring price reported by the Land Agency [Koji Kakaku], the assessment for bequest-tax purposes by the National Tax Agency [Rosen Ka], the assessment for property-tax purposes by the prefectural government, and the monitoring of representative places conducted by the prefectural government. There is also the land-price index of urban districts surveyed by the Japan Real Estate Institute, a non-government agency. The last is believed to reflect the market value best, and it is used in this section because it has a long time series and because the survey is conducted every 6 months (as opposed to once a year).

The Koji Kakaku has been reported by the Land Agency every January 1 since 1970. The price is determined by actual transactions in neighboring places. The points at which prices are monitored currently number about 17,000 nationwide. (The number of monitoring locations was not expanded until the mid 1970s.) There exists significant overlap in monitoring points every year, although there have been several substitutions. It is widely believed that the Koji Kakaku is below market value by 20–30 percent.

Assessments for property-tax and bequest-tax purposes are much lower than the Koji Kakaku. The Rosen Ka, for bequests, is about 50–70 percent of the Koji Kakaku. Homma and Atoda (1989, pp. 134–135) investigated the gap between the Koji Kakaku and Rosen Ka at the places reporting the highest Rosen Ka in the capital cities of prefectures. They found that in 1988 the gap ranged from 33.5 percent (in Kyoto) to 94.1 percent (in Kofu), with an average gap of 56.4 percent.

A major policy discussion erupted in Japan after the large increase in land prices in 1986–87. Most policy makers and a few economists blamed speculation. It is not clear, however, whether this land price increase was the result of a speculative bubble. Recall figure 14.1. The land price trend line was much steeper during the 1950s and the 1960s. After the mini-bubble-cum-crash of 1974–75, the land price was amazingly stable until the mid 1980s. It is understandable that the land price trend has a kink around 1973–74, when the Japanese economy shifted to slower growth. The increase in real land prices since 1974 has been very small. It is a reasonable assumption that the land price would increase at a rate close to the increase in the real GNP rate. In fact, one study shows that a 1 percent increase in GNP will immediately cause land price increases in a range between 0.6 and 0.7 percent (Ito 1990). In the long run, however, the income

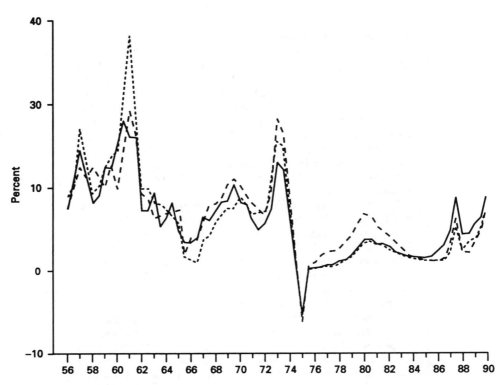

Figure 14.3
Inflation rates of residential (-----), commercial (————), and industrial
(———) land.

elasticity of land is about 2.5—a very large value. This shows how
sensitive the land price is to real economic growth. If this inference
is correct, then the recent increase in land prices in Japan represents
a process of catching up to the post-oil-crisis trend line. This
observation will be overlooked if one concentrates only on the land
price problem of 1986–87. (A similar observation could be applied to
the Tokyo stock prices for the same period.) It remains to be seen
whether the 1986–87 episode represents another mini-bubble to be
followed by a mini-crash, a catch-up to the trend line, or some
structural change in the housing market.

Do Japan's higher land prices also imply higher rents than in the
United States? Not necessarily. Noguchi (1989, pp. 75–78) compares
land prices and rents in Tokyo with those in London and concludes

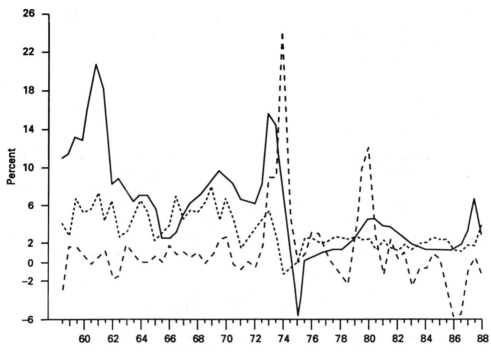

Figure 14.4
Land inflation (————), WPI inflation (— — —), and GNP growth rate
(— — — —).

that, whereas the representative price of Tokyo land is about ten
times that of London land, rents in Tokyo are only twice as high as
rents in London. A casual perusal of newspaper advertisements
in Tokyo and New York produces a similar observation. Land in
Japan as an asset is priced higher, but it yields lower flows of earnings (rents). How can landlords in Tokyo afford to keep this expensive asset with its low earnings? The real puzzle is not why the
land price is higher, but why the price-earning ratio (PER) of land is
higher in Japan.

In order to understand this puzzle in a formal framework, we can
use the concept of the "required rate of return"—the return on holding assets, such as bonds, equities, and land. Since investors try to
maximize the returns on their assets, the returns (net of any risk
premium) to various assets become equal. Landholding yields a return in the form of rent and capital gains. With the price of land

denoted by q_t and rent by R_t, the arbitrage condition between land and other assets yields the following relationship:

$$r = \frac{R_t + (q_{t+1} - q_t)}{q_t},$$

or

$$r = R_t/q_t + (q_{t+1} - q_t)/q_t.$$

The first term is the earning/price ratio (the reciprocal of the PER); the second term is the (expected) capital gain. The low earning/price ratio implies either that the required rate of return is low or that the expected capital gain is large. Suppose that the required rate of return on land is the same in Tokyo, New York, and London. Then, if the earning/price ratio (R/q) in Tokyo is one-fifth of that in London or New York, the expected capital gains must be much higher in Tokyo than those in London and New York.

The required rate of return in Tokyo may be lower, because real-estate taxes are much lower in Japan than in the United States or the United Kingdom. It is a well-known rule of thumb that the assessment of real estate for the purpose of calculating real-estate taxes (the equivalent of the US property tax) is about one-third to one-half of market value. Put differently, even though before-tax rental income is lower in Tokyo, in principle this income net of real-estate and income taxes could be comparable to that in New York and London. In fact, the PER gap is too large to be explained by the difference in tax treatment alone.

Another well-known rule of thumb is that the assessment of real estate for the purpose of calculating inheritance taxes (the equivalent of the US estate tax) is also about one-half of market value. Hence, if parents want to bequeath a given yen amount, real estate is the best instrument to use. (Recall chapter 6.) This observation works to justify the apparently low rate of return on investments in rental property.

Now suppose all of the above adjustments were made. Then the real question would be reduced to whether the corrected rate of return is high enough to bring down the amount of (expected) future capital gains to a reasonable level. Even though the postwar capital gains in Tokyo were in fact much higher than those in New York and in London, it may not be reasonable to assume that the real land price will increase at the rate at which it has been increasing. This question is now more serious than ever, as the price/wage ratio indicates that owner-occupied housing is an impossible dream for the average Japanese wage earner who does not inherit a piece of land. If the land price is increasing simply because everyone believes that others think it will in the future, then there is a bubble. In fact, Noguchi (1989) thinks that about half of the land price must be attributed to a bubble.

POLICY IMPLICATIONS

What Is the Problem?

The problem of high land prices has many aspects. As explained, the high PER of land is a puzzle. Even well-informed visitors would likely be surprised to find that many of the commercial buildings have only three or four stories, and that many one- and two-story residential buildings are scattered around downtown Tokyo. At the opposite extreme, some prime locations are occupied by space-inefficient "pencil buildings," large portions of which must be reserved for elevators and stairs. Moreover, in the first-tier suburbs of Tokyo there are many patches of "agricultural" land in the middle of residential areas. Why is the expensive land underused?

Many economists in Japan think that the apparent underuse is symbolic of the reasons behind the high land prices, rather than being a puzzle by itself. The following discussions explain why the misallocation of land has occurred, and what kinds of policies would mitigate the high-land-price problem.

Property Taxation, Capital-Gains Taxation, and the Lock-in Effect

Assessments of real estate for property taxation are systematically below market value by as much as 50 percent. The low property tax encourages hoarding when prices are expected to rise. The capital-gains tax is levied when property is sold. The tax schedule is higher for property held for fewer than five years, and another tax (a surcharge) has been levied since 1987 to capture profits from land held for fewer than two years. These provisions are intended to prevent speculative (short-term) demands for land. In the past, during the periods in which land prices rose sharply, many real-estate companies made quick profits through quick turnovers. The surcharge on short-term gains now prevents this kind of behavior.

When all these provisions are combined, however, the taxes on the property and on capital gains have a "lock-in effect." That is, once an investor has purchased land and expects capital gains, the investor requires a higher selling price in order to realize the same yield. Since property taxes are lower, the land could easily be held without being developed. When land tends to be "locked in" by the tax system, it is difficult to plan large-scale housing or commercial development projects.

On the basis of the reasons given above, property taxes should be raised and capital-gains taxes on real properties should be lowered. Those who think land prices increase as a result of speculative activities, on the other hand, oppose the lowering of capital-gains tax rates. The key to resolving these conflicting views is to check whether, and to what extent, speculative bubbles exist in land prices. If land-price increases are mostly a bubble phenomenon, transaction taxes and short-term capital-gains taxes are an effective way to curb bubbles. If land prices rise because of changes in fundamentals, however, then a high capital-gains tax impedes the efficient allocation of land.

Bequest Taxes on Real Estate

The inheritance tax is much heavier in Japan than in the United States. The marginal rate goes up to 70 percent quickly, and there is no simple way to create a tax-exempt trust for one's heirs. Since the *inter vivos* transfer (gift) tax is even stricter, most intergenerational gifts take place at the time of death.

Whereas bonds and other securities are assessed at market value for the purposes of the inheritance tax, real estate is assessed below its market value. The favorable treatment of real estate is due partly to special legal provisions under which the assessment of the first 200 square meters of property used for residences or for rental housing is reduced by 50 or 60 percent and partly to the tradition of assessing inherited land according to a valuation map [Rosen Ka] kept in the local Tax Bureau's office rather than according to the land-price survey [Koji Kakaku] done by the Land Agency of the Japanese government or the land valuation used for the municipal property tax. Any of these three government assessments is below the market value of the property; the question is one of magnitude. (See the discussion of land prices above.)

In planning a bequest, it is preferable from a tax standpoint to hold real assets rather than financial assets at the time of death. This helps explain why the elderly in Japan retain housing and other real estate until death. It also discourages elderly landowners who plan to make bequests from selling their property, even at market prices.

To the extent that real estate is a vehicle for bequests, land and housing prices are likely to contain a premium relating to this practice. This explains, at least partly, a high PER of land. It is not clear how significant this premium is in actual land prices; however, from the viewpoint of efficient resource allocation there is no question about the need to adjust the assessment of real property to its market value.[2]

Overprotection of Tenants

Tenants are heavily protected by laws regarding the leasing of land and the renting of houses and apartments (the Land Lease Law and the House Lease Law). If land is leased indefinitely and the lessee builds a concrete building, the lease must extend 60 years; if the structure is not of concrete, the lease must extend 30 years. (In fact, the maturity of a lease cannot be set at less than 30 years for a concrete structure and 20 years for a non-concrete one.) Even if the original lease expires, if the building is in good condition the lease on the land is automatically extended and cannot be terminated at the will of the landlord.

A lease on a house or an apartment extends at least a year, and the landlord cannot terminate the lease unless he moves into the unit or has some other "rightful cause." "Rightful cause" has been interpreted very narrowly in many court decisions. Essentially, the landlord must prove that he has no alternative but to move into the property.[3] This particular amendment to the law was enacted during World War II, when there was an acute shortage of housing. Several difficulties result from this law. First, there is a shortage of large and high-quality rental housing in Japan, as landlords are afraid to risk large investments. Second, it has become a common practice to require a renter to pay the equivalent of two months' rent to initiate a lease. This can be interpreted as a risk premium for the landlord. Third, redevelopment is impeded when it is difficult to get a few remaining residents to vacate a run-down apartment building despite large vacancies, or when a large development project (perhaps covering an entire block) contains a few renters of land. Public housing is no exception. Even when a local government agency wants to scrap an old low-rise apartment and build a high-rise, a few tenants can block the plan. (There have been a few examples of this in the central districts of Tokyo.)

Sunshine and Cubic-Size Restrictions

In most cases, the height and the total cubic size of a building are regulated. For example, if an area is designated as a Class 1 residential area, then a new structure must be under 10 meters high. And there are sunshine restrictions limiting the sizes of houses and other structures that might deprive a neighboring house of sunlight—typically, at least 3 hours a day of sunlight during the wintertime are guaranteed.

Of course, zoning laws are established for good reasons, and the sunshine laws protect residents from negative externalities. On the other hand, a Pareto-optimal solution (that is, one in which everybody gains) could be arranged in most cases. If regulations do not intervene, lots for many small houses may be merged so that a high-rise can be built.

Agricultural Land in Cities

As was mentioned above, agricultural land is taxed much more lightly than residential or commercial land. Although some justifications (such as national security) have been put forth in support of this, there is little ground for permitting preferential treatment of small agricultural lots in cities. From the viewpoint of city planning, agricultural plots in urban residential areas should be taxed at the same rate as residential plots. This was what the tax law of 1982 was supposed to have achieved: In the three largest metropolitan areas (Tokyo, Osaka, and Nagoya), agricultural lots in areas that city planners designate as residential/commercial and for which the appraisal value is more than 30,000 yen per 3.3 square meters are supposed to be taxed at the residential rate, in order to release land from agriculture. There is a loophole in this provision, however. If a

Table 14.10
Sizes (in hectares) of agricultural lots in residential/commercial zones.

	Tokyo[a]			Three metropolitan areas[b]		
	Applicable (A)	Exempted (B)	(B)/(A)	Applicable (A)	Exempted (B)	(B)/(A)
1982	30,261	24,510	90.0%	42,472	35,030	82.5%
1983	29,065	24,191	83.2	40,922	34,526	84.4
1984	28,299	23,484	83.0	39,904	33,592	84.2
1985[c]	29,612	24,709	83.4	44,975	38,120	84.8
1986	28,824	23,970	83.2	43,932	37,121	84.5

a. The Tokyo area includes Tokyo, Ibaragi, Saitama, Chiba, and Kanagawa prefectures.
b. The Tokyo, Osaka, and Nagoya areas.
c. There was an appraisal change in 1985 and more land was appraised at more than 30,000 yen/3.3 sq. meters.
Source: Namekawa 1988; p. 98.

lot is more than 990 square meters and the owner plans to continue farming for more than 10 years, the lot is exempted from the higher rate. The fraction of all land defined as being used for farming is 1/37 in the three metropolitan areas together, and 1/57 in Tokyo. Since the definition of farming is rather arbitrary, the loophole is taken advantage of: Only 15.5 percent of urban agricultural lots are taxed at residential rates (table 14.10).

Many economists and policy makers suggest that releasing agricultural lands, especially those in cities, for residential purposes would be a good idea. In order to do this, it is essential to repeal the special treatment of agricultural land in cities. Whether political opposition to such measures can be overcome remains to be seen.[4]

WHY ARE JAPANESE STOCK PRICES SO HIGH?

Whether Japanese stock prices are "too high" depends on their expected or proper level. Since the stock price of a company is the equity value of the firm divided by the number of stocks, there are at least two ways to approach this question.

Traditional theory assumes that the stock price is determined as the discounted sum of future dividend streams. (See the box on Cross-Holding and PERs for a formal presentation.) From this point of view, the appropriateness of any stock's price depends on the unknown future stream of dividends. Tautologically, therefore, any price can be justified: A high price implies that the market regards a company's future as bright, a low price that the market believes that the company will reduce its dividend payout. One problem for this tautological explanation is that Japanese corporations do not pay out large dividends. Worse still, the payout ratio has been declining.

There is another way to look at the value of a firm. Suppose that a firm can adjust its capital stock and employment to the optimal level immediately without costs. Then the market value of the firm—that is, the stock price times the number of shares of stock—equals the value of its assets. Under more realistic conditions, fixed investment takes place according to the discrepancy between the market value of the firm and the asset value. When a deviation occurs, the ratio of a firm's market value to its asset value is called the *q-ratio*. (The name is borrowed from the investment-function literature of macroeconomics. Since it is not quite the same as the investment ratio, some authors call it the *market value/corporate asset ratio*.)

If the q-ratio is greater than 1, which means that the market value exceeds the value of assets already in place, then either the stock price is overvalued or the asset value is not properly measured for some reason. If there is a bubble in the stock market, then the q-ratio will be more than 1. But a q-ratio above 1 could also mean that the stock market foresees that the company has profitable opportunities that have not yet been capitalized upon. If the q-ratio is less than 1, then the market believes that the firm needs to trim its inefficient assets. If the q-ratio is larger than 1, then the market expects that the firm will earn more than just its liquidation value. This is the basic understanding of how stock prices are determined.

Unfortunately, unrealized capital gains in the balance sheet [fukumi] pose a measurement problem. As was noted above, land prices in Japan have recently increased rapidly. The balance sheet of a Japanese firm, however, often uses the book (historical purchase) value for assets. In measuring firms' assets, it is essential to correct land values from book value to market value.

When the price of a Japanese stock is said to be too high, it is a long-run phenomenon. Therefore, the traditional theory of stock-price determination may be used to assess this question. The following discussion will try to explain how factors that influence the future streams of earnings and the discount rate may influence the q-ratio.

Stylized Facts

It is well known that Japanese stock prices went up sharply in the latter half of the 1980s. In particular, in the wake of the worldwide stock-price decline triggered by Black Monday in 1987, Japanese stocks came back to their previous record highs much faster than US stocks, and they continued to climb. In fact, many investors and economists—particularly outside Japan—considered stock prices in Japan to be too high both when compared against the earnings or dividends of their respective companies and when compared against similar measures for other countries. This was true even after the downward "adjustment" that occurred during the first quarter of 1990 and the "Black August" episode of 1990 (see below). Are

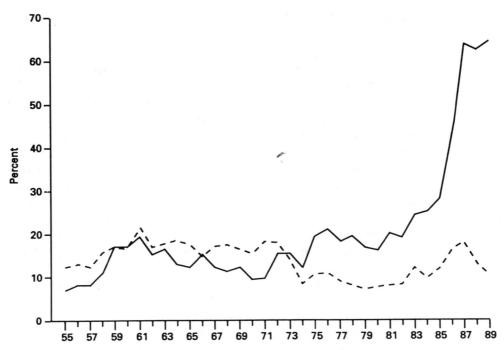

Figure 14.5
Price-earning ratios of Japan (solid line) and United States (broken line).
Adapted from Ueda 1990.

foreign investors missing the "uniqueness" of the Japanese stock market, which seems to allow it to defy the law of gravity?

Ueda (1990) examined the traditional theory of stock-price determination, using the price-earning ratio (PER), the price-dividend ratio (PDR), and the q-ratio. He concluded that it is difficult to explain, using the traditional theory, why Japanese stock prices took off in the mid 1980s and why the PERs of Japanese stocks became much higher than those of American stocks.

As figure 14.5 shows, the Japanese PER was below its US counterpart until the mid 1970s. The two PERs show similar fluctuations throughout most of the 1950s and the 1960s. Hence, the rapid economic growth of Japan (the prospect of a brighter future) during the 1960s did not produce high PERs. After 1975, however, the Japanese PER became roughly twice as high as its US counterpart. Then, after 1986, the Japanese PER simply skyrocketed. (Recall that Japanese land prices skyrocketed at the same time. Several economists have noted the parallel.) In comparison with US stock prices, Japanese prices were "normal" until the mid 1980s. Any explanation of "too-high stock prices" in Japan must explain what happened during the second half of the 1980s.

The PER of Japan is not readily comparable to that of the United States. First, the Japanese PER must be corrected for cross-holding. In Japan, about 40–50 percent of all outstanding shares of stock are held by other corporations. (See chapter 7 for details of cross-holding, or interlocking shares represented by the matrix of cross-holding among firms in an enterprise group. Now imagine that the matrix is extended to cover all listed firms and sum up the ratio of stocks held by other firms.)

The mechanism by which cross-holding raises a stock price in Japan is similar to (but not quite the same as) the mechanism by which stock-buyback schemes raise stock prices in the United States. The latter occurs because a smaller number of shares represents the same quantity of assets after the buyback; the former occurs through the holding of stocks of other firms. Earnings are automatically retained in the corporate sector instead of being paid out as dividends. Suppose that two identical firms, A and B, which expect identical market returns from their operations in the future, distribute part of their profits to shareholders and reinvest the rest of their profits toward the growth of the firm. At the end of the fiscal year, firms A and B decide not to distribute dividends but to use the funds to purchase each other's stocks in the market. Instead of the price decline due to dividend distributions, the stock prices of firms A and B remain the same, since the retained earnings are invested in high-earning projects. From the viewpoint of future dividend flows, cross-holding implies that the same dividends from the respective operations are now divided by a smaller number of ultimate shareholders, and more funds are reinvested for growth. It can be shown that the multiplier for the effect of cross-holding on the PER, denoted by y (see table 14.11), is a function of the dividend-payout ratio and the cross-holding ratio. (See the box on Cross- Holding and PERs.)

French and Poterba (1990) and Ueda (1989) attempted to correct the PER by taking cross-holding into account and found that cross-holding would increasingly raise the PER over time—by about 40 percent by the end of the 1980s.

Cross-Holding and PERs

Suppose that the stock price, p_t, is determined as the discounted sum of future dividend streams:

$$p_t = \sum_{j=0}^{\infty} (1 + r)^{-1-j} dE^{t+j} \tag{1}$$

where d is the dividend payout ratio, E is earnings, and r is the interest rate (which equals the discount rate). Suppose also that the earnings of the firm are determined by the returns r on its assets A_t:

$$E_t = rA_t. \tag{2}$$

The assets increase by the amount of the firm's retained earnings, $(1 - d)E_t$:

$$A_{t+1} = A_t + (1 - d)E_t. \tag{3}$$

From (2) and (3),

$$A_{t+j} = [1 + (1 - d)r]^j A_t. \tag{4}$$

Substituting (2) and (4) into (1), we obtain the stock price:

$$P_t = \frac{(drA_t)/(1 + r)}{1 - [1 + (1 - d)r]/(1 + r)}. \tag{5}$$

By transforming (5), we obtain

$$P_t = A_t; \tag{6}$$

that is, the market value equals the value of the assets ($q = 1$):

$$P_t/E_t = 1/r. \tag{7}$$

Now assume cross-holding of equities. Suppose that each of two identical firms holds a fraction h ($0 < h < 1$) of the shares of the other firm. Since dividends of the other firm are now counted as a part of each firm's cash flows and vice versa, earnings E_t^* under cross-holding are a function of "virtual" earnings E_t plus dividends from the other firm: $E_t^* = E_t + dhE_t^*$. Hence,

$$E_t^* = E_t/(1 - dh) = rA_t/(1 - dh). \tag{8}$$

The stock-price equation is now

$$p_t^* = \sum_{j=0}^{\infty} (1 + r)^{-1-j} dE_{t+j}^*. \tag{1'}$$

Retained earnings, taking into account the receipt of dividends, now become

$$A_{t+1} = A_t + (1 - d)E_t^* = A_t + (1 - d)rA_t/(1 - dh). \tag{9}$$

Therefore,

$$A_{t+j} = \{1 + [r(1 - d)/(1 - dh)]\}^j A_t. \tag{10}$$

Substituting (8) and (10) into (1'), we obtain

$$P_t^* = P_t/(1 - h). \tag{11}$$

Calculate the PER under cross-holding:

$$P_t h^*/E_t^* = (1 - dh)/(1 - h)r = [(1 - dh)/(1 - h)]P_t/E_t. \tag{12}$$

Therefore, the PER under cross-holding, which is the left-hand side of (12), is higher than the PER without cross-holding if $0 \leq d < 1$. The ratio $(1 - dh)/(1 - h)$ is shown in table 14.11.

Table 14.11
Cross-holding and dividend payout ratios (for listed companies only).

Ratio	1970	1975	1980	1981	1982	1983	1984	1985	1986
h^a	0.385	0.415	0.432	0.423	0.435	0.433	0.450	0.457	0.477
d^b	0.501	0.499	0.399	0.366	0.394	0.408	0.385	0.356	0.350
y^c	1.31	1.36	1.46	1.46	1.47	1.45	1.50	1.54	1.59

a. Cross-holding ratio.
b. Dividend payout ratio, Dividends/Earnings.
c. Cross-holding multiplier, $(1 - hd)/1 - h$.
Source: Ueda 1990.

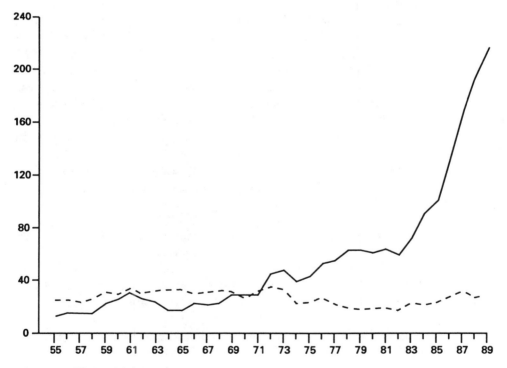

Figure 14.6
Equity price-dividend ratios of Japan (solid line) and United States (broken line). Adapted from Ueda 1990.

Table 14.12
The q-ratio for equities (market value/corporate assets).

Equities	1970	1975	1980	1981	1982	1983	1984	1985	1986
all private[a]	0.40	0.34	0.40	0.41	0.37	0.47	0.57	0.60	0.87
listed[a]			0.75	0.90	0.86	1.04	1.27	1.28	1.73
listed[b]		0.26	0.35	0.35	0.34	0.36	0.42	0.42	0.45

Source: Ueda 1990, citing (a) Ueda 1989 and (b) Konya and Wakasugi 1987.

Figure 14.6 shows the price-dividend ratios (PDRs) of the two countries. Ueda argues that, unlike PERs, PDRs will not be affected by cross-holding of equities. Again, until 1970 the PDRs in the two countries remained close. Slowly over the 1970s, Japanese PDRs moved above US PDRs; then, after 1980, Japanese PDRs soared while US PDRs remained relatively flat. The similar pattern of PER and PDR behavior implies that cross-holding is not the major cause of the difference between stock prices in Japan and the United States.

By the way, one of the reasons why the Japanese PDR seems to have an upward trend since 1965 is that in Japan a stable dividend means, say, 10 percent of the *face* value of the stock, whereas in the United States the *market* value is considered.

The q-ratios presented in table 14.12 are corrected, with various assumptions, for land-price valuation. This table shows that the q-ratio tends to be below 1 for all private corporations, implying that there is no evidence that Japanese stock prices are too high. For listed companies, however, there is disagreement between the estimates of Ueda (1989) and Kon-ya and Wakasugi (1987). Ueda believes that the q-ratio went up sharply during the 1980s, reaching 1.73 in 1986, which strongly implies that Japanese stock prices became too high (even at 1986 levels). Kon-ya and Wakasugi believe that the ratio is stable around 0.45. The difference is due to the use of different methods of estimation (i.e., the use of aggregate or disaggregated data) and different methods of tax adjustment and land valuation. The dispute has not been resolved. (See Hoshi and Kashyap 1990 and Hayashi and Inoue 1991 for more recent evidence.)

In comparing the behavior of Japanese and American stock prices, the following institutional differences must be noted:

• The dividend-payout ratio is much smaller in Japan, so investors almost uniformly expect capital gains.

• Cross-holding raises the PER in Japan, and it is difficult to know exactly how stocks are cross-held.

• It is difficult to estimate the market value of land held as a part of assets by firms.

Are Japanese Stock Prices Too High?

Cross-holding tends to raise PERs, but the evidence suggests that corrections reduce the Japanese PER by 25–35 percent (Ueda 1989; French and Poterba 1990). This still does not bring Japanese PERs down to the levels of American PERs (recall figure 14.5).

Some argue that the rising value of land owned by corporations can explain the level of Japanese stock prices. However, it is difficult to estimate how much land corporations are holding at which book value and then to adjust for its market value. Different methods of correction yield different results.

Those who suspect that Japanese stock prices are too high must explain when they became too high and what kept them so high. The mini-crashes of early 1990 seem to suggest that there may have been some overvaluation in Japanese stock prices. Even after losing one-fourth of its value, the Nikkei 225 average stood at its 1988 level, which many foreign investors considered too high at the time.

Black August, 1990

The Tokyo stock market enjoyed a sharp increase from 1986 to 1989, as PERs soared. Although foreign investors were scared away by the high prices, domestic investors continued to pour funds into the stock market during 1989. Stock prices rose about 30 percent for the year 1989. The trend turned in 1990, however. Sharp decreases in February, March, and April were only a hint of what was to come. After the Iraqi invasion of Kuwait, the Tokyo stock market dropped more than 16 percent over the month of August. Table 14.13 shows the roller-coaster ride of Japanese stock prices in 1989 and 1990.

If the high PERs cannot be explained even after adjustment for cross-holding, the rise and fall of Japanese stock prices may reflect the forming and bursting of bubbles. Of course, one might attribute the changes to hikes in the discount rate and to fundamental changes in the world economy implied by the Iraqi invasion. As of

Table 14.13

		Nikkei 225 monthly average (yen)	Change (%)
1988	Dec	29,720	
1989	Jan	31,170	+ 4.9
	Feb	32,005	+ 2.7
	Mar	31,955	− 0.2
	April	33,226	+ 4.0
	May	33,989	+ 2.3
	June	33,373	− 0.7
	July	33,843	+ 0.3
	August	34,808	+ 2.9
	Sept	34,649	− 0.5
	Oct	35,323	+ 1.9
	Nov	36,038	+ 2.0
	Dec	38,130	+ 5.8
1990	Jan	37,404	− 1.9
	Feb	36,517	− 2.4
	March	32,305	−11.5
	April	29,237	− 9.5
	May	31,826	+ 8.9
	June	32,264	+ 1.4
	July	32,170	− 0.3
	August	26,908	−16.4
	Sept	23,935	−11.0
	Oct	23,816	− 8.9
	Nov	23,468	− 1.5
	Dec	23,740	+ 2.0

the end of 1990, it was not clear whether the episode was a bubble forming and bursting or whether it reflected fundamental changes in the Japanese economy.

Volatility Spillovers among the World's Stock Markets

In discussing stock prices, it may be appropriate to differentiate between long-run trends and short-run fluctuations. The above descriptions were mainly concerned with the former. Short-run movements in stock prices, however, cannot be understood by means of the theory we have considered thus far. There are several deficiencies in the standard theory. Some argue that stock-price movements cannot be explained by subsequent changes in dividends (Shiller 1981). Others argue that stock-price volatility cannot be attributed to the arrival of news (French and Roll 1986). Cutler, Poterba, and Summers argue that relatively small market responses were observed on *a priori*-chosen major news dates in history, and that large market moves often occurred on days without any identifiable major news. This and their finding that only one-third of the variance in stock-market returns can be attributed to changes in macroeconomic variables cast some doubt on the views discussed in the preceding subsection.

Other economists have investigated volatility spillovers between the world's capital markets. When New York stock prices decline sharply on one day, a lot of anxiety prevails in the Tokyo stock market, which opens several hours after the New York closing (but on the next calendar day). A sharp drop in stock prices in Tokyo sends a shock to the stock markets in Hong Kong, London, and New York, which open later on the same calendar day. This kind of international spillover was most prominent in the Black Monday episode of October 19, 1987. A sharp drop in stock prices in New York was reinforced in Tokyo and in other markets on October 20, and fed back to New York the following day. Econometric investigations reveal that the spillover from New York to Tokyo was much more pronounced than the reverse spillover (Hamao et al. 1989).

CONCLUDING REMARKS

In the midst of increases in land and stock prices in Japan in the second half of the 1980s, the following circular argument was often presented in the popular press: Land-price increases imply a rise in asset values in the balance sheet of a firm. This will immediately raise stock prices, given the q-ratio. Higher land prices also mean higher collateral values, which enable the firm to obtain more bank loans. Loans may be used to invest in structures and machinery. But some loans were used to purchase land, or stocks of other companies, in a speculative quest for capital gains. Higher stock prices also created an "equity finance" boom in 1988–89, which halted in 1990. (Convertible bonds and warrants were also issued with very low capital costs for Japanese firms.) Some of the funds obtained through equity finance were used for speculation. More speculation led to another round of increases in the prices of land and stocks. Although this explanation lacks a real cause for the initial price increases, it is suggestive of a kind of multiplier process that works through the financial market once one asset price starts to increase.

A few factors are suspected as the ultimate causes of the increases in land and stock prices. First, the several steps taken to lower the official discount rate during 1986–87 may have lowered capital costs too much. Financial deregulation is a second suspect. The land-price increase of 1986–87 was led by increases in the Tokyo metropolitan area, especially in the prices of commercial land. Profits as well as stock prices in the financial sector soared at the same time. Thus, the demand for land brought on by the idea of Tokyo's becoming the center of the world's financial markets and requiring more office space could be a factor. The price of land in other sectors and places is set by pure arbitrage from Tokyo's commercial district. Third, "restructuring" of the Japanese economy in favor of more information-intensive and consumer-oriented industries was a buzz-word after the Plaza Agreement. In order for the surpluses on the Japanese current account to be reduced, domestic demand had to increase more than external demand. At the same time, export-oriented industries were encouraged either to invest directly in the United States or to start producing more for domestic sales.

The search will undoubtedly continue for the common factor behind asset-price inflation in Japan. "Too-high" land prices have made it very difficult for ordinary employees to buy owner-occupied housing, and "too-high" stock prices have kept foreign investors sidelined. Many are still puzzled as to whether the problem will be resolved.

APPENDIX: GUIDE TO DATA

Land Prices

A reliable annual series on the Koji Kakaku (official posted prices) has been published by the Land Agency since the mid 1970s. Koji Kakaku are investigated at around 16,000 locations in the country on January 1 of every year. Locations may vary over time. It is speculated widely that Koji Kakaku are lower than the market (transaction) price by about 30 percent.

A longer time series containing twice-a-year observations since the mid 1950s is available from the Japan Real Estate Institute. The observations are taken on March 31 and September 30 of each year. This series is composed of 10 locations in each of 140 cities. Recent data from both series are reprinted in the Economic Statistics Annual of the Bank of Japan.

For the purpose of the bequest tax, the Rosen Ka, determined by the Tax Collection Bureau, is used. The price indicated by the Rosen Ka is known to be lower than the Koji Kakaku by 30–40 percent. The real estate (property) tax is based on property-tax assessment value, determined by municipal governments. This assessment value in relationship to the market value varies depending on the municipalities (Homma and Atoda 1989).

Stock Prices

There are two popular indices of stock prices: the Nikkei 225 and the TOPIX. The Nikkei 225 includes 225 companies in the "first" section of the Tokyo Stock Exchange (TSE), and represents more than 50 percent of the equity capitalization of the TSE. The index is a share-price-weighted index without dividend adjustment (similar to the Dow-Jones stock index in the United States). Dividend payout ratios in Japan, however, are low. The TOPIX is an equity-value-weighted index for the Tokyo Stock Exchange.

Any large securities house, in Japan or the United States, maintains a time series of stock prices. Commercial data companies such as Nikkei NEEDS and Data Resources Inc. have daily stock-price series. One can also find intradaily data in newspapers. Nihon Keizai Shinbun prints the Nikkei 225 index at 9:15, 10:00, 11:00, 13:15, 14:00, and 15:00 every day. Note that there is a lunch break from 11:00 to 13:00, during which the market is closed. Most annuals of economic statistics, such as those from Toyo Keizai Shinposha and the Bank of Japan, contain monthly and quarterly series.

NOTES

1. However, financial assets that pay no dividends or rents can have value if for some reason their current price is expected to increase, in which case the prospect of a capital gain creates value. This is a source of "bubbles."

2. There is a viewpoint that advocates lowering bequest-tax rates in the face of land-price increases. This argument emphasizes the fact that unexpected rises in land prices jeopardize the bequest plans of ordinary citizens. If the bequest motive of handing down family assets from one generation to the next should be respected, then the unexpected burden in inheritance taxes from speculative bubbles should be lightened. If the land-price increase is within the range of expectations reflecting "fundamentals," then the increase in the tax burden just reflects the increased value in the resource allocation. There is no reason to reduce the tax burden in this case.

Note that, as a part of the tax reform of 1987, bequest taxes were reduced by increasing the standard deduction and by adjusting the tax-rate schedule. (See Barthold and Ito 1990 for details.) Although the Japanese government claimed that this was intended as a compensation for the new value-added (consumption) tax, it was actually a technical correction for the government's not having indexed tax brackets and deductions, since the bequest-tax schedule had not changed since 1975. The ratio of "taxable" bequest wealth to total wealth was reduced in 1988 to its 1985 level, which meant that the technical correction pushed back the clock only by two (out of thirteen) years.

3. There are many horror stories involving a landlord's "losing" a principal residence to tenants. Consider a professor taking a leave to go abroad for two years, or a professional banker being assigned to a position in a foreign subsidiary for two years. If he owns a house, he typically shuts it up for the two years, because a two-year lease (even with a mutual understanding) to another person may result in his losing the house to the tenant after two years. Suppose, for example, that the professor has a second house, or an apartment or two as investments, and that the tenant does not have any real estate. If after two years the tenant reneges on the "understanding" and declares his intention to stay, the court will definitely grant an automatic extension of the lease to the tenant. There are many court decisions of this sort. In this case, the Japanese legal system does not honor a voluntarily signed contract between individuals.

4. Sachs and Boone (1988) presented an interesting twist on this issue in contending that eliminating the farm subsidy will increase the current account. In their model, removing land from production would reduce labor

income and, thus, reduce both consumption and saving. The decrease in saving dominates the decrease in domestic wealth (investment) due to the lower value of land. There is no substitution between land and labor in production; thus, removing land from production does not change the productivity of human capital (labor income). Consequently, saving does not change in the new steady state, wealth in land decreases, and external wealth has to rise. See Ito 1990 for an opposite conclusion obtained under slightly different assumptions.

BIBLIOGRAPHY

Barthold, T., and T. Ito. 1991. "Bequest taxes and accumulation of household wealth: US-Japan comparison." In *Political Economy of Tax Reforms*, ed. T. Ito and A. Krueger. University of Chicago Press.

Building Center of Japan. 1985. *A Quick Look at Housing in Japan*.

Cutler, D. M., J. M. Poterba, and L. H. Summers. 1989. "What moves stock prices?" *Journal of Portfolio Management*, spring: 4–12.

Economic Planning Agency. 1985. White paper. Government Printing Office.

French, K. R., and J. M. Poterba. 1990. Are Japanese Stock Prices Too High? Working paper 3290, National Bureau of Economic Research.

French, K. R., and R. Roll. 1986. "Stock return variances: The arrival of information and the reaction of traders." *Journal of Financial Economics* 17: 5–26.

Hamao, Y., R. W. Masulis, and V. Ng. 1989. Correlations in Price Changes and Volatility across International Stock Markets. Mimeo.

Hayashi, F., and T. Inoue. 1991. "The relation between firm growth and Q with multiple capital goods: Theory and evidence from panel data on Japanese firms." *Econometrica* 59: 731–753.

Hayashi, F., T. Ito, and J. Slemrod. 1988. "Housing finance imperfections, taxation, and private saving: A comparative simulation analysis of the US and Japan." *Journal of the Japanese and International Economies* 2, no. 3: 215–238.

Homma, M., and M. Atoda (eds.) 1989. *Zeisei Kaikaku no Jisho Bunseki* [Empirical Analysis of Tax Reform]. Toyo Keizai Shinpo.

Horioka, C. Y. 1988. "Saving for Housing Purchase in Japan." *Journal of the Japanese and the International Economics* 2: 351–384.

Hoshi, T., and A. K. Kashyap. 1990. "Evidence on q and investment for Japanese firms." *Journal of the Japanese and International Economies* 4, no. 4: 371–400.

Ito, T. 1990. The Land/Housing Problem in Japan. Discussion paper 228, Institute of Economic Research, Hitotsubashi University.

Konya, F., and T. Wakasugi. 1987. "Tobin's q and Stock Prices" (in Japanese). *Research on Securities* 80: 149–162.

Ministry of Construction. 1986. *Nihon no Jutaku Jijo [Housing in Japan]*. Gyosei.

Namekawa, M. 1988. *Economics of Problems of Land and Its Price* (in Japanese). Toyo Keizai Shimpo.

Noguchi, Y. 1989. *Economics of Land* (in Japanese). Nihon Keizai Shinbunsha.

Sachs, J., and P. Boone. 1988. "Japanese structural adjustment and the balance of payments." *Journal of the Japanese and International Economies* 2, no. 3: 286–327.

Sawamoto, M., and K. Minohara 1987. *Housing in Japan*. JCIF Policy Study Series, no. 8.

Shiller, R. 1981. "Do stock prices move too much to be justified by subsequent changes in dividends?" *American Economic Review* 71, no. 3: 421–436.

Ueda, K. 1989. "On the recent movement of Japanese stock prices" (in Japanese). *JCER Economic Journal* 18: 4–12.

Ueda, K. 1990. "Are Japanese stock prices too high?" *Journal of the Japanese and International Economies* 4, no. 4: 351–370.

INDEX

Accelerator-multiplier process, 81
Agency theory, 195
Agricultural land in cities, 421, 424–426
Agriculture
  under Meiji emperor, 22–23, 27
  under Tokugawa, 18
  and unemployment, 244–245, 249
Agri-Forest Central Bank, 111
Akaji Kōsai (deficit-financing bonds), 165
Akihito, Emperor, 14
Anti-Monopoly Law, 54, 179, 180, 204–205, 377
Anti-trust policies, 54, 200
Arai, Hakuseki, 10
Article 9 of constitution, 60
Assessments of land values, 417, 420
Assets. *See* Land and real estate; Stock prices
Automobile industry
  exports by, 296–297
  and MITI policy, 201–202
  success in, 368
  VER for, 370–371

Balance of payments, 291–296
  and business cycles, 78–79, 83
  and capital accounts, 331
Bank of Japan, 31, 112–114
  dollars held by, 313
  executive committee of, 114
  and exchange rates, 345–347, 351–353

loan regulation by, 114
  monetarism in, 129–132
  notes from, 21
  policy board of, 112
Banks
  central, 20, 112–114
  commercial, 107–108
  in enterprise groups, 177, 180, 194
  long-term credit, 108
  trust, 109
  working hours in, 230
Basic Survey on Trade Unions, 254
Basic Survey on Wage Structure, 254
Bill discount market, 121, 123
Black August, 433–435
Black Monday, 133, 353
Blue-collar workers, 212, 216, 367
Bonds
  construction, 150, 165
  corporate, 105
  government, 106, 120–121, 150, 165–166, 170
Bonuses, 212, 231–239
  and layoffs, 215–216
  and saving, 271–272
Bretton Woods system, 69, 313–316
Budgets, 145–146, 149. *See also* Deficits
Bureaucracies, in Japan vs. in US, 203
Business cycles
  dating of, 77–78
  estimation of, 79–89
  political, 89–95

Business cycles (contd.)
  theories of, 79–89, 96–100
  before World War II, 17–18
  after World War II, 59, 78–80

Cabinet members, 57
Call market, 121, 136
Capital
  budget for, 146, 148
  controls on, 313, 316–321, 323–
    325
  exporting of, 330–333
  foreign reserves for, 68
  and growth, 47–50
  mobility of, 157
  and saving, 259, 277–280
  under Tokugawa, 18
Capital gains
  on business balance sheets, 427
  on land, 279
  taxes on, 152, 421
Cartels, 204–205, 371
Carter, Jimmy, 315
Cash vs. credit cards, 108
Caste system, 8–9
Central banks, 20, 112–114. See
  also Bank of Japan
Certificates of deposit, 122, 135–
  136
Checkable accounts, 135
Checks, 108
Chihō (local) governments, 145
Chihō ginkō (regional banks), 107
China
  communism in, 59
  war with, 13, 15
Chingin Kōzō Kihon Tōkei Chosa
  (Basic Survey on Wage Structure),
  254
Chochiku Dōkō Chōsa (Family
  Saving Survey), 264–268, 281
Chōshū clan, 11–12
Chrysler Corporation, 370–371
Chūō (national) government, 145
Chūritsu Rōren union, 227
City banks, 107
Cliometrics, 34

Coal industry, 58, 199
Cobb-Douglas production function,
  49
Coeducation, 55
Cold War, 59–60
Colleges, 56
Columbia Pictures, purchase of, 333
Cominform, 59
Commerce Law, 191
Commercial banks, 107–108
Commercial paper, 105
Commodity taxes, 150–151, 154
Comparative advantage, 291
Compliance, tax, 153
Composite index, 77–78
Comprehensive Survey of Living
  Conditions of the People on
  Health and Welfare, 282
Computers, tariffs on, 372
Confucianism, 12–13
Constitution
  current, 60
  under Meiji emperor, 13
Construction industry
  bonds for, 150, 165
  labor shortages in, 230
  US access to, 373
Consumption taxes, 150
Contract negotiations, 212, 239–
  241
Copper currency, 10
Corporations
  bonds issued by, 105
  taxes on, 149–151, 156–157
Cotton spinning, 31–33
Covered interest parity, 321–327
Cram schools, 56, 244
Credit banks, 111
Credit cards, 108
Credit rationing. See Loans
Credit unions, 111
Cross-holding of shares. See Inter-
  locking shares
Culture and savings, 270–271
Current-account balance, 291–293,
  330–331
Custom duties, 150–151

Daie stores, 397
Daihatsu company, 371
Daiichi-Kangyo Bank, 182, 191
Daimyōs (provincial lords), 9–10
Daiten Hō (Large-Scale Retail Store Law), 394–397
Daiwa Securities Company, 109
Deductibility of expenses, 153
Defense forces
  and Cold War, 59–60
  spending for, 69, 159
Deficits, budget, 165–170
  bonds for, 106, 120–121, 150, 165–166, 170
  and growth, 64
  and saving, 171–173, 283
  and trade deficits, 379
Deflation, 10–11
Dejima, trading at, 8, 10
Demand
  and business cycles, 80–81
  and growth, 47, 50–52, 63
Demand deposits, 135
Department Store Law, 394
Depository Institutions Deregulation and Monetary Control Act, 105
Deposits, taxes on, 272
Depreciation and savings rate, 268
Depression cartels, 205
Deregulation
  of capital control, 317–321
  of financial markets, 104, 124–125
  of imports, 200
  of international finance, 329–330
  pressures against, 366–367
Developing countries, Japan as model for, 34–35
Development Bank, 68, 146, 164
Diet, 57
Diffusion index, 77–78
Distribution system, 385
  efficiency measurements for, 398–403
  and enterprise groups, 392–394
  and Large-Scale Retail Store Law, 394–397

personal relationships in, 397
  in SII, 377
  sole-representative importers, 397
  surveys on, 386–392
Diversification, 4
Dividends
  payout ratios on, 431
  taxes on, 152, 157
Dodge, Joseph, 59
Dodge Plan, 52, 59
Dōjima, futures market in, 30
Dōmei union, 227
Dual enterprise structure, 178, 195–196
Dual labor structure, 212
Dumping, 290, 365, 370, 372
Dynastic years, 14

Earthquake of 1923, 14
Eclectic gradualism, 130
Economic Planning Agency, 64–65, 77
Economic Statistics Annual, 174
Edo, government in, 8–9. See also Tokyo
Educational system, 56
  under Meiji emperor, 19
  reforms in, 55
  under Tokugawa, 18
  and youth unemployment, 244
Elections, 91–95
Election timing curve, 93–94
Electoral districts, 57
Electricity Development Corporation, 164
Electronic bank transfers, 108
Elimination of Excessive Concentration of Economic Power Law, 54, 179
Emperor, powers of, 55, 60
Employment Status Survey, 254
Energy savings, 296. See also Oil crisis
Enterprise Group in Japan, 206
Enterprise groups, 4, 177–178
  banks in, 177, 180, 194
  current status of, 180–189

Enterprise groups (contd.)
dual structure of, 195–196
independent, 189–190
interlocking shares in, 181, 183, 191–195
trading practices of, 392–394
after World War II, 179–180
vs. Zaibatsu, 190
Enterprise taxes, 150
Enterprise unions, 212, 226–228
Environment, 70–71, 200
Equality of life, 408
Equilibrium business-cycle theory, 98–100
Equity, evaluation of, 193
European Currency Unit, 314–315
European Monetary System, 314
Exchange Rate Mechanism, 315
Exchange rates, 4
under Bretton Woods system, 69, 313–316
and business cycles, 83
and covered interest parity, 321–327
and current accounts, 294–295
fixing of, 52, 59
floating, 69–70
and imports, 82
and J-curve effect, 299–300, 303
under Meiji emperor, 21–22
and monetary policy, 126–127, 133
and news, 333–341
and oil crisis, 347–348
and Plaza Agreement, 341–349
and pricing to market, 303–304
target zones for, 349–355
and trade, 289–290
and Yen/Dollar Working Group, 329–330
Export-Import Bank, 146, 164
Exports, 4, 296–299
of capital, 330–333
of cotton goods, 32
and growth, 50–51, 64
under Meiji emperor, 23–26
voluntary restraints on, 370–371

Family business, 244–245, 249
Family Income and Expenditure Survey, 280
Family Saving Survey, 264–268, 281
Feudalism, 7
Final Report of Structural Impediments Initiatives, 376
Finance Act, 165
Financial Bills, 106, 134
Financial markets, 103–106. See also International finance
banks, 107–109, 112–114
data for, 134–138
deregulation of, 104, 124–125
disequilibrium in, 119
government, 111–112
insurance companies, 110–111
and monetary policy, 125–134
in 1950s and 1960s, 114–118
in 1970s, 119–121
securities companies, 109–110
short-term, 103, 121–124
time differences in, 335–337
First Iron and Steel Rationalization Plan, 68
Fiscal Investment and Loan Program, 64
as capital budget, 146
distributions by, 162–165
funds for, 111
in industrial restructuring, 199
Fiscal reforms, 19–20
Fiscal years, 147
Foreign Exchange and Foreign Trade Control Law, 321
Foreign Exchange Fund Special Account, 82
Foreign investment, 4–5, 321
Foreign pressure in trade, 378–380
Foreign technology under Meiji emperor, 20
Forward markets, 357–358
Four tigers, 35
Franchises, 385
Free-banking era, 31

Friedman, Milton
  on GNP and money supply, 139
  on Meiji emperor, 28
  on monetarism of Bank of Japan,
    129–130
Fringe benefits, 225
Fudai daimyō (old allies), 9
Fuel, imports of, 296–297
Fukoku-Kyōhei (wealthy nation and
    strong army), 13
Futures markets, 29–30, 357–358
Fuyo enterprise group, 180–182,
    186–189, 191

Gaiatsu (foreign pressure), 378–380
Gasoline taxes, 150–151
General-account budget, 145
General Agreement on Tariffs and
    Trade, 376
General elections, 91–92
General trading companies, 190
Gensaki (repurchase agreements)
    market, 121–123
  foreign investment in, 321
  rates for, 134, 136–138
Germany, intra-industry trade by,
    306–307
Glass-Steagel Act, 103
Gold
  Meiji government and, 20–21
  Tokugawa government and, 10–
    11
Golden week, 231
Gold standard, 13–14, 21, 69, 127,
    313–314
Gōrika (rationalization) plans, 199
Government
  bonds issued by, 106, 120–121,
    150, 165–166, 170
  in Edo, 8–9
  financial institutions in, 111–112
  formation of, 7
  industrial policy of, 196–204
  infant-industry protection by, 68,
    178, 300–301, 366
  levels of, 145

and Ricardian neutrality, 167, 170–
    173
  and saving, 261–263
  securities from, 122, 124
  spending by, 146–150, 159–165
  taxation by, 150–159
  transitional, under Meiji emperor,
    19–20
Government-agencies budgets, 145
Great Depression, 14
Gross national product, 3
  and government spending, 147
  after World War II, 43–46
Gross profit margin, in distribution
    system, 400–403
Group of Five, 341–343
Group of Seven, 350–352
Growth, 43. See also Business cycles
  in aggregate demand, 50–52
  under Meiji emperor, 15–18
  1950–1973, 61–69
  and politics, 89–95
  rate of, 3
  and reform, 52–61
  and saving, 274–275
  scales for, 25
  slowdown in, 69–72, 87–89
  sources of, 46–50
  takeoff off, 15–16
  after World War II, 43–46
Growth recessions, 79
Gulf War (1991)
  Self-Defense Forces and, 60
  and stock prices, 433
  technology and, 368

Hakodate, 11
Health conditions, survey on, 282
Hedging, 317
Heirs, 158–159
Highway Corporation, 164
Holidays, paid, 228
Honda, 371
Hong Kong, 34–35
House Lease Law, 377, 423
House of Councilors, 55, 57

House of Representatives, 57, 91
Housing. *See also* Land and real
  estate
  cost of, 5, 408, 411–412
  international comparisons of, 408–
  411
  loans for, 412–413
  quality of, 411–412
  savings for, 272–274
Housing Finance Corporation, 164,
  412

Iemochi (Shōgun), 12
Ikeda, Hayato, 61
Ikkan enterprise group, 180–182,
  186–189
Imports, 296–299
  deregulation of, 200
  and exchange rates, 82
  pressure for, 374–375
  in retail stores, 394
  through sole-representative
  importers, 397
Income
  and expenditures, survey on, 280
  and saving, 275–276
Income taxes, 149–153, 156–157
Independent enterprise groups, 189–
  190
Indirect financing, 117
Industrial Bank of Japan, 108
Industry. *See also* Enterprise groups
  under Meiji emperor, 20
  policy toward, 33, 67–69, 196–204
  structure of, 177–178
Infant-industry protection, 68, 178,
  300–301, 366
Inflation
  and bonuses, 233
  and business cycles, 79–80
  and exchange rates, 126–127
  and growth, 61–62
  and labor negotiations, 240
  of land prices, 414–421
  under Meiji emperor, 20
  from oil crisis, 70–71, 84–85

and politics, 89–93
after World War II, 52–53, 58–59
Infrastructure
  industrial, 197
  under Meiji emperor, 20
Inhabitants taxes, 150
Inheritance
  of land, 417, 423
  savings for, 276–277
  taxes on, 150–151, 158–159, 422–
  423
Input-output approach to profit
  margins, 403
Insurance companies, 110–111
Interest
  on government bonds, 159
  taxes on, 152, 272–274
Interest rates
  and balance of payments, 79
  and business cycles, 82
  on certificates of deposit, 122
  on consumer deposits, 105–107
  control of, 323
  and credit rationing, 119
  deregulation of, 124
  and enterprise groups, 194
  and exchange rates, 327–328
  for housing loans, 412
  and investments, 114
  and saving, 259, 277
Intergenerational transfers
  of land, 417, 423
  savings for, 276–277
  taxes on, 150–151, 158–159, 422–
  423
Interlocking Enterprise Annual,
  205
Interlocking shares, 178
  in enterprise groups, 181, 183,
  191–195, 205
  and long-term profits, 368
  and price-earnings ratio, 429–433
  and returns to capital, 279
International finance, 103–104
  under Bretton Woods system, 313–
  316

and capital controls, 316–321, 323–325
and capital exports, 330–333
and covered interest parity, 321–327
deregulation of, 329–330
and exchange-rate target zones, 349–355
forward and futures markets, 357–358
International Monetary Fund, 313
Inter vivos transfer taxes, 159, 422
Intragroup loan ratio, 181, 184
Intra-industry trade, 290–291, 305–308, 373
Inventory investments, 87, 89
Investment, 3
  and business cycles, 82
  and enterprise groups, 195
  foreign, 4–5, 321
  and growth, 50–52, 63–64
  and interest rates, 114
  in inventory, 87, 89
  loans for, 68
  and saving, 259–260, 277–280, 283
Ippan kaikei (general-account budget), 145
IS-LM model, 96–98
Isolationism, 7–8

Jackson, Andrew, 31
Japan Real Estate Institute, 417, 437
J-curve effect, 299–300, 303
Joint Japan-US Ad Hoc Group on Yen/Dollar Exchange Rate, Financial and Capital Market Issues, 329–330
Joint ventures, 385
Juglar cycles, 78

Kaikoku ("open the country"), 11
Kakei Chōsa (Family Income and Expenditure Survey), 280
Kanagawa, 11
Kanren gaisha (affiliates), 189
Kansai Airport, 373

Kansetsu Kinyū no Yūi (indirect financing), 117
Kazu, Princess, 12
Keiretsu. *See* Enterprise groups
Keisha Seisan Hōshiki (Preferential Production Plan), 199
Kensetsu Kōsai (construction bonds), 165
Keynesian view
  of business cycles, 81–85, 96–99
  of monetary policies, 138
Kitchin cycles, 78
Kōdo seichō (high-speed growth), 43
Kogaisha (subsidiaries), 189
Koito company, 192
Kōji Kakaku (Land Agency), 417, 437
Kokumin Seikatsu Kiso Chōsa (Comprehensive Survey of Living Conditions of the People on Health and Welfare), 282
Kōmei, Emperor, 12
Kome kitte (rice coupons), 30
Korea
  control and annexation of, 13
  emulation of Japan by, 34–35
Korean War, 60–61
Krugman effect, 354
Kyōran Bukka (wild inflation), 70, 84–85
Kyoto, imperial court moved from, 12
Kyushu, cotton-spinning mills at, 31–33

Labor credit unions, 111
Labor Force Survey, 253–254
Labor market, 209
  blue-collar workers, 212, 216, 367
  bonuses in, 231–239
  for enterprise groups, 196
  and enterprise unions, 226–228
  and growth, 47–49
  lifetime employment in, 214–226
  under Meiji emperor, 19, 23–24
  reforms in, 55

Labor market (contd.)
  rotation of, 214–216, 367
  shortages in, 230
  spring offensive, 239–241
  statistics for, 253–255
  theories of, 250–253
  training of, 214–216, 367
  unemployment in, 212–213, 241–246, 248–253
  women in, 33, 209–210, 231–232
  working hours of, 4–5, 47–49, 212, 228–231
Labor Relations Adjustment Act, 55
Labor Standards Law, 55
Labor Union Law, 55
Land Agency, 417, 437
Land and real estate
  agricultural, in cities, 421, 424–426
  assessment of, 417, 420
  capital gains on, 279
  cost of, 5, 407–408, 414–421, 437
  and inheritance taxes, 158, 422–423
  policy toward, 421–426
  reforms for, 54, 375
  savings for, 273–274
  and stock prices, 433
  sunshine and size restrictions on, 424
  taxes on, 20
Land Lease Law, 377, 423
Land Legend, 414
Landlords, risks of, 423–424
Laptop computers, tariffs on, 372
Large-amount time deposits, 124
Large Scale Retail Store Law, 394–397
Layoffs, 215–216, 245
League of Nations, withdrawal from, 15
Leases, protection of, 423–424
Liberalization in financial markets, 104–105
Life-cycle theories
  of consumption, 264
  of saving, 275–276, 284–285
Life-insurance companies, 110–111
Lifetime employment, 210–211, 214–226
Limits of Growth report, 70
Liquor taxes, 150–151
Living conditions, survey on, 282
Loans
  for housing, 273, 412–413
  for investment, 68
  rationing of, 119
  regulation of, 114–115, 120
Logarithmic scale, 25
Long-Term Credit Bank of Japan, 108
Long-term financial markets, 103
Long-term relationships, 369, 397
Louvre agreement, 351–353
Lump-sum severance payments, 152, 213, 268

MacArthur, Douglas, 54
Machine tools, negotiations over trade of, 370
Macroeconomics
  and monetary policies, 140
  for planning, 64–67
  and stabilization, 161–163
Maekawa, Haruo, 374
Main banks, 116
Main Economic Indicators table, 134
Maitsuki Kinrō Tōkei Chōsa (Monthly Labor Survey), 253–254
Major business cycles, 78
Management, success of, 367–369
Manchuria, control of, 13–14
Mandatory retirement, 217–218
Manipulative model of business cycles, 89–91
Manufacturing under Meiji emperor, 22–23, 27
Market failures, 197
Market-Oriented Sector-Specific talks, 373

Market value of businesses, 426–427

Maru-yu (deposits), taxes on, 272

Mass production vs. product development, 368

Matsushita, 397

Medical care, 170

Medium and Small-size Business Corporations, 164

Medium-size firms, government handling of, 198

Medium-term business cycles, 78

Meiji, Emperor, 7
economic growth under, 15–18
heritages from Tokugawa era, 18–19
industrial structure under, 22–24
political events under, 13–15
prices under, 21–22
restoration of, 12–13
trade under, 24–28
transition policies of, 19–21

Meiji Ishin (Meiji Restoration), 12–13

Mein banku (main banks), 116

Merged households, 409–410

Merit pay, 236

Military
and Cold War, 59–60
under Meiji emperor, 13–15
spending for, 69, 159

Ministry of International Trade and Industry, 196–197, 200–201

Mitchell, George, 368

Mitsubishi enterprise group, 180–185, 188–189, 191
purchases by, 333
US factories built by, 371

Mitsui enterprise group, 180–182, 185, 188–189, 191

Miyazawa-Baker agreement, 350–351

Modern economic growth, 15–17, 34

Monetarists
in Bank of Japan, 129–132

business cycle view of, 98–99
monetary policy of, 138–139
in United States, 128–129

Monetary aggregates, 135–137

Monetary policy, 4
in 1971–1975, 125–127
in 1975–1989, 128–134
theories of, 138–140

Money, forms of, 108

Money-market certificates, 124

Money Market Deposit Accounts, 105, 136

Money-market mutual funds, 104–105, 136

Money supply, and business cycles, 98–99

Monopolies, reform of, 54, 179, 204–205, 377

Monthly Labor Survey, 253–254

Mortgages, availability of, 273

Multi-Fiber Agreement, 369–370

Municipal governments, 145
autonomy of, 148–149
taxes for, 150

Mutual banks, 111

Nagasaki, 11

Nakasone, Y., 105, 374–375

National Railway, 164

National saving rate, 261–264, 267

National security, 368

National Survey of Family Income and Expenditure, 281

National Tax Agency, 417, 437

Nenko Joretsu (seniority-based wages), 211–212, 216–218, 222–224

News and exchange rates, 333–341

New trade theory, 366

Night shifts, 32–33

Niju Kozo (dual structure), 195–196, 212

Nikkei 225 stock index, 437

Nissan company, US factories built by, 371

Nissay life-insurance company, 110

Nixon, Richard
  China visit by, 70
  and gold standard, 69, 127, 314
Nonbank enterprise groups, 189–190
NOW accounts, 135

Oba, Tomomitsu, 329
Occasional income, taxes on, 152
Occupation forces, reforms imposed by, 54, 179
Oil, imports of, 296–297
Oil crisis
  and business cycles, 79, 83
  and deficit financing, 150, 167
  and exchange rates, 315, 347–348
  and financial markets, 119–120
  and GNP, 43–46
  and growth, 65
  inflation from, 70–71, 84–85
  and investment, 51
  and monetary policy, 127
  and spring offensive, 241
Oil Industry Law, 201
Omnibus Trade and Competitiveness Act, 375–376
One set principle, 182
Ordinary deposits, 135
Osaka, 9, 30
Osaka Boseki Company, 32
Overborrowing, 115–117
Overloans, 114–115, 120

Paper money, 10, 20–21
Parliament, 13, 57
Partisan model of business cycles, 89–91
Pass-through, 301–305
Peasant class, 9
Peerage, 13
Pension and Welfare Corporation, 164
Pensions
  and saving, 271–272
  and severance payments, 213
  and trust banks, 109

Permanent-income hypothesis, 274
Perry, Matthew, 11–12
Personal saving rate, 261–267
Persons on loan, 393–394, 398
Phillips curve, 90–91
Pickens, T. Boone, 192
Planning
  industrial, 67–69
  macroeconomic, 64–67
Plaza Agreement, 341–343
Politics
  and business cycles, 83, 89–95
  reforms in, 55, 57, 60
Pollution, 71, 200
Postal savings accounts, 111–112, 136, 163–165, 272
Postal Saving Special Account, 164
Postal system under Meiji emperor, 20
Potential workers, 248
Prefectural governments, 145, 150
Preferential Production Plan, 199
Presidents' Club, 180
Price-dividend ratios, 431–432
Price-earnings ratios, 407
  of land, 423
  of stocks, 428–433
Pricing to market, 301–305
Private saving rate, 261, 264, 267, 269–270
Product development vs. mass production, 368
Productivity, measurements of, 398–403
Profits
  sharing of, 236–237
  short-term vs. long-term, 367–368
Promotions, 211–212, 215
Property taxes, 150, 421–422
Public Finance Corporation, 164
Public Finance Law, 59
Public housing, 424
Public works, 161

Q-ratio, 426–427, 432
Quantitative economic history, 34

Quantity-based managed trade, 378

Rationalization plans, 199
Reagan, Ronald
  and foreign investment, 328
  free trade position of, 366
  meeting with Nakasone, 105
  and VERs, 370–371
  and Yen/Dollar Working Group,
    329
Real demand principle, 321
Real estate. *See* Land and real estate
Reconstruction Bank, 58–59
Reconstruct the Japanese Archipelago Plan, 127
Reform
  fiscal, 19–20
  growth from, 52–61
  land, 54, 375
Regan, Donald, 329
Regional banks, 107
Rengo union, 228
Rentals
  cost of, 418–419
  protection of tenants, 423–424
  quantity of, 410
Repurchase agreements, 121–123
  foreign investment in, 321
  rates for, 134, 136–138
Required rate of return, 419–420
Reservation strategy, 250–251
Resource allocation, industrial,
  197–198
Restructuring, industrial, 198
Retail stores
  approval for, 394–397
  size of, 387–392
Retirement, 217–218
  saving in, 275–277
  taxes on income from, 152
Returns policies, 393
Revisionist argument, 377–378
Ricardian equivalence, 167, 170–
  173, 264
Rice
  futures market for, 29–30

for tax payments, 9
Road system, 9, 18
Rockefeller Center, purchase of, 333
Rōdō kinko (labor credit unions),
  111
Rōdōryoku Chōsa (Labor Force
  Survey), 253–254
Rosen Ka (National Tax Agency),
  417, 437
Rotation of workers, 214–216, 367
Russia, war with, 13

Sakhalin Island, control of, 13
Sakoku (isolationism), 8
Sales as productivity measurement,
  398–399
Samurai (warriors), 9–10
San Francisco peace treaty, 61
Sangyo Seisaku (industrial policy),
  196
Sankin-Kotai (alternating attendance of local lords), 8–9
Sanwa enterprise group, 180–182,
  186–189, 191
Satsuma clan, 11–12
Saturdays, work on, 228, 230
Saving, 3
  and bonuses, 238, 271–272
  data on, 280–282
  and deficits, 171–173, 283
  and growth, 63
  and inheritance taxes, 158–159
  interest rates on, 105–107
  and investment, 259–260, 277–
    280, 283
  Japan vs. US, 262–264, 268–270,
    275
  and land prices, 273–274, 375
  life-cycle hypothesis of, 275–276,
    284–285
  location of, 117–118, 125
  rates of, 260–262
  reasons for, 268–277
  and saving-investment identity,
    259, 282–284
  survey of, 264–267, 281

Saving-investment identity, 259, 282–284
Savings accounts, postal, 111–112, 136, 163–165, 272
Scale economies, 50, 301
Search theory, 250–251
Second Association of Regional Banks, 107
Second Rationalization Plan, 68
Securities companies, 109–110
Securities Transaction Law, 103
Security-transaction taxes, 150–151
Seifu kankei kikan (government-agencies budgets), 145
Seigniorage, 10–11
Self-Defense Forces
    and Cold War, 59–60
    spending for, 69, 159
Self-employment income, taxes on, 153
Semi-logarithmic scales, 25
Seniority-based wages and promotions, 211–212, 216–218, 222–224
Service industries
    under Meiji emperor, 22–23
    shift to, 89
Severance payments, 152, 213, 268
Share economy, 236–237
Shinō-Kōshō (caste system), 8–9
Shinpan (relatives of Shōgun), 9
Shinsan betsu union, 227
Shinyo kinko (credit banks), 111
Shinyo kumiai (credit unions), 111
Shōgun (military general), 7, 9
Shōhi zei (value-added taxes), 154–156
Shokusan-Kōgyō (industrialization), 13
Short-term financial markets, 103, 121–124
Showa years, 14
Shugyo kozo kihon chosa (Employment Status Survey), 254
Shunto (contract negotiations), 212, 239–241

Silk exports, 23–24
Silver
    under Meiji emperor, 20–21
    in Tokugawa government, 10–11
Silver standard, 21
Singapore, 34–35
Small firms, government handling of, 198
Smithsonian Agreement, 69, 127, 314
Social security
    reform in, 170
    and savings, 271
    taxes for, 154
Social wealth, 3
Sōgō ginko (mutual banks), 111
Sōgō Shosha (general trading company), 190
Sōhyō union, 227
Sole-representative importers, 397
Sonnō-jōi ("revere the emperor and expel the barbarians"), 11
Sony enterprise group, 189, 333
Special-account budgets, 145–146, 148
Specialization and Grouping Plan, 202
Speculation
    in land prices, 417
    in trade, 317
Spillovers of stock markets, 435
Spot labor market, 250
Spring offensive, 212, 239–241
Sprinkel, Beryl W., 329
Stabilization policy, 85–86, 161–163
Stamp revenues, 150–151
Standard of living, 4–5
Statutory heirs, 158–159
Steel, negotiations over trade of, 369–370
Stock prices, 426–433
    in Black August, 433–435
    indices of, 437–438
    and interlocking shares, 192–193
    and price-earnings ratio, 407

volatility of, 435
Structural Impediments Initiatives, 376–377
Subsidiaries, 189
Subsidizing of US industries, 378
Sumita, S., 346
Sumitomo enterprise group, 180–182, 185, 188–189, 191
Sunk costs, 303–304
Sunrise-industry protection, 68, 178, 300–301, 366
Sunshine restrictions, 424
Super-301 clause of Omnibus Trade Act, 375–376

Taishoku kin (severance pay), 152, 213, 268
Taisho period, 13–14
Taiwan
  control of, 13
  emulation of Japan by, 34–35
Takahashi, Korekiyo, 14
Takeovers and interlocking shares, 192
Takeshita, Noboru, 329, 347
Tanaka, K., 70, 127
Target zones for exchange rates, 349–355
Tariffs, 204
  under Meiji emperor, 27–28, 33
  by US, 372
Tax Collection Bureau, 437
Taxes, 145, 150–151
  on agricultural land, 424–426
  on capital gains, 152, 421
  consumption, 154–156
  income, 152–153, 156–157
  and industry development, 199
  inheritance, 158–159, 422–423
  on land and real estate, 20, 417, 420–421
  levels of, 149
  rice for, 9
  and saving, 272–273
  on security transactions, 122
Tax identification numbers, 152

Tea exports, 23–24
Technology
  conflicts in, 366
  and enterprise groups, 194
  and export prices, 305
  and growth, 47–50, 63, 72
  under Meiji emperor, 13, 20
  under Tokugawa, 7–8, 18
Tegata (bill discount) market, 121, 123
Telegraph service, 20
Televisions
  dumping of, 370
  tariffs on, 372
Tenants, protection of, 423–424
Textiles
  exports of, 24–25
  negotiations over trade of, 369–370
Thailand, 34
Time deposits, 135
Time differences in financial markets, 335–337
Tokubetsu kaikei (special-account budgets), 145–146, 148
Tochi Shinwa (Land Legend), 414
Tokugawa, Ieyasu, 8
Tokugawa family, 7–12, 18–19
Tokurei Kosai (deficit-financing bonds), 165
Tokyo. See also Edo
  imperial court moved to, 12
  land usage in, 421
TOPIX stock index, 437
Toshi ginko (city banks), 107
Toyota, 189, 196, 371
Tozama daimyō (recent allies), 9
Trade, 289–290. See also Exports; Imports
  and balance of payments, 78–79, 83, 291–296, 331
  and capital controls, 316–321
  by commodity, 296–297
  and comparative advantage, 291
  conflicts over, 5, 365–383
  by destination, 296, 298–299

Trade (contd.)
and exchange-rate adjustments,
299–300
and general trading companies, 190
and infant-industry protection, 68,
178, 300–301, 366
intra-industry, 290–291, 305–308,
373
under Meiji emperor, 24–28
negotiations over, 369–375
pricing to market and pass-through
with, 301–305
and saving, 259, 283
under Tokugawa government, 11–
12
US access to, 371–373
Trade Act, 375
Training of workers, 214–216,
367
Transition quarter, 147
Transportation account, 293
Travel account, 293
Treasury Bills, 106, 134
Treaty of Versailles, 13
Trigger-price system, 370
Tripartite Pact, 15
Trust banks, 109

Unemployment, 212–213, 241–246,
248–253
and bonuses, 233, 237
and elections, 91–92
and family businesses, 244–245,
249
Unfair trading partners, naming of,
375–376
Unions
enterprise, 212, 226–228
formation of, 55
in labor market theory, 251–253
and spring offensive, 239–241
statistics on, 254–255
Unitary tax system, 157
United States
central bank of, 31
comparative advantage in, 291

and Japanese industrial policy,
202–204
political business cycles in, 89–90
United States vs. Japan
bureaucracies, 203
corporate financing, 115
corporate income taxes, 156–157
current accounts, 294–295
deficits, 167–169
dividend payout ratios, 431–432
economic conflicts, 5, 365–381
education system, 56
fiscal years, 147
government expenditures, 146, 148
gross national product, 43–45
gross profit margins, 401
growth rates, 87–89
housing, 409–411
industry structure, 177
inheritance taxes, 159
interest on bond payments, 159
labor market, 210–213
land values, 408
location of savings, 118, 125
monetary policies, 128–134
price-earnings ratio of stocks, 428–
429
productivity, 399
rents, 418–419
returns to capital, 277–280
savings, 262–264, 268–270, 275
size of retail stores, 388
sources of growth, 46–48
tenure of workers, 217–222
trade commodities and destinations, 297–298
trust banks, 109
unemployment, 241–245
union membership, 226–227
wholesale sales, 391
working hours, 229–230
Universities, 56
US Trade Representative, 375–376

Vacations, 228
Valuation of businesses, 426–427

Value-added taxes, 154–156
Vector autoregression, 86
Videocassette recorders, 368
Vogel, Ezra, 367
Volcker, Paul, 128
Voluntary export restraints, 5, 370–
   371
Voting rights, 13, 55, 60

Wholesale industry, 389–391, 402
Withholding taxes, 152–153
Women
  in cotton mills, 33
  in labor market, 209–210, 231–
   232
  and unemployment, 245, 249
  voting rights of, 55, 60
Working hours, 4–5, 47–49, 212,
   228–231
World War II, recovery after, 52–
   61

Yamaichi Securities Company,
   109–110
Yaohan company, 157
Yearbook of Labor Statistics, 255
Yen, exchange rates of. *See*
   Exchange rates
Yen/Dollar Working Group, 105,
   124, 329
Yobiko (cram schools), 56
Youth, unemployment of, 243–244

Zaibatsu Dissolution, 179–180. *See
   also* Enterprise groups
Zaikei (housing and pension
   savings), taxes on, 272
Zaisei Toyushi. *See* Fiscal Invest-
   ment and Loan Program
Zenkoku Shohi Jittai Chosa
   (National Survey of Family In-
   come and Expenditure), 281
Zenro-ren union, 228